Running
Microsoft
Access™

Running
Microsoft
Access™

John L. Viescas

The Authorized Edition

PUBLISHED BY
Microsoft Press
A Division of Microsoft Corporation
One Microsoft Way
Redmond, Washington 98052-6399

Library of Congress Cataloging-in-Publication Data
Viescas, John, 1947–
    Running Microsoft Access / John L. Viescas.
      p.   cm.
    Includes index.
    ISBN 1-55615-507-7 : $29.95
    1. Data base management.   2. Microsoft Access.   I. Title.
QA76.9.D3V55   1992
005.75'65--dc20   92-29928
                                      CIP

Printed and bound in the United States of America.

 2 3 4 5 6 7 8 9   8 7 6 5 4 3

Distributed to the book trade in Canada by Macmillan of Canada, a division of Canada Publishing Corporation.

Distributed to the book trade outside the United States and Canada by Penguin Books Ltd.

Penguin Books Ltd., Harmondsworth, Middlesex, England
Penguin Books Australia Ltd., Ringwood, Victoria, Australia
Penguin Books N.Z. Ltd., 182-190 Wairau Road, Auckland 10, New Zealand

British Cataloging-in-Publication Data available.

Companies, names, and data used in examples herein are fictitious unless otherwise noted.

Acquisitions Editor: Dean Holmes
Project Editor: Rich Gold
Technical Editor: Jim Fuchs

In memory of my father, Albert H. Viescas,
who taught me the patience, perseverance,
and attention to detail required to successfully
complete a project like this book.

Contents

PART IV: USING FORMS

Acknowledgments

No one can produce a 500-plus page book on a technical subject without a lot of assistance from a great many people.

First I'd like to thank key members of the Microsoft Access development team who not only gave me "access" to beta copies of the software but also contributed personal time to help me better understand the product and work through the examples I used in this book. Thanks to David Risher and Jonathan Biard who introduced me to the beta team and kept me on top of the latest developments. Thanks also to Product Support Specialists MariEsther Burnham, Kim Abercrombie, Dan Madoni, and all the other members of the PSS team who helped me sort out bugs from problems in my sample application design. Special thanks to Ross Hunter, Microsoft Access Program Manager, whose vision and quest for excellence has been crucial to delivering an incredibly exciting new software product to market.

On the book production side, there's Dean Holmes, acquisitions manager, who had the confidence to entrust such a key book about a new Microsoft product to my hands. JoAnne Woodcock nursed my early chapters to life and set me on the path toward producing a quality product. Richard Gold, my manuscript editor, worked many extra hours to polish my work and keep it on schedule. Jim Fuchs, technical editor, toiled over the many technical details that are part of my description of this complex product, ensuring technical accuracy for our readers. There's also a whole host of people "behind the scenes" at Microsoft Press who ably handled all the many, many tasks that go into producing a book. Thanks to you all.

Finally, special thanks to David Rygmyr and Craig Parsons whose small business, Prompt Computer Solutions, provided a "true to life" background for the sample application I built for this book.

Introduction

Although many people will view Microsoft Access as the long-awaited Windows-hosted database from Microsoft, Access is really just one part of Microsoft's overall data management product strategy. Microsoft Access is not just a database; it also complements other database products because of several powerful features. Microsoft Access *does* have a data storage system and, like all good relational databases, it allows you to easily link related information—for example, customer and order data that you enter. But one of the real strengths of Microsoft Access, as its name implies, is that it can work with data from other sources, including many popular PC database programs (such as dBASE, Paradox, FoxBase, or Btrieve) and many SQL (structured query language) databases on servers, minicomputers, or mainframes. Also, Microsoft Access has a very sophisticated application development system for the Microsoft Windows operating system that makes extensive use of information about your data—whatever the data source—to help you build applications quickly. In fact, you can build simple applications by defining (literally drawing on the screen) forms and reports based on your data and linking them together with a few simple macros—no need to write any code in the classical programming sense.

For small businesses (and for consultants creating applications for small businesses), Microsoft Access is all you'll need to store and manage the data you use to run the business. For many medium-sized companies, Microsoft Access coupled with the Microsoft SQL Server is an ideal way to build new applications for Windows very quickly and inexpensively. For large corporations that have a big investment in mainframe relational database applications and also have a proliferation of desktop applications that rely on PC databases, Microsoft Access provides the tools to easily link host and PC data in a single Windows-based application.

ABOUT THIS BOOK

If you're developing a database application, this book gives you a thorough understanding of "programming without writing code" using Microsoft Access. The book provides a solid foundation for designing databases, forms, and reports and getting them all to work together. You'll discover you can create moderately complex applications by linking design elements with Microsoft Access's powerful macro facilities. After you master these concepts, you'll be ready to selectively add modules in the Microsoft Access Basic programming language to fully customize your application. And, even if someone else has built most of the application for you, you'll find this book useful for understanding how to use an Access application and for extending that application to suit your changing needs.

Running Microsoft Access is divided into six major parts:

- Part I gives you a thorough overview of Microsoft Access. Chapter 1 describes how Microsoft Access fits into the world of PC database systems. Chapter 2 describes how you might use Microsoft Access, and Chapter 3 takes you on a tour of Microsoft Access, introducing you to the basic concepts and terminology.

- Part II tells you how to design, define, and modify database definitions in Microsoft Access. Chapter 4 explains a fairly simple, yet methodical technique that you can use to design a good relational database with little effort. Even old pros might appreciate this technique. Starting with a good design is the key to building easy-to-use applications.

- Part III focuses on working with data. Here you'll learn not only how to add, update, delete, or replace data in a Microsoft Access database but also how to design queries to work with data from multiple tables, calculate values, or update many records with one command. Perhaps the heart of the book is Chapter 10, "Importing, Attaching, and Exporting Data." Here you'll learn how Microsoft Access can connect you to many other popular databases, spreadsheets, and even text data.

- Part IV is all about forms. Chapter 11 introduces you to forms—what they look like and how they work. The remaining chapters provide you with an extensive tutorial on designing, building, and implementing simple and complex forms, including use of the FormWizards feature.

- Part V gives you detailed information about reports. The first chapter in this part leads you on a guided tour of reports and explains the major features you can use. The following chapters teach you how to design, build, and implement both simple and complex reports in your application.

- Part VI teaches you how to bring together tables, queries, forms, and reports. This part introduces you to Microsoft Access macros and shows you how to use them to link together forms and reports into an application.

Throughout this book, you'll see examples that explain how to build a Microsoft Access application for a small computer company called Prompt Computer Solutions, Inc. If you're a CompuServe member, you can find a copy of the PROMPT database in the libraries of the Microsoft Access forum. Type *Go Microsoft* at any ! prompt. For an introductory CompuServe membership kit specifically for users of Microsoft software, call (800) 848-8199 and ask for operator 230.

CONVENTIONS USED IN THIS BOOK

The following conventions are used throughout this book to represent keystroke and mouse operations:

Convention	Meaning
Alt-F	Press and hold down the Alt key and then, while holding down Alt, press the F key.
Alt,F	Press the Alt key, release it, and then press the F key.
Choose	Pick and execute an item in a menu or option group.
Select	Highlight a field in a table or an item in a list.
Click	Move the mouse pointer to the named item and press the left mouse button once.
Double-click	Move the mouse pointer to the named item and press the left mouse button twice in rapid succession.
Drag	Move the mouse pointer to the named item, press the left mouse button, and then move the mouse pointer while holding down the left mouse button.
Enter	Type in a value, as in "Enter a name for the file in the File Name text box."
Press	Press the named key on your keyboard, as in "Select the file you want to open and press the Enter key."

PART I

UNDERSTANDING MICROSOFT ACCESS

The first part of this book is an introduction to Microsoft Access. Use this part of the book to gain an overview of the product, its uses, and its major features.

Chapter 1 explains the concept of a database management system from the perspective of a personal computer user. It explains the position of Microsoft Access in the PC database world.

Chapter 2 explores three major scenarios for using Microsoft Access.

This part concludes with Chapter 3, a tour of the Microsoft Access components.

1

Microsoft Access Is a Database and More

Database programs have been available for personal computers for a long time. Unfortunately, these programs have been so complex and difficult to use that even many computer-literate people have avoided database systems unless they were handed a complete, custom-built database application. But Microsoft Access represents a significant turnaround in ease of use, and many people will be drawn to create their own useful databases and full database applications.

Microsoft Access is an easy-to-use, Microsoft Windows-hosted product that combines powerful database features with the ability to access data in many different files and on other types of computers. In addition, Microsoft Access is a full *application development system* that generates forms and reports within its graphical user interface. Microsoft Access can manage data for you on your PC, in applications of your own creation, and it accomplishes this without forcing you to learn complex features or a programming language.

WHAT IS A DATABASE?

Quite simply, a database is a collection of records and files that are organized for a particular purpose. You maintain databases all the time. On your computer system, your company might keep the addresses of all your customers. Perhaps you collect all the letters you write and organize them by recipient. You might have another set of files in which you keep all your financial data—accounts payable and accounts receivable. The word processor documents that you organize by topic are one database. The spreadsheet files that you organize according to their uses are another database.

If you're very organized, you can probably manage several hundred documents or spreadsheets by using directories and subdirectories. But what do you do when your business grows beyond this level? How can you easily collect information about all customers and their orders when the data might be stored in several document and spreadsheet files? How do you ensure that data is being entered correctly? What if you need to share your information with many other people but don't want two people to try updating the same data at the same time? Faced with these challenges, you need a *database management system,* or *DBMS.*

Nearly all modern database management systems store and handle information using the *relational* database management model. In a relational database, sometimes called an *RDBMS,* the system manages all data in tables. Tables store information about a subject (such as customers) and have columns that contain the different kinds of information about the subject (such as customer address) and rows that describe all the attributes of a single instance of the subject (data on a specific customer). Even when you use one of the DBMS facilities to fetch information from one or more tables (often called a *query*), the result is always something that looks like another table. In fact, you can execute one query that uses the results of another query.

The name *relational* stems from the fact that each record in the database contains information *related* to a single subject and only that subject. Also, data about two classes of information (such as customers and orders) can be manipulated as a single entity based on *related* data values in the tables that store that information. For example, each entry in an Orders table should contain a column that stores data, such as a customer number, that can be used to connect each order with customer information in the Customers table.

MICROSOFT ACCESS AS A DBMS

A database management system gives you complete control over how you define your data, work with it, and share it with others. This system also provides you with sophisticated features that make it easy to catalog and manage large amounts of data in many files. A DBMS generally has three main types of capabilities: data definition, data manipulation, and data control. All of this functionality is contained in the powerful features of Microsoft Access.

Data Definition

A DBMS allows you to define what kind of data you have and how the data should be stored. You can also usually define rules that the DBMS can use to ensure the integrity of your data. In its simplest form, an integrity rule might ensure that you can't accidentally store alphabetic characters in a field that should contain a number. Other rules might define valid values or ranges of values for your data. In the most sophisticated systems, you can define the relationship between different collections of data (usually called tables or files) and ask the DBMS to ensure that your data remains consistent. For example, you could have the system automatically check to ensure that every order is entered for a valid customer.

4

With Microsoft Access, you have complete flexibility to define your data (as text, numbers, dates, times, currency, pictures, sounds, documents, spreadsheets), to define how Microsoft Access stores your data (string length, number precision, date/time precision), and to define what the data looks like when you display or print it. You can define simple or complex validation rules to ensure that only accurate values exist in your database. You can request that Microsoft Access check for valid relationships between files or tables in your database.

Because Microsoft Access is a state-of-the-art application for Windows, you can use all the facilities of *Dynamic Data Exchange* (*DDE*) and *Object Linking and Embedding* (*OLE*). DDE lets you use the familiar Cut/Copy/Paste commands to share information between Microsoft Access and any other application for Windows that supports DDE. You can also make DDE connections to other applications using macros or Access Basic. OLE is an advanced Windows capability that allows you to link to or embed in your Microsoft Access database objects (such as pictures, graphs, spreadsheets, or documents) from other applications for Windows that also support OLE. Figure 1-1 shows you a display of data from the sample Northwind Traders database (NWIND) that Microsoft ships with Microsoft Access. You can see an employee record that not only has the typical name and address information but also a picture and biographical text.

Microsoft Access also has the ability to understand and use a wide variety of other data formats, including many other database management system file structures. You can import and export data from word processing files or spreadsheets. Microsoft Access can directly access and update Paradox, dBASE III, dBASE IV, Btrieve, FoxBase, and other files. You can also import data from these files into a

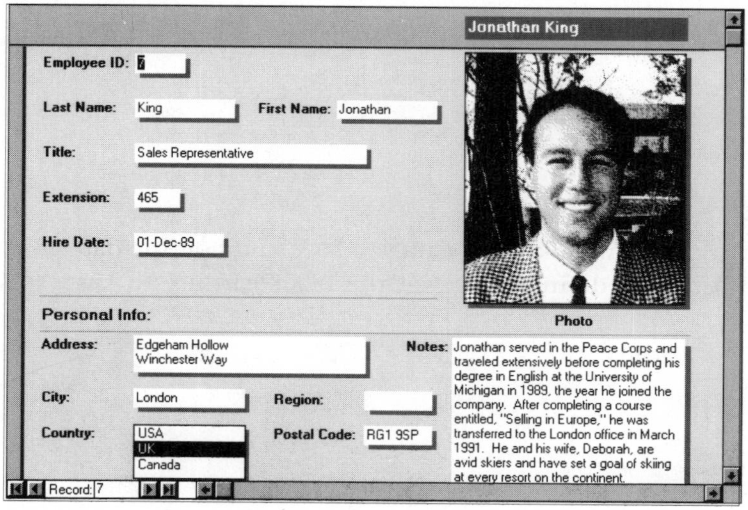

Figure 1-1.
An employee record form in Microsoft Access.

Microsoft Access table. In addition, Microsoft Access can work with most popular databases that support the *Open Database Connectivity* (*ODBC*) *standard*, including Microsoft SQL Server, Oracle, DB2, and Rdb.

Data Manipulation

A DBMS provides you with many ways to work with your data. You can, for example, search a single table for information or request a complex search across several related tables or files. You can update a single field or many records with a single command. You can write programs that use DBMS facilities to read and update your data. Many systems provide you with data entry and report generation facilities.

Microsoft Access uses the powerful *SQL* (*structured query language*) database language to process data in your tables. Using SQL, you can define the set of information that you need to solve a particular problem, including data from perhaps many tables. But Microsoft Access simplifies data manipulation tasks. You don't even have to understand SQL to get Microsoft Access to work for you. Microsoft Access uses the relationship definitions you provide to automatically link the tables you need. You can concentrate on how to solve information problems without having to worry about building a complex navigational system between all the data structures in your database. Microsoft Access also has an extremely simple yet powerful graphical query definition facility (called *graphical query by example*, or *QBE*) that you can use to specify the data you need to solve a problem. Using point and click, drag and drop, and a few keyboard strokes, you can build a complex query in a matter of seconds.

Figure 1-2 shows you a complex query under construction in Microsoft Access. Microsoft Access displays field lists from selected tables in the top of the window, and the lines between field lists indicate the automatic links that Microsoft Access will use to solve the query. To create the query, you simply select the fields you want from

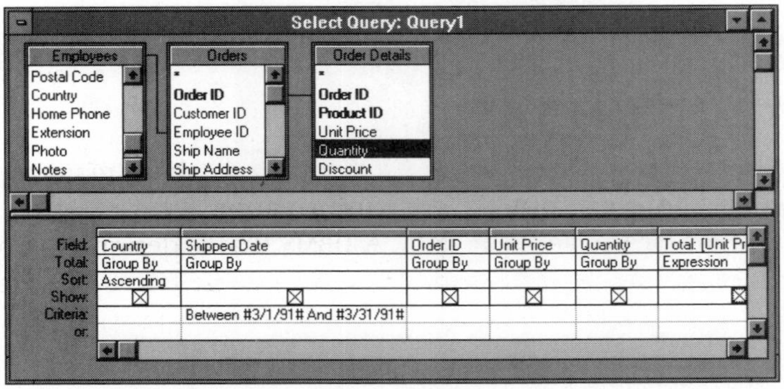

Figure 1-2.
A Query window in Microsoft Access.

the top of the window and drag them to the QBE grid in the bottom of the window. Select a few options, type in any criteria, and you are ready to have Microsoft Access select the information you desire. Figure 1-3 shows you an example of an SQL statement that Microsoft Access automatically creates from your specifications in the QBE grid. Figure 1-4 shows you the result of running the query.

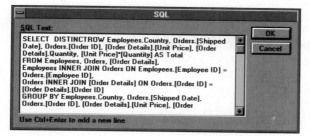

Figure 1-3.
The SQL text generated by the query in Figure 1-2.

Country	Shipped Date	Order ID	Unit Price	Quantity	Total
UK	01-Mar-91	10475	$10.00	35	$350.00
UK	01-Mar-91	10475	$13.60	60	$816.00
UK	01-Mar-91	10475	$14.40	42	$604.80
UK	04-Mar-91	10496	$10.00	20	$200.00
UK	04-Mar-91	10497	$10.40	25	$260.00
UK	04-Mar-91	10497	$27.80	25	$695.00
UK	04-Mar-91	10497	$30.40	14	$425.60
UK	06-Mar-91	10489	$13.90	18	$250.20
UK	06-Mar-91	10489	$16.80	15	$252.00
UK	13-Mar-91	10501	$7.45	20	$149.00
UK	13-Mar-91	10503	$21.05	20	$421.00
UK	13-Mar-91	10503	$23.25	70	$1,627.50
UK	14-Mar-91	10500	$15.50	12	$186.00
UK	14-Mar-91	10500	$45.60	8	$364.80
UK	19-Mar-91	10507	$12.75	15	$191.25
UK	19-Mar-91	10507	$46.00	15	$690.00
UK	21-Mar-91	10512	$4.50	10	$45.00
UK	21-Mar-91	10512	$9.50	6	$57.00

Figure 1-4.
The result of running the query in Figure 1-2.

Data Control

When you need to share your information with others, true database management systems have features that allow you to make your information secure so that only those you authorize can read or update your data. A DBMS that is designed to allow data sharing also provides features to ensure that no two people try to change the same data at the same time. The best systems also allow you to group changes (a series of changes is sometimes called a *transaction*) so that either all of the changes or none of the changes appear in your data. For example, while entering a new order for a customer, you probably would like to know that all items are recorded, or if you encounter an error, that none of the changes are saved. You would also like to be sure that no one else can view any part of the order until you have entered all of it.

Microsoft Access is designed to be used as either a stand-alone DBMS on a single workstation or in a shared client-server mode across a network. Because you can share your Microsoft Access data with other users, Microsoft Access has excellent data security and data integrity features. You can define which users or groups of users can have access to objects (tables, forms, queries) in your database. Microsoft Access automatically provides locking mechanisms to ensure that no two people can update an object at the same time. Microsoft Access also understands and honors the locking mechanisms of other database structures (such as Paradox, dBASE, or SQL databases) that you attach to your database.

MICROSOFT ACCESS AS SOMETHING MORE

Being able to define exactly what data you need, how it should be stored, and how you want to access it solves the data management part of the problem. You also need a simple way to automate all the most common tasks you want to perform. For example, each time you need to enter a new order, you don't want to have to run a query to search the Customers table, execute a command to open the Orders table, create a new record, and enter the data for the order. And what about scanning the table that contains all your products to verify sizes, colors, and prices?

So, you not only need a powerful relational database management system, but you also need an *application development system* to help you automate your tasks. Virtually all database systems include application development facilities to allow programmers or users of the system to define the procedures needed to automate the creation and manipulation of data. Unfortunately, many of these application development systems require knowledge of a programming language, such as C or COBOL, to define these procedures. Although these languages are very rich and powerful, they require special training before they can be used properly. To really take advantage of the DBMS, you have to learn programming, hire a programmer, or buy a ready-made database application (which might not exactly suit your needs) from a programming company.

Fortunately, Microsoft Access makes it easy to design and construct database applications without requiring you to know a programming language. Although you begin in Microsoft Access by defining the relational tables and the fields in those tables that will contain your data, you'll see that you will quickly branch out to defining actions on the data in these tables via forms, reports, and macros.

Microsoft Access provides advanced database application development facilities to process not only data in its own database structures but also information stored in many other popular database formats. Perhaps Access's biggest strength is its ability to handle data from spreadsheets and text files, dBASE files, Paradox, Btrieve and FoxBase databases, and any SQL database supporting the ODBC standard. This means you can use Access to create an application for Windows to process data from a network SQL server or a mainframe SQL database.

In the next chapter you'll read about some uses of the Microsoft Access application development system in different professional settings. Then in Chapter 3 you'll open the sample application distributed with the product (Northwind Traders, the NWIND database) to explore some of the many features and functions of Access.

2

The Uses of
Microsoft Access

Microsoft Access has all the features of a classic database management system and more. Access is not only a powerful, flexible, and easy-to-use DBMS, but also a complete database application development facility. You can use Access to create and run under Windows an application system tailored to your specific data management needs. Access enables you to create forms for viewing and changing your data. You can also use Access to create simple or complex reports. Both forms and reports "inherit" the properties of the underlying table or query so that in most cases you need to define such things as formats and validation rules only once. Among the most powerful features of Access are the FormWizards and ReportWizards that you can use to create and customize a wide variety of forms and reports simply by choosing from options with your mouse. Access makes it easy to link data to forms and reports using macros to fully automate your application. You can build most applications without ever having to write anything that looks remotely like computer program code. But if you need to get really sophisticated, there's also a comprehensive programming language, Microsoft Access Basic, that you can use to add complexity to your applications.

Finally, you get all of these sophisticated development facilities not only for working with the Access database but also to attach to and work with data stored in many other popular formats. You can build an Access application to work directly with dBASE files, Paradox, Btrieve, and FoxBase databases, and any SQL database that supports the Open Database Connectivity (ODBC) standard.

This chapter describes three scenarios in which Microsoft Access is used to meet the database and application-development needs of the owners of a small business, a PC application developer or consultant, and a management information systems (MIS) coordinator in a large corporation.

IN A SMALL BUSINESS

If you're the owner of a small business, you can use the simple yet powerful capabilities of Microsoft Access to manage the data you need to run your business. In addition, you will soon find dozens of Access-based applications available that will add to your productivity and make running your business much simpler. Because Access's application design facilities are so simple to use, you can be confident in creating your own applications or customizing applications provided by others for your specific needs.

Throughout much of the rest of this book, you'll read about the progressive design and creation of a database for a small computer business called Prompt Computer Solutions, Inc. This business is real and is owned by a couple of my friends.

Prompt Computer Solutions is like many small businesses. The two partners got started a couple of years ago custom-assembling personal computer systems and local area networks for their friends and other small businesses. Even though they understand computers very well, most of their business is run out of a filing cabinet. They do use tools like Microsoft Excel and Microsoft Word to automate some of their information and to produce price lists and fliers for their customers. They have taken the time to build templates in Excel that they use to prepare invoices for customers—one template for each major type of computer system that they build. When assembling a price quotation, they cut and paste or enter by hand the add-on items to their base computer systems.

Ultimately, each order spreadsheet becomes a build record and customer invoice. They've become pretty smart about creating subdirectories on their hard disks and using naming conventions to manage their files. Nonetheless, they practically had to shut down for two weeks last March to gather information for their accountant so that they could file their tax return. To make things a bit more complex, they've recently added some rental business. The situation was pretty simple when they took an order, recorded it in a Microsoft Excel file, built the computer system, and recorded the payment. Now they must produce monthly invoices for their rental customers and keep track of computer system serial numbers and ongoing payments.

When it was suggested that maybe it was time for them to buy an application or a database system to simplify their lives, their reaction was swift: "Forget it. We don't have the time to go searching for an application that would work for us, and we can't afford to hire a consultant to custom-build an application from scratch. Most databases we've looked at would take us aeons to learn to use, and even if we knew a database, it would take us too much time to write something that could help us out."

Enter Microsoft Access. It took almost no time to lay out the tables they needed to keep track of everything for their business. They were even able to import some of their old data directly from Microsoft Excel. In just a few days they created several forms, a couple of reports, and some macros to link them together, and they had solved a big piece of their data-management problem. See Figure 2-1.

The bottom line? Yes, the folks at Prompt Computer Solutions are pretty comfortable working with computers. But you'll notice that before Microsoft Access, they didn't dream they'd ever be able (or have the time) to tackle a PC database system. Now they have the database they need for their growing business. If you're a small business owner who understands that computers should be able to do more than spreadsheets and word processing, perhaps Access is for you, too. Even if you don't have the time (or the patience) to fully develop a PC database system for yourself, you'll want to know more about Access. You'll soon find a lot of computer consultants ready and able to put together a Microsoft Access application for you in record time and at low cost.

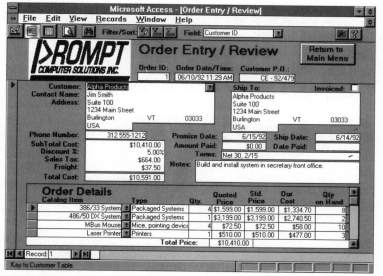

Figure 2-1.
The Order Entry form in the database application for Prompt Computer Solutions.

IN CONTRACT WORK

In today's highly competitive consulting marketplace, the developer who can deliver custom applications quickly and inexpensively will win the lion's share of the business. If you're a PC application developer or consultant, you will find that the forms, reports, and macro facilities of Microsoft Access allow you to create complete applications for your clients in record time. You can also take advantage of Microsoft Access Basic to satisfy unique requirements and produce truly custom applications. If you have worked with products like Microsoft Visual Basic for Windows, you will find the Access application development features very familiar, with the added benefit of a full-function relational database management system.

If you're a consultant building applications for a vertical market, you'll especially appreciate how Access makes it easy to build your core application and modify the application for each client's needs. You can create optional add-on features that you can price separately. Whether you're building a custom application from scratch or modifying an existing one, your clients will appreciate the fact that you can sit down with them and use Access to prototype the finished application so that they can see exactly what they'll be getting.

You can scale your application to your client's needs by taking advantage of the fact that Microsoft Access can connect to and work with other database management systems. For smaller clients, you'll find the native Access database system more than adequate. For larger clients, you can connect your application to Microsoft SQL Server or other host databases without having to change any of the forms, reports, macros, or modules in your application.

Imagine a local bookstore chain that has personal computers in each store for use by customers to locate a book by title, subject, or author. Suppose the database system was built by you several years ago using an xBase product. The bookstore chain would like to upgrade by converting the system to run under the Microsoft Windows operating system. The chain would also like to connect the database system to the current inventory information that is kept in a SQL Server database. Your client wants the new database system to tell customers whether a book is in stock. If a book is in stock, the new system should tell customers where they can find the book in the bookstore using a graphical map.

Sounds like Microsoft Access might be a perfect solution. You can use the existing xBase data or convert it easily to Microsoft Access format. You can also connect the new application to the existing SQL Server inventory data. Adding a map of the store is easy—and you can even include location indicators that show the customers where they are and where they have to go to find the book they want. See Figure 2-2.

What if you have an even larger problem to solve? The next section describes how large corporations might use Microsoft Access.

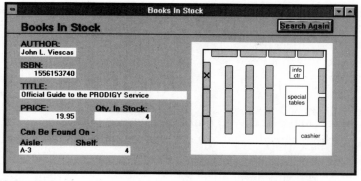

Figure 2-2.
A bookstore application.

IN A LARGE CORPORATION

All companies today recognize that one of the ways to remain competitive is to use computer-stored data for more than just the day-to-day operation of the company. Creative managers are constantly looking for ways to "turn data into information." As a result, companies no longer have "data processing" organizations, they have vast MIS departments charged with the care and feeding of the company's valuable computer-stored information.

Nearly all corporations start by building operational data processing systems. These systems collect and process the individual transactional data required to run the business on a day-to-day basis. Examples of transactional data include:

- Checks cleared and money withdrawn and deposited in a banking demand deposit system

- Incoming inventory and items sold in a retail system

- Raw materials ordered and received and finished goods shipped in a manufacturing system

- Energy consumed, raw product delivered, and service-connected or service-disconnected data in a utility system

These systems are relatively simple to design and implement in terms of the data input, the processes required on this data, and the data output. They are also easy to cost-justify in terms of reducing clerical tasks, handling rapidly growing volumes (imagine trying to post 10 million checking accounts manually), or achieving efficiency.

After operational systems are in place and management begins to become aware of the vast amounts of data being collected, it is a natural consequence to begin examining the data to gain a better understanding of how the business interacts with its customers, suppliers, and competitors—to learn how to become more efficient and/or more competitive. Information processing in most MIS departments usually begins quite innocently as an extension of operational systems. In fact, some informational processing almost always gets defined as part of an operational application system design. While interviewing users of a system during systems analysis, the system designer usually hears requests such as: "When the monthly invoices are produced, I'd also like to see a report that tells me which accounts are more than 90 days past due." Printing the invoices *is not* information processing. Producing the report *is* information processing.

On the surface, it would seem simple to answer a question about delinquent accounts given the data about all accounts receivable. However, the operational system might require only 30 days of "current" data to get the job done. The first information request almost always begins to put demands on the data processing systems, and these demands far exceed the data and processing power needed to merely run the business. At some point, the MIS organization decides consciously to reserve additional data storage and processing capability to meet growing informational needs. However, managing the transition of data collected in operational systems into the data required to support informational systems is complex indeed. While operational systems are well understood in terms of the inputs available, the outputs required, and the processes necessary to go from input to output, information systems are defined only by the next question that might be asked.

This growing thirst for information has led companies to build vast networks of departmental systems, which are in turn linked to desktop systems on employees' desks. As more and more data spreads down through the corporation, the data becomes more difficult to manage, locate, and access. See Figure 2-3. Multiple copies of the same data proliferate, and it becomes hard to figure out who has the most current and accurate data. Why do so many copies exist? Many copies of data exist because the vast majority of existing tools aren't designed to work with data in more than one format or to connect to data from multiple sources. Employees must resort to obtaining a copy of the data they want and then converting it to the format understood by their tool of choice.

The main strength of Access in a corporate environment is its ability to link to a variety of database formats on the workstation, on database servers, or on host computers. A manager trying to solve a problem no longer has to figure out how to get copies of data from several different sources to plug into a spreadsheet graph for analysis. Using Microsoft Access, the manager can connect directly to the source data, build a query to extract the necessary information, and create a report with an embedded graph—all with one tool.

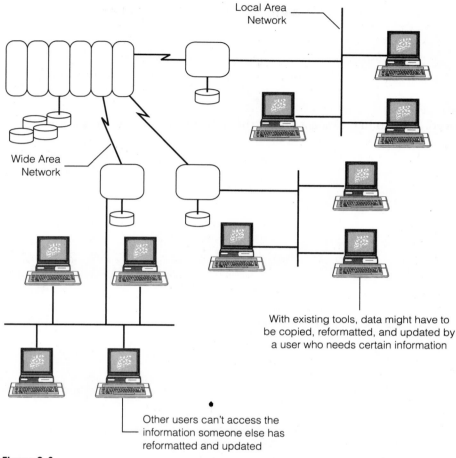

Local Area
Network

Wide Area
Network

With existing tools, data might have to
be copied, reformatted, and updated by
a user who needs certain information

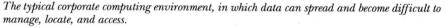

Other users can't access the
information someone else has
reformatted and updated

Figure 2-3.
The typical corporate computing environment, in which data can spread and become difficult to manage, locate, and access.

Large corporations will also find Microsoft Access especially suited for creating the workstation portion of client-server applications. Unlike many other Windows client application development systems, Microsoft Access uses its knowledge of the application data and structure to simplify the creation of forms and reports. Applications developed using Access can be made available to users at all levels of the corporation. And with Access it's easy to design truly "user-friendly" applications that fully utilize the investment in employee workstations.

In the next chapter, you'll explore some of Microsoft Access's many features in a quick tour of the product.

3

Touring
Microsoft Access

Before you plunge into the many facets of Microsoft Access, it's worthwhile to spend a little time looking it over and "kicking the tires." This chapter helps you understand the relationships between the main components in Access and shows you how to move around within the product.

WINDOWS FEATURES

Microsoft Access takes advantage of the many easy-to-use features of the Microsoft Windows operating system. If you have used other Windows products, such as Microsoft Excel or Microsoft Word for Windows, you'll be right at home with Access's use of menus, tool bars, and drop-down lists. Even if you are new to the Windows operating system, you'll discover that all the techniques you quickly learned in the first chapter of the *Microsoft Windows User's Guide* apply just as easily to Access. When working with data, you will find familiar cut/copy/paste capabilities for moving and copying data and objects within Access. In addition, Access supports useful *drag and drop* capabilities to assist you in designing queries, forms, reports, and macros. For example, you can select a field in a table, and then drag the field and drop it where you want that data to appear in a report.

THE ARCHITECTURE OF MICROSOFT ACCESS

Microsoft Access calls anything that can have a name an *object*. Within an Access database, the main objects are tables, queries, forms, reports, macros, and modules.

If you have used other database systems on desktop computers, you might have seen the term *database* used to refer to just the files in which you store data. In Microsoft Access, a database also includes all the major objects related to the stored data, including those objects you define to automate the use of your data. Inside a Microsoft Access database, these major objects are

Table   An object you define and use to store data. Each table contains information about a particular subject, such as customers. Tables contain *fields* that store the different kinds of data, such as a customer name or address, and *records* that collect all the information about a particular instance of the subject, such as all the information about a customer named Jane Smith. You can define a *primary key* (one or more fields that have a unique value for each record) and one or more *indexes* on each table to help speed access to your data.

Query   An object that provides a custom view of data from one or more tables. In Microsoft Access, you can either use its graphical query by example (QBE) facility, or you can write SQL statements to create your queries. You can define queries to select, update, insert, or delete data. You can also define queries that create new tables from data in one or more existing tables.

Form   An object designed primarily for data input, display, or control of application execution. You use forms to completely customize the presentation of data that is extracted from queries or tables. You can also print forms. You can design a form to run a *macro* or *module* (see below) in response to any of a number of events—for example, to run a macro when the value of data is changed.

Report   An object designed for formatting, calculating, printing, and summarizing selected data. You can view a report on your screen before you print it.

Macro   An object that is a structured definition of one or more actions that you want Access to perform in response to a defined event. For example, you might design a macro that opens a subform in response to the selection of an item on a main form. You might have another macro that validates the contents of a field whenever the value in the field changes. You can include simple conditions in macros to specify when one or more actions in the macro should be performed or skipped. You can use macros to open and execute queries, open tables, or print or view reports. You can also run other macros or modules from within a macro.

Module   An object that is a custom function you code using Microsoft Access Basic, a variant of the Microsoft Basic language that is designed to work with Access. You do not need to create modules unless your application requires a function not covered by standard macro actions.

Figure 3-1 shows you a conceptual overview of how objects in Microsoft Access are related.

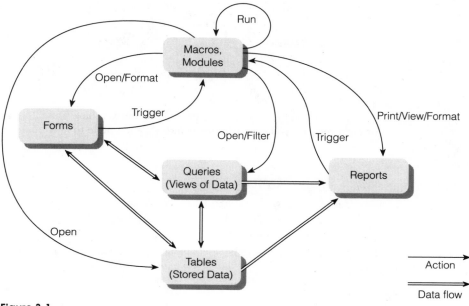

Figure 3-1.
Microsoft Access's main objects and their relationships.

THE TOUR

Now that you know a little bit about the major objects that make up a Microsoft Access database, a good next step is to spend some time exploring the extensive Northwind Traders (NWIND) sample database application that you received with the product. Start Access, and choose the Open Database command from the File menu, as shown in Figure 3-2. In the Open Database dialog box, shown in Figure 3-3 on the next page, select the file NWIND.MDB in your Microsoft Access directory. You will see the *Database window* for the NWIND database, as shown in Figure 3-4 on the next page.

Figure 3-2.
The File menu.

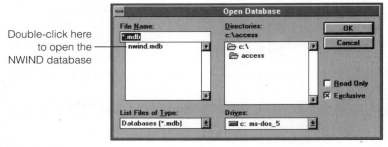

Double-click here
to open the
NWIND database

Figure 3-3.
The Open Database dialog box.

The Database window always opens in the upper left corner of the Access workspace. The title bar shows you the name of the database that you have open. Although you can have only one Access database open at any one time, you can connect that open database (and its forms, reports, macros, and modules) to tables in other Access databases, to data in Paradox, dBASE, or Btrieve databases, or to data in SQL Server databases on a network.

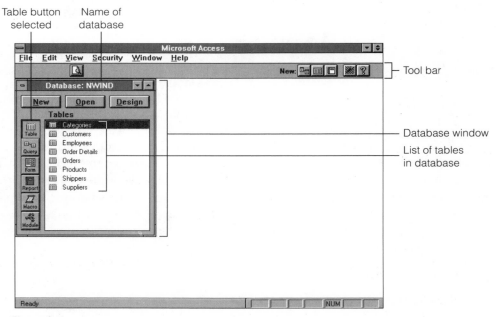

Figure 3-4.
A Database window.

Notice that Access displays a few additional buttons on the tool bar after you open a Database window. As you explore Microsoft Access, you'll see that Access customizes the tool bar to provide you with buttons that are most appropriate for the work you are currently doing. In all, Microsoft Access has 11 different tool bars. Each one will be described in detail in the appropriate chapters later in this book.

Down the left side of the Database window are buttons that allow you to choose one of the six major object types: tables, queries, forms, reports, macros, or modules.

Tables

When you first open a Database window, Microsoft Access automatically selects the Table button and shows you the list of available tables in this database. See Figure 3-4. Across the top of the window, just under the title bar, you can see three command buttons. One allows you to create a new table, and the other two allow you to open the two views of existing tables:

 Allows you to define a new table.

 Lets you view and update the data in the selected table from the table list. Clicking this button opens a Table window in Datasheet View.

Design Lets you view and modify the selected table's definition. Clicking this button opens a Table window in Design View.

When the Database window is active, you can select any of these command buttons from the keyboard by pressing the first letter of the command button name while holding down the Alt key. You can also open a table in Datasheet view by double-clicking the table name in the Database window with your *left* mouse button, or you can open the table in Design view by double-clicking the table name using your *right* mouse button.

Table Window in Design View

When you want to change the *definition* of a table (the structure or design of a table, as opposed to the data in a table), you must open the Table window in Design view. With the NWIND database open, double-click the table named Customers with your right mouse button to open the Customers table in Design view. See Figure 3-5 on the next page. Notice that the NWIND Database window appears behind the active Table window. You can click in any part of the Database window to make it active and bring it to the front. You can also use the F11 key to make the Database window active (or use Alt-F1 on keyboards with 10 or fewer function keys).

Notice that in Design view each row in the top portion of the Table window defines a different field in the table. You can use your mouse to select any field that you want to modify. You can also use the Tab key to move left to right across the

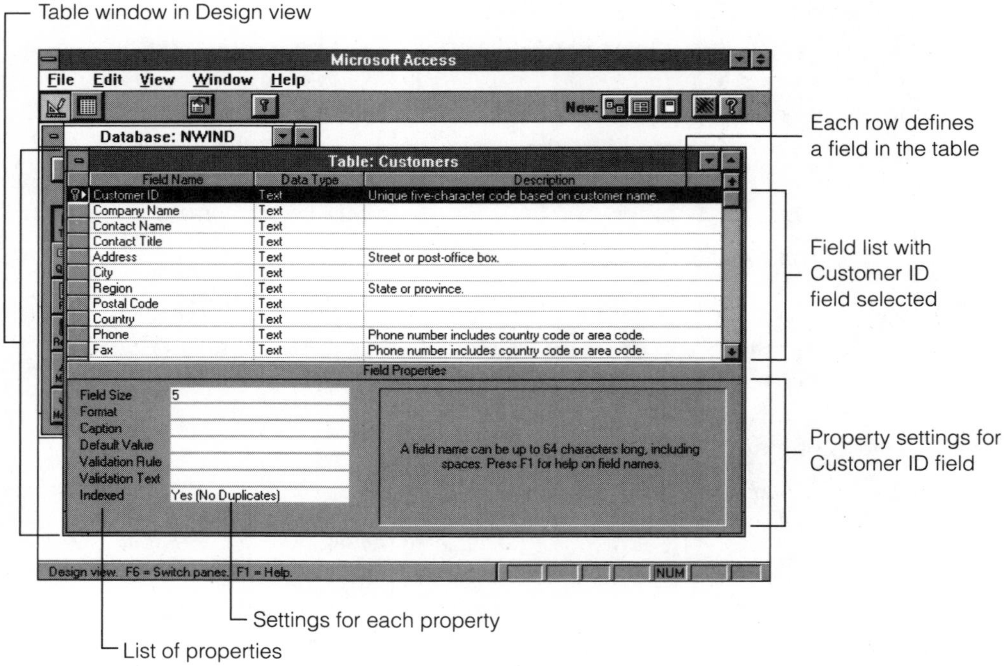

Table window in Design view

Each row defines
a field in the table

Field list with
Customer ID
field selected

Property settings for
Customer ID field

Settings for each property

List of properties

Figure 3-5.
A Table window in Design view.

screen from column to column. Use Shift-Tab to move right to left across the screen from column to column. Use the up and down arrow keys to move from row to row in the field list. As you select a different row in the field list in the top portion of the window, you can see the property settings for the selected field in the bottom portion of the Table window. Use the F6 key to move between the top (the field list) and bottom (the property settings) portions of the Table window in Design view.

Microsoft Access has many features that make it easy to use. Wherever you can choose from a limited list of valid values, Access provides a drop-down list box to assist you in selecting the proper value. For example, when you tab to an area in the Data Type column you should notice that a small gray down arrow button appears at the far right of the column. Click the arrow or press Alt-down arrow to see the list of available valid data types, as shown in Figure 3-6.

You can open as many as 254 tables, or as limited by your computer's memory. You can also minimize any of the windows to an icon by clicking the down arrow in the upper right corner of the window, or you can maximize the window to fill the Access workspace by clicking the up arrow in that same corner. See Figure 3-7. If you don't see a window you want, you can use a list of active windows in the Window menu

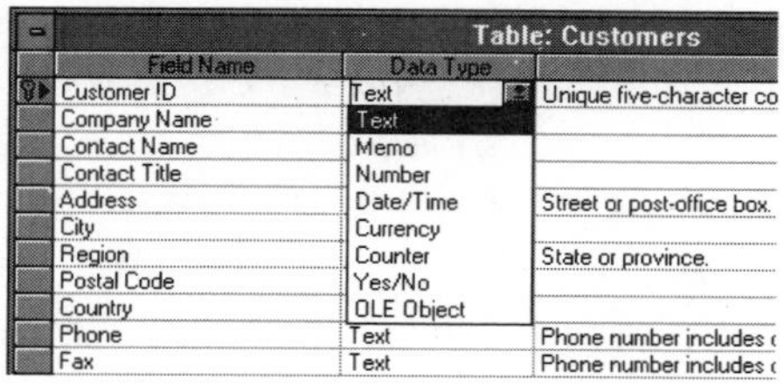

Figure 3-6.
The Data Type drop-down list box.

to bring the window to the front. You can use the Hide command in this menu to make selected windows temporarily disappear, or use the Show command to make visible any windows that you have previously hidden. Choose the Close command from the File menu or the Control menu to close any window.

Table Window in Datasheet View

To view, change, insert, or delete data in a table, you can use the table's Datasheet view. A datasheet is a simple way to look at your data in rows and columns without

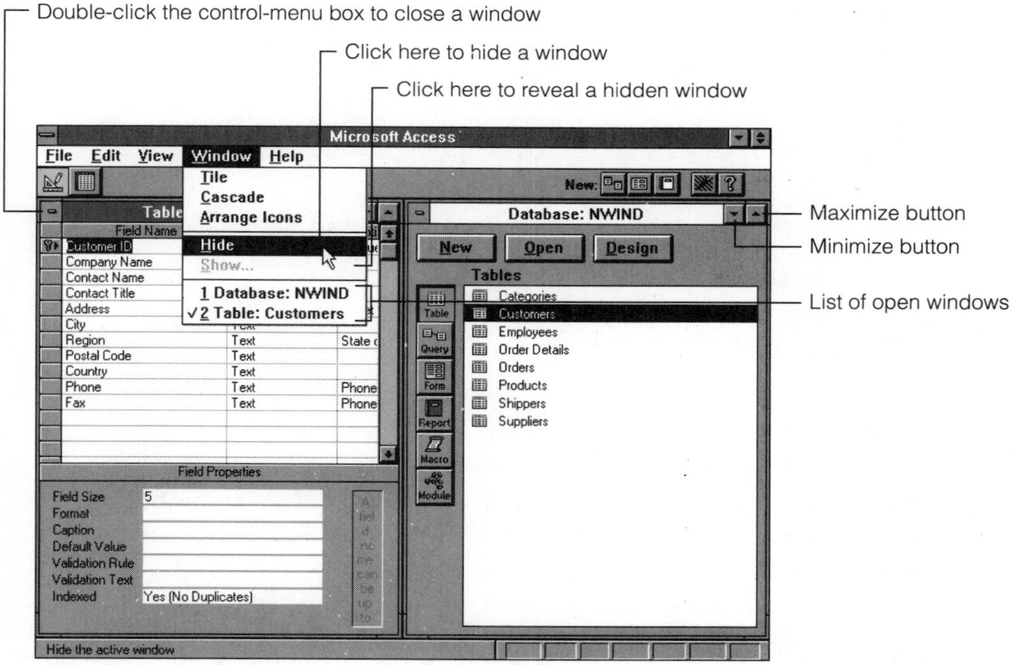

Figure 3-7.
Some ways to manage windows in Microsoft Access.

any special formatting. You can open a table's Datasheet view by selecting the name of the table you want in the Database window and clicking the Open button. When you open a table in Design view, such as the Customers table in Figure 3-5, you can also go directly to the Datasheet view of this table by clicking the Datasheet button on the tool bar, as shown in Figure 3-8.

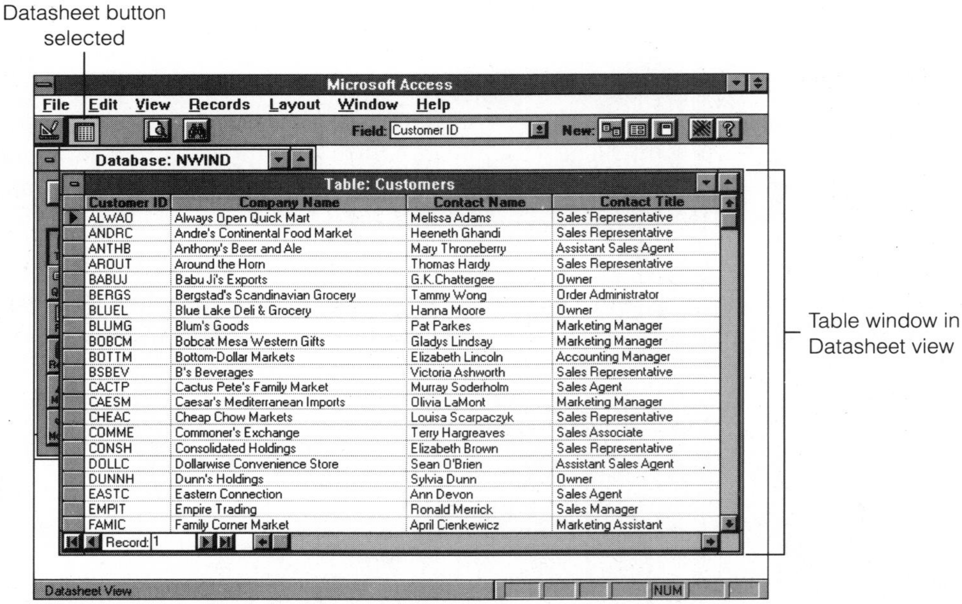

Figure 3-8.
A Table window in Datasheet view.

As in the Table window in Design view, you can move from field to field with the Tab key and move up and down the records with the arrow keys. You can also use the scroll bars at the bottom and on the right side to move around in the datasheet. To the left of the bottom scroll bar, Access shows you the current record number. You can select the record number with your mouse (or press the F5 key), type a new number, and press Enter to go to that new record number. You can use the arrows on either side of this record number box to move up or down one record or to the first or last record in the table. See Figure 3-9. You'll read more about working with data in Datasheet view in Chapter 7, "Using Datasheets."

Close the Customers window now by double-clicking the window's control-menu box or by choosing the Close command from the File menu. You should now be back in the Database window for NWIND.

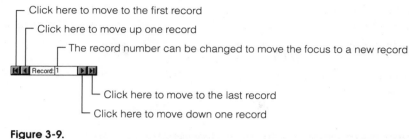

Figure 3-9.
The record number box.

Queries

You probably noticed that the Datasheet view of the Customers table gave you all the fields and all the records in the table. What if you want to see just the customer names and addresses? Or maybe you'd like to see information about customers and all of their outstanding orders in one view. To solve these problems, you can create a *query*. Click the Query button to see the list of queries available in NWIND, as shown in Figure 3-10.

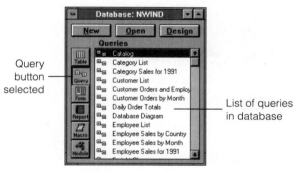

Figure 3-10.
A query list in the Database window.

Across the top of the Database window, just under the title bar, you can see three command buttons:

New	Allows you to define a new query.
Open	Lets you view and possibly update the data gathered by the query selected in the query list. Clicking this button opens a Query window in Datasheet view. You might not be able to update all data in a query.
Design	Lets you view and modify the definition of the query selected in the query list. Clicking this button opens a Query window in Design view.

When the Database window is active, you can select any of these command buttons from the keyboard by pressing the first letter of the command button name while holding down the Alt key. You can also open a query in Datasheet view by double-clicking the query name in the window using your left mouse button, or you can open the query in Design view by double-clicking the query name using your right mouse button.

Query Window in Design View

When you want to change the definition of a query (the structure or design, as opposed to the data represented in the query), you must open the Design view of the query. Take a look at one of the more complex queries in the NWIND query list by scrolling to the Order Review query. Double-click the Order Review query with your right mouse button to see the query in Design view, as shown in Figure 3-11. You can also select the query name with your mouse, and then click the Design button at the top of the Database window.

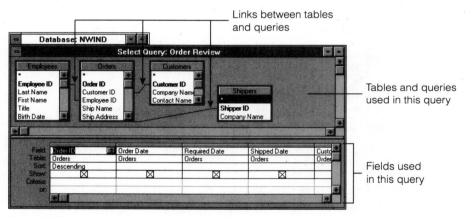

Figure 3-11.
A Query window in Design view.

At the top of a Query window in Design view, you can see the field lists of the tables or other queries that this query uses. The lines between the field lists show you how Microsoft Access links the tables to solve your query. If you define relationships between tables in your database design, Access draws these lines automatically. See Chapter 5, "Building Your Database in Microsoft Access," for details. You can also define relationships when you build the query by dragging a field from one table or query and dropping it on a field in another table or query.

At the bottom of the Query window, you can see the fields that Access uses in this query, the tables or queries from which the fields come, any sorting criteria, whether fields show up in the result, and any selection criteria for the fields. You can use the bottom scroll bar to bring other fields in this query into view. As in the Design view of tables, you can use the F6 key to move the cursor between the top and bottom portions of the Query window.

Query Window in Datasheet View

Click the Datasheet button on the tool bar to run the query and see the results in a query datasheet, as shown in Figure 3-12.

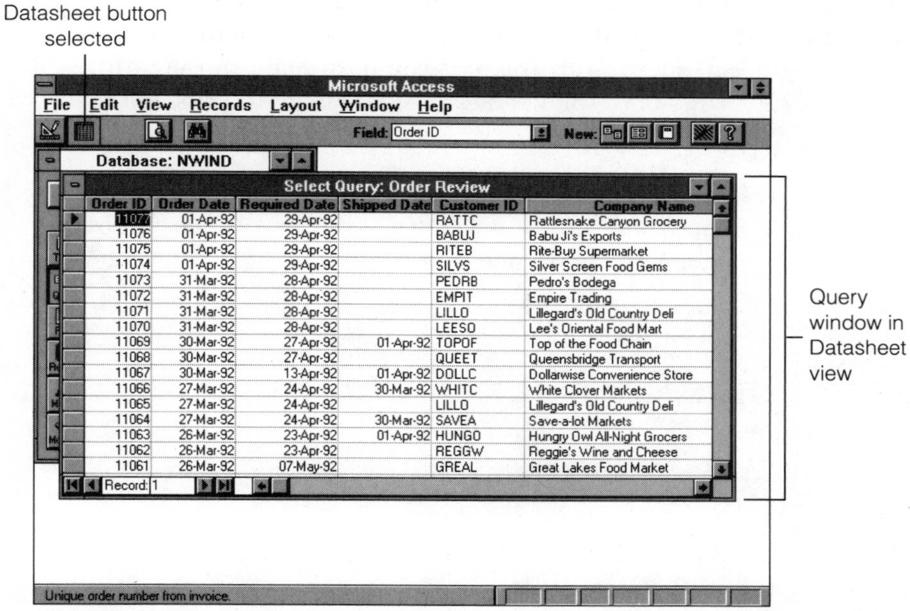

Figure 3-12.
A Query window in Datasheet view.

Query windows in Datasheet view are similar to Table windows in Datasheet view. Even though the fields in the datasheet in Figure 3-12 are from four different tables, you can work with the fields as though they were in a single table. If you're designing an Access application for another person, you can use queries to hide much of the complexity of the database and make the application much simpler to use. Depending on how you designed the query, you might also be able to update some of the data in the underlying tables simply by typing in new values as you would in a Table window in Datasheet view. See Chapter 8, "Adding Power with Select Datasheets," for details.

Close the Query window to see only the Database window.

Forms

Datasheets are useful for looking at and changing data in your database, but they're not particularly attractive or simple to use. If you want to format your data in any special way or automate how your data is used and updated, you need to use a *form*. Forms provide several key capabilities:

- You can control and enhance the way your data looks on the screen. For example, you can add color and shading or add number formats. You can add controls such as a drop-down list or a check box. You can display OLE objects such as pictures and graphs directly on the form. And you can calculate and display values based on data in a table or query.

- You can perform extensive editing of data using a form with macros.

- You can link multiple forms or reports together with macros or modules that are run from buttons on a form. You can also customize the menu bar using macros associated with your form.

Click the Form button in the NWIND Database window to see the list of available forms, as shown in Figure 3-13.

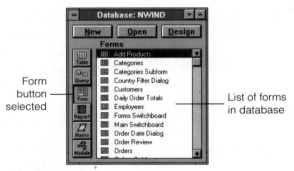

Figure 3-13.
A forms list in the Database window.

Across the top of the window, immediately under the title bar, you can see three command buttons:

 Allows you to define a new form.

Lets you view and update your data through the form you have selected in the form list. Clicking this button opens a Form window in Form view.

 Lets you view and modify the definition of the form you have selected in the form list. Clicking this button opens a Form window in Design view.

When the Database window is active, you can select any of these command buttons from the keyboard by pressing the first letter of the command button name while holding down the Alt key. You can also open a form in Form view by double-clicking the form name in the window using your left mouse button, or you can open the form in Design view by double-clicking the form name using your right mouse button.

Form Window in Design View

When you want to change the definition of a form (the structure or design, as opposed to the data represented in the form), you must open the form in Design view. Take a look at the Order Review form in the NWIND database; it's designed to display the data from the Order Review query just discussed. Scroll down through the list of forms in the Database window and double-click the Order Review form with your right mouse button to see the design for the form, as shown in Figure 3-14 on the next page. You can also select the form name with your mouse, and then click the Design button at the top of the Database window. Don't worry if what you see on your screen doesn't exactly match Figure 3-14. In this figure a few things have been moved around and several options have been selected so that you can see all the main features of the Form window in Design view.

When you first open this form in Design view, you should see the toolbox near the lower left of the screen. If you don't see the toolbox, select the Toolbox command from the View menu. This is the action center of form design; you'll use the tools here to add to your form the controls you want, to display data, and to trigger macros or modules. See Chapter 11, "Form Basics," and Chapter 12, "Building a Form," for details.

In the lower right of the window shown in Figure 3-14 you can see a field list labeled Order Review Query. This is the query you looked at earlier in this chapter. You might see the field list near the top of the Form window when you first open the form. If you don't see the field list, choose the Field List command from the View menu or click the Field List button on the tool bar. You can move the field list by dragging the title bar. When you read about form design in Chapter 11, you'll see that you can pick a tool from the toolbox, then drag and drop a field from the field list to place a field-display control on the form.

After you place all the controls on a form, you might want to customize some of them. You'll do this by opening the property sheet, which you can see in the lower left of Figure 3-14. To see this window, select the Properties command from the View menu or click the Properties button on the tool bar. The property sheet always shows the property values for the currently selected control in the Form window. In the example shown in Figure 3-14, the text box called Freight has been selected,

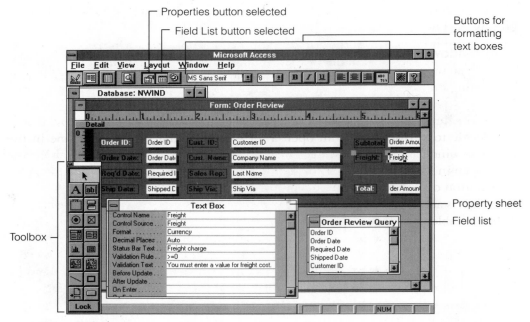

Figure 3-14.
A Form window in Design view.

toward the right side of the form. Looking at the property sheet, you can see that Access displays the Freight field from the query in a Currency format. The designer specified a validation rule and a validation message to be displayed if the validation rule fails. The designer could have named a macro or module to perform a more complex data validation. If you scroll down the list of other properties for this text box, you can see the wide range of conditions for which you can specify a macro or initiate a Microsoft Access Basic module.

You might have noticed that Access displayed some additional boxes and buttons on the tool bar when you selected the Freight control. When you select a text box on a form in Design view, Access shows you drop-down boxes to make it easy to select a font and font size, and Access shows you three buttons to let you set values for a property: Bold, Italic, and Underline. To the right of these are four buttons to set text alignment: Left, Center, Right, or General. (General Alignment will left-align text and right-align numbers.)

If all of this looks just a bit too complex, don't worry! Building a simple form is really quite easy. In addition, Access provides you with a *FormWizard* that you can use to automatically generate a number of standard form layouts based on the table or query you choose. You'll find it simple to customize a form to your needs once the FormWizard has done most of the hard work. See Chapter 13 for details.

Form Window in Form View

To view, change, insert, or delete data via a form, you can use the form's Form view. Depending on how you've designed the form, not only can you work with your data in an attractive, clear context, but you can also have the form validate the information you enter, or you can use it to trigger other forms or reports based on actions you decide to perform. You can open a form by selecting the form's name in the Database window and clicking the Open button. Since you have the Order Review form open in Design view, you can go directly to the Form view by clicking the Form View button on the tool bar. See Figure 3-15.

This is actually a fairly simple form that brings together information from four different tables into a display that's easy to use and understand. This form includes

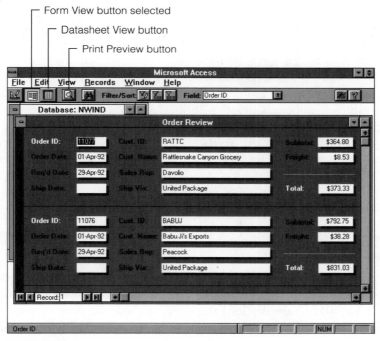

Figure 3-15.
A Form window in Form view.

all the fields from the Order Review query. In addition, the form calculates a total that didn't exist in the query. You can tab or use the arrow keys to move through the fields, but you'll discover that the form is designed so that the user cannot accidentally enter data.

There are two other ways to look at a form: Datasheet view and Print Preview. You can use the Datasheet View button on the tool bar to see all the fields on the form arranged in a datasheet—similar to a datasheet for a table or a query. You can click the Print Preview button on the tool bar to view on your screen what the form will look like on a printed page. You'll read more about Print Preview in the next section on reports. For now, close the Order Review window so that only the Database window is visible on your computer screen.

Reports

Although you can print information in a datasheet or form, neither of those formats provides the flexibility you need to produce complex printed output such as invoices or summaries that might include many calculations and subtotals. Formatting in datasheets is limited to sizing the rows and columns and specifying fonts. You can do a lot of formatting in a form, but because forms are designed primarily for viewing and entering data on your screen, they are not suited for extensive calculations, grouping of data, or multiple totals and subtotals in print. If your primary need is to print data, you should use a report. Click the Report button to see the list of reports available in NWIND, as shown in Figure 3-16.

Across the top of the window, just under the title bar, you can see three command buttons:

> **New** Allows you to define a new report.

> **Preview** Lets you see how the report you selected will look on a printed page. Clicking this button initiates the Print Preview command.

> **Design** Lets you view and modify the definition of the report you selected. Clicking this button opens a Report window in Design view.

When the Database window is active, you can select any of these command buttons from the keyboard by pressing the first letter of the command button name while holding down the Alt key. You can also look at the report in Print Preview by double-clicking the report name in the window using your left mouse button, or you can open the report in Design view by double-clicking the report name using your right mouse button.

Report Window in Design View

When you want to change the definition of a report, you must open the report in Design view. In the reports list for NWIND, double-click the Alphabetical List of

Figure 3-16.
The Reports list in the Database window.

Products report with your right mouse button to see the design for the report, as shown in Figure 3-17. You can also select the report name with your mouse and then click the Design button at the top of the Database window. Don't worry if what you see on your screen doesn't exactly match Figure 3-17. A few things were moved around and several options were selected so that you could see all the main features of the Report window in Design view.

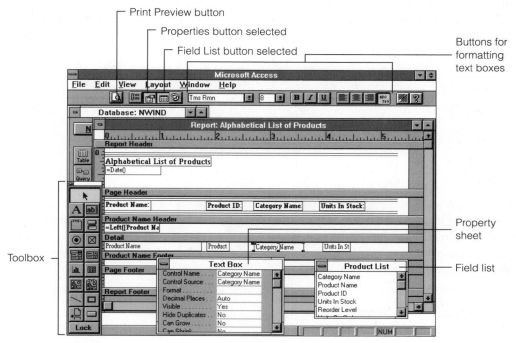

Figure 3-17.
A Report window in Design view.

You can see that the Design view for reports is similar to the Design view for forms. (Refer to Figure 3-14.) Reports provide additional flexibility, allowing you to group items and to total them (either across or down). You can also define header and footer information for the entire report, for each page, and for each subgroup.

When you first open this report in Design view, you should see the toolbox near the lower left of the screen. If you don't see the toolbox, select the Toolbox command from the View menu.

In the lower right of Figure 3-17 you can see a window titled Product List. This is a field list containing all the fields from the Product List query that provides the data for this report. You might see this list near the top of the report's Design view when you first open it. If you don't see the field list, select the Field List command from the View menu or click the Field List button on the tool bar. You can move the field list by dragging the title bar. When you read about report design in Chapter 15, "Report Basics," you'll see that you can pick a tool from the toolbox and then drag and drop a field from the field list to place the field-display control on the form.

After you place all the controls on a report, you might want to customize some of them. You'll do this by opening the property sheet, which you can see in the lower center of Figure 3-17. To see this window, select the Properties command from the View menu or click the Properties button on the tool bar. The property sheet always shows the property settings for the currently selected control in the Report window. In the example shown in Figure 3-17, the text box called Category Name is selected. You can see that Access displays the Category Name field from the query as the input data for this control. You can also specify complex formulas that calculate additional data for report controls.

You might have noticed that Access displayed some additional boxes and buttons on the tool bar when you selected the Category Name control. When you select a text box in a report in Design view, Access shows you drop-down boxes to make it easy to select a font and font size, and Access displays three buttons—Bold, Italic, and Underline—to let you set the values for a property. To the right of these are four buttons to set text alignment: Left, Center, Right, or General. (General alignment left-aligns text and right-aligns numbers.)

Reports can be even more complex than forms, but building a simple report is really quite easy. As with forms, Access provides you with a *ReportWizard* that you can use to automatically generate a number of standard report layouts based on the table or query you choose. You'll find it simple to customize a report to suit your needs after the ReportWizard has done most of the hard work. See Chapter 16, "Constructing a Report," for details.

Report Window in Print Preview

Reports do not have a Datasheet view. To see what the finished report looks like, choose the Print Preview button (shown in Figure 3-17) on the tool bar when you are in the Report window in Design view. From the Database window, you can also select the report name and then click the Preview button. The Alphabetical List of Products looks like Figure 3-18 in Print Preview.

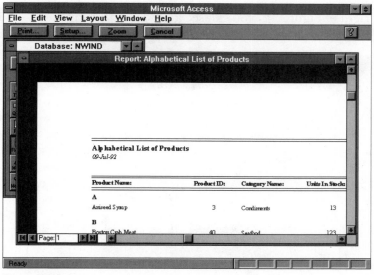

Figure 3-18.
A Report window in Print Preview.

Microsoft Access initially shows you the upper left corner of the report. To see the report centered in full-page view in the Print Preview window, click the Zoom button on the tool bar. The full-page view is a reduced picture, which gives you an overall idea of how Access arranges major areas of data on the report; but unless you have a large monitor, you won't be able to read any of the data. See Figure 3-19 on the next page. When you move the mouse pointer over the window, the mouse pointer changes into a magnifying glass icon. To zoom in, you can place this icon in an area that you want to see more closely, and click. You can also click the Zoom button on the tool bar to again see a close-up view of the upper left corner of the report. Use the scroll bars to move around in the magnified report.

Close the Report window to return to the Database window.

Macros

You can make working with your data much easier within forms and reports by triggering a macro action.

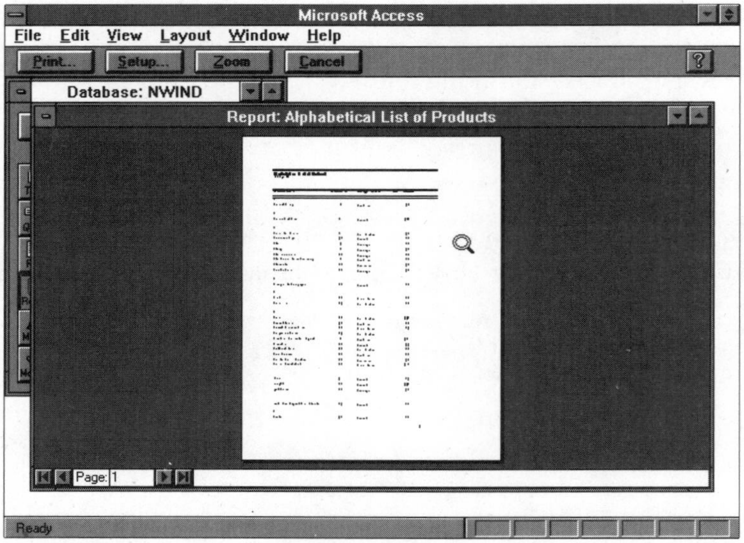

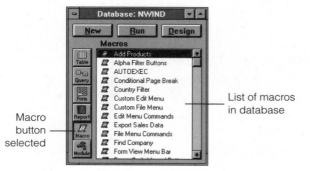

Figure 3-19.
A "zoomed" report in Print Preview.

Microsoft Access provides more than 40 actions that you can include in a macro. They perform actions such as opening tables and forms, running queries, running other macros, selecting options from menus, and sizing open windows. You can even start other applications that support Dynamic Data Exchange (DDE), such as Microsoft Excel, and exchange data from your database with that application. You can group multiple actions in a macro and specify conditions that determine when each set of actions will or will not be executed by Access.

In the Database window, click the Macro button to see the list of available macros in the NWIND database, as shown in Figure 3-20.

Figure 3-20.
A Macros list in the Database window.

Across the top of the window, just under the title bar, you can see three command buttons:

 Allows you to define a new macro.

Lets you execute the actions in the macro you have selected in the Database window. A macro file can consist of a single set of commands or multiple named sets. If you select a macro file from the Macro list and then click the Run button, Access runs the first macro in the file.

Lets you view and modify the definition of the macro you have selected in the Database window. Clicking this button opens a Macro window in Design view.

When the Database window is active, you can select any of these command buttons from the keyboard by pressing the first letter of the command button name while holding down the Alt key. You can also run a macro by double-clicking the macro name in the window using your left mouse button, or you can open the Macro window in Design view by double-clicking the macro name using your right mouse button.

One of the most useful things you can do with a macro is to validate data entered on a form. You can even check the value in one control based on the value of another control. For example, take a look at the Validate Postal Codes macro in the NWIND database. Scroll down in the Database window until you see this macro name, select it, and click the Design button. You'll see a window similar to Figure 3-21.

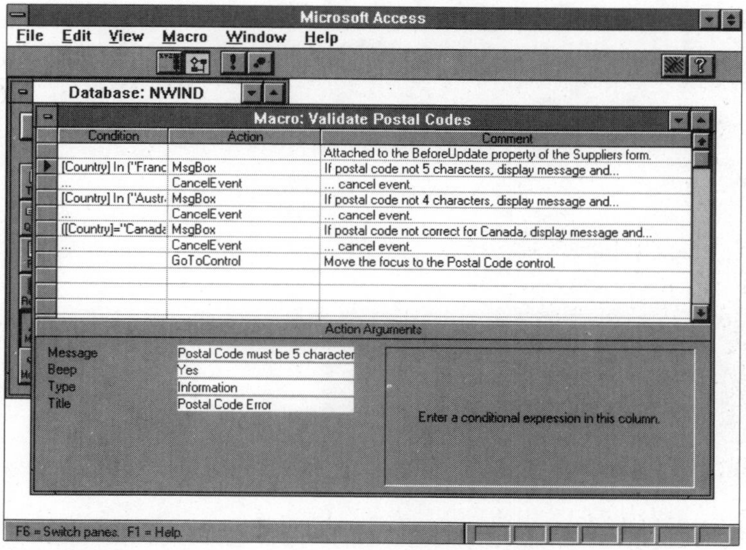

Figure 3-21.
A field-validation macro.

This macro is designed to validate the length of the postal code when a postal code is entered along with the country in a form. In France, Italy, and Spain, the postal code must be five characters long. In Australia and Singapore, the postal code is only four characters long. The postal codes in Canada consist of a letter-number-letter combination, a space, and a number-letter-number combination. In the macro shown in Figure 3-21, when any condition is not true, the MsgBox action opens a window and displays an appropriate error message. The CancelEvent action prevents the record update and returns you to the erroneous field. You can just begin to imagine some of the possibilities with macros. See Chapter 18, "Adding Power with Macros," for details. Close the Macro window to return to the Database window.

Modules

You might find that you keep coding the same complex formula over and over in some of your forms or reports. Although you can easily build a complete Microsoft Access application using only forms, reports, and macros, you might find there are some actions that are difficult or impossible to define in a macro. To solve these problems, you need a Microsoft Access Basic module. You can create modules that perform a series of calculations, and then you can use that module as a function in a form or report. Since the Microsoft Access Basic language is a complete programming language with complex logic and the ability to link to other applications and files, you can solve unusual or difficult programming problems with a module.

Click the Module button in the Database window to display the window shown in Figure 3-22. The complete NWIND database application does not require any modules. However, Microsoft includes a sample module in NWIND called Introduction To Programming that helps you understand the programming examples in the manuals.

Figure 3-22.
A module list in the Database window.

From the Database window you can either start a new module with the New button or open the design of an existing module with the Design button. You can run a module only from a macro or a form, except that you can also run a module as a validation function from a table or a form.

Select the Introduction To Programming module and click the Design button to open a window containing the Microsoft Access Basic code in the module. Use the Procedure drop-down list box on the tool bar or choose the Procedures command from the View menu to look at the procedure names available in the sample. One of the more simple, yet interesting functions in this module, called DueDate, calculates the first weekday in the month following the date supplied by the routine or macro that calls the function. This routine might be useful to calculate the first business day of the following month to display as a payment due date on an invoice. You can see this function in Figure 3-23.

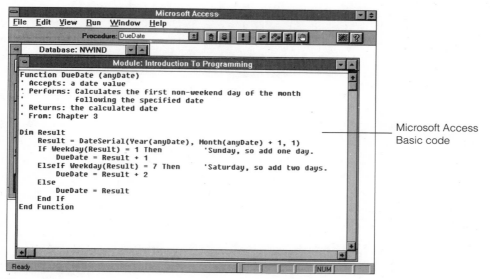

Microsoft Access Basic code

Figure 3-23.
A Microsoft Access Basic module.

When you have completed this book, you will find that you can perform most tasks you need without modules, using only forms, reports, and macros. Refer to *Microsoft Access Basic: An Introduction to Programming* in your product documentation for more information about Microsoft Access Basic and modules.

Now that you have had a chance to look at the major objects in the NWIND sample database, you should be getting comfortable with how you will go about working with Access. Perhaps the most important aspect of building an application is designing the database that will support your application. The next chapter describes how you should design your application data structures. Building a solid foundation makes creating the forms and reports for your application easy.

PART II

BUILDING A DATABASE

This part of the book teaches you how to design a database, how to define the database in Microsoft Access, and how to change an existing Access database. Anyone planning to build a Microsoft Access application should read these chapters in detail.

Chapter 4 covers the fundamentals of good relational database design. The procedure covered here teaches you how to identify major tasks that you'll implement in your application and how to design the data structures you'll need to support those tasks.

Once you've designed a database, Chapter 5 shows you how to define the database in Microsoft Access.

Chapter 6 covers all the major types of changes that you might want to make to your database design once it's been defined.

4

Designing
Your Database

You could begin building a database in Microsoft Access much as you might begin creating a simple single-sheet problem in a spreadsheet application like Microsoft Excel—just start organizing your data into rows and columns and throw in calculation formulas where you need them. If you have ever worked extensively with a database or spreadsheet application before, you already know that this unplanned technique will work for only the most trivial situations. Solving real problems takes some planning, or you end up rebuilding your application over and over again. One of the beauties of a relational database like Access is that it is much easier to make mid-course corrections; however, it is well worth your while in the long run to spend time up front designing the data structures you need to support the job you want to do.

You don't have to go deeply into database design theory to build a solid foundation for your database project. In this chapter you'll read about design fundamentals in the first section, "Basic Design Concepts," and then apply those fundamentals in the second section, "Coming Up with Your Design."

BASIC DESIGN CONCEPTS

In a relational database system like Microsoft Access, you should begin by designing each database around a specific set of tasks or functions. For example, you might have one database designed for order processing, and this database would contain information about customers, orders, the items each customer ordered, how the orders were shipped, how much the customers owe for each order, who supplied the items you sold, and so forth. In Access, the NWIND sample database is this sort of database. You might have another database that handles your company's human resources tasks and contains all the relevant information about your employees— their names, job titles, employment history, dependents, insurance coverage, and the like.

It's at this point that you face your biggest design challenge: How do you organize information within each task-oriented database so that you take advantage of the relational capabilities of the tool and avoid inefficiency and waste?

Waste Is the Problem

You use a table within your database to store the information you need for the tasks you want to perform. A table is made up of columns or *fields* that each contain a specific kind of information (such as customer name or item price), and rows or *records* that collect all the information about a particular person, place, or thing. You can see this organization in the NWIND database's Customers table, as shown in Figure 4-1.

Company Name	Contact Name	Contact Title	Address	City	
Always Open Quick Mart	Melissa Adams	Sales Representative	77 Overpass Ave.	Provo	UT
Andre's Continental Food Market	Heeneth Ghandi	Sales Representative	P.O. Box 209	Bellingham	WA
Anthony's Beer and Ale	Mary Throneberry	Assistant Sales Agent	33 Neptune Circle	Clifton Forge	WA
Around the Horn	Thomas Hardy	Sales Representative	Brook Farm	Colchester	Ess
Babu Ji's Exports	G.K.Chattergee	Owner	Box 29938	London	
Bergstad's Scandinavian Grocery	Tammy Wong	Order Administrator	41 S. Marlon St.	Seattle	WA
Blue Lake Deli & Grocery	Hanna Moore	Owner	210 Main St.	Port Townsend	WA
Blum's Goods	Pat Parkes	Marketing Manager	The Blum Building	London	
Bobcat Mesa Western Gifts	Gladys Lindsay	Marketing Manager	213 E. Roy St.	Seattle	WA
Bottom-Dollar Markets	Elizabeth Lincoln	Accounting Manager	23 Tsawassen Blvd.	Tsawassen	BC
B's Beverages	Victoria Ashworth	Sales Representative	Fauntleroy Circus	London	
Cactus Pete's Family Market	Murray Soderholm	Sales Agent	87 Yuca Dr.	Albuquerque	NM
Ceasar's Mediterranean Imports	Olivia LaMont	Marketing Manager	9308 Dartridge Ave.	San Francisco	CA
Cheap Chow Markets	Louisa Scarpaczyk	Sales Representative	1225 Zephyrus Rd.	Anacortes	WA

Figure 4-1.
The NWIND Customers table in Datasheet view.

For the purposes of this design exercise, assume you need to build a brand new database for order processing for the ACME Corporation. You might be tempted to put all the information about the task you want to do—processing orders—in a single Orders table whose fields are represented in Figure 4-2.

There are basically three things wrong with this technique:

1. Every time the same customer places another order, you have to duplicate the Customer Name and Address fields in another record for the new order. Storing the same name and address over and over in your database wastes a lot of space—and you can easily make a mistake if you have to enter basic information about a customer more than once.

2. There's no way to predict how many items a customer might order at one time. If you try to keep track of each item the customer orders in one record, you have to guess what the largest number of items in an order might be and leave space for Item-1, Item-2, Item-3, Item-4, and more, all the way up to the maximum number. Again, you are wasting valuable space in your database. If you guess wrong, you will have to

change your design just to accommodate an order that has too many items. Also, if you later want to find out which customers ordered what products, you will have to search each Item field in every record.

3. There's no need to waste space in the database storing data that can easily be calculated when it's time to print a report or produce an invoice. For example, you certainly want to keep track of how many items were ordered and the unit price that was quoted to the customer, but you don't need to calculate and keep the total amount owed in a Total Price field.

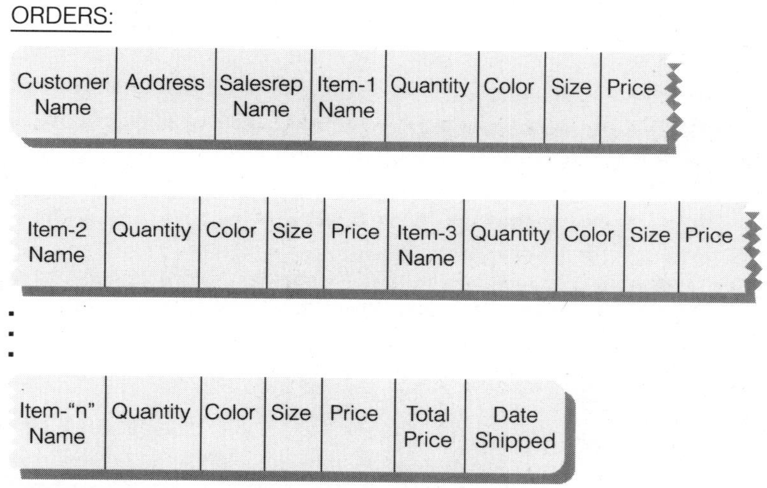

ORDERS:

Figure 4-2.
The design for ACME order processing that uses a single table.

Normalization Is the Solution

To minimize the kinds of problems noted above (although it might not always be absolutely desirable to eliminate all duplicate values), you'll use a process called *normalization* to organize data fields into a group of tables. The mathematical theory behind normalization is rigorous and complex, but the tests you can apply are quite simple, to determine whether you have a design that makes sense and is easy to use.

Rule 1: Field Uniqueness

The first test is a rule about field uniqueness.

Rule 1: Each field in a table should contain a unique type of information.

This rule means that you should get rid of the repeating Item fields in the ACME Orders table. You can do this by creating a row in this table for each item ordered

ORDERS:

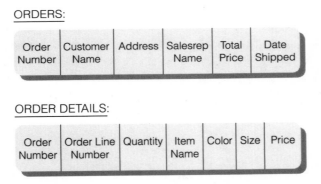

Figure 4-3.
A design for ACME order processing that eliminates repeating item fields.

and inserting an Order Line Number field to uniquely identify the individual rows in each order. The result might be represented by Figure 4-3.

This table is much simpler because it's now easy to process one record per item ordered—whether you are pulling items from inventory to ship or creating a detailed bill for the customer. Also, you don't have to worry about having enough "buckets" in your records to hold large orders. And if you want to find out who has ordered a particular item, you need to look in only one place in each record.

However, the problem is now somewhat worse because you are repeating the Customer Name, Address, Salesrep Name, Total Cost, and Date Shipped fields on each and every line. You can solve that problem by assigning a unique code number to each order and moving the information about items out to another table. The result is represented in Figure 4-4.

ORDERS:

Figure 4-4.
A design for ACME order processing that includes a separate table for item information.

Although it appears that you have created duplicate data with the Order Number field in each table, you have actually significantly reduced the total amount of data stored. The Customer Name and Address fields have to be stored only once in the Orders table for each order and not for each and every item ordered. You have duplicated only a small piece of information, the Order Number field, which allows you to *relate* the Order Details data to the appropriate Orders data. Relational databases are especially equipped to support this design technique by giving you powerful tools to bring related information back together easily. (You'll take a first look at some of these tools in Chapter 8, "Adding Power with Select Queries.")

But you still have the Customer Name field stored in each and every order. You are also repeating the Item Name field in each and every order detail. To solve this, you need to understand a few additional rules about relational tables.

Rule 2: Primary Keys

To qualify as a good relational database design, each record in any table must be unique. That is, there must be no two rows in a table that can possibly be identical. For example, it doesn't make sense to keep two records that both describe the same customer.

Rule 2: Each table must have a unique identifier, or primary key, that is made up of one or more fields in the table.

In the Orders table, the Order Number field is probably unique in the ACME order processing system, so the Order Number field could well be the primary key of that table. See Figure 4-5.

ORDERS:

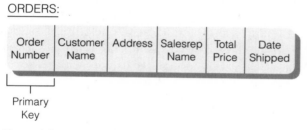

Primary
Key

Figure 4-5.
The primary key for the ACME Orders table.

In the ACME Order Details table, Order Number might be repeated many times—once for each line item in the order. The Order Line Number is also not unique—every order has a line number 1. However, the combination of Order Number and Order Line Number is unique and can serve as the primary key for this table. See Figure 4-6.

ORDER DETAILS:

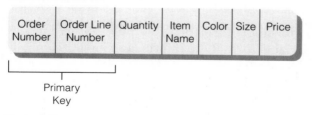

Primary
Key

Figure 4-6.
The primary key for the ACME Order Details table.

Whenever you build a table in an Access database, Access always recommends that you define a primary key for a table. You can let Microsoft Access build an artificial primary key, in which case Access adds a counter field to each record; Access increments that counter by 1 each time you add a new record.

Rule 3: Functional Dependence

Once you have a primary key in each table, you can check to see if you have included all the information relevant to the subject of the table. In terms of relational database design theory, you should check to see whether each field is *functionally dependent* on the primary key.

Rule 3: For each unique primary key value there must be one and only one value in any of the data columns, and that value must be relevant to the subject of the table.

This rule works in two ways. First, you shouldn't have any data in a table that is not relevant to the subject (as defined by the primary key) of the table. For example, you don't need an employee salary in your customer orders table. Second, the information in the table should completely describe the subject. For example, if some of your customers have both a billing and a shipping address, one address field in the Orders table is not going to be sufficient. Or perhaps your sales representatives work in teams; then one Salesrep Name field is not enough. Fortunately, the information in the ACME Orders table is all relevant.

If you need a more complete address, simply adding another address field might work, as shown in Figure 4-7.

ORDERS:

Figure 4-7.
A second address is added to the ACME Orders table to make the information more complete.

In the second example of missing information (multiple sales rep names), you should probably create another table to hold the information about the members of each sales team, as shown in Figure 4-8.

You might be tempted to create the Sales Teams table with a single Sales Team ID field and multiple columns to contain the Salesrep Name fields. If you do that, you are violating Rule 1 on page 47, which calls for unique information in each field. However, if all of your sales teams are made up of exactly two or exactly three

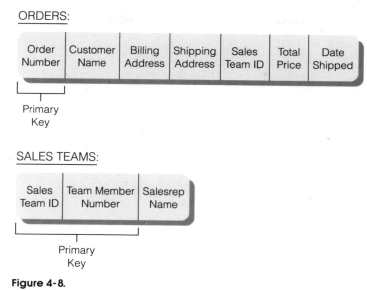

Figure 4-8.
A Sales Teams table is added to the database.

people, it is acceptable to do this. Notice that in this design there's a Team Member Number field as part of the primary key to accommodate sales teams of any size.

Rule 4: Field Independence

The last rule checks to see if you will have any problems when you make changes to the data in your tables.

> *Rule 4: You must be able to make a change to any field (other than fields in the primary key) without affecting any other field.*

Take a look again at the Orders table in Figure 4-8. The first field outside the primary key is Customer Name. If you need to correct the spelling of a name, you can do so without affecting any other fields in this record. If you got the customer wrong (the order is really for Jameson Labs on Main Street, not James Company on First Street), you can't change Customer Name without also fixing Billing Address and Shipping Address. The Customer Name, Billing Address, and Shipping Address fields are not *independent* of one another. In fact, Billing Address and Shipping Address are *functionally dependent* on Customer Name (see Rule 3 above). Customer Name describes another subject, different from the subject of orders. When you have this situation, it calls for another table in your design. You need a separate Customers table, as shown in Figure 4-9 on the following page.

Now if you have spelled the name incorrectly, you just change the Customer Name field in the Customers table. Note that instead of using Customer Name (which might be 40 or 50 characters long) as the primary key of the Customers table,

ORDERS:

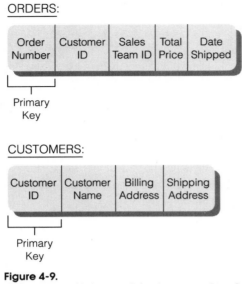

Primary
Key

CUSTOMERS:

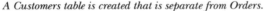

Primary
Key

Figure 4-9.
A Customers table is created that is separate from Orders.

you create a shorter Customer ID field (perhaps a 5-digit number) to minimize the size of the relational data you need in the Orders table.

Another (although less rigorous) way you can check for this condition of field independence is to see if you have the same information repeated over and over in your records. In the previous design, you would soon notice that whenever a customer had placed more than one order, you had to enter the customer's name and the addresses in multiple order records. Now that you have a separate Customers table, if you need to correct the spelling or change an address, you only have to make the change in one field of one record in the Customers table. If you find you have the wrong customer, you only have to change the Customer ID field in the Orders table to fix the information.

What about the other fields in the Orders table? You can make a change to Sales Team ID or Date Shipped independently of the other fields. You can also change the Total Price field without affecting other fields in *this* record, but Total Price is related to two fields, Quantity and Price, in the Order Details records. In fact, Total Price is one of those calculated fields (the sum of the quantity times price for all items in the order) that you would be better off not including in your table.

The only reason to keep a calculated field in your table is to improve performance. For example, if you frequently produce a report that lists outstanding orders and the amount owed, and you never need to show the details of the items ordered, then keeping the calculated total in the Orders table saves searching the Order Details table each time you want that report. However, you must be sure to build your application so that you always update Total Price whenever you add a new item to the order or change Quantity or Price in Order Details.

If you look at the Order Details table in Figure 4-6, you can see that the Item Name, Color, Size, and Price fields probably also belong in another table. Be careful that the Price you charge a customer is always the latest Price in the new Items table. If you have a policy of charging the price quoted at the time of the order, or you have different discounts that you give to each customer, you might need to keep a Quoted Price in the Order Details table that is different from the Price in the Items table. See Figure 4-10.

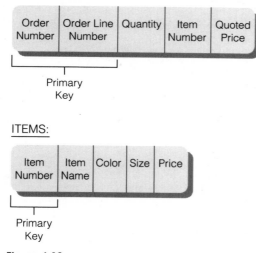

Figure 4-10.
A new Items table is created that is separate from Order Details.

After applying all the rules, the database design includes five tables, which are all shown in Microsoft Access in the query in Figure 4-11 on the following page.

Efficient Relationships Are the Result

When you apply good design techniques, you end up with a database that efficiently links your data. You probably noticed that when you normalize your data as recommended, you tend to get lots of separate tables as a result. Before relational databases were invented, you either had to compromise your design or manually keep track of the relationships between files or tables. For example, you either had to put customer information in your Orders table, or you had to write your program to first open and read a record from the Orders table and then search for the matching record in the Customers table. Relational databases solve those problems. With a good design you don't have to worry about how to bring the data together when you need it.

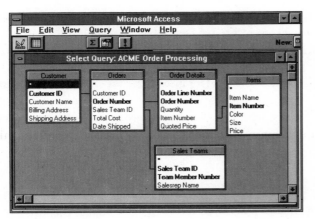

Figure 4-11.
The ACME Corporation order processing tables are shown in a Microsoft Access query.

Foreign Keys

You probably noticed as you followed along in the ACME example above that each time you created a new table, you left behind a small piece of information that could link you to the new table—Customer ID and Sales Team ID fields in the Orders table, and an Item Number field in the Order Details table. These "linking" fields are called *foreign keys.*

In a well-designed database, foreign keys result in efficiency. You keep track of related foreign keys as you lay out your database design. When you define your tables in Access, you link primary keys to foreign keys to tell Access how to automatically join the data when you need to get information from more than one table. To improve performance, you also instruct Access to build indexes on your foreign keys. (For details on defining indexes, see the section in Chapter 5 titled "Building Your Database in Microsoft Access.")

One-to-Many and One-to-One Relationships

In most cases, the efficient relationship between any two tables is one-to-many. That is, for any one record in the first table, there are many related records in the second table, but for any record in the second table, there is exactly one matching record in the first table. You saw many instances of this pattern of relationship in the ACME design. For example, each customer might have several orders, but an order applies to only one customer. An order has many order details, but each order detail is a part of only one order. An item might appear in many different order details, but an order detail has only one Item.

Occasionally, it might be useful to further break down a table because you use some of the information in the table infrequently or because some of the data in the table is highly sensitive and should not be available to everyone. For example, you might want to keep track of some descriptive information about each of your customers for marketing purposes, but you don't need that information all the time. Or you might have data such as credit rating or amount of credit that should only be accessible to certain authorized people in your company. In either case, you can create a separate table that also has a primary key of Customer ID. The relationship between the original Customers table and the Customer Info or Customer Credit tables is one-to-one. That is, for each record in the first table, there is exactly one record in the second table. Like the one-to-many relationship, the one-to-one relationship of tables is an efficient design.

COMING UP WITH YOUR DESIGN

Now that you understand the fundamentals of relational database design, the rest of this chapter shows you a method for gathering and organizing your tasks and data. You'll follow the design of a new order-processing application for Prompt Computer Solutions, Incorporated, a small business.

Throughout the rest of the book this Prompt Computer Solutions application will be used as an example, and you will build pieces of the application as you explore the architecture and features of Microsoft Access. This sample application (PROMPT) for Prompt Computer Solutions is somewhat more complex than the Northwind Traders sample (NWIND) provided with the product. PROMPT is designed to show you some techniques not found in the product documentation. The PROMPT database is described in Appendix B. If you don't want to build the PROMPT database yourself, you can find a copy on the Microsoft Access forum on CompuServe. See the Introduction of this book for details.

There are two major schools of thought when it comes to designing databases: *process-driven design* (also known as *top-down design*) that focuses on the functions or tasks you need to perform, and *data-driven design* (also known as *bottom-up design*) that concentrates on identifying and organizing all the bits of data you need. The method used here incorporates ideas from both philosophies.

This book starts by having you identify and group tasks to help you decide whether you need only one or more than one database. (This is a top-down approach.) As explained previously, databases should be organized around a group of related tasks or functions. For each task, you then choose the individual pieces of data you need. Next, you gather all the data fields for all related tasks and begin organizing them into subjects. (This is a bottom-up approach.) Each subject forms the foundation for the individual tables in your database. Finally, you apply the rules you learned in the "Basic Design Concepts" section of this chapter in order to create your tables.

Identifying Tasks

Assume you have been given an assignment to act as Microsoft Access database consultant to a small company, Prompt Computer Solutions, Incorporated. This company custom builds and resells personal computer systems, software, and components. The owners of the company need a better way to keep track of customers, of the computer systems and components they order, and of the many suppliers from which Prompt Computer Solutions gets the parts, boards, software, and peripherals that the company resells. The owners need to

- Record customer orders
- Schedule customer order fulfillment
- Calculate charges
- Bill customers
- Record customer payments
- Manage inventory
- Order parts and components from suppliers
- Keep track of money owed to suppliers
- Pay supplier bills
- Prepare monthly income statements
- Analyze quarterly sales
- Produce a sales catalog
- Track profit margins

To start, this chapter will introduce you to an application design worksheet that you would fill out for each task. A blank worksheet is shown in Figure 4-12. Consider the first task—Record Customer Orders. Your purpose with this task is to provide a list of available company products and then to enter the ordered items on an order form (and in the database) when a customer calls or sends in an order. Looking at the other tasks identified by the business owner, the list of related tasks probably includes fulfilling orders, calculating charges, billing customers, and recording payments. You would fill out one task worksheet for each related task, and then you'd be ready to start working on the data you need.

Selecting the Information You Need

After you have identified all tasks, you would list for each task the data items you need to do that task. On the task worksheet, you enter a name for each data item, how the data item will be used, and a brief description. The Usage column on the

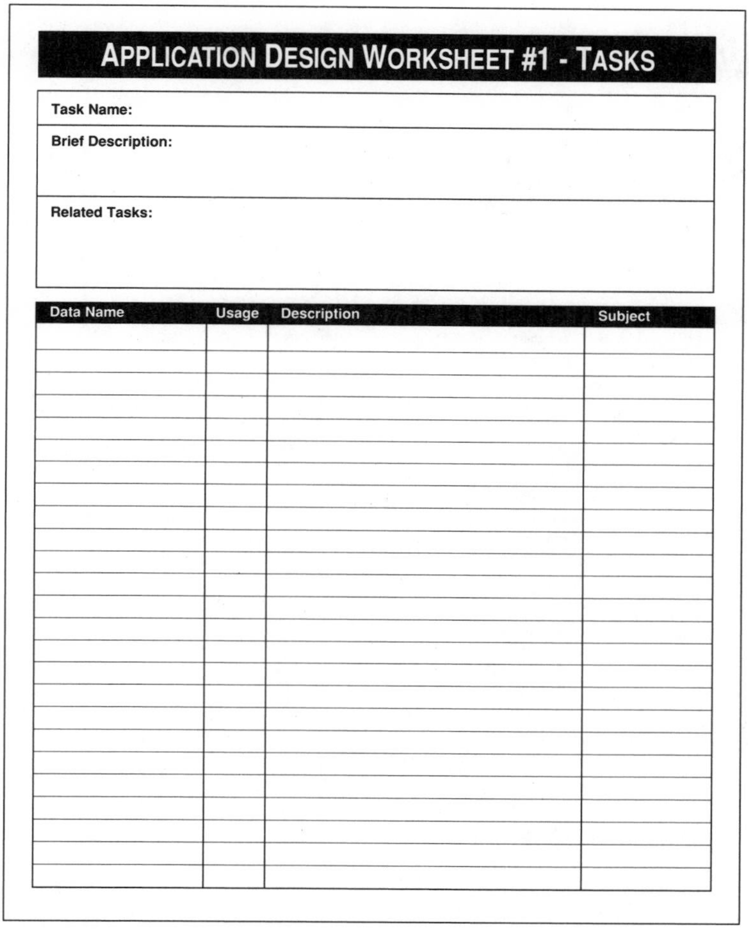

APPLICATION DESIGN WORKSHEET #1 - TASKS

Task Name:

Brief Description:

Related Tasks:

Data Name	Usage	Description	Subject

Figure 4-12.

An application design worksheet for use with tasks.

form has five codes—I, O, U, D, C—that stand for Input, Output, Update, Delete, and Calculate. In the Subject column, you enter the name of the Microsoft Access object to which you think each data item belongs. For example, an Address might belong to a Customer table. A completed application design worksheet for the Record Customer Orders task might look like Figure 4-13 on the following page.

Choosing the Database Subjects

If you have been careful in identifying the subject for each data item you need, your next step is very easy. You would create another set of worksheets similar to Figure 4-14 on page 59 to help you collect all the data items that belong to each subject. At

APPLICATION DESIGN WORKSHEET #1 - TASKS

Task Name:	Record Customer Orders
Brief Description:	Capture customer orders when they call in Help customer choose items Inform customer of total price
Related Tasks:	Schedule customer order fulfillment Calculate charges Bill customers Record customer payments

Data Name	Usage	Description	Subject
Company Name	I	Name of company	Customer
Customer Name	I	Name of company contact	Customer
Address	I, U	Street address	Customer
City	I, U	City	Customer
State/Province	I, U	State or province	Customer
Postal Code	I, U	Zip or postal zone code	Customer
Country	I, U	Country	Customer
Phone Number	I, U	Phone number	Customer
Fax Number	I, U	Fax number	Customer
Credit Limit	I	Maximum credit allowed	Customer
Amount Owed	I, U	Amount customer currently owes	Customer
Last Pay Date	I	Date of last payment	Customer
Item Name	I	Description of item	Items
Item Description	I	Name of item we're selling	Items
Item Components	I	Parts of this item	Items
Days to Build	I	Time to assemble item	Items
Cost	I	Our cost	Items
Quantity on Hand	I	In-stock amount	Items
Quantity Ordered	O	Amount customer wants	Order
Price Quoted	O	Price charged this customer	Order
Sales Tax	C	Tax we have to charge	Order
Shipping Charge	C	Cost to send the items	Order
Total Cost	C	Total for the order	Order

Figure 4-13.
A completed application design worksheet for the Record Customer Orders task.

the top of the form for each subject, you list the related subjects that appear in any given task. Under the Relationship column, you enter the kind of relationship (one-to-many or one-to-one). For example, the Customer subject might have "many" Orders. A completed application design worksheet for the Customer subject is shown in Figure 4-15 on page 60.

As you copy each data item to the subject worksheet, you decide the data type (text, number, currency, memo, and so on) and how large the stored data needs to be. The data item description is a short descriptive phrase that you can enter into the design for your table. Access will use the description as the default information that will be displayed in the status bar at the bottom of the screen whenever the field is selected on a datasheet, form, or report.

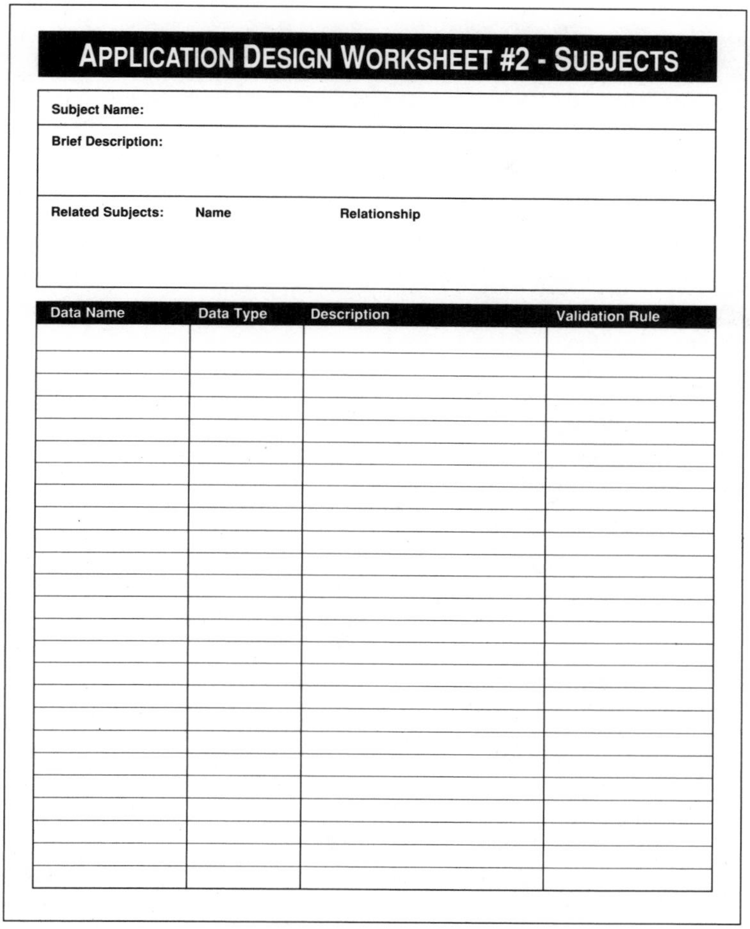

APPLICATION DESIGN WORKSHEET #2 - SUBJECTS

Subject Name:

Brief Description:

Related Subjects: Name   Relationship

Data Name	Data Type	Description	Validation Rule

Figure 4-14.
An application design worksheet for use with subjects.

Finally, you might make a note of any validation rules that should always apply to the data field. Later you can define these rules in Microsoft Access, and Access will check each time you create new data to ensure you haven't violated any of the rules. Validating data can be especially important when you create a database application for other people to use.

Mapping Subjects to Your Database

After you fill out all of your subject sheets, each sheet becomes a candidate to be a table in your database design. For each table you must confirm that all of the data you need is included. You must also be sure you don't have any unnecessary data.

APPLICATION DESIGN WORKSHEET #2 - SUBJECTS

Subject Name:	Customer
Brief Description:	Information about customers

Related Subjects:	Name	Relationship
	Orders	Many
	Sales Reps	One
	Sales History	Many

Data Name	Data Type	Description	Validation Rule
Company Name	Text (25)	Name of company	
Customer Name	Text (25)	Name of company contact	
Address	Text (30)	Street address	
City	Text (20)	City	
State/Province	Text (12)	State or province	
Postal Code	Text (10)	Zip or postal zone code	USA: nnnnn-nnnn
			Canada:xnx nxn
Country	Text (6)	Country	Canada, USA
Phone Number	Number (10)	Phone number	>100000000
			2nd digit 0 or 1
Fax Number	Number (10)	Fax number	(same as Phone)
Credit Limit	Currency	Maximum credit allowed	<5000000
Amount Owed	Currency	Amount customer currently owes	
Last Pay Date	Date	Date of last payment	

Figure 4-15.
A completed application design worksheet for the Customer subject.

For example, if any customers need more than one line for an address, you can add a second data field. If you regularly have more than one contact person within a company, you might need to create a separate Contact table that contains records for each name and phone number. The Contact table would be linked back to the Customer table. You would then apply each of the four rules that you learned in the section "Basic Design Concepts":

1. Each field in a table should contain a unique type of information. If you have a subject with repeating items, you need to break up that subject into smaller component parts. Or you might have confused a task and a

subject; in other words, you have chosen a task like Order Processing as your subject instead of separate Customers, Orders, and Order Details subjects. If you have a subject table that looks like the one in Figure 4-1, you have probably made this error.

2. Each table must have a unique identifier, or primary key, that is made up of one or more columns in the table. In many cases, you will have to create a code number to use as an identifier. For example, you might think that the Company Name field in the Customer table can serve as your unique identifier. However, you might do business with some individuals who do not have a company name. Or, there might be several companies with very similar names. In any case, you probably don't want to use a 30-character field as a primary key because you will have to copy that field into related tables that you link together.

3. For each unique primary key value there must be one and only one value in any of the data columns, and that value must be relevant to the subject of the table.

4. You must be able to make a change to any field (other than fields in the primary key) without affecting any other field. If you have carefully mapped out subjects at a low enough level of detail, you should have no problem with this rule.

Creating Table Links

The last step in designing your database is to create the links between each of your tables. For each subject, look at the subjects for which you wrote Many in the Relationship column of the worksheet. Be sure that the corresponding relationship for the other table is One. If you find Many in both Relationship columns, you must create a separate *intersection* table to handle the relationship. In this example of the Record Customer Order task, one order can contain "many" items, and any given item can appear in "many" orders. The Order Details table is an intersection table that clears up this many-to-many relationship between the Orders and Items tables. Order Details works as an intersection table because it is in a one-to-many relationship with both Orders and Items.

After you have straightened out the many-to-many relationships, you need to create the links between tables. To complete the links, place a copy of the primary key from the "one" tables into the "many" tables. For example, by looking at the worksheet for Customers shown in Figure 4-15, you can surmise that the primary key for the Customer table (probably a field called Customer ID) also needs to be in the Orders table (a "many") and the Sales History table (a "many"). On the other hand, the primary key from the Sales Reps table (a "one") should appear in the Customer table.

ORGANIZING TASKS

You now have enough information to be able to lay out the design for your tables and to define them in your database. Before you wade in to do that task, it's useful to go back to your task sheets and lay out an initial structure for your application. Part of the planning you did on the task worksheets was to consider usage—whether a piece of information might be needed as input, for update, or as output of a given task. Wherever you have something that is required as input, you should have a *precedent* task that creates that data item as output.

For example, in the Record Customer Orders task worksheet in Figure 4-13, you clearly must create catalog items to be able to sell to a customer before you can record customer orders. Similarly, you need the customer information created in some other task before you can use that information (or update it) in this task. So, you should have a task for creating catalog items and a task for creating customer lists. You'll find when you look at catalog items that some of them might be made up of several components. So, even before defining catalog items you need a task to create components.

You might also be able to combine some tasks with others. On the example in Figure 4-13, you can see a reference to a Calculate Charges task that might well be handled within the Record Customer Orders task. You can also see tasks on the worksheet that are subordinate to Record Customer Orders: Bill Customers (print an invoice), Schedule Order Fulfillment, and Record Customer Payments. It's useful to lay out all your defined tasks in a relationship diagram. The relationships of the tasks in the Prompt Computer Solutions database are shown in Figure 4-16.

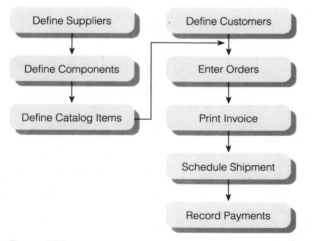

Figure 4-16.
The relationships between the tasks in the Prompt Computer Solutions database.

Now that you understand the fundamentals of good database design, you are ready to move on to doing something a little more fun with Access—actually building a database. The next chapter shows you how to create a new database and tables, and Chapter 6 shows you how to make changes later if you discover you need to modify your design.

In the following chapters, you'll learn about the mechanics of defining queries, forms, and reports using Microsoft Access. You'll find that you're building some pieces of the database to satisfy the tasks shown in Figure 4-16. In the final part of the book, you'll learn about macros and how to link together the queries, forms, and reports you have built to create a working application.

Building Your Database in Microsoft Access

After you have designed the tables for your database, defining them in Microsoft Access is incredibly easy. This chapter shows you how. Continuing the exercise (begun in Chapter 4, "Designing Your Database") of building a database for Prompt Computer Solutions, this chapter shows you how to define the Customer–Chap 5 table and relate it to other tables. For a complete description of the PROMPT database, refer to Appendix B, "Sample Database Schemas."

CREATING A NEW DATABASE

When you first start Microsoft Access, you see only File and Help on the menu bar and the Help button (a question mark) on the tool bar. Open the File menu to see the commands shown in Figure 5-1. If you have previously opened other databases such as the NWIND sample, you might see a "most recently used" list of up to four numbered database selections just above the Exit command.

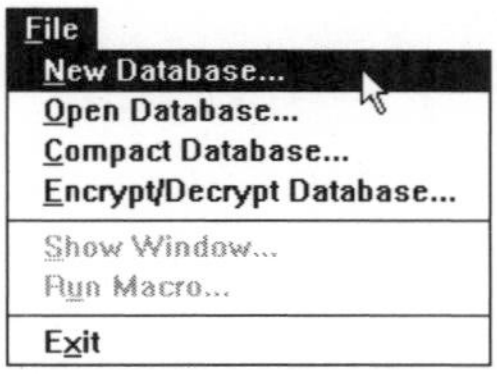

Figure 5-1.
The File menu.

To begin creating a new database, simply choose the New Database command from the File Menu. This command opens the dialog box shown in Figure 5-2 on the following page. Select the drive you want from the Drives drop-down list box and select a directory from the Directories list box. The drive and directory will be the location for the new database. In this example, the directory *access* is selected on the C drive. Finally, go to the File Name text box and type in the name of your new database. Access automatically supplies an MDB extension to the filename for you. If you are creating a database for Prompt Computer Solutions, you could name the database PROMPT.MDB. If you have copied the PROMPT database from CompuServe, you could name your new database MYPROMPT.MDB. Click the OK button to create your database.

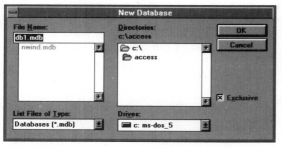

Figure 5-2.
The New Database dialog box.

Microsoft Access takes a few moments to create the system files in which it keeps all the information about the tables, queries, forms, reports, macros, and modules that you might create. When Access has completed this process, you see the Database window for your new database displayed in the upper left corner of your Access workspace, as shown in Figure 5-3.

Figure 5-3.
The Database window for a new database.

When you open any database, Access automatically selects the Tables button and shows you the available tables in the Database window. Because this is a new database, no tables exist yet and the Database window is empty.

THE TOOL BAR FOR THE DATABASE WINDOW

Before you get right down to defining tables in your new database, it is worth spending just a few moments to look at the Database tool bar that Microsoft Access displays when the Database window is active. The buttons are described below.

 Print Preview button. Select a table, query, form, or report and then click this button to see what the selected item will look like in printed form.

New Query button. Click this button to start designing a new query. If you have selected a table or query in the Database window, Access starts you off with the selected table or query as the basis for your new query. See Chapter 8, "Adding Power with Select Queries," for details on building a query.

 New Form button. Click this button to begin a new form. See Chapter 11, "Form Basics," for details on building a report.

 New Report button. Click this button to begin a new report. See Chapter 15, "Report Basics," for details on constructing a report.

Undo button. Click this button to undo your last action. Undo has the same effect as Ctrl-Z or the Undo command on the Edit menu. The button is disabled when there are no changes that can be undone.

 Help button. Click this button to open Access Help at the Contents window. See Figure 5-4 on the following page.

MORE ABOUT MICROSOFT ACCESS HELP

In addition to the Help button on the Database window tool bar, there are several other ways of opening Microsoft Access Help. You can use the commands on the Help menu. The Contents command opens the Contents screen for Help, as shown in Figure 5-4.

You can also bring up context-sensitive help by pressing the F1 key. Whenever you press F1, a Help window opens with information on the active window or the highlighted keyword. To get context-sensitive help on a button or other screen control, press Shift-F1. A special mouse pointer appears that you use to click the screen element about which you have a question. The Help window then opens with the information about the screen element you clicked.

On the Contents screen for Help, you can see a button that runs a special feature in Access Help called Cue Cards. Cue Cards can walk you through the individual steps required to perform any one of six important tasks, as shown in Figure 5-5 on the following page.

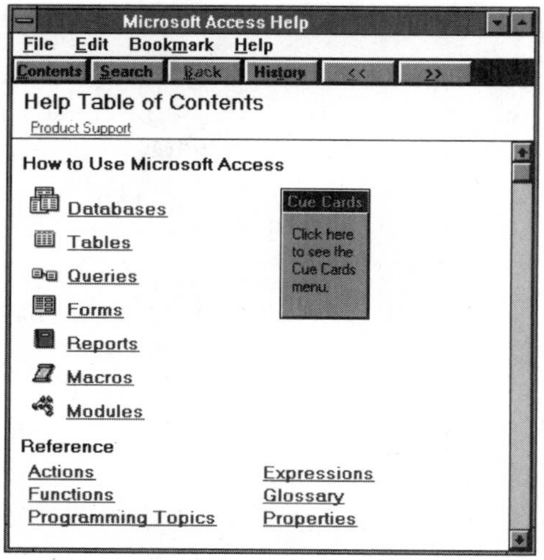

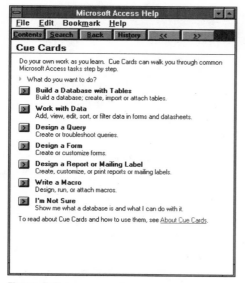

Figure 5-4.
The Contents screen in Microsoft Access Help.

Figure 5-5.
The Cue Cards list in Microsoft Access Help.

DEFINING TABLES

To define a new table in a database, the Database window (as shown in Figure 5-3) must be active. Click the Table button (the top button on the left side of the Database window) and then click the New button at the top of the Database window. Access shows you a blank Table window in Design view, as shown in Figure 5-6. At the top of the window are columns where you can enter each field name, the data type for the field, and a description of the field. Once you select a data type for a field, Access allows you to set field properties in the lower left corner of the Table window. In the lower right corner of the Table window is a box where Access displays informative messages about fields or properties. The contents of this box changes as you move your cursor from one location to another within the Table window.

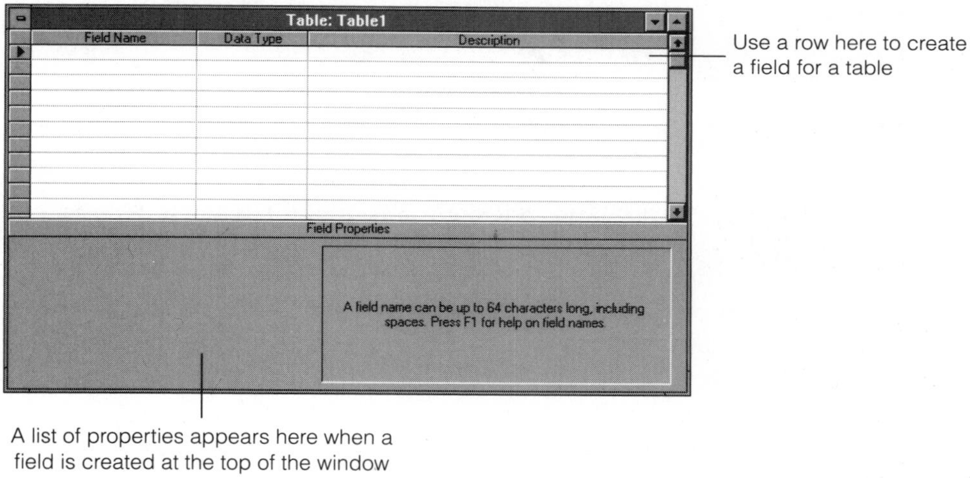
Table: Table1
Field Name
Data Type
Description
Field Properties
A field name can be up to 64 characters long, including spaces. Press F1 for help on field names.
Use a row here to create a field for a table
A list of properties appears here when a field is created at the top of the window

Figure 5-6.
A blank Table window in Design view.

The Tool Bar for the Table Window in Design View

When you open a Table window in Design view, the tool bar changes. From left to right, you can see the following buttons:

Design View button. This button initially appears activated, indicating you are in Design view. Click this button to return to Design view from Datasheet view.

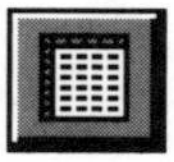

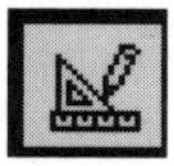

Datasheet View button. Once you have finished designing your table and have saved the design, you can use this button to enter Datasheet view to begin entering data in your table. See Chapter 7, "Using Datasheets," for more details on Datasheet view.

(continued)

Table Properties button. Click this button to open the Table Properties window. See below for details.

Primary Key button. Click this button to define a selected field or fields as the primary key for this table. See below for more details.

Table Properties

Click the Table Properties button on the tool bar or choose the Table Properties command from the View menu to open the window shown in Figure 5-7.

Table Properties
Description . . . . .
Primary Key . . . . .
Index1 . . . .
Index2 . . . .
Index3 . . . .
Index4 . . . .
Index5 . . . .

Figure 5-7.
The Table Properties window.

In the Table Properties window you can enter a description of the table on the first line. You can also enter the field names for the Primary Key and up to five multiple-field indexes. Although the Primary Key field in the Table Properties window is handy for changing the Primary Key later, it's easier the first time to use the Primary Key button on the tool bar to define a primary key. See the "Adding Indexes" section later in this chapter for details on defining a multiple-field index. For now, just enter *Customer–Chap 5* in the first field, and then double-click the control-menu box to close the Table Properties window.

DEFINING FIELDS

Now you're ready to begin defining the fields for the Customer–Chap 5 table. Be sure the cursor is in the first position of the Field Name column, and then type the name of the first field, *Customer ID*. Press the Tab key once to move to the Data Type column. A little gray box with a down arrow appears on the right side of the Data Type column. Here and elsewhere in Microsoft Access this type of box signifies the presence of a drop-down list. Click the down arrow or press Alt-down arrow to open the list of data type options, as shown in Figure 5-8. In the Data Type column you can either type a valid value or select from the list of values in the drop-down list box. The data type values are explained in the "Field Data Types" section below.

Once you have selected a data type, Access shows you some property boxes in the Field Properties area at the bottom of the window. These boxes allow you to set properties and thereby customize a field. Access shows you different boxes, depending on the data type selected, and when the boxes appear they have some default properties in place, as shown in Figure 5-8. The various property settings for each property box are explained in the "Field Properties" section below.

In the Description column for each field (in the upper right of the Table window), you have the option of entering a descriptive phrase for each field. Microsoft Access displays this description in the status bar whenever you select this field in a query in Datasheet view or in a form in Form view or Datasheet view.

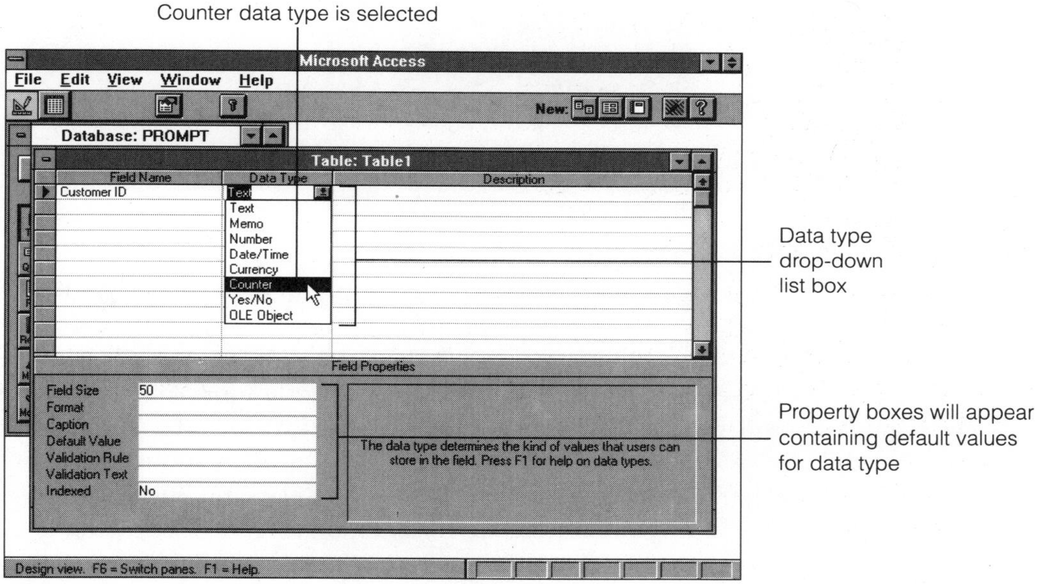

Figure 5-8.
The open list of data type options.

Field Data Types

Microsoft Access supports eight different types of data, each with a specific purpose. These data types are described in Figure 5-9 on the following page.

Choose the data type for each field in your tables that is most appropriate for how you will use that field's data. For character data, you should normally choose the Text data type. You can control the maximum length of a Text field by using a field property, as explained below. Use Memo only for long text that might exceed 255 characters or that might contain formatting characters such as tabs or carriage returns.

Data Type	Usage	Size
Text	Alphanumeric data	Up to 255 bytes
Memo	Alphanumeric data—sentences and paragraphs	Up to 32,000 bytes
Number	Numeric data	1, 2, 4, or 8 bytes
Date/Time	Dates and times	8 bytes
Currency	Monetary data, stored with 4 decimal places of precision	8 bytes
Counter	Unique number generated by Access for each new record	4 bytes
Yes/No	Boolean data	1 bit
OLE Object	Pictures, graphs, or other OLE objects from another application for Windows	Up to 128 megabytes

Figure 5-9.
Microsoft Access data types.

When you choose the Number data type, you'll need to think carefully about what you enter as the Field Size property, because these choices will affect precision as well as length. (For example, integer numbers do not have decimals.) Always use the Currency data type to store money. Currency has the precision of integers, but with a fixed number of decimal places. The Date/Time data type is useful for calendar or clock data and has the added benefit of allowing calculations in minutes, seconds, hours, days, months, or years. For example, you can find out the difference in days between two Date/Time values. The Counter data type is a special kind of number specifically designed for automatic generation of Primary Key values. You can include only one Counter data type in any table.

Use the Yes/No data type to hold Boolean or true/false values. This data type is particularly useful for "flagging" accounts paid or not paid or tests passed or not passed. Finally, the OLE Object data type allows you to store complex data such as pictures, graphs, or sounds that can be maintained by a dynamic link to another application for the Microsoft Windows operating system. For example, Access can store and allow you to edit pictures created using the Paintbrush or Draw applications.

Field Properties

You can customize each field with specific properties you set. These properties vary according to the data type you choose. Properties include:

Field Size	You can specify the length of *Text* and *Number* data types. *Text* can be from 1 through 255 characters long, with a default length of 50 characters. For *Number*, the field sizes are as follows:

Byte	A single-byte integer containing values from 0 through 255
Integer	A 2-byte integer containing values from −32,768 through +32,767
Long Integer	A 4-byte integer containing values from −2,147,483,648 through +2,147,483,647
Single	A 4-byte floating-point number containing values from -3.4×10^{38} through $+3.4 \times 10^{38}$
Double	An 8-byte floating-point number containing values from -1.797×10^{308} through $+1.797 \times 10^{308}$

Format	You can control how your data is displayed or printed. The format options vary by data type.

For *Text* and *Memo* data types, you can specify a custom format that controls how Access displays the data. For details on custom formats, see "Setting Control Properties" in Chapter 13 or the "Format Property–Text and Memo Data Types" topic in Access Help.

For *Number*, *Currency*, and *Counter*, standard format options are:

General Number	The default (no commas or currency symbols; decimal places shown depend on the precision of the data)
Currency	Currency symbols and two decimal places
Fixed	At least one digit and two decimal places
Standard	Two decimal places and separator commas
Percent	Percentage
Scientific	Scientific notation (as in 1.05×10^3)

For the *Date/Time* data type, the format options follow the patterns of the examples below:

General Date	The default 04/15/92 05:30:10 PM (US) 15/04/92 17:30:10 (UK)
Long Date	Wednesday, April 15, 1992 (US) 15 April 1992 (UK)
Medium Date	15-Apr-92
Short Date	4/15/92
Long Time	5:30:10 PM
Medium Time	5:30 PM
Short Time	17:30

(continued)

For the *Yes/No* data type, the options are:

Yes/No   The default

True/False

On/Off

Decimal Place	For *Number* and *Currency* data types, you can specify the number of decimal places that Access displays. The default specification is Auto, which causes Access to display two decimal places for *Currency, Fixed, Standard,* and *Percent* format, and the number of decimal places necessary to show the current precision of the numeric value for *General Number* format. You can also request a fixed display of decimal places, ranging from 0 through 15.
Caption	You can enter a more fully descriptive field name that Access displays on form labels and in report headings.
Default Value	You can specify a default value for all data types except *Counter* and *OLE Object.* For numbers, the standard default value is 0. Access provides a standard empty string for *Text* and *Memo* data types.
Validation Rule	You can supply an expression that must be true whenever you enter or change data in this field. For example, *<100* specifies that a number must be less than 100. You can also check for one of a series of values. For example, you could have Access check for a list of valid cities by specifying *"Chicago" Or "New York" Or "San Francisco"*. In addition, you can specify the name of a macro or a Microsoft Access Basic function to perform more complex validation tests. See the section "Defining Simple Field Validation Rules" later in this chapter. Also see Chapter 18, "Adding Power with Macros."
Validation Text	You can have Microsoft Access display text whenever the data entered does not pass your validation rule.
Indexed	You can ask that an index be built to speed access to data values for *Text, Number, Date/Time, Currency, and Counter* data types. You can also require that the values in the indexed field always be unique for the entire table.

Completing the Fields in Your First Table

You now know enough about field data types and properties to enable you to finish designing the Customer–Chap 5 table for the PROMPT database example. The table you create now will be changed in Chapter 6, "Modifying Your Database Design," so that it is more like the final PROMPT Customer table. (To build the entire PROMPT database, you can use the first database schema in Appendix B. You can also obtain the complete PROMPT database from CompuServe, as described in the Introduction to this book.) Use the information listed in Figure 5-10 to define the table shown in Figure 5-11.

Field Name	Data Type	Description	Field Size
Customer ID	Counter	Customer Identifier	–
Company Name	Text	Customer Company Name	30
Customer Name	Text	Name of Company Contact	25
Address	Text	Street address	30
City	Text	City	20
State	Text	State or province	12
Postal Code	Text	Zip or postal zone code	10
Country	Text	Country name	6
Phone Number	Number	Phone number	20
Fax Number	Number	Fax machine phone number	20
Credit Limit	Currency	Maximum credit allowed	–
Amount Owed	Currency	Amount currently owed	–
Last Pay Date	Date/Time	Date of last payment	8

Figure 5-10.
The field definitions for the Customer–Chap 5 table.

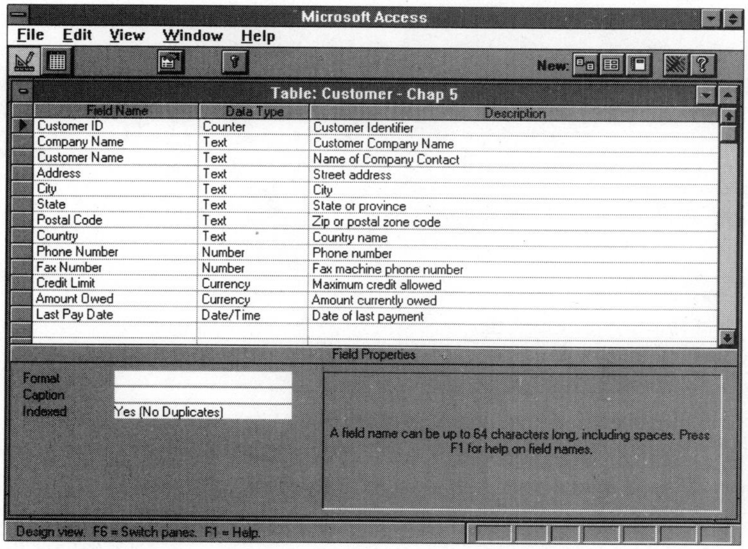

Figure 5-11.
The fields in the Customer–Chap 5 table.

Defining Simple Field Validation Rules

In Figure 5-12, you can see a validation rule for the Country field. To define a simple check on the values that you allow in a field, enter an expression in the validation rule property box for the field. To check for a list of values, enter each value separated by the word *Or*. If one of your values is a text string containing blanks or special characters, be sure to enclose the entire string in quotes. For example, you might enter a validation rule for states surrounding our nation's capital as *"Maryland" Or "Virginia" Or "District of Columbia"*. If you are comparing date values, you must enclose date constants in pound sign (#) characters, as in #01/15/92#.

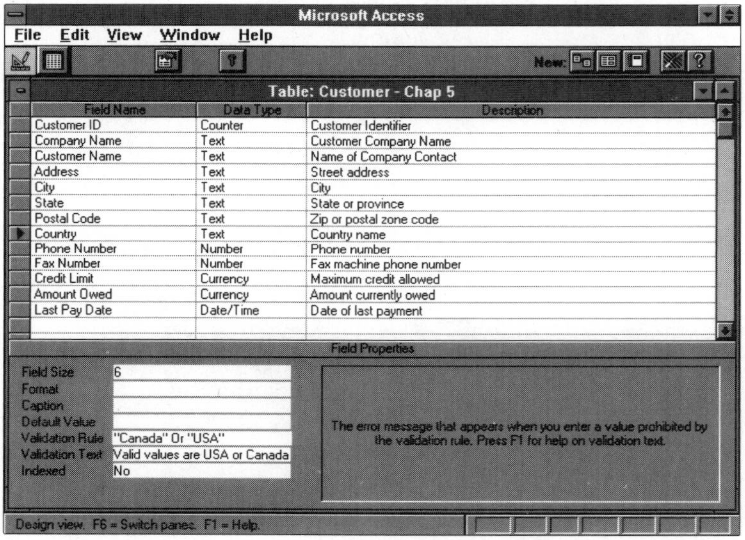

Figure 5-12.
A validation rule for the Country field.

You can also use comparison symbols to compare the value in the field to a value or values in your validation rule. Figure 5-13 shows you the comparison symbols you can use. You might want to check that a numeric value is always less than 1000. To do this, enter *<1000*. You can use one or more pairs of comparisons to check that the value falls within certain ranges. For example, if you want to verify that a number is between 50 and 100, enter *>=50 And <=100*. You can compare the value in a field to a value in any other field. To indicate that you are comparing to a field name, enclose the name in brackets. In the Customer table, you might want to have Access automatically check to be sure that the amount a customer owes cannot exceed the established credit limit. See the example shown in Figure 5-14.

Symbol	Meaning
<	Less than
<=	Less than or equal to
>	Greater than
>=	Greater than or equal to
=	Equal to
<>	Not equal to

Figure 5-13.
Some comparison symbols that can be used in validation rules.

Note that Microsoft Access performs any value comparison between fields using the values stored in the database. Access doesn't store any new values until all validations complete successfully. For example, if a customer's Credit Limit is $5,000 and the customer's Amount Owed is $4,000, your validation rule fails if you change the customer's Credit Limit to $6,000 and the customer's Amount Owed to $5,500 in the same update step. The new Amount Owed ($5,500) exceeds the previous Credit Limit. You must first change the Credit Limit and save the record and then change the Amount Owed.

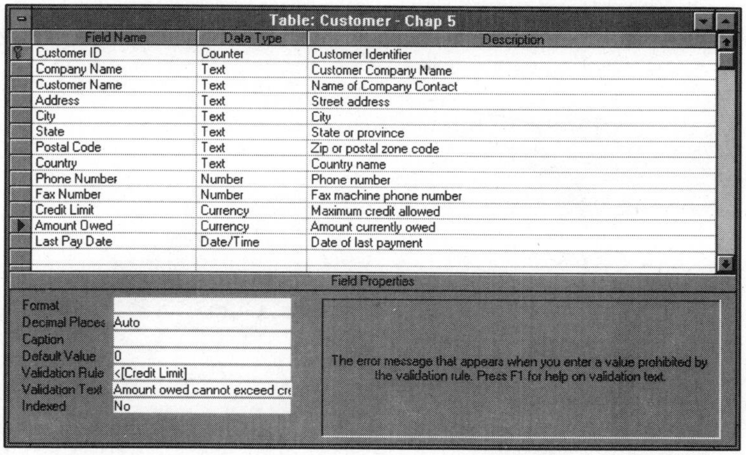

Figure 5-14.
A validation rule that uses another field.

If you're familiar with SQL, you can create a validation rule using any valid SQL predicate. For example, you can also test for a list of values using the In predicate. Finally, you can use an Access macro or an Access Basic module in a form to perform more complex validations. See Chapter 18, "Adding Power with Macros,"for information about creating a macro to do data validation.

DEFINING A PRIMARY KEY

Every table in a relational database should have a primary key. If you used the procedure outlined in Chapter 4, "Designing Your Database," you should know what fields must make up the primary key for each of your tables. Telling Microsoft Access how to define the primary key is quite simple. Select the first field in the primary key by clicking the button to the left of that field's name in the Table window in Design view. If you need to select multiple fields for your primary key, hold down the Ctrl key and click each button of the additional fields you need. When you have selected all the fields for the primary key, click the Primary Key button on the tool bar, or choose the Set Primary Key command from the Edit menu. Access displays a key symbol to the left of the selected fields to acknowledge your definition of the primary key. (To eliminate all primary key designations, you can click the Table Properties button and delete the entry in the Primary Key properties box.) When you finish creating the Customer table for Prompt Computer Solutions, the primary key should be the Customer ID field, as shown in Figure 5-14.

SAVING A NEW TABLE AND ENTERING DATA

The last step you need to perform for a new table is to save it. From the File menu choose the Save command or the Save As command. Microsoft Access will open the Save As dialog box, as shown in Figure 5-15. Type the name of your table, *Customer–Chap 5*, and click OK to save the table.

Figure 5-15.
The Save As table dialog box.

Now you're ready to enter some data into your table. Click the Datasheet button on the tool bar, or choose the Datasheet command from the View menu. Then enter the data shown in Figures 5-16 and 5-17 for Alpha Products, Beta Consulting, and Condor Leasing. You'll notice that the figures below do not show the Customer ID field. Microsoft Access will automatically enter unique numbers for Customer ID because it is set to the Counter data type.

Next spend a few minutes defining the Orders table in the PROMPT database, as defined in Appendix B. You can also go ahead and define all the other tables if you like.

Figure 5-16.
The data in some fields of the Customer–Chap 5 table.

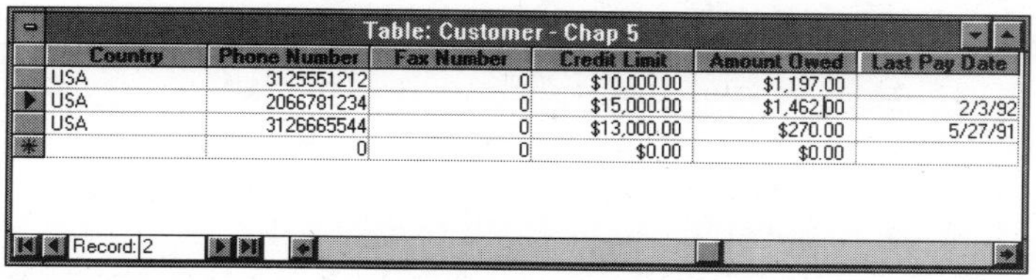

Figure 5-17.
The data in the remaining fields of the Customer–Chap 5 table.

DEFINING RELATIONSHIPS

Once you have defined two or more related tables, you should tell Microsoft Access how the tables are related. If you do this, Access will know how to link all your tables when you need to use them later in queries, forms, or reports.

To define relationships, you need to return to the Database window by closing any Table windows and by clicking the Database window to make it active. Then choose the Relationships command from the Edit menu to open the dialog box shown in Figure 5-18.

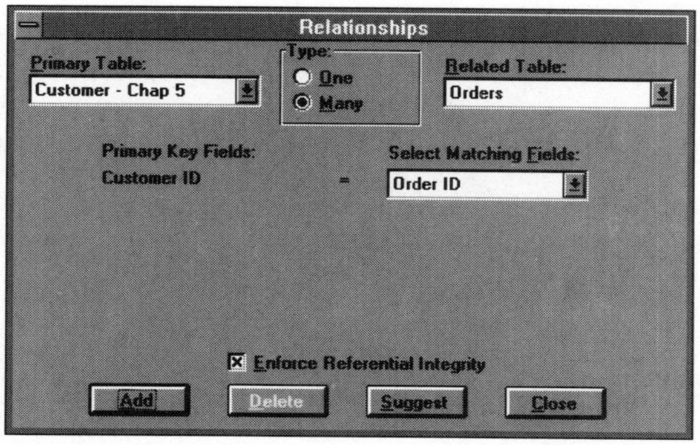

Figure 5-18.
The Relationships dialog box.

On the left side of the dialog box, choose the primary table of the relationship (the table on the "one" side of a one-to-many relationship or either of the tables in a one-to-one relationship) from the Primary Table drop-down list box. (Refer to your subject application design worksheets for design information.) The dialog box shows you the Primary Key fields of the Primary Table. Select the option button in the center Type group box (One or Many) that defines the type of relationship. On the right side, select the related table name from the Related Table drop-down list box. Access displays the available fields with a compatible data type in that table in the Select Matching Fields drop-down list box. You can select the correct matching field or click the Suggest button at the bottom of the dialog box to ask Access for a recommendation. When you ask for a recommendation, Access chooses any field with a matching name and data type.

If you want Microsoft Access to always validate the foreign key values on the "many" side of a relationship, check the Enforce Referential Integrity check box. When you choose this option, Access won't allow you to create a record in the "many" table that doesn't have a matching value in the "one" table. For example, you can't create an order for a nonexistent customer. Also you can't delete a record from the "one" table when you still have records in the "many" table. For example, you can't delete data for a customer that still has outstanding orders.

When you have selected the correct fields, click the Add button to set the relationship definition in Access. That's all there is to it. Later, when you use multiple tables in a query in Chapter 8, "Adding Power with Select Queries," you'll see that Access builds the relationships between tables based on the relationships you have defined.

ADDING INDEXES

The more data you have in your tables, the more you need indexes to help Access search your data efficiently. An index is simply an internal table that contains two columns: the value in the field or fields being indexed and the location of each record containing that value in your table. Assume that you often want to search your Customer table by state. Without an index, when you ask Access to find all the customers in the state of Utah, Access has to search every record in your table. This search is fast if you have only a dozen or so customers, but very slow if you have hundreds or thousands of customers. If you create an index on the State field, Access can use the index to directly find the records for the customers in the state you want.

Single Field Indexes

Most of the indexes you need to define will probably contain the values from only a single field. Access uses this type of index to help narrow the number of records it has to search whenever you provide search criteria on the field—criteria such as *State = WA* or *Item Type Code = 005*. If you have defined indexes on multiple fields and provided search criteria for more than one of the fields, Access uses the index that is most likely to yield the fewest records to search. For example, if you have indexes on State and City and you ask for *State = CA* and *City = San Francisco*, Access uses the City index because there are likely to be fewer entries for the city of San Francisco than for the entire state of California. A request for *State = IL* and *City = Springfield* might use the State index because there are at least 21 cities in the U.S. named Springfield and so there actually might be fewer records for the state of Illinois.

Creating an index on a single field in a table is easy. Open the table in Design view and select the field for which you want an index. Click in the Indexed property box in the bottom half of the Table window and drop down the list of choices as shown in Figure 5-19.

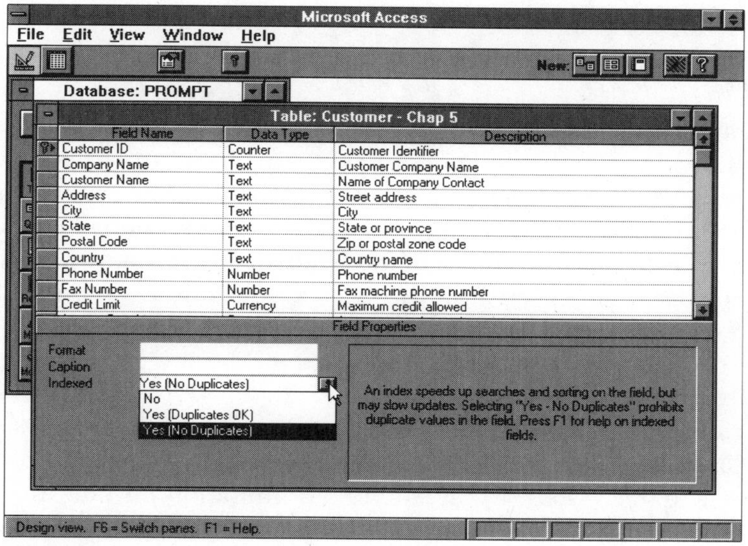

Figure 5-19.
The Indexed property box is used to set an index on a single field.

The default indexed property setting for all fields except the primary key is *No.* If you wish to set an index for a field, there are two *Yes* choices. In most cases, a given field will have multiple records with the same value—such as multiple customers in the state of Texas or multiple products that come in red. You should select *Yes (Duplicates OK)* to create an index on this type of field. Note that you can use Microsoft Access to enforce unique values in any field by creating an index that doesn't allow any duplicates— *Yes (No Duplicates)*. Access performs this check automatically for the primary key index.

Multiple Field Indexes

If you often provide multiple criteria in searches against large tables, you might want to consider creating a few multiple field indexes to help Microsoft Access narrow the search quickly. For example, suppose you often perform a search for customers who live in a specific state and city and who work for a particular company. If you create an index that has all three of these fields, as shown in Figure 5-20, Access can satisfy your query very rapidly.

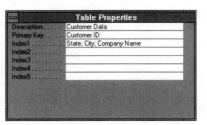

Figure 5-20.
A multiple field index is defined in the Table Properties window.

To create a multiple field index, you must open the Table window in Design view and open the Table Properties window by clicking the Properties button on the tool bar or by choosing the Table Properties command from the View menu. As you can see in Figure 5-20, you can define up to five indexes on a single table. Choose one of the index fields and enter the names of the fields you want indexed, in order, separated by semicolons. Access creates this index when you save the table definition.

Access will also use a multiple field index even if you don't provide search values for all the fields. Access can use a multiple field index as long as you provide search criteria for consecutive fields starting with the first field. In the multiple field index of Figure 5-20, therefore, you can search for state, or state and city, or state and city and company name. There is one additional limitation on multiple field indexes: Only the last search criteria can be an inequality such as >, >=, <, or <=. In other words, Access can use the index shown in Figure 5-20 when you specify searches like

        State = CA
        State > CA
        State = CA And City = Los Angeles
        State = CA And City >= San
        State = CA And City = San Francisco And Company Name > Ma

But Access cannot use the index shown in Figure 5-20 if you ask for

        State = CA And Company Name = Marble Industries   *(Can't skip a field, in this case City)*
        State > CA And City > San   *(Only the last field you search can be an inequality, in this case City)*
        City = San Diego   *(Must include the first field, in this case State)*

DATABASE LIMITATIONS

As you design your database you should keep in mind the following limitations:

- A table can have up to 255 fields.

- A table can have up to 32 indexes, including up to 5 multiple field indexes.

- A multiple field index can have up to 10 columns. The sum of the lengths of the columns cannot exceed 255 bytes.

- There is no limit on the number of records in a table, but a Microsoft Access database cannot be larger than 128 megabytes. If you have several large tables, you might need to define each one in a separate Microsoft Access database and then attach them to the database that contains the forms, reports, macros, and modules for your applications. See Chapter 9, "Modifying Data with Action Queries," for details.

Now that you have started building PROMPT, you can read the next chapter to learn how to make modifications to an existing database.

6
Modifying Your Database Design

No matter how carefully you design your database, you can be sure that you'll need to change it at some later date. Some of the reasons you might need to change your database include

- You find that you have some tables you don't need any longer.

- You want to be able to do some new tasks that require not only creating some new tables but also inserting some linking fields in existing tables.

- You have discovered that you use some fields in a table much more frequently than others, so it would be easier if those fields appeared first in the table design.

- You thought you would need to keep track of a certain kind of data when you first designed your database, but you discover that you don't need that data after all.

- You want to add some new fields that are very similar to fields that already exist.

- You discover that some data you defined would be better stored as a different data type—for example, a field that you originally designed to be all numbers (such as a U.S. zip code) must now contain some letters (as in a Canadian postal code).

- You have a number field that needs to hold larger values or have a different number of decimal places than originally planned.

- You find you could improve your database design by splitting an existing table into two tables or by joining two tables into a single table.

- You discover that the field you defined as a primary key isn't always unique, so you need to change your key definition.

- You find that some of your queries take too long and might run better if you added an index to your table.

This chapter takes a look at how you can make these changes easily and relatively painlessly with Microsoft Access. If you want to follow along with the examples in this chapter, you should create a database named PROMPT and then define the Customer table as described in Chapter 5, "Building Your Database in Microsoft Access." (You can also make similar changes to the Customers table in the sample NWIND database supplied with Microsoft Access.)

> **NOTE:** *You might have noticed that the Customer–Chap 5 table you defined for Prompt Computer Solutions in the previous chapter is different from the Customer table in the PROMPT database as defined in Appendix B, "Sample Database Schemas" (and located on CompuServe). In this chapter you will modify the first version of the Customer table so that it is more like the second.*

BEFORE YOU GET STARTED

Microsoft Access makes it easy for you to change the design of your database, even when you already have data in your tables. However, you should understand the potential impact of any changes you plan and take steps to ensure you can recover if you make a mistake. Things to consider before you make changes include

- Microsoft Access does not automatically propagate changes you make in tables to any queries, forms, reports, macros, or modules. You must make changes to dependent objects yourself. You can find out which other objects use the table or fields you plan to change by running the DataAnalyzer utility included with Access. See Appendix C, "The Data Analyzer Tool," for details.

- You cannot change the data type of a field that is part of a relationship definition between tables. You must first delete the relationship definition.

- You cannot change the definition of any table that you have open in a query, form, or report. You must first close any other objects that refer to the table you want to change before you open that table in Design view. If you allow other users on a network access to your database, you must be sure no one has your table open before you try to change it.

- One helpful feature of Access is that it always prompts you for confirmation before committing any changes that permanently alter or delete data in your database. If any changes would result in losing any data, Access informs you and gives you a chance to cancel the operation.

Making a Backup Copy

The safest way to make changes to your database design is to make a backup copy before you begin. If you plan to make extensive changes to several tables in your database, you should make a copy of the MDB file that contains your database using a utility such as File Manager in the Windows operating system. If you created (copied from CompuServe) the PROMPT database for use as you work through examples in this book, or if you plan to use NWIND for that purpose, now would be a good time to make a backup copy of the MDB file.

If you want to change a single table, you can easily make a backup copy of that table right in your database. You can use the procedure described below to copy any table structure (the contents of the Table window in Design view), table data (the contents of the Table window in Datasheet view), or structure and data together.

1. Open the database containing the table you want to copy. If the database is already open, click the Table button in the Database window.

2. Select the table you want to copy by clicking on it in the Database window. The table listing will be highlighted.

3. Choose the Copy command from the Edit menu. See Figure 6-1. This operation copies the entire table (structure and data) to the Clipboard.

4. Choose the Paste command from the Edit menu. Access opens the Paste Table As dialog box shown in Figure 6-2 on the following page. Type in the new name for your table. (When making a backup copy, you can add *Backup* and the date to the original table name, as shown in Figure 6-2.) The default option is to copy both the structure and the data. You also have options to copy only the table's structure or to append the data to another table.

Figure 6-1.
The Copy command will copy a table from the table list.

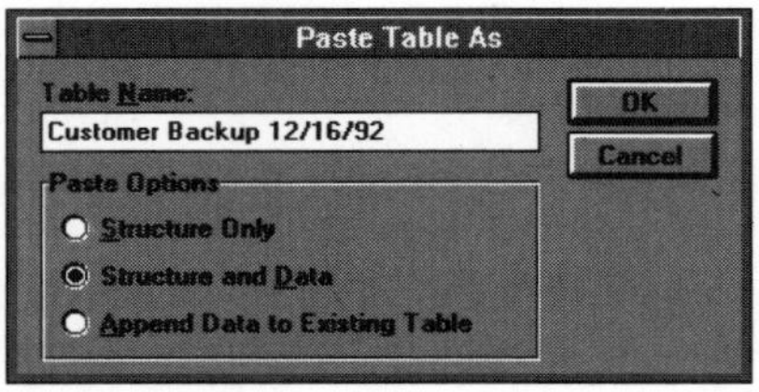

Figure 6-2.
The dialog box that appears when you paste a table into your database.

Reversing Changes

You can always take back the last change you made by choosing the Undo command from the Edit menu. If you make several changes and then decide you don't want any of them, you can close the Table window without saving it. When you do that, Access opens the dialog box shown in Figure 6-3. Simply click the No button to abort all of your changes. Click the Cancel button to return to the Table window without saving or aborting your changes.

Figure 6-3.
A dialog box gives you the option to abort the unsaved changes to a table.

DELETING TABLES

You probably won't want to delete an entire table very often. However if you set up your application to collect historical information—for example, to collect sales history in tables by month—you will eventually want to delete old information that you no longer need. You also might want to delete a table if you have made extensive changes that are incorrect and you decide it would be easier to delete your work and restore the table from a backup.

To delete a table, select it in the Database window and press the Del key or choose the Delete command from the Edit menu. Access opens the dialog box shown in Figure 6-4 to give you a chance to confirm or cancel the delete operation. Even if you mistakenly confirm the deletion, you can immediately select the Undo command from the Edit menu to get your table back.

Figure 6-4.
A dialog box gives you the option to cancel the deletion of a table.

RENAMING TABLES

If you keep transaction data (such as receipts, deposits, or checks written), you might want to capture that data at the end of each month in a table with a unique name. One way to save your data is to rename the existing table (perhaps by adding a date to the name). You can then create a new table (perhaps by making a copy of the table structure) to start collecting information for the next month. It's also useful to rename a table when you want to restore a table from a backup copy.

To rename a table, select it in the Database window and choose the Rename command from the File menu. Microsoft Access prompts you with the dialog box shown in Figure 6-5. Type in the new name and click OK to rename the table.

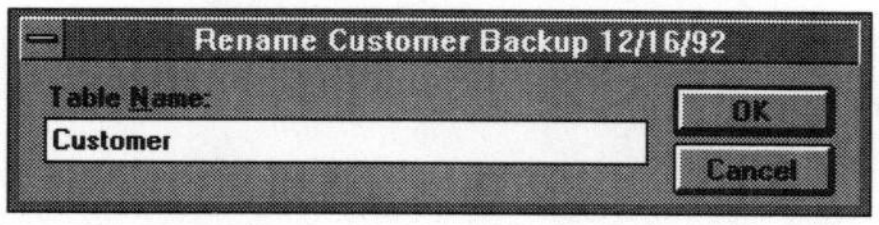

Figure 6-5.
A dialog box allows you to rename a table.

If you enter the name of a table that already exists, Access asks you if you want to replace the existing table. If you click the OK button, Access deletes the old table before performing the rename operation. Even if you replace an existing table, you can undo the rename operation by immediately choosing the Undo command from the Edit menu.

CHANGING FIELD NAMES

Perhaps you misspelled a field name when you first created one of your tables. Or maybe you decide that one of your field names isn't quite descriptive enough. You won't want the work of giving the field a new name every time it appears in a query, form, or report. Fortunately, Microsoft Access makes it easy to change a field name in a table—even if you already have data in the table.

Assume that you are maintaining the database for Prompt Computer Solutions and that you have run into some customer addresses that need a mail stop or suite number right after the Company Name line. The current Address field in the Customer table contains a street address, so the new address line should go after Company Name but before the existing Address field. As the first step, you decide to rename the Address field and call it *Address 2*.

Open the Customer–Chap 5 table in Design view, move the cursor to the Address field, and at the end of the name type a space followed by a *2*. Next change the Description field. Update this line to read *Street Address Line 2*. Figure 6-6 shows these changes.

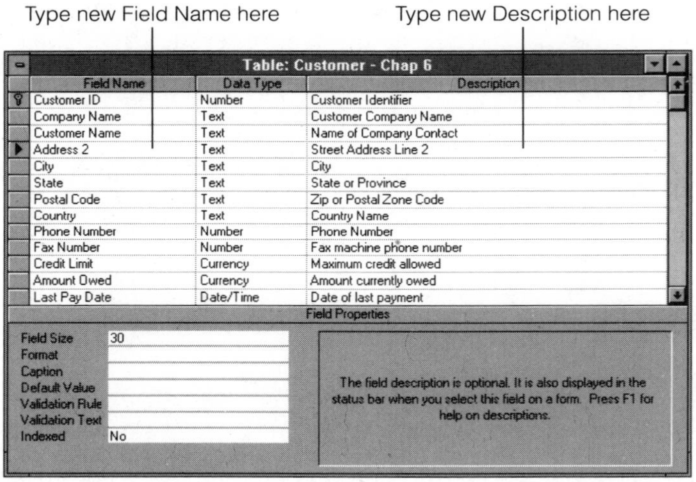

Type new Field Name here   Type new Description here

Figure 6-6.
A field name is changed by simply typing in a new name.

Once you have changed the name—and, optionally, the description—of the field, choose the Save As command from the File menu and type a new name for the table, *Customer–Chap 6*. You won't lose any data in your table when you change the name of a field. You can now reference the data in the old field by its new name.

NOTE: *If you have defined any queries, forms, reports, modules, or macros that use this field, you must also change the field name in those other objects. You can find out which other objects use this field by running the DataAnalyzer utility included with Access. See Appendix C for details.*

INSERTING FIELDS

Perhaps one of the most common changes you will make to your database is to insert a new field in a table. In the exercise above, you changed the name of the Address field to Address 2 so that you could have two separate address fields. Now you're ready to insert a field for the new first line of the address.

First you must select the row or move your cursor to the row that defines the field *after* the point where you want to insert the new field. In this case, if you want to insert a new row between Customer Name and Address 2, you should place your cursor anywhere in the row that defines the Address 2 field or select that row. If the cursor is in the bottom half of the Table window in Design view, press F6 to move the cursor to the field definition area in the top half of the window. Using your arrow keys or mouse, move the cursor anywhere in the Address 2 row. To select the Address 2 row, click the row selector at the far left of the row. Next choose the Insert Row command from the Edit menu. See Figure 6-7.

Row selector

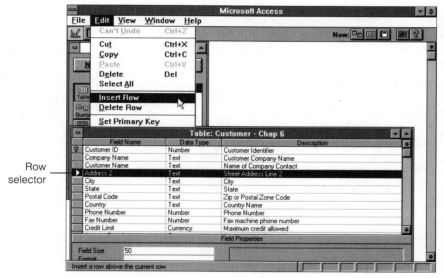

Figure 6-7.
The Insert Row command will insert a new row above a selected row.

Microsoft Access gives you a new blank row that you can use to define your new field. Type in the definition for the Address 1 field. When you are finished, your Table window in Design view should look like the one shown in Figure 6-8 on the following page.

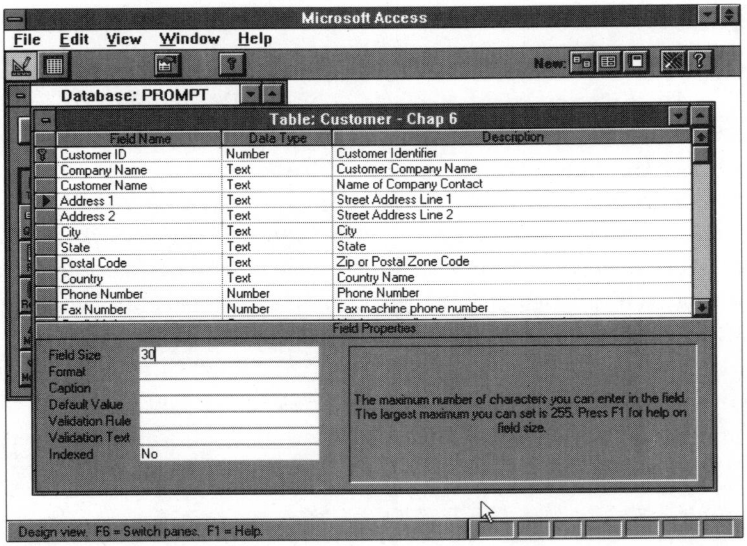

Figure 6-8.
A new field is created by inserting a blank row and typing a field definition.

MOVING FIELDS

There are a number of reasons why you might want to move a row in a table definition. You might make an error as you are entering or changing the information in a table. Or you might discover that you're using some fields you defined at the end of a table quite frequently in forms or reports, in which case it would be easier to find and work with those fields if they were nearer the beginning of your table definition.

You can use your keyboard or your mouse to move one or more rows that define the fields. To use your keyboard, do the following:

1. Open the table you want to change in Design view.

2. Use F6 (if necessary) to move your cursor to the top half of the Table window.

3. Use your arrow keys or Tab key to move the cursor anywhere in the row that defines the first field that you want to move.

4. Press Shift-Spacebar to select the entire row.

5. If you want to move a group of rows, hold down the Shift key and extend the selection using the arrow keys.

6. Press Ctrl-F8 to turn on Move mode. You will see *MOV* appear on the status bar to show you that you have activated this mode.

7. Use your up and down arrow keys to move the selected fields up or down until you have placed them where you want them. Press Esc to turn off Move mode.

Using a mouse can be quicker but requires a sure eye. To select a field definition you want to move, first click the row selector for the row. If you want to move multiple consecutive fields, scroll until you can see the last row in the group. Hold down the Shift key and click the row selector for the last row. The first and last rows and all the rows in between will be selected. Release the Shift key and click any of the row selectors in the highlighted rows and drag the field definitions to a new location. A small shaded box attaches to the bottom of the mouse pointer, and you will see a highlighted line appear to indicate the position to which the rows will move when you release the mouse button.

In our sample Customer–Chap 6 table in the Prompt Computer Solutions database, suppose the Address 1 row were incorrectly placed so that it followed Address 2, as shown in Figure 6-9. You can select the Address 1 line with your mouse by clicking the row selector. You can click the row selector again and drag the Address 1 field above the Address 2 field. In Figure 6-10, you can see that the mouse pointer has

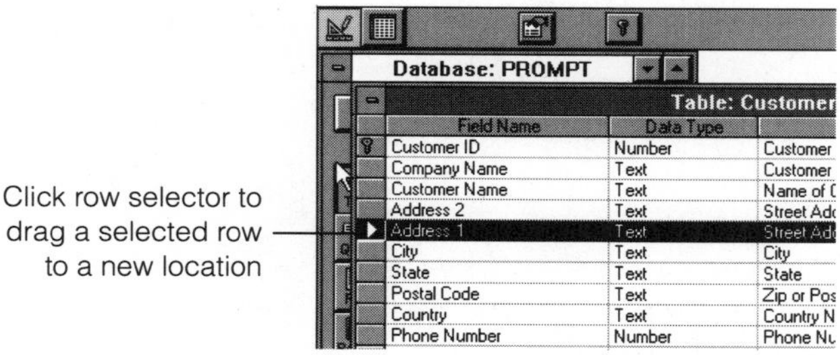

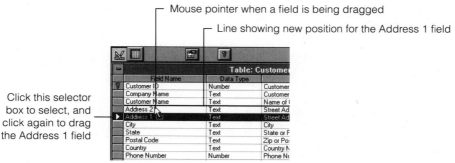

Figure 6-9.
The Address 1 field is incorrectly placed after Address 2.

Figure 6-10.
The Address 1 field has been selected and is being dragged (using the selector box) to precede Address 2.

changed and that the line above the Address 2 field is highlighted just before you release the mouse button. In Figure 6-11 the row is positioned correctly.

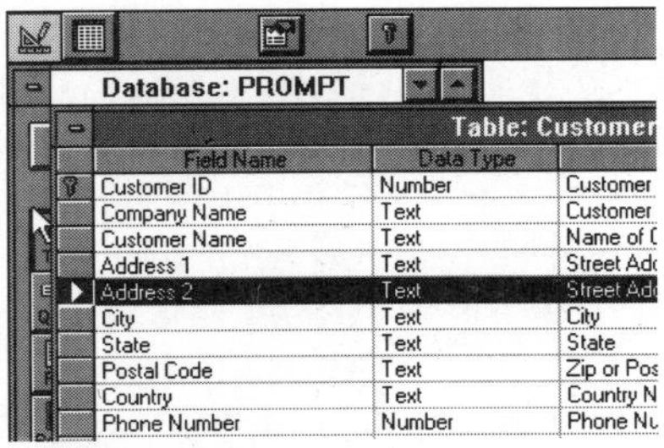

Figure 6-11.
The Address 1 field is correctly placed.

When it comes to moving fields, you might find a combination of mouse and keyboard methods a bit easier. Use your mouse to select the row you want. Then activate Move mode by pressing Ctrl-F8. Use the arrow keys to position the rows. As you experiment with Access, you'll discover more than one way to perform many tasks. You can choose the techniques that are easiest for you.

COPYING FIELDS

As you create table definitions, you might find that several field definitions in your table are similar. Rather than enter each field definition separately, you can enter one field definition and copy it as many times as necessary.

If you look at the version of the Customer table in the Prompt Computer Solutions sample database in Appendix B, you will see several "amount owed" fields at the end of the table. You could type in each one separately, or you could enter one of them and then copy the field as many times as necessary.

One way to make some of the changes for the Customer table in Appendix B is to create the definition for the Amount Owed Current field and then copy the definition several times to create the other fields for past due amounts. Select the entire row containing the field definition that you want to copy by clicking the row selector or by moving the cursor to that row with an arrow key and pressing Shift-Spacebar. Next choose the Copy command from the Edit menu to copy the row. See Figure 6-12. Move the cursor to the row that should follow your new inserted row. Choose the Paste command from the Edit menu to insert the copied row. See Figure 6-13. You can use the Paste command multiple times to insert the row more than once. Remember to change the names of the fields so that they are unique before you save the modified table definition.

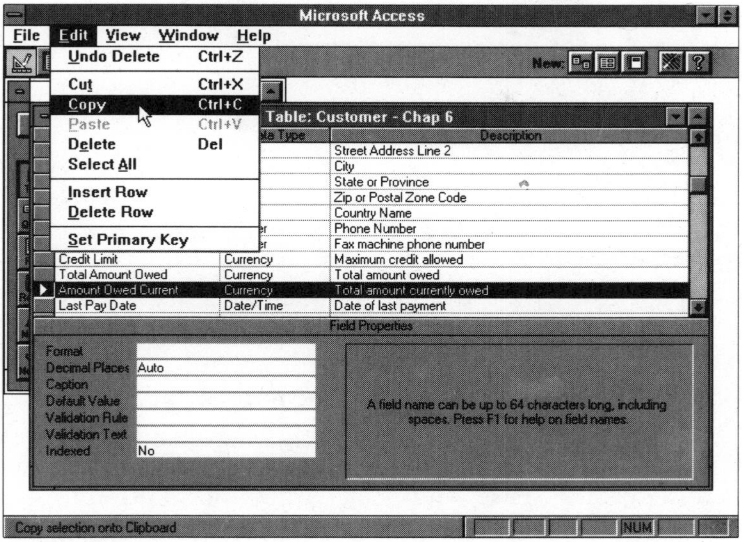

Figure 6-12.
The Amount Owed Current field is selected and copied.

Choose this command to insert
the field copied in Figure 6-12

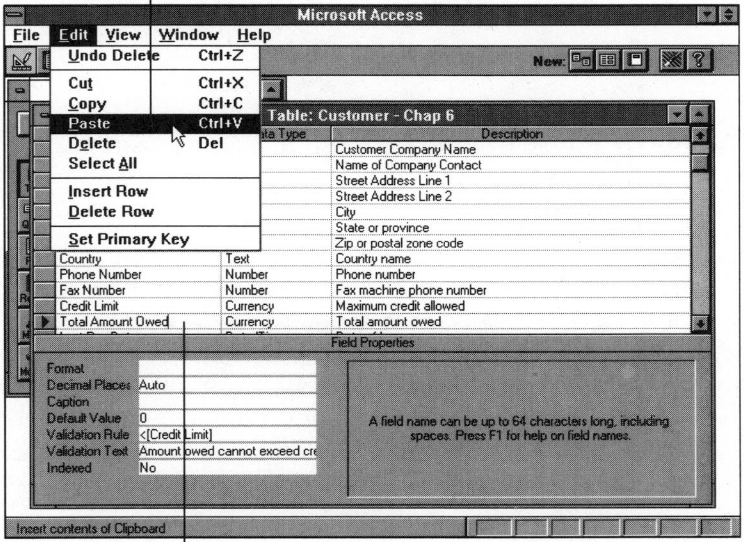

Field will be inserted above
the row with the cursor

Figure 6-13.
The field copied in Figure 6-12 can be inserted above the row with the cursor.

NOTE: *If a row is selected when the Paste command is chosen, the copied row will replace the selected row. Should you make this replacement in error, you can choose the Undo command from the Edit menu to restore the original row.*

DELETING FIELDS

Removing unwanted fields is easy. With the Table window open in Design view, select the field definition that you want to delete by moving to that row with the arrow keys and pressing Shift-Spacebar or by clicking the row selector. You can extend the selection to multiple fields as you did earlier when selecting a group of field definitions to move. You can also make multiple selections that are not contiguous by holding down the Ctrl key while you click different row selectors. Choose the Delete command from the Edit menu or press the Del key to remove the selected rows.

If a table has one or more rows of data, Access prompts you when you delete field definitions, as shown in Figure 6-14. Click the OK button to complete the deletion of the fields and the data in those fields. Click the Cancel button if you think you made a mistake.

Figure 6-14.
A dialog box allows you to confirm a field deletion.

CHANGING DATA ATTRIBUTES

As you learned in the previous chapter, Microsoft Access provides you with a number of different data types. These different data types help Access work more efficiently with your data and also provide a base level of data validation—for example, you can enter only numbers in a Number or Currency field.

When you initially design your database, you should match the data type and length of each field to its intended use. You might discover, however, that a field you thought would contain only numbers (such as a U.S. zip code) must actually contain some letters (when your business expands to Canada). You might find that one or more number fields need to hold larger values or a different number of decimal places. Access allows you to change the data type and length of many fields, even after you have entered data in them.

Changing Data Types

Changing the data type of a field in a table is very simple. Open the table in Design view, click in the data type column of the field definition you want to change, click the down arrow button at the right to see the available choices, and choose a new data type. In Figure 6-15 the data type for the Phone Number field is being changed from Number to Text in order to accommodate parentheses around area codes and hyphens in local numbers. (You should change the data type of the Fax Number field to Text as well.)

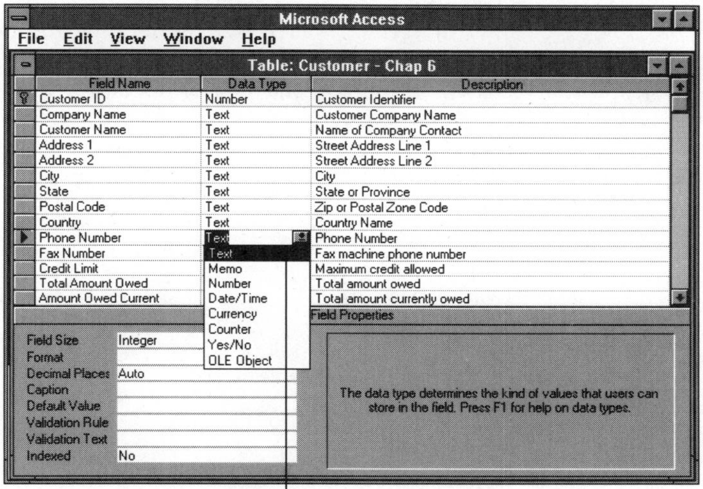

Phone Number data type is being
changed from Number to Text

Figure 6-15.
A data type can be changed by selecting from the drop-down list.

With a few limitations, Access can successfully convert every data type to any other data type, with the exception of OLE Object. Figure 6-16 shows you the possible conversions and potential limitations.

Convert From	Convert To	Limitations
Text	Memo	Access deletes indexes that include the text field
	Number	Text must contain only numbers and valid separators
	Date/Time	Text must contain a recognizable date and/or time, such as 11-Nov-92 5:15 PM
	Currency	Text must contain only numbers and valid separators
	Counter	Not possible if table contains data
	Yes/No	Text must contain only Yes, True, On, No, False, Off

Figure 6-16. *(continued)*
The data type conversion limitations.

Figure 6-16. *continued*

Convert From	Convert To	Limitations
Memo	Text	Access truncates text longer than 255 characters
	Number	Memo must contain only numbers and valid separators
	Date/Time	Memo must contain a recognizable date and/or time, such as 11-Nov-92 5:15 PM
	Currency	Memo must contain only numbers and valid separators
	Counter	Not possible if table contains data
	Yes/No	Memo must contain only Yes, True, On, No, False, Off
Number	Text	No limitations
	Memo	No limitations
	Date/Time	Number must be between −657,434 and 2,958,465.99998843
	Currency	No limitations
	Counter	Not possible if table contains data
	Yes/No	Zero or Null = No; any other value = Yes
Date/Time	Text	No limitations
	Memo	No limitations
	Number	No limitations
	Currency	No limitations, but value might be rounded
	Counter	Not possible if table contains data
	Yes/No	Null or 12:00:00 AM = No; any other value = Yes
Currency	Text	No limitations
	Memo	No limitations
	Number	No limitations
	Date/Time	Number must be between −$657,434 and $2,958,465.99
	Counter	Not possible if table contains data
	Yes/No	Null or Zero = No; any other value = Yes
Counter	Text	No limitation
	Memo	No limitation
	Number	No limitation
	Date/Time	Value must be less than 2,958,466
	Currency	No limitation
	Yes/No	All values evaluate to Yes

(continued)

Figure 6-16. *continued*

Convert From	Convert To	Limitations
Yes/No	Text	Converts to text "Yes" or "No"
	Memo	Converts to text "Yes" or "No"
	Number	No = 0; Yes = −1
	Date/Time	No = 12:00:00 AM; Yes = 12/29/1899
	Currency	No = 0; Yes = −$1
	Counter	Not possible

Changing Length

For text and number fields, you can define the maximum length of the data that can be stored in the field. Although a text field can be up to 255 characters long, you can restrict the length to as little as 1 character. If you don't specify a length for text, Access assigns a default length of 50. Access won't let you enter in a text field data longer than the defined length. If you find you need more space in a text field, you can increase the length at any time. If you try to redefine the length of a text field so that it's shorter, you might get a warning that Access will truncate a number of the data fields when you try to save your change.

Sizes for numbers can vary from a single byte (that can contain a value from 0 through 255) up to eight bytes (necessary to hold very large floating-point or currency numbers). You can change the size of numbers at any time, but you might get errors if you make the size smaller. Access also rounds and truncates numbers when converting from floating-point data types (Single or Double) to Integer or Currency values.

Conversion Errors

Access always warns you when you try to save a changed table definition if any changes in data type or length will cause conversion errors. For example, if you change the Field Size property of a Number field from Integer to Byte, Access warns you if any of the records contain a number larger than 255. You'll see a dialog box like the one shown in Figure 6-17 on the following page to warn you about fields that Access will set to a null value (empty) if you proceed with your changes. Click the OK button to complete the changes. You will have to examine your data to correct any conversion errors.

If you click the Cancel button when you receive conversion errors, Access shows you the dialog box in Figure 6-18 on the following page. If you deleted any fields or indexes, added any fields, or renamed any fields, Access will save those changes. Otherwise, the database will be unchanged. You can correct any data type or length changes you made and try to save the table definition again.

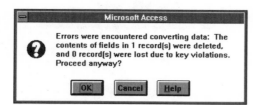

Figure 6-17.
A dialog box informs you of conversion errors.

Figure 6-18.
A dialog box appears when you decide not to save a changed table definition because of conversion errors.

SPLITTING A TABLE

After you have worked with your application for a while, you might discover one or more tables that have an excessive number of fields. If most of your queries or forms use data from only a part of a table and rarely from the whole table, you might get better performance if you split your table into two or more tables.

Another reason to split a table is if some of the fields contain sensitive information that you don't want all users of your application to see. Examples of sensitive information include employee salaries and customer credit ratings. Although you can create views and secure your table so that only authorized people can access certain data, it is easier to control sensitive information if it is placed in separate tables.

In the Prompt Computer Solutions database, you might want to separate the credit and payment information about a customer from the less sensitive data such as address and phone numbers. Start by backing up your entire database just in case you ever need the combined Customer–Chap 6 table again. Simply switch to File Manager and make a copy of the PROMPT.MDB file.

The easiest way to split the Customer–Chap 6 table is to create two copies of the original, including all the data. Use the same copy and paste procedure that you read about earlier in this chapter to make two backup copies of the Customer–Chap 6 table. Name one copy *Customer Info* and name the other copy *Customer Credit.* In the

Customer Info table, select all the credit and amount owed fields and delete them. Microsoft Access warns you that you are about to permanently delete data, but that's OK. In the Customer Credit table, choose all the name, address, and phone number fields and delete them. Be sure to keep the Customer ID field in both tables—that's how you'll link them together.

Having created two new tables, you might want to create a backup of just the definition of the old combined Customer–Chap 6 table for future reference. From the Database window, select the Customer–Chap 6 table and then choose the Copy command from the Edit menu. Choose the Paste command from the Edit menu, and the Paste Table As dialog box will open. Type in a name such as *Old Customer Structure–Chap 6*, click the Structure Only option button, and then click OK. Now you can delete the Customer–Chap 6 table.

To make it easier to create queries on the two new tables, you should choose the Relationships command from the Edit menu. In the dialog box set the values as shown in Figure 6-19. Be sure to click the One option button in the Type group box to tell Access that there's a one-to-one relationship between the two tables. Click the Add button to create the new relationship definition.

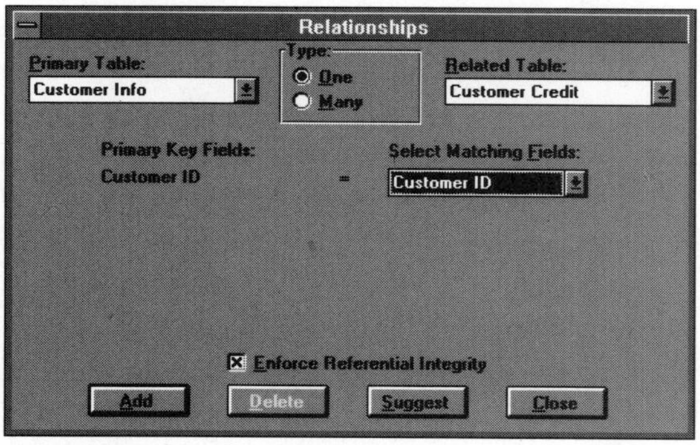

Figure 6-19.
The Relationships dialog box allows you to set the one-to-one relationship between the two parts of a split table.

You should also define relationships between your two new tables and the other tables in your database. For example, you should define a one-to-many relationship between Customer Info and Orders after entering their data. You must also find and update any queries, forms, or reports that referenced the old Customer table. You can use the Data Analyzer tool to do this, as explained in Appendix C. Click the Close button when you've finished defining relationships.

COMBINING TABLES

As you discovered in Chapter 4, "Designing Your Database," you use a process called *normalization* to come up with a good relational database design. If you follow all the rules rigorously, it is possible to end up with lots of little tables—known as an *over-normalized database*. That's not a serious problem in Access because Microsoft Access has an excellent query capability that allows you to easily work with data from many tables in a single view. However, whenever Access has to join multiple tables, performance is likely to be slower than if Access were working with data in a single table.

One way to detect whether you have over-normalized your database is to check whether you are always using two or more tables together and very rarely separately. If you are, and especially if one of the tables has a lot of data, you can probably improve performance by combining tables. For example, you might have items for sale that you normally group into a number of categories—such as Products and Categories in the NWIND database or Components and Types in the PROMPT database. In the case of NWIND, if the category names are long, it's a good idea to use a code in the products table to refer to the category rather than carry the long name in each record. The shorter code will save you a lot of disk space. However, if you have thousands of products and dozens of categories and you always retrieve the category name with the product, you might want to sacrifice disk storage space in exchange for speed by eliminating the Categories table and putting the full category name in the Products table.

Whatever your reason for combining two tables, it's a fairly simple procedure when you use a query and save the result as a physical table. In the following example, you can put the Customer Info and Customer Credit tables in the PROMPT database back together. For the full details on creating and using queries, see Chapter 8, "Adding Power with Select Queries."

Start by opening the PROMPT database and highlighting the Customer Info table in the Database window. Click the New Query button on the tool bar to open the Query window in Design view. Access places the field list from the table you selected in the top half of the window. By default, you are creating a select query, but you really want to make a new table with the results of this query. To do that, choose the Make Table command from the Query menu, as shown in Figure 6-20.

When you use a Make Table command on a query, Access asks you for the name of the table you want to build. You are creating a combined customer table from two tables, so enter *Customer–Chap 6* for the table name, as shown in Figure 6-21. Click the OK button to save the name.

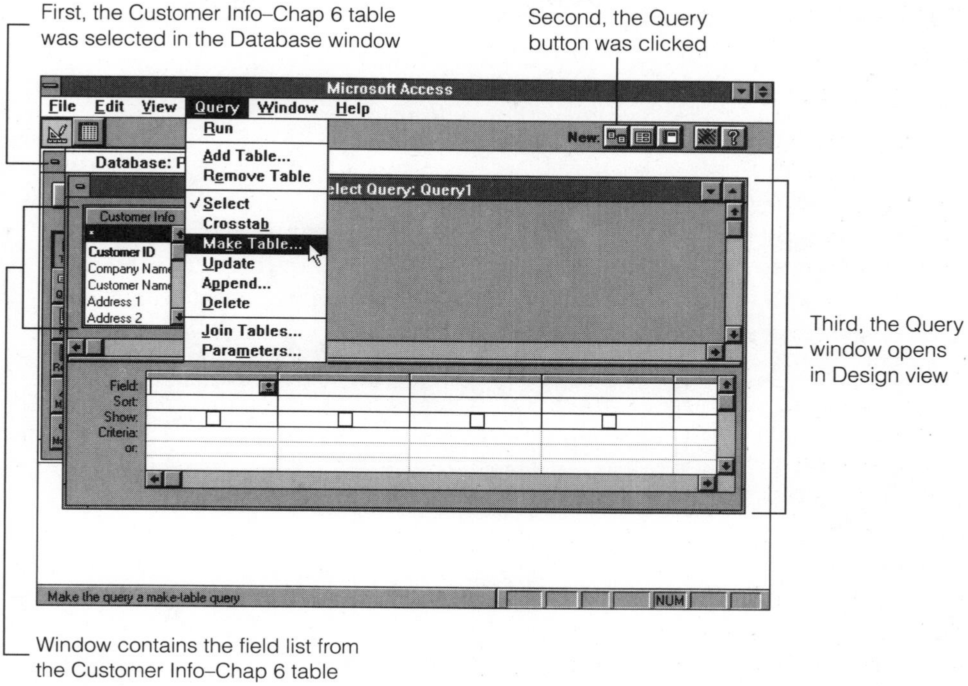

First, the Customer Info–Chap 6 table
was selected in the Database window

Second, the Query
button was clicked

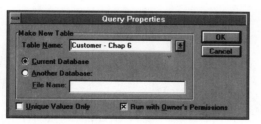

Third, the Query
window opens
in Design view

Window contains the field list from
the Customer Info–Chap 6 table

Figure 6-20.
The Make Table command is used to combine tables using a query.

Figure 6-21.
The Query Properties dialog box is used to name a new table.

Next you need to add the second table to the query. Drag the title bar of the query window aside until you can see the Database window, or choose the Tile command from the Window menu to line up the two windows side-by-side. Use your mouse to drag the name of the Customer Credit table from the table list in the Database window to the top part of the Query window in Design view. See Figure 6-22 on the following page. If you created the relationship between the two tables properly, you should see a line connecting the Customer ID field in the Customer Info field list to the Customer ID field in the Customer Credit field list. This connection must exist for the query to execute properly. If the line is not there, you can create the relationship now by dragging the Customer ID field from one field list and dropping it on the Customer ID field in the other field list.

Customer Credit table is being
dragged to Query window

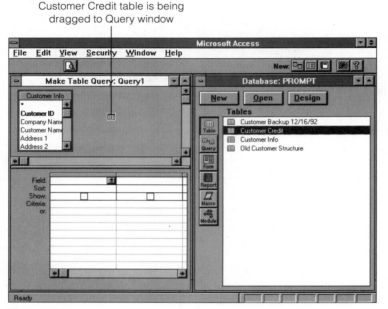

Figure 6-22.
A second table is dragged to the Query window in Design view as the next step in making a combined table.

Now you need to tell Microsoft Access which fields you want in the resulting table. You want all the fields from both tables, except that you want only one Customer ID field. At the top of the field list for each table there is an asterisk that is shorthand for "give me all the fields in this table." Use your mouse to drag the asterisk from the Customer Info QBE field list to the first Field box in the grid at the bottom half of the Query window in Design view. See Figure 6-23. Access shows you "Customer Info.*" in this field. You could have typed this yourself, but dragging and dropping is much quicker and easier. Now you need all the fields from the Customer Credit field list except Customer ID. Click the field Credit Limit to select it in the field list, and then scroll down until you see the last field, Last Pay Date, in the field list. Hold down the Shift key and click this last field to highlight all the fields from Credit Limit to Last Pay Date. Drag any of the highlighted fields to the second Field box in the QBE grid at the bottom half of the Query window. Your mouse pointer changes to show you that you've grabbed a set of fields. When you release your mouse pointer, Access fills in all the field names you selected from the Customer Credit table. Your completed query should look like Figure 6-23.

Figure 6-23.
The fields from two tables are dragged to the grid in a Query window in order to make a combined table.

Now you are ready to create the new table with data combined from the two old tables. Simply click the Run button on the tool bar to run your query. Access retrieves the data you asked for and then shows you how many rows you are creating in the new table, as shown in Figure 6-24. Click the OK button to finish creating the table. If you didn't delete the old table, Access also prompts you to confirm whether you want to replace the existing Customer–Chap 6 table.

Figure 6-24.
A dialog box asks you to confirm the Make Table query.

CHANGING THE PRIMARY KEY

Chapter 4, "Designing Your Database," discussed the need to have one or more fields that provide a unique value to every row in your table. This field with unique values is identified as the *primary key*. If you don't have a primary key, you can't define a relationship with other tables, and Microsoft Access can't automatically link tables for you. Even when you choose a primary key in your initial design, you might discover later that it doesn't really contain unique values. In that case, you might have to define a new field or fields to be the primary key.

Suppose that in designing the Components table in the PROMPT database, you used the item code from each manufacturer as a unique key for items in the table. Later you discover that some of the item codes from a couple of the manufacturers are the same. All you need to do is to add a counter field that will enter a unique number in each record. To do this, insert a row at the beginning of the table, give it the field name *Component ID*, and give it the data type *Counter*. Then click the row selector and press the Primary Key button. See Figure 6-25.

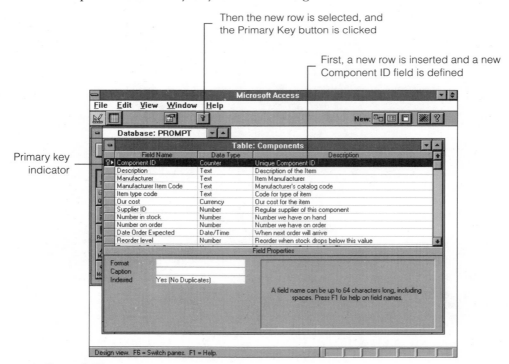

Figure 6-25.
The Components table is given a new field to be its primary key.

To remove an existing primary key without selecting a new primary key, you have to open the property sheet for the table. While the Table window is in Design view, click the Properties button on the tool bar or choose the Table Properties command from the View menu. Either operation will open the table's property sheet, as shown in Figure 6-26.

To remove the existing primary key, clear the name from the Primary Key field in the property sheet and then close the property sheet by clicking the Properties button on the tool bar again. You should see the primary key indicator disappear from the rows in the Components table.

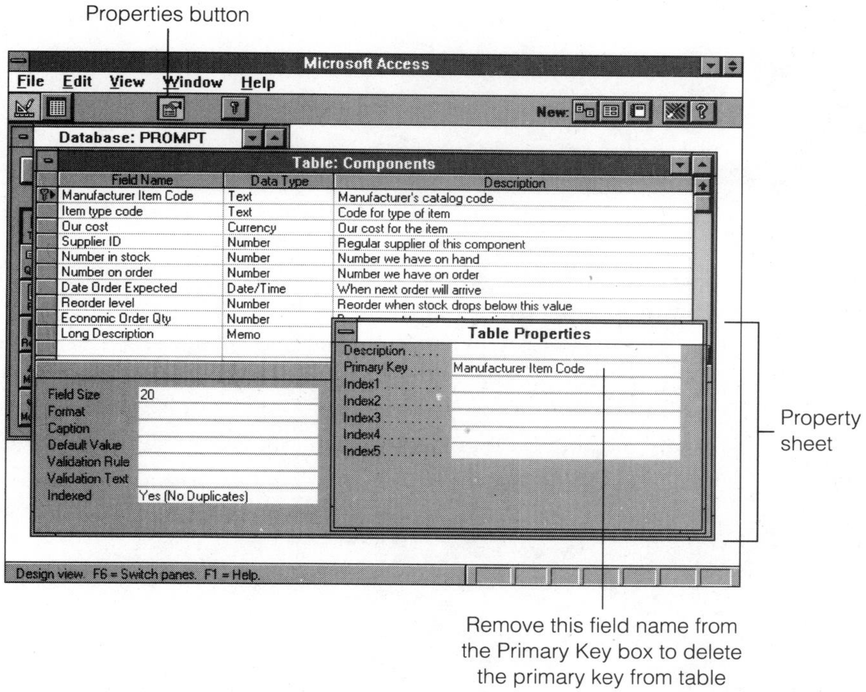

Properties button

Property sheet

Remove this field name from the Primary Key box to delete the primary key from table

Figure 6-26.
A primary key designation is removed using the property sheet.

COMPACTING YOUR DATABASE

Microsoft Access reuses blocks as much as possible within the space allocated to the file that contains your database. Whenever you change a definition, Access saves the new definition and deletes the old one. If you delete records or object definitions, Access can use that space again later for new records or object definitions. However, over time the file allocated to your database can grow larger than it needs to be to store all your definitions and data.

To regain unused space, you should compact your database periodically. No database can be open when you run the compact utility. Also, no other users should be accessing the database you intend to compact. To execute the compact utility, open the File menu in the Microsoft Access window after all databases have been closed. Choose the Compact Database command. Access opens the dialog box shown in Figure 6-27.

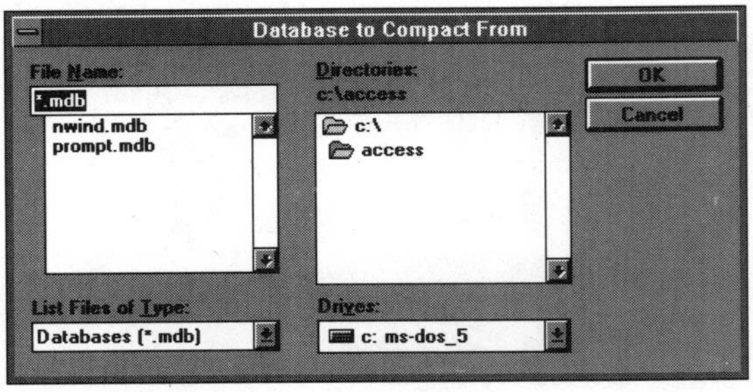

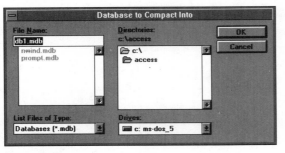

Figure 6-27.
The dialog box for specifying a database to compact.

Choose the database you want to compact and then click OK. Access then asks you for a database name to compact into, as shown in Figure 6-28. You can create a compacted copy of your database under another name, or you can enter the same name as the database you are compacting. When you choose the same name, Access compacts your database into a temporary file. When compaction is successfully completed, Access deletes your old database and automatically gives its name to the new compacted copy.

Figure 6-28.
The dialog box in which you name a compacted database.

You now have all the information you need to modify and maintain your database table definitions. In the next chapter, you'll explore working with the data in your tables.

PART III

WORKING WITH DATA

The next four chapters cover everything you need to know about entering data in your database, designing queries to read and modify your data, and working with data in external data formats.

Chapter 7 introduces you to displaying, updating, and printing data in a datasheet format.

Chapters 8 and 9 cover designing and running queries. Chapter 8 discusses all the ways you can ask Microsoft Access to find data in your database, including joining multiple tables and performing calculations. Chapter 9 shows you how to add, delete, or insert sets of records quickly and easily by running an action query.

The last chapter in this section, Chapter 10, explores one of the primary strengths of Microsoft Access—the ability to work directly with data stored in many different formats. This chapter shows you how to connect to data stored in dBASE, Paradox, FoxBase and Btrieve files. You'll also learn how to connect to other Microsoft Access databases or SQL databases on servers or host computers. Finally you will find out how to import and export spreadsheet and text files.

7

Using Datasheets

The simplest way to look at your data is to open a table in Datasheet view. When you build your application, you probably will work with your data mostly through forms that you design. However, studying datasheets is useful because it improves your understanding of basic concepts such as viewing, updating, inserting, and deleting data. Microsoft Access performs these functions in the same way whether you're using a datasheet or a specially designed form to work with your data. On some forms, you might decide to embed a Datasheet view to make it easy to look at several rows and columns of data at once. Even after you have built an application to work with your data, you'll find that Datasheet view is often useful to verify data at the

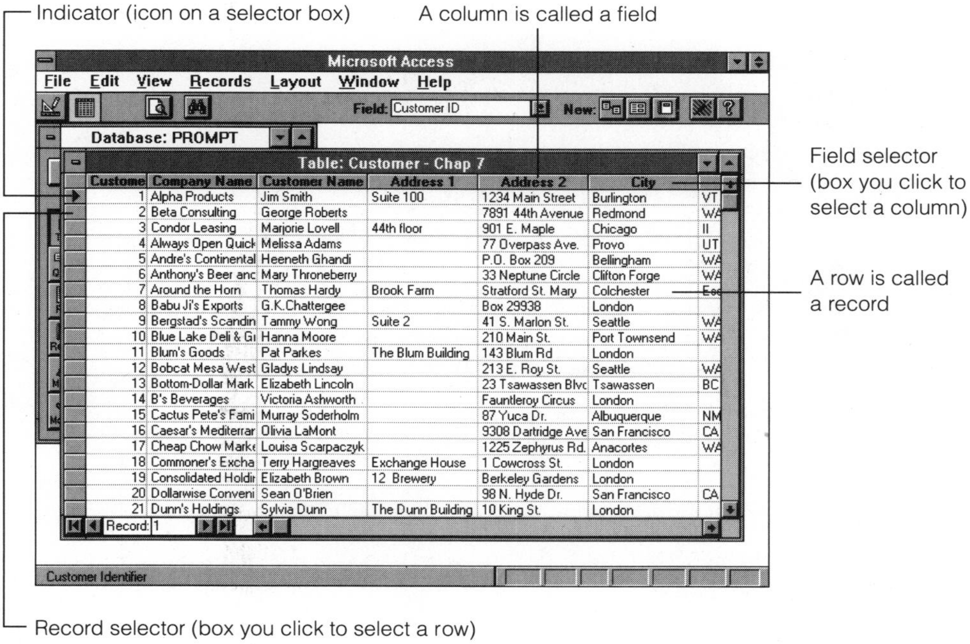

Figure 7-1.
A table in Datasheet view consists of fields (columns) and records (rows).

basic table level. Throughout this chapter, you'll look at examples of operations using the Customer table in the PROMPT database that you designed using Appendix B—or that you copied from CompuServe. Take a moment now to copy the Customer table. The copy procedure is described in Chapter 6, "Modifying the Database Design." Name your copy *Customer–Chap 7*. (If you don't have the PROMPT database, you can use the Customers table from the NWIND database that came with Microsoft Access.) Figure 7-1 shows the table in Datasheet view and explains some key terms.

THE TOOL BAR IN DATASHEET VIEW

Before you go exploring datasheets, it's useful to take a moment to look at the tool bar that Microsoft Access displays when you open any table in Datasheet view. The tool bar is shown in Figure 7-2.

Figure 7-2.
The tool bar in Datasheet view.

From left to right, the buttons are

 Design View button. Click this button to see the Table window in Design view.

 Datasheet View button. This button appears pressed when you are looking at a Table window in Datasheet view.

 Print Preview button. You can print the data displayed in a datasheet. Click this button to see a preview of the printed page.

 Find button. Click this button to initiate a search for particular values in the table.

 New Query button. Click this button to begin designing a new query based on the current table. See Chapter 8, "Adding Power with Select Queries," for details.

 New Form button. Click this button to begin designing a new form based on the current table. See Chapter 11, "Form Basics," for details.

 New Report button. Click this button to begin designing a new report based on the current table. See Chapter 15, "Report Basics," for details.

 Undo button. Click this button to undo the last change you made to data in the table.

Help button. Click this button to access context-sensitive help.

There is one additional element on the tool bar, a drop-down list of fields.

| Field: Customer ID ▼ | Field box. Shows the currently selected field. Click the down arrow button to drop down a list of available fields. You can select a different field using this list. |

VIEWING DATA

To look at data in one of your tables in Datasheet view, do the following:

1. Open your database. By default, Microsoft Access will display the list of tables in the database within the Database window.

2. Double-click on the name of the table you want. If you want to use the keyboard, press the up or down arrow keys to move the highlight to the table you want, and then press Alt-O.

Figure 7-3 shows you the Datasheet view of the Customer–Chap 7 table from the PROMPT database. Open this table on your computer now. If you like, you can make the datasheet fill the workspace by clicking the Maximize button in the upper right corner of the window. Or you can press Alt-Hyphen to open the Control menu and then press X to choose the Maximize command.

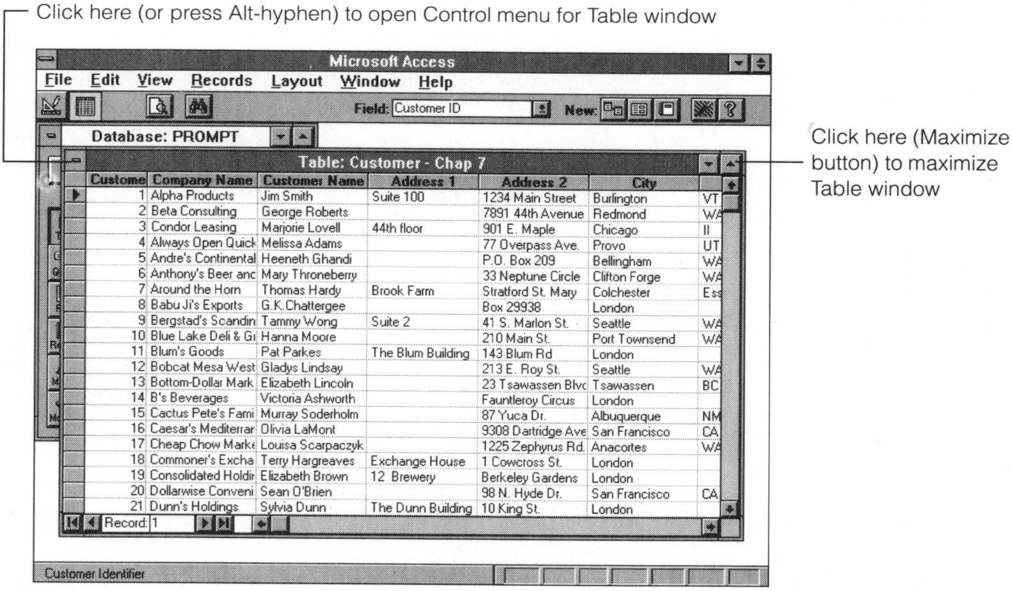

Figure 7-3.
The Datasheet view of the PROMPT Customer–Chap 7 Table.

Moving Around

Changing the display to show you different records or fields is very simple. You can use the vertical or horizontal scroll bars, as illustrated in Figure 7-4.

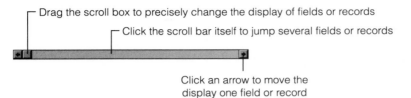

Figure 7-4.
The scroll bars can be used to change the display of records and fields in a window.

In the lower left corner of the table in Datasheet view, you can see a record number box, as shown in Figure 7-5. The record number box shows you the *relative record number* of the current record (meaning the number of the record where the cursor is located or where some data is selected). Note that you might not see the current record in the window if you have scrolled the display.

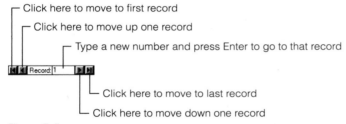

Figure 7-5.
The record number box is at the bottom left of a table in Datasheet view.

You can use the record number box to quickly move to the record you want. As you will read a bit later, you will usually select some data in a record in order to change it. You can also choose the Go To command from the Records menu to move to the next, previous, first, or last records. You can also make any record current by clicking anywhere on its row, and the number in the record number box will change to indicate the new row you have selected.

To select a different field (even one you can't currently see in Datasheet view), you can choose it from the Field drop-down list box on the tool bar. (See Figure 7-2.) As with records, you can also select any field you can see in Datasheet view by clicking anywhere in its column.

Keyboard Shortcuts

You might find it easier to use the keyboard rather than your mouse to move around on the datasheet especially if you have been typing in new data on the keyboard. Some of the keyboard shortcuts are listed in Figures 7-6 and 7-7.

Keys	Scrolling Action
Page Up	Up one page
Page Down	Down one page
Ctrl-Page Up	Left one page
Ctrl-Page Down	Right one page

Figure 7-6.
The keyboard shortcuts for scrolling in a datasheet.

Keys	Selecting Action
Tab	Next field
Shift-Tab	Previous field
Home	First field, current record
End	Last field, current record
Up arrow	Current field, previous record
Down arrow	Current field, next record
Ctrl-up arrow	Current field, first record
Ctrl-down arrow	Current field, last record
Ctrl-Home	First field, first record
Ctrl-End	Last field, last record
F5	Record number box

Figure 7-7.
The keyboard shortcuts for selecting data in a datasheet.

MODIFYING THE DATASHEET LAYOUT

You can make a number of changes to the appearance of your datasheet. You can change the height of rows or the width of columns. You can rearrange or hide columns. You can set the display or printing font and decide whether you want to see gridlines. You can make most of these changes from the Layout menu shown in Figure 7-8 on the next page.

Figure 7-8.
The Layout menu in Datasheet view.

Changing Row Height and Column Width

Microsoft Access initially displays all the columns and rows using a default width and height. The standard width is probably wider than it needs to be for some columns that contain a small amount of data, but not wide enough for other columns. For example, the first column in the PROMPT Customer–Chap 7 table is wider than it needs to be to display the Customer ID field. However, the second column is not wide enough to display the typical Company Name entry.

One way to fix the column width is to select any value in the column that you want to change and choose the Column Width command from the Layout menu. You will see a dialog box similar to the one shown in Figure 7-9. You can type in a new width value in number of characters. The default width is approximately 1 printed inch based on the current font selection.

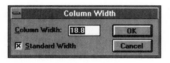

Figure 7-9.
The Column Width dialog box.

You can also modify the column widths directly on the screen by placing your mouse pointer on the gray line between the column names at the top of the Table window. When you do this, your mouse pointer changes into a vertical bar with arrows pointing to the left and right. By dragging the column boundary, you can adjust the size of the column. See Figure 7-10.

If you plan to print your datasheet, you might want to increase the height of the rows to create some space between each record on the report. Choose the Row Height command from the Layout menu to see a dialog box similar to the one shown in Figure 7-11. The row height is measured in points, units of approximately $\frac{1}{72}$ inch ($\frac{1}{28}$ centimeter). To allow space between rows, Access calculates a standard height that is approximately 30% larger than the current font point size. You can enter a new height in the text box. If you choose a number that is smaller than the font size, your rows will overlap when printed. You can also change the row height by dragging the row boundary from within the record selector on the left, in the same way you changed the column width with the mouse, as shown in Figure 7-10.

To widen the Company Name field, drag the column
boundary to the right when the mouse pointer looks like this

		Microsoft Access			▼ ♦
File	**Edit** **View** **Records**	**Layout** **Window** **Help**			

Field: Customer ID ▼ New: ▫▫ ▦ ▫ ▧ ?

Database: PROMPT ▼ ▲

Table: Customer - Chap 7 ▼ ♦

Custome	Company Name	Customer Name	Address 1	Address 2	City	
1	Alpha Products	Jim Smith	Suite 100	1234 Main Street	Burlington	VT
2	Beta Consulting	George Roberts		7891 44th Avenue	Redmond	WA
3	Condor Leasing	Marjorie Lovell	44th floor	901 E. Maple	Chicago	Il
4	Always Open Quick	Melissa Adams		77 Overpass Ave.	Provo	UT
5	Andre's Continental	Heeneth Ghandi		P.O. Box 209	Bellingham	WA
6	Anthony's Beer and	Mary Throneberry		33 Neptune Circle	Clifton Forge	WA
7	Around the Horn	Thomas Hardy	Brook Farm	Stratford St. Mary	Colchester	Ess
8	Babu Ji's Exports	G.K.Chattergee		Box 29938	London	
9	Bergstad's Scandin	Tammy Wong	Suite 2	41 S. Marlon St.	Seattle	WA
10	Blue Lake Deli & Gr	Hanna Moore		210 Main St.	Port Townsend	WA
11	Blum's Goods	Pat Parkes	The Blum Building	143 Blum Rd	London	
12	Bobcat Mesa West	Gladys Lindsay		213 E. Roy St.	Seattle	WA
13	Bottom-Dollar Mark	Elizabeth Lincoln		23 Tsawassen Blvc	Tsawassen	BC
14	B's Beverages	Victoria Ashworth		Fauntleroy Circus	London	
15	Cactus Pete's Fami	Murray Soderholm		87 Yuca Dr.	Albuquerque	NM
16	Caesar's Mediterran	Olivia LaMont		9308 Dartridge Ave	San Francisco	CA
17	Cheap Chow Marke	Louisa Scarpaczyk		1225 Zephyrus Rd.	Anacortes	WA
18	Commoner's Excha	Terry Hargreaves	Exchange House	1 Cowcross St.	London	
19	Consolidated Holdir	Elizabeth Brown	12 Brewery	Berkeley Gardens	London	
20	Dollarwise Conveni	Sean O'Brien		98 N. Hyde Dr.	San Francisco	CA
21	Dunn's Holdings	Sylvia Dunn	The Dunn Building	10 King St.	London	

I◀ ◀ Record: 1 ▶ ▶I ♦

Customer Identifier

Figure 7-10.
A mouse can be used to adjust the column width.

Row Height	
Row Height: 10.5	**OK**
☒ **Standard Height**	**Cancel**

Figure 7-11.
The Row Height dialog box.

Arranging Columns

The default order of fields from left to right in Datasheet view is the order in which the fields were defined in the table. You can easily change the column order for viewing or printing. Select the column you want by clicking the field selector. Microsoft Access highlights the entire column. You can select multiple columns by dragging across several selector boxes in either direction before you release the mouse button. To select columns with the keyboard, use the Tab or arrow keys to move to any row in the column you want and press Ctrl-Spacebar. To extend the selection, hold down the Shift key while using the left or right arrow keys to expand the highlighted area.

To move the selected columns, drag a selector box to the desired new location. See Figure 7-12. To move the columns using the keyboard, press Ctrl-F8 to turn on Move mode. Access displays *MOV* in one of the areas on the status bar. Shift the columns to the left or right using the arrow keys. Press Esc to turn off Move mode.

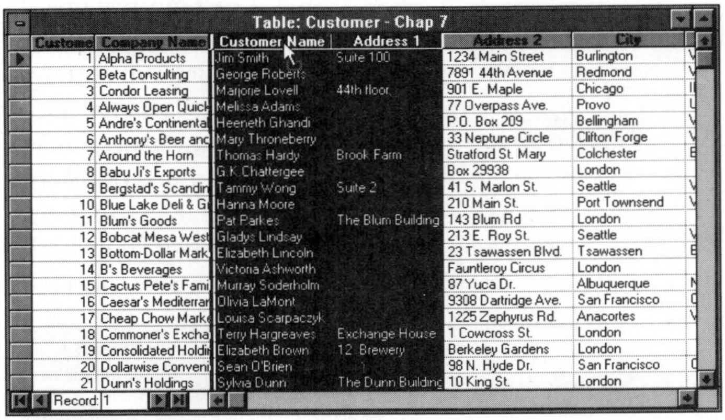

Figure 7-12.
A column is moved by first selecting it and then dragging the selector box.

Hiding and Showing Columns

By default, Microsoft Access displays all of the columns in the table in Datasheet view, though you might have to scroll to see some of them. If you are not interested in looking at or printing all of these fields, you can hide some of them. One way to hide a column is to drag the right column boundary to the left (from within the field selector) until the column disappears. You can also select one or more columns and choose the Hide Columns command from the Layout menu.

You can use the Show Columns dialog box (available from the Layout menu) to reveal hidden columns or to hide additional ones. See Figure 7-13. Select a column from the list and then click the appropriate option button. The checked columns are already showing. You can select multiple contiguous fields by clicking one field, scrolling up or down in the dialog box until you see the first or last field in the range

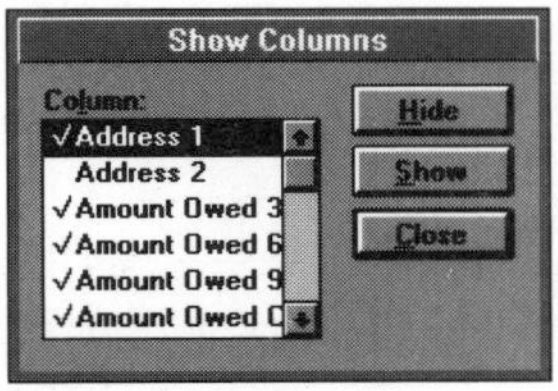

Figure 7-13.
The Show Columns dialog box.

you want, and then clicking that field while holding down the Shift key. You can select multiple noncontiguous fields by clicking each one while holding down the Ctrl key. Click Close to close the dialog box.

Freezing Columns

Sometimes while viewing data, you might want to keep one column on the screen while scrolling left or right through the other columns. For example, you might want to keep the Customer Name column on the screen as you scroll all the way to the right to see the phone numbers. You can freeze one or more columns by selecting them (as a group of contiguous selected columns or one column at a time) and then choosing the Freeze Columns command from the Layout menu. Access moves the selected columns to the far left and "freezes" them there. Those fields do not scroll off the left of the window when you scroll right. To release frozen columns, choose the Unfreeze All Columns command from the Layout menu. Figure 7-14 shows the Company Name field frozen to the left with the rest of the display scrolled right to show the postal code, country, and phone number.

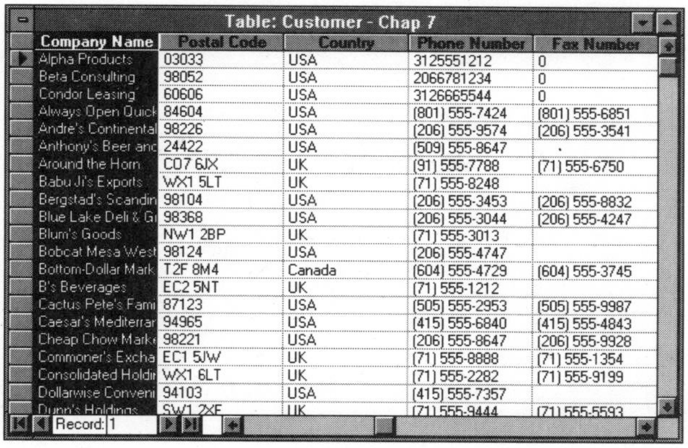

Figure 7-14.
A datasheet with a frozen column.

Removing Gridlines

The Datasheet view normally has gridlines between the columns and rows. Microsoft Access also includes these gridlines if you print the datasheet. You can easily remove the gridlines by choosing the Gridlines command from the Layout menu. Choose it again to turn the gridlines back on. Figure 7-15 on the next page shows you the datasheet from Figure 7-14, but without the gridlines. Notice that a line is present to indicate that the Company Name column is frozen to the left. Access includes this line if you decide to print a report with frozen columns.

Company Name	Postal Code	Country	Phone Number	Fax Number
Alpha Products	03033	USA	3125551212	0
Beta Consulting	98052	USA	2066781234	0
Condor Leasing	60606	USA	3126665544	0
Always Open Quick	84604	USA	(801) 555-7424	(801) 555-6851
Andre's Continental	98226	USA	(206) 555-9574	(206) 555-3541
Anthony's Beer and	24422	USA	(509) 555-8647	
Around the Horn	CO7 6JX	UK	(91) 555-7788	(71) 555-6750
Babu Ji's Exports	WX1 5LT	UK	(71) 555-8248	
Bergstad's Scandin	98104	USA	(206) 555-3453	(206) 555-8832
Blue Lake Deli & Gr	98368	USA	(206) 555-3044	(206) 555-4247
Blum's Goods	NW1 2BP	UK	(71) 555-3013	
Bobcat Mesa West	98124	USA	(206) 555-4747	
Bottom-Dollar Mark	T2F 8M4	Canada	(604) 555-4729	(604) 555-3745
B's Beverages	EC2 5NT	UK	(71) 555-1212	
Cactus Pete's Fami	87123	USA	(505) 555-2953	(505) 555-9987
Caesar's Mediterrar	94965	USA	(415) 555-6840	(415) 555-4843
Cheap Chow Marke	98221	USA	(206) 555-8647	(206) 555-9928
Commoner's Excha	EC1 5JW	UK	(71) 555-8888	(71) 555-1354
Consolidated Holdir	WX1 6LT	UK	(71) 555-2282	(71) 555-9199
Dollarwise Conveni	94103	USA	(415) 555-7357	
Dunn's Holdings	SW1 2XF	UK	(71) 555-9444	(71) 555-5593

Record: 5

Figure 7-15.
A datasheet without gridlines.

Selecting Fonts

The last thing you can do to customize the look of a datasheet is to select a different font. Choose the Font command from the Layout menu to see the dialog box shown in Figure 7-16.

Font

Font: Book Antiqua

Arial
Arial Narrow
AvantGarde
Book Antiqua
Bookman

Font Style: Regular

Regular
Italic
Bold
Bold Italic

Size: 8

8
9
10
11
12

[OK]
[Cancel]

Effects
☐ Underline

Sample

AaBbYyZz

This is a TrueType font. This same font will be used on both your printer and your screen.

Figure 7-16.
The Font dialog box.

In the list box at the upper left of the dialog box, you can see all the fonts that you have installed in your Windows operating system. You can scroll down through the list box and select the font name that you want.

The icon to the left of the font name indicates whether the font is a screen font (blank), a printer font (printer icon), or a TrueType font that you can use for both screen display and printing (a TT icon). If you select a printer font, Access uses the closest matching screen or TrueType font to display the datasheet on your screen. If you choose a screen font, Access uses the closest matching printer or TrueType font when you print. In either case, your printed result might look different from the image on your screen.

When you select a font, Access shows you a sample of the font in the lower right Sample box. Depending on the font you choose, you might also see a wide range of font styles (such as italic or bold) and font sizes. Click the Underline check box at the lower left if you want all the characters underlined. Click OK to set the new font for the entire datasheet. Click Cancel to dismiss the dialog box without changing the font.

Saving the Datasheet Layout and Setting Defaults

After you have the datasheet formatted the way you want it, you don't have to lose your work when you close the table. Choose the Save Layout command from the File menu to keep the format. Access also will ask whether you want to save a new layout when you try to close a table that's been changed.

You can also reset the default font for all datasheets. To do this, choose the Options command from the View menu. In the Datasheet category in the Options dialog box you can set the font name, size, weight (light, normal, or bold), italics, and underline. You'll also find options here to reset the default column width and display of gridlines.

CHANGING DATA

Not only can you view and format data in a datasheet, you can also insert new records, change data, and delete records.

Record Indicators

You might have noticed as you moved around the datasheet that occasionally icons were displayed on the record selector at the far left of each row. (See Figure 7-1.) These *indicators* and their meanings are listed below.

 Indicates this is the current row.

 Indicates you have made a change to one or more entries in this row. Microsoft Access saves the changes when you move to another row. Before moving to a new row you can press Esc once to undo the change to the current value or press Esc twice to undo all changes in the row. If you are updating a database that is shared on a network with other users, Access locks this record so that no one else can update it until you are finished. (See the last indicator below.)

 Indicates the blank row at the end of the table that you can use to create a new record.

Indicates that another user might be changing this record. You will see this icon only when you are accessing a database that is shared by other users on a network. You should wait until this indicator disappears before attempting to make changes to this record.

Adding a New Record

As you are building your application, you might find it useful to place some data in your tables so that you can test the forms and reports that you design. You might also find it convenient from time to time to add data directly to your tables by using the Datasheet view rather than by opening a form. If your table is empty, Microsoft Access shows you a single blank row when you open the Datasheet view. If you have data in your table, Access shows a blank row beneath the last record. You can jump to the blank row to begin adding a new record by selecting the Go To command from the Records menu and then choosing New, or by pressing Ctrl-+. Access places the cursor in the first column when you start a new record. As soon as you begin typing, Access changes the indicator to the pencil icon to show that updates are in progress. You can press Tab to move to the next column.

If you violate a validation rule, Access notifies you as soon as you attempt to leave a column. You must provide a correct value before you can move to another column. Note that if your validation rule checks data in this field against data in another field, Access compares to the previously saved value of the other field and does not use any changed value you might have entered but not saved. For example, if field A must always be less than field B and the original values were A=20 and B=25, you cannot change A to 30 and B to 50 at the same time. You must first change B to 50 and save the record, then change A to 30. Press Shift-Enter at any place in the record or press Tab in the last column in the record to commit your new record to the database. You can also choose the Save Record command from the File menu. If you want to cancel adding the record, press Esc twice.

Access provides several keyboard shortcuts to assist you as you enter new data, as shown in Figure 7-17.

Keys	*Data Action*
Ctrl-;	Enters the current date
Ctrl-:	Enters the current time
Ctrl-' or Ctrl-"	Enters the value from the same field in the previous record
Ctrl-Enter	Inserts a carriage return in a memo or text field

Figure 7-17.
The keyboard shortcuts for entering data in a datasheet.

Selecting and Changing Data

After you have data in your table, you can easily change the data by editing it in Datasheet view. You must first select a value before you can change it. If you click at the lower left corner of a box in the grid (that is, when the mouse pointer turns into an arrow pointing up to the right), Access selects the entire contents of the box. Any data you type replaces completely the old, selected data. In Figure 7-18 the address value for Piccadilly Foods in the PROMPT Customer–Chap 7 table has been selected. In Figure 7-19 that value has been changed prior to saving the record.

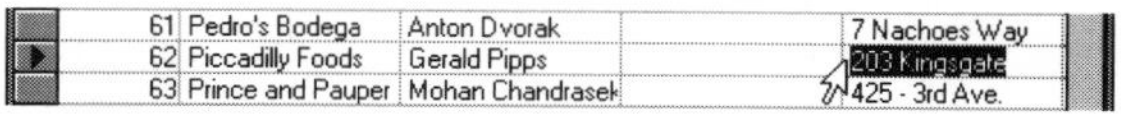

Figure 7-18.
The old data is selected.

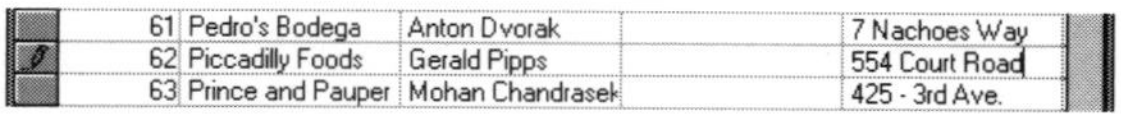

Figure 7-19.
The new data is typed in, replacing the old.

Microsoft Access also selects the entire entry if you tab into the box on the datasheet grid. If you want to change only part of the data (for example, to correct the spelling of a street name), you can shift to single character mode by pressing F2 or by clicking at the location where you want to start your change. Use the Backspace key to erase characters to the left of the cursor and the Delete key to remove characters to the right of the cursor. Press Shift and the right or left arrow keys to select multiple characters to replace. You can press F2 again to select the entire entry. A useful keyboard shortcut to change data is Ctrl-Alt-Spacebar to restore the data to the default value you specified in the table definition.

You can set two options to control how the left and right arrow keys and the Enter key work as you move from entry to entry. Choose the Options command from the View menu and select the Keyboard category in the Options dialog box, as shown in Figure 7-20. To control what happens inside an entry using the right or left arrow keys, you can set the Arrow Key Behavior item to Next Character (cursor moves over one character), or Next Field (selection moves to next field in record). If you set the Move After Enter item to Next Field, pressing the Enter key completes

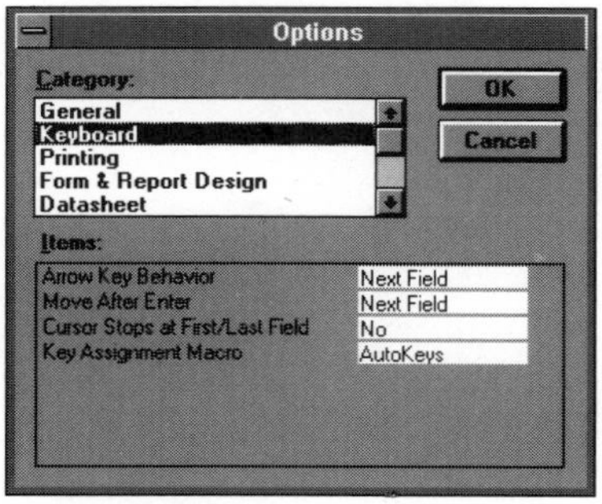

Figure 7-20.
The Options dialog box with the Keyboard category selected.

the update of the current field in the record and tabs to the next field. If you set the Move After Enter item to Next Record, pressing Enter moves you to the next row in the datasheet. If you set the Move After Enter item to No, pressing Enter selects the current entry.

Replacing Data

What if you need to make the same change in multiple records? Microsoft Access has a way to make that kind of change too. Select any entry in the column whose values you want to change (pick the entry in the first row if you want to start at the beginning of the table) and then choose the Replace command from the Edit menu or press Shift-F7 to see the dialog box in Figure 7-21. For example, to fix the spelling of *Seatle* in the City field in the PROMPT Customer–Chap 7 table you would select an entry in the City column, choose the Replace command, and fill in the dialog box as shown in Figure 7-21. Click the Find Next button to search for the next occurrence of the text in the Find What text box. Click the Replace button to change data selectively, or click the Replace All button to change all the entries that match the Find What text. Note that you have the option to search all fields, to exactly match the case for text searches (because searches in Access are normally case insensitive), and to select an entry only if the Find What text matches the entire entry in the field.

Figure 7-21.
The Replace dialog box.

Copying and Pasting Data

You can copy or cut any selected data to the Clipboard in the Windows operating system. In Access this data can be pasted into another field or record. To copy data, tab to the entry or click on the lower left corner of the box in the datasheet grid to select it. Choose the Copy command from the Edit menu or press Ctrl-C. You can also choose the Cut command from the Edit menu or press Ctrl-X to delete (cut) the data you have selected. To insert the data into another location, select the data you wish to replace in that location and choose the Paste command from the Edit menu or press Ctrl-V. If the new location is blank, move the cursor to the new location before choosing the Paste command.

To select an entire record to copy or cut, click the record selector at the far left of the row. You can also move to any entry in the row with the Tab or arrow keys and then select the entire row by pressing Shift-Spacebar. If you happened to click the wrong record selector, you can use the up and down arrow keys to move the selection highlight. You can drag through the record selectors or press Shift-up arrow or Shift-down arrow to extend the selection to multiple rows. Choose the Copy command from the Edit menu or press Ctrl-C to copy the contents of multiple rows to the Clipboard. You can paste copied rows into existing rows in another table, or you can use the Paste Append command on the Edit menu to paste the rows at the end of another table. You can paste copies of records into the same table only if the table has no primary key or if the primary key is a Counter data type. When the primary key is a Counter, Access automatically generates new counter values for you.

Note that cutting the rows from the table is the same as deleting them. (See the next section.) However, using the Cut command is handy for moving data you don't want any more in an active table to another backup table. You can have the other table open in Datasheet view at the same time. Simply switch to that window and paste the cut rows.

Whenever you paste rows into a table, Microsoft Access warns you that you will not be able to undo the paste operation. See Figure 7-22. Click the OK button to proceed or click Cancel if you decide to abort the operation.

Figure 7-22.
The dialog box warns you that a paste operation can't be undone.

Deleting Rows

To delete one or more rows, select them using the record selectors at the left of the rows and then delete. For details on selecting multiple rows, see the previous discussion on copying and pasting data. You can also use Ctrl-− to delete just the current row. When you delete rows, Access gives you a chance to change your mind if you made a mistake. See Figure 7-23. Choose OK in the dialog box to delete the rows. Click Cancel to abort the deletion.

Figure 7-23.
The dialog box that appears when you delete a row.

NOTE: *After you choose OK, you cannot restore the deleted rows. You will have to re-enter them or copy them from a backup.*

PERFORMING A SIMPLE SEARCH

If you want to look for data anywhere in your table, Microsoft Access provides you with a powerful search capability. To perform a search on a particular field, select that field first. Open the Find dialog box shown in Figure 7-24 by choosing the Find command from the Edit menu, or by pressing F7, or by clicking the Find button on the tool bar.

Figure 7-24.
The Find dialog box.

In the Find What text box within the Find dialog box, you can type the data that you want Access to find. You can include wildcard characters to perform a generic search. Use an asterisk (*) to indicate a string of unknown characters of any length, and a question mark (?) to indicate exactly one unknown character. For example, "*AB??DE*" matches "Aberdeen" and "Tab idea" but not "Lab department." If you're searching a date field for dates in January, you can specify *-Jan-* provided that you check the Search Fields As Formatted check box and provided that you chose the Medium Date format when you designed the table.

By default, Access searches the field your cursor was in before you opened the Find dialog box. Click All Fields in the Search In group box to check the entire table. Access searches down from the current record position unless you choose the up direction. Click the Match Case check box if you want to find text that exactly matches the uppercase and lowercase letters you typed. By default, Access is case insensitive unless you check this check box.

As noted above, check the Search Fields As Formatted check box if you need to search the data as it is displayed rather than as the data is stored by Access. Although searching this way is slower, you probably should check this check box any time you are searching a date/time field. You might also want to use "as formatted" when searching a yes/no field for *yes* because any value except 0 is a valid indicator of *yes*.

Click Find First to start the search from the beginning of the table. Click Find Next to start searching from the current record. Once you establish search criteria, you can press Shift-F4 to execute the search from the current record without having to open the Find dialog box again.

PRINTING FROM THE DATASHEET

You can use Datasheet view to print information from your table. Although you cannot limit which records Microsoft Access prints, you can control which fields are printed. (You also cannot perform any calculations; you need to create a form or report to do that.) As you discovered earlier in this chapter, you can format the fields you want to print, including setting the font, adjusting the spacing between columns, and the spacing between rows. If you use the Caption property when defining fields in Design view, you can also customize the column headings.

To produce the datasheet layout shown in Figure 7-25 for the PROMPT Customer–Chap 7 table, you can hide all but the columns shown, select a 10-point serif font (such as Bookman or Times Roman), and size the columns so that you can see all the information. You also should eliminate the gridlines by making sure that the Gridlines command is unchecked in the Layout menu. It's a good idea to maximize the window in Datasheet view so that you can see as many columns as possible.

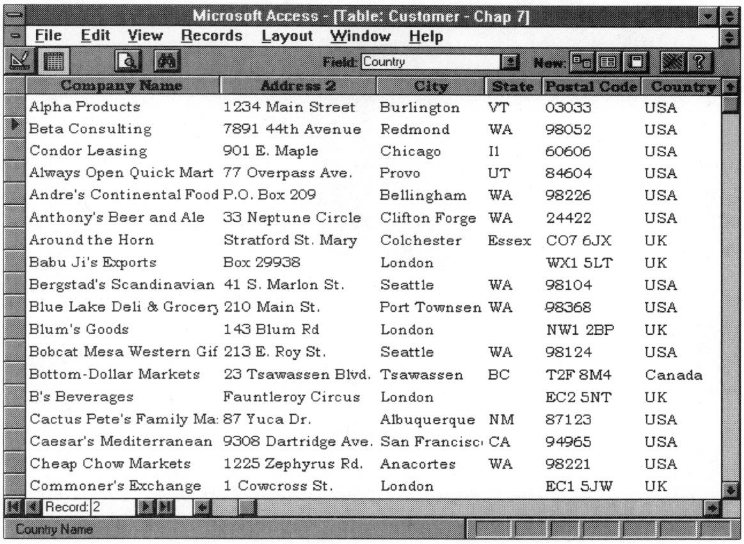

Company Name	Address 2	City	State	Postal Code	Country
Alpha Products	1234 Main Street	Burlington	VT	03033	USA
Beta Consulting	7891 44th Avenue	Redmond	WA	98052	USA
Condor Leasing	901 E. Maple	Chicago	Il	60606	USA
Always Open Quick Mart	77 Overpass Ave.	Provo	UT	84604	USA
Andre's Continental Food	P.O. Box 209	Bellingham	WA	98226	USA
Anthony's Beer and Ale	33 Neptune Circle	Clifton Forge	WA	24422	USA
Around the Horn	Stratford St. Mary	Colchester	Essex	CO7 6JX	UK
Babu Ji's Exports	Box 29938	London		WX1 5LT	UK
Bergstad's Scandinavian	41 S. Marlon St.	Seattle	WA	98104	USA
Blue Lake Deli & Grocery	210 Main St.	Port Townsen	WA	98368	USA
Blum's Goods	143 Blum Rd	London		NW1 2BP	UK
Bobcat Mesa Western Gif	213 E. Roy St.	Seattle	WA	98124	USA
Bottom-Dollar Markets	23 Tsawassen Blvd.	Tsawassen	BC	T2F 8M4	Canada
B's Beverages	Fauntleroy Circus	London		EC2 5NT	UK
Cactus Pete's Family Ma	87 Yuca Dr.	Albuquerque	NM	87123	USA
Caesar's Mediterranean	9308 Dartridge Ave.	San Francisc	CA	94965	USA
Cheap Chow Markets	1225 Zephyrus Rd.	Anacortes	WA	98221	USA
Commoner's Exchange	1 Cowcross St.	London		EC1 5JW	UK

Figure 7-25.
A datasheet that's ready to print.

Print Preview

After you have a datasheet formatted the way you want, you can activate Print Preview to verify that the data you want fits on a printed page. Choose the Print Preview command from the File menu, or click the Print Preview button on the tool bar, to see the display shown in Figure 7-26 on the next page. Notice that the mouse pointer changes to a small magnifying glass. You can move the mouse pointer to any part of the report and click to zoom in and see the data up close. You can also click the Zoom button on the tool bar to magnify the report and display the upper left corner of the current page. While zoomed in, you can use the arrow keys to move around the displayed page in small increments. Press the Page Up or Page Down key to move in larger increments. You can press Ctrl-down arrow to move to the bottom of the page, Ctrl-up arrow to move to the top, Ctrl-right arrow to move to the right margin, and Ctrl-left arrow to move to the left margin. Ctrl-Home puts you back in the upper left corner, and Ctrl-End moves the display to the lower right corner. Click the Zoom button again or click the left mouse button to zoom out.

If your printed output has multiple pages, you can use the Page Up and Page Down keys while zoomed out to move between pages. Click the Cancel button to exit Print Preview without printing. Click the Print button to send your formatted datasheet to a printer. Click the Setup button to specify printer setup options, as explained in the next section.

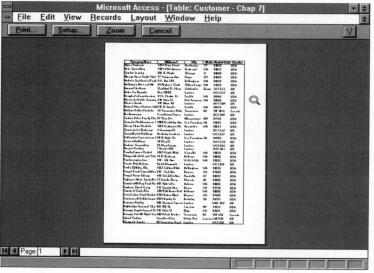

Figure 7-26.
The datasheet in Print Preview.

Print Setup

Using the Print Setup command can be difficult, particularly if your system is connected to more than one printer. When you click the Print Setup button on the tool bar from Print Preview, or choose the Print Setup command from the File menu, Microsoft Access opens the dialog box shown in Figure 7-27.

Access initially chooses your default printer in the Printer group box. If you have more than one printer, you can select the one to which you want to print from

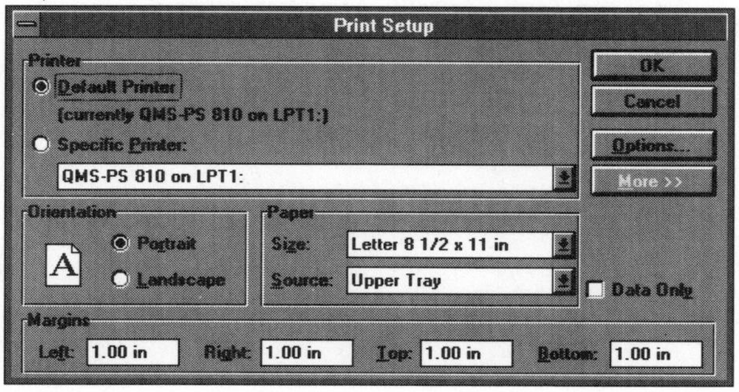

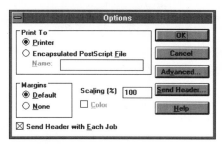

Figure 7-27.
The Print Setup dialog box.

the Specific Printer drop-down list. Other options in this dialog box let you pick the paper size and tray source (if your printer supports multiple trays), the margins, and the orientation—Portrait or Landscape.

If you have a PostScript printer and click the Options button, Access displays the dialog box shown in Figure 7-28. When printing in PostScript mode, you can send your output directly to the printer or you can create a file that you can print later. If the data you chose doesn't fill the full width of the page, you can specify a scale larger than 100% to use more of each page. If the printed data is too wide or long, you can scale it down to fit on one page. However, you won't be able to see the results in the Print Preview window. Later, when you design forms using color, you can check the Color check box in this dialog box in order to print colors on your form if you have a color printer. Although it might take a bit longer to start printing each report, it's a good idea to always send the PostScript header every time to ensure that your printer is set up properly.

Figure 7-28.
The PostScript options for printer setup.

If you click the Advanced button in the PostScript Options dialog box, you will see the dialog box shown in Figure 7-29 on the next page. You can send output to a PostScript printer as either Adobe or Bitmap. If your documents are printing correctly when they include graphics, or if your documents include only text (as should be the case when printing a datasheet), use Adobe to print faster. If all the TrueType fonts you use have printer equivalents, you can check the Use Printer Fonts check box. Otherwise, you should check the Use Substitution Table check box in order to map fonts for printing. Click the Edit Substitution Table button to scan your available fonts and change the mapping from TrueType to your printer. You can force your printer driver to download a soft font specification for all TrueType fonts, but this will cause your documents to print more slowly. In general, Setup establishes good font mapping when you install Windows, so you shouldn't need to change these settings unless you are having problems.

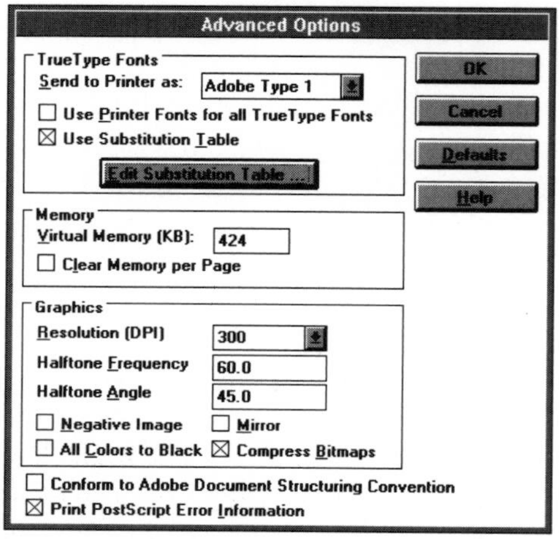

Figure 7-29.
The Advanced Options dialog box for PostScript printer setup.

In the Memory section, you can enter the value for how much memory you have installed on your printer. If your printer has more memory than shown, you can improve performance by correcting this number. If you are having problems printing documents with multiple fonts, try checking the Clear Memory Per Page check box. In the Graphics section, you can select a coarse or fine printer resolution. (Most PostScript printers can handle a full 300 dots per inch easily.) You can also select halftone frequency (density) and angle if you have pictures in your documents. Check the Negative Image check box to reverse black and white in your document. Check the Mirror check box to swap the print image from left to right. Check the All Colors To Black check box if images with multiple colors are not being printed properly. Check the Compress Bitmaps check box to speed the printing of graphics. Then click the OK button to save changes, the Cancel button to abort any changes, and the Defaults button to restore all settings to the default.

If you have a LaserJet or compatible printer, the Options dialog box is a bit less daunting. See Figure 7-30. For colored pictures, you can set the level of dithering to control the relative gray variation between colors. Choose the None option to print colors in black. Choose the Line Art option to print only the outline of colored areas. You can also control graphic printing by adjusting the Intensity Control. Choose this option for forms and reports if you print white characters on a black or colored background. At the bottom of the window, you can see a check box titled Print TrueType As Graphics. Normally, the LaserJet printer driver maps TrueType fonts to available printer fonts. If you check this check box, you'll see TrueType font text printed as you actually see it on the screen, but printing will be much slower.

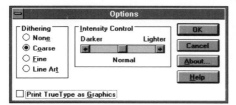

Figure 7-30.
The HP LaserJet printer setup options.

Printing

To send the datasheet to your printer, click the Print button on the Print Preview tool bar. You can also print a datasheet directly from the Database window by selecting the table you want and choosing the Print command from the File menu. Microsoft Access shows you a Print dialog box similar to Figure 7-31. This dialog box varies depending on your printer.

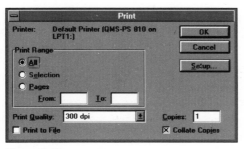

Figure 7-31.
The Print dialog box.

In all Print dialog boxes, you can choose to print multiple copies. You can also choose to print all pages or a range of pages. If you ask Access to collate multiple copies, Access prints the first through last pages in sequence and repeats for each copy. If you deselect the Collate Copies check box, Access prints the number of copies you requested for the first page, then the number of copies you requested for the second page, and so on. You can also tell Access to send your output to a file that you can copy to your printer later.

When you tell Access to send the output to a printer, Access formats and sends the pages to the Windows operating system Print Manager if you've selected the Use Print Manager check box in the Control Panel's Printers option. You can see the printing progress in a dialog box, as shown in Figure 7-32. After all pages are sent to Print Manager, you can generally continue with other activities in Access while your pages are printing.

Figure 7-32.
The Printing dialog box that shows the printing status.

Now that you're familiar with working with data directly out of tables by using datasheets, it's time to move on to dealing with data from multiple tables and to updating many rows in a table in one operation. To do these operations, you need the power of queries, as explained in the next chapter.

8

Adding Power with Select Queries

In the previous chapter you learned about working with the data in your tables in Datasheet view. Although there's a lot you can do with datasheets—including browsing, updating, or printing your data—you'll find that most of the time you need to look at only part of your data in one table or else specific data from multiple related tables. To select a set of data to work with, you use queries.

When you define and run a *select query* (one that selects information from the tables and queries in your database, as opposed to an *action query* that inserts, updates, or deletes data), Microsoft Access creates a *dynaset* of the selected data. In most cases, you can work with a dynaset in the same way you work with a table; you can browse through it, select information from it, print it, and even update the data in it. But, unlike a real table, a dynaset doesn't really exist in your database. Access creates a dynaset from the data that exists in your tables and queries at the time you run the query. When you update data in a dynaset, Access reflects your changes in the tables underlying your query.

As you learn to design forms and reports later in this book, you'll find that queries are the best way to focus in on just the data you need for the task at hand. When you get into advanced form design, you'll find that queries are also useful for providing lists of choices for list boxes, which will make entering data into your database much easier.

To open a new Query window in Design view, click the Query button in the Database window, and then click the New button above the query list. To open an existing query in Design view, click the Query button in the Database window, select the query you want, and click the Design button. See Figure 8-1 on the next page.

Figure 8-2 on the next page shows an existing query whose window has been opened in Design view. The Query window contains field lists and a Query By Example or QBE grid.

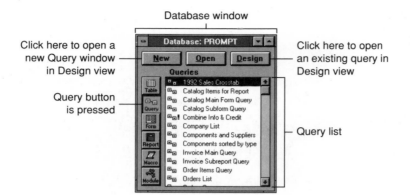

Figure 8-1.
The Database window is used to open the Query window in Design view.

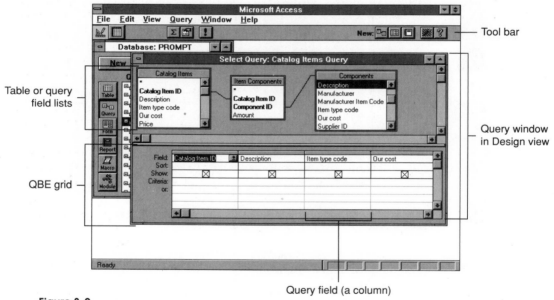

Figure 8-2.
An existing query opened in Design view.

All of the examples in this chapter, including the query shown in Figure 8-2, use data from the database for Prompt Computer Solutions that you designed using Appendix B or that you copied from CompuServe. You can also follow along in this chapter using the tables in the sample NWIND database provided with Microsoft Access.

THE TOOL BAR FOR
THE QUERY WINDOW IN DESIGN VIEW

Figure 8-3 shows you the tool bar for the Query window in Design view. Microsoft Access displays this tool bar whenever a Query window in Design view has the current focus.

Figure 8-3.
The tool bar for the Query window in Design view.

You can see the following action buttons from left to right on the tool bar:

 Design View button. This button appears pressed, indicating you are in Design view.

 Datasheet View button. Click this button to see the Query window in Datasheet view, a view of the dynaset. Datasheets are discussed in Chapter 7. This button is not available for action queries, which are described in Chapter 9.

 Totals button. Click this button to open the totals row in the QBE grid. You can create a query to calculate totals across groups of data. See the section "Totals Queries" later in this chapter for more information. This button is not available for action queries, which are described in Chapter 9.

Properties button. Click this button to open the Query Properties window. You can change various query properties in the window, depending on the type of query you are designing.

Run button. For select queries (as described in this chapter), this button does the same thing as the Datasheet View button, displays the dynaset. For action queries (as described in Chapter 9), click this button to run the query.

 New Query button. Click this button to design a new query based on the current query. You must save the current query before you can design another query based on it.

 New Form button. Click this button to design a new form based on the current query. You must save the current query before you can design a new form based on it.

 New Report button. Click this button to design a new report based on the current query. You must save the current query before you can design a new report based on it.

Undo button. Click this button to undo the latest change. This button is not available if a change cannot be undone.

Help button. Click this button to open the context-sensitive Help window.

QUERY OPTIONS

Before you get started designing queries, you can set an environment option in the Options dialog box that will help you work with QBE grids in Design view. To avoid confusion, especially when working with multiple tables or other queries in a new query, it's useful to see the table or query name in the QBE grid. Microsoft Access doesn't show you the table or query names by default. To set this option, choose the Options command from the View menu. Within the Options dialog box, select Query Design from the Category list, as shown in Figure 8-4. Select the Yes setting for the Show Table Names option, and you will see the table and query names in the QBE grid for all queries, as shown in Figure 8-5.

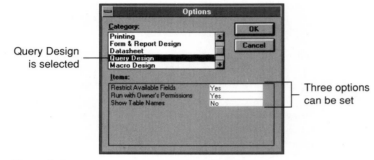

Figure 8-4.
The Query Design options within the Options dialog box.

There are two other Query Design options you can set in the Options dialog box. They are the Restrict Available Fields option and the Run with Owner's Permissions option.

You will normally select only specific fields that you want returned in the dynaset when you run a select query. However, if you're designing the query to be used in a form and you want all fields from all tables in the query available to the form, set the Restrict Available Fields option to No. It's a good idea to keep the default setting of Yes and change this option only on specific queries.

If you have designed your database to be shared by multiple users across a network, you might want to secure the data tables and only grant access to other users through queries. The owner of the table always has full access to any table. You can deny access to the tables to everyone and still let authorized users see certain data. You accomplish this by setting the Run with Owner's Permissions option to Yes. See your *Microsoft Access User's Guide* for details on securing your Access database.

The Restrict Available Fields option and the Run with Owner's Permissions option can also be set in a different dialog box, by choosing the Properties button from the tool bar. The Show Table Names option can also be set by choosing the Table Names command from the View menu.

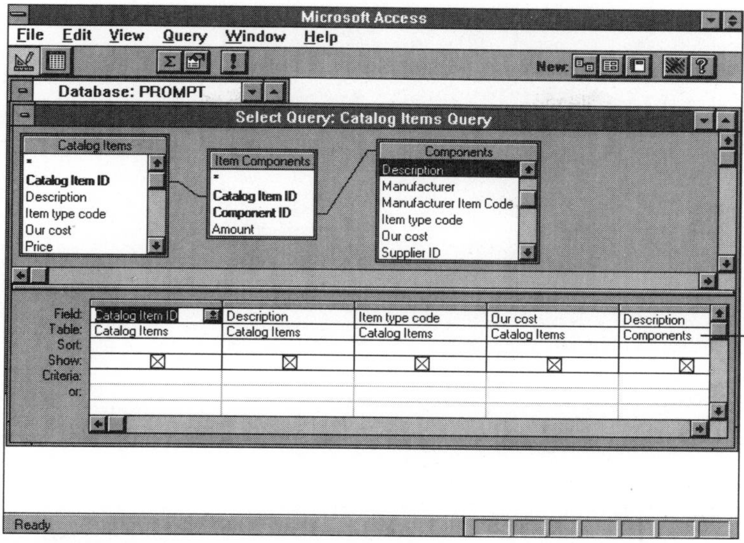

Table or query names are shown here

Figure 8-5.
The QBE grid shows table and query names after the Show Table Names option is set.

SELECTING DATA FROM A SINGLE TABLE

One of the advantages of using queries is that they allow you to find data in multiple related tables easily. However, you'll also find queries useful for sifting through the data in a single table. And all the techniques you use for working with a single table apply equally to more complex multiple-table queries. So, this chapter begins by using queries to select data from a single table.

The easiest way to start building a query on a table is to open the Database window, select the table you want, and click the New Query button on the tool bar. Do that now with the Customer table in the PROMPT database, and you will see the window shown in Figure 8-6. (If you want to create similar queries using the sample NWIND database, select the Orders table.)

The Query window in Design view has two main sections. In the top you can see field lists with the fields for the tables or queries you have chosen for this query. The bottom part of the window is the QBE grid in which you will do all your design work. Each column in the grid represents one field that you'll be working with in this query. As you'll see later, a field can be a simple field from one of the tables, a calculated field based on several fields in the tables, or a totals field using one of the functions provided by Access.

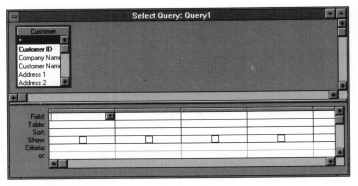

Figure 8-6.
The Query window in Design view.

You'll use the first line in the QBE grid to select fields: the fields you want in the resulting dynaset, the fields you want to sort, and the fields you want to test for values. Because the Show Table Names option is set, Access displays the table name (which is the source of the selected field) in the second line of the QBE grid. On the next line, you can specify whether Access should sort the selected or calculated field in Ascending or Descending order.

On the Show line, you can use the check boxes to determine the fields that will be returned in the dynaset. By default, Access shows all the fields you selected on the QBE grid. Sometimes you want to include a field in the query to allow you to screen out the records you want (such as the customers or shippers in a certain state), but you don't need that field in the dynaset. You can add that field to the QBE grid so that you can define criteria, but deselect the Show box underneath to exclude the field from the dynaset.

Finally, you can use the Criteria line and the lines labeled *or* to enter the criteria you want to use as filters. Once you understand how it's done, you'll find it easy to specify exactly the fields and records that you want.

Specifying Fields

The first step in building a query is to choose the fields you want in the dynaset. You can select the fields you want in several ways. Using the keyboard, you can tab to an available column in the QBE grid and press Alt-down arrow to open up the list of available fields. (If you need to move the cursor to the bottom half of the design window, first press F6.) Use the up and down arrow keys to move the highlight to the field you want and press Enter to select the field.

Another way to select a field is to drag it from one of the field lists in the top of the window to one of the columns on the QBE grid. In Figure 8-7, the Credit Limit field is being dragged to the QBE grid. When you drag a field, the mouse pointer turns into a small rectangle.

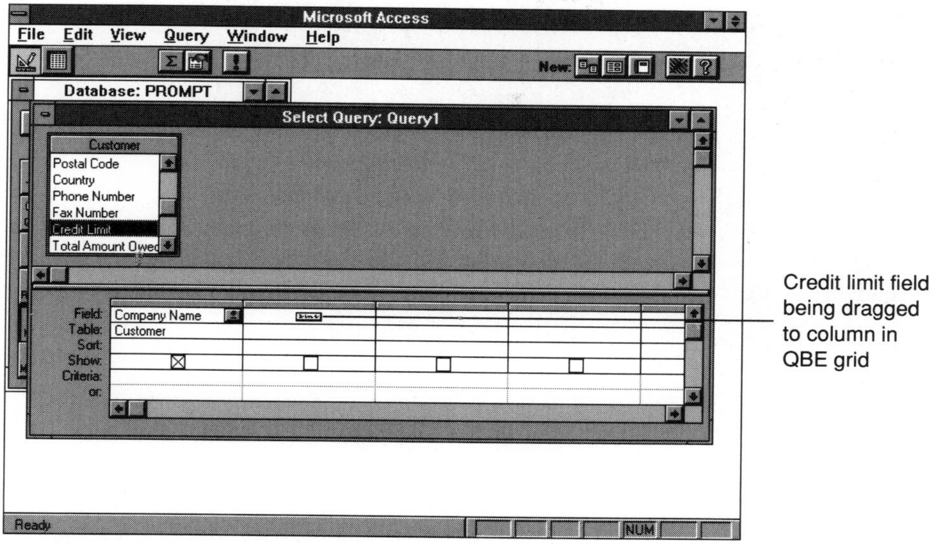

Figure 8-7.
A field being dragged to a column in the QBE grid.

At the top of each field list in the top portion of the Query window (and also the first entry in the Field drop-down list on the QBE grid) is a special asterisk (∗) symbol. This symbol is shorthand for "all fields in the table or query." Whenever you want to include all the fields in the table or query, you don't have to define each one individually on the QBE grid (unless you also want to define some sorting or selection criteria for specific fields). You can simply add the asterisk to the QBE grid to include all the fields from a list. Note that you can add individual fields to the grid in addition to the asterisk in order to define criteria for those fields, but you should deselect the Show box for the individual fields so that you don't see them twice in the dynaset.

In this exercise, pick Company Name, State, Credit Limit, and Total Amount Owed from the PROMPT Customer table. (If you're following along with NWIND, pick Ship Name, Ship Region, Order Amount, and Freight from the Orders table.) If you switch the Query window to Datasheet view at this point, you'll see only the fields you selected from all the records in the underlying table.

Entering Selection Criteria

The next step is to further refine the values in the fields you want. In the example in Figure 8-8, you focus in on customers in the state of Washington. (In NWIND, you can look for shipping addresses in the Orders table in Washington in the same way by applying this test to the Region field.)

To look for a single value, simply type it on the Criteria line below the field you want to test. If the field you're testing is a text field and the value you're looking for has any blanks in the middle, you must enclose each value in quotes. Note that Access automatically adds quotes for you around single text values. (In Figure 8-8, *WA* was typed, but the field shows "*WA*" after Enter was pressed.)

If you want to test for the existence of any of several values, simply enter each of them on the Criteria line separated by the word *Or.* For example, specifying *WA Or CA* searches for records for either of the two states. You can also test for any of several values by entering each one on a separate Criteria or Or line under the field you want to test. For example, enter *CA* on the Criteria line, *WA* on the next line (the first Or line), and so on. But you have to be careful if you're also specifying criteria in other fields, as explained below.

In the next section you'll also see that you can include a comparison operator on the Criteria line to look for values less than (<), less than or equal to (< =), greater than (>), greater than or equal to (> =), or not equal to (< >) the value that you specify.

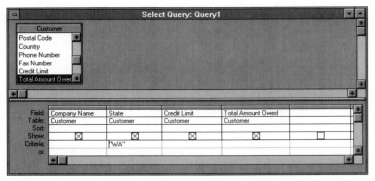

Figure 8-8.
A QBE grid that specifies WA as a selection criteria.

AND vs. OR

When you enter criteria under several different fields, all of the tests on a single Criteria line or an Or line must be true for a record to be included in the dynaset. That is, Microsoft Access performs a logical AND between multiple criteria on the same line. So, if you enter *WA* under State (or Region in the NWIND Orders table) and *>5000* under Credit Limit (or Order Amount in NWIND Orders), the record must be for the state of Washington AND have a credit limit greater than 5000 in order to be selected. If you enter *WA Or CA* under State and *>=1000 And <=1500* under Credit Limit, the record must be for the state of Washington OR California, and the credit limit must be between 1000 AND 1500, inclusive.

Figure 8-9 shows you the result of applying a logical AND between any two tests. As you can see, both tests must be true for the result of the AND to be true and the record selected.

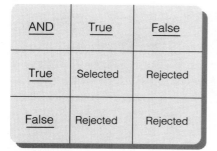

Figure 8-9.
The result of applying the logical AND between two tests.

When you specify multiple criteria for a field separated by a logical OR, only one of the criteria must be true for the record to be selected. You can specify several OR criteria for a field by either entering them all in a single Criteria box separated by the OR logical operator, as shown earlier, or by entering each of the criteria on a separate Or line. When you use multiple Or lines, all the criteria *on only one of the Or lines* must be true for a record to be selected. If, for example, you enter criteria on three different lines in the QBE grid (call them A, B, and C), you have asked Access to include a record in the result set whenever all the criteria on line A are true OR all the criteria on line B are true OR all the criteria on line C are true. Figure 8-10 shows you the result of applying a logical OR between any two criteria or sets of criteria. As you can see, only one of the tests must be True for the result of the OR to be true and the record selected.

OR	True	False
True	Selected	Selected
False	Selected	Rejected

Figure 8-10.
The result of applying the logical OR between two tests.

Look at a specific example. In Figure 8-11, you specify *WA* on the first Criteria line of the State field. On the next line (the first Or line), you specify *CA* in the State field and *>5000* in the corresponding Or line of the Credit Limit field. When you run this query, you'll get all the records for the state of Washington. You'll also get any records for the state of California in which the credit limit is more than 5000.

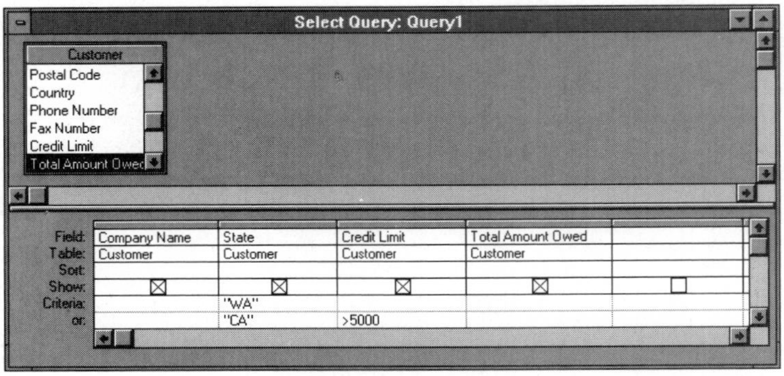

Figure 8-11.
A QBE grid that specifies multiple AND and OR selection criteria.

In Figure 8-12, you can see the dynaset that results from running this query (the Datasheet view). (You can see similar results in the NWIND Orders table if you set up criteria for the Ship Region and Order Amount fields.)

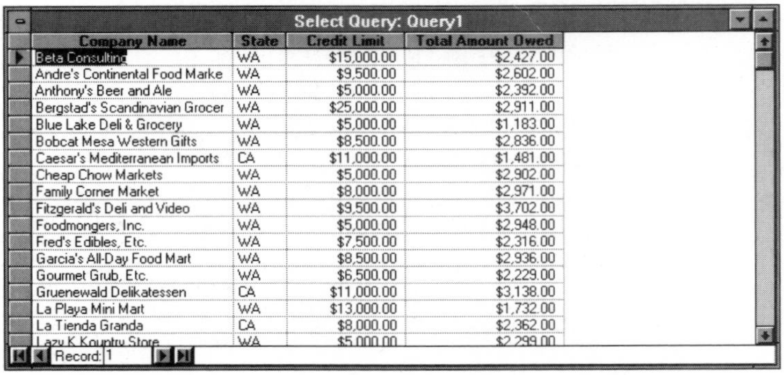
Select Query: Query1

Company Name	State	Credit Limit	Total Amount Owed
Beta Consulting	WA	$15,000.00	$2,427.00
Andre's Continental Food Marke	WA	$9,500.00	$2,602.00
Anthony's Beer and Ale	WA	$5,000.00	$2,392.00
Bergstad's Scandinavian Grocer	WA	$25,000.00	$2,911.00
Blue Lake Deli & Grocery	WA	$5,000.00	$1,183.00
Bobcat Mesa Western Gifts	WA	$8,500.00	$2,836.00
Caesar's Mediterranean Imports	CA	$11,000.00	$1,481.00
Cheap Chow Markets	WA	$5,000.00	$2,902.00
Family Corner Market	WA	$8,000.00	$2,971.00
Fitzgerald's Deli and Video	WA	$9,500.00	$3,702.00
Foodmongers, Inc.	WA	$5,000.00	$2,948.00
Fred's Edibles, Etc.	WA	$7,500.00	$2,316.00
Garcia's All-Day Food Mart	WA	$8,500.00	$2,936.00
Gourmet Grub, Etc.	WA	$6,500.00	$2,229.00
Gruenewald Delikatessen	CA	$11,000.00	$3,138.00
La Playa Mini Mart	WA	$13,000.00	$1,732.00
La Tienda Granda	CA	$8,000.00	$2,362.00
Lazy K Kountry Store	WA	$5,000.00	$2,299.00

Record: 1

Figure 8-12.
The dynaset of the query shown in Figure 8-11.

BETWEEN, IN, and LIKE

In addition to comparison operators, Access provides you with three special predicate clauses that are useful for specifying the data you want in the dynaset. These are

BETWEEN	Useful for specifying a range of values. The clause *Between 10 And 20* is the same as specifying *>=10 And <=20*.
IN	Useful for specifying a list of values, any one of which can match the field being searched. The clause *In ("WA", "CA", "ID")* is the same as *"WA" Or "CA" Or "ID"*.
LIKE	Useful for searching for patterns in text fields. You can include special characters and range values in the Like comparison string to define the character pattern you want. Use *?* to indicate any single character in that position. Use *** to indicate zero or more characters in that position. The character *#* specifies a single numeric digit in that position. Include a range in brackets to test for a particular range of characters in a position, and use *!* to indicate exceptions. The range [0–9] tests for numbers, [a–z] tests for letters, [!0–9] tests for any characters except 0–9. As an example, a phrase such as *Like "?[a–k]d[0–9]*"* tests for any single character in the first position, any character a through k in the second position, the letter d in the third position, any character 0 through 9 in the fourth position, and any number of characters after that.

Suppose that in your Customer table you want to find all companies in Washington or Idaho whose names begin with *F* and who have a credit limit greater than or equal to 5000 but less than or equal to 15,000. Figure 8-13 shows how you would enter these criteria. And Figure 8-14 shows the dynaset of this query.

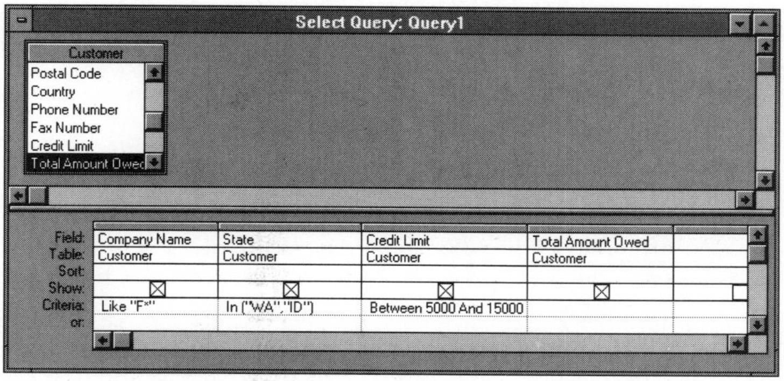

Figure 8-13.
A QBE grid that uses BETWEEN, IN, and LIKE.

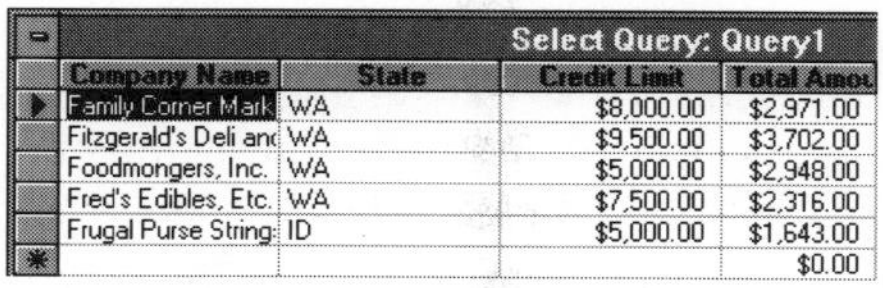

Figure 8-14.
The dynaset of the query shown in Figure 8-13.

Working with Dates and Times in Criteria

Microsoft Access stores dates and times as double precision floating-point numbers. The value to the left of the decimal point represents the day, and the fractional part of the number stores the time as a fraction of a day. Fortunately, you don't have to worry about converting internal numbers to specify a test for a particular date value. Access handles date and time entries in several different formats.

In general, you should always surround date and time values with the pound-sign character (#) to help Access determine that you are entering a date or time. To test for a specific date, use the date notation that is most comfortable for you to use. For example, #April 15, 1992#, #4/15/92#, and #15-Apr-1992# are all recognized as the same date by Access when you set your date format to U.S. in the Control Panel of Windows. Also, #5:30 PM# and #17:30# both specify 5:30 in the evening.

Access has several useful functions to assist you in testing date and time values. These are explained below with examples that use the Last Pay Date field in the PROMPT database:

Day(*date*)	Returns a value from 1 through 31 for the day of the month. For example, if you want to select records with Last Pay Date values after the 10th of any month, enter *Day([Last Pay Date])>10* in the Last Pay Date field criteria.
Month(*date*)	Returns a value from 1 through 12 for the month of the year. For example, if you want to find all records that have a Last Pay Date value of June, enter *Month([Last Pay Date])=6* in the Last Pay Date field criteria.
Year(*date*)	Returns a value from 100 through 9999 for the year. If you want to find a Last Pay Date value in 1990, enter *Year([Last Pay Date])=1990* in the Last Pay Date field criteria.
Weekday(*date*)	Returns from 1 (Sunday) through 7 (Saturday) for the day of the week. To find business day dates, enter the phrase *Weekday([Mydate]) Between 2 and 6* in the field criteria for a field named Mydate.
Hour(*date*)	Returns the hour (0 through 23). To find a payment made before noon, enter *Hour([Last Pay Date])<12* in the Last Pay Date field criteria.
Datepart(*interval, date*)	Returns the portion of the date or time depending on the interval code you supply. Useful interval codes are "q" for quarter of the year (1 through 4) and "ww" for week of the year (1 through 52). For example, to select dates in the second quarter, enter *Datepart("q",[Mydate])=2* in the field criteria for a field named Mydate.
Date()	Returns the current system date. To select dates more than 30 days ago, enter *<Date() −30* in the field criteria.

Calculating Values

You can specify a calculation on any of the fields in your table and make that calculation a new field in the dynaset. In an Order Item record, for example, you might have a Quantity field and a Price field, but not the extended price (quantity times price). You can include that value in your dynaset by typing in the calculation in the field of an empty column in the QBE grid.

Try calculating the remaining credit for each customer in the PROMPT database by subtracting Total Amount Owed from Credit Limit, as shown in Figure 8-15. (If you're working with the NWIND Orders table, you might want to find out the total bill by adding Order Amount and Freight.) Notice that when you enter a calculation formula, Access assigns a temporary field name followed by a colon. In this case, the field name begins with *Expr1*.

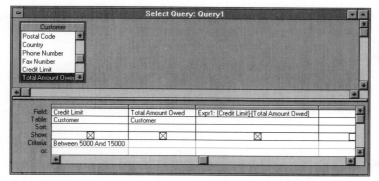

Figure 8-15.
A calculation added to a QBE grid.

Specifying Field Names

You can change or assign field names that will appear in the dynaset of a query. This feature is particularly useful when you have calculated a value in the query. In Figure 8-15, you calculated a value and Access assigned a temporary name. In Figure 8-16 on the next page, the name has been changed to something more meaningful.

You can change the name of any column in your query by prefixing the field name in the QBE grid with a new name followed by a colon. Figure 8-17 shows the dynaset with a new name assigned to the calculated field.

Sorting Data

Normally, Access presents the rows in your dynaset in the order that they're retrieved from the database. You can add sorting information to determine the sequence of the data. To specify sorting criteria, click in the Sort line under the field you want to sort and choose Ascending or Descending from the drop-down list. In the example, shown in Figure 8-18, the query results are sorted in descending sequence based on Total Amount Owed. The dynaset will list the customers who owe the most first.

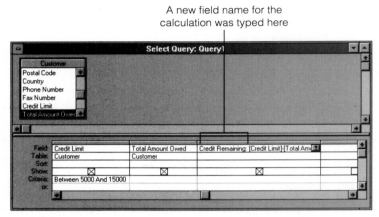

A new field name for the calculation was typed here

Figure 8-16.
A calculation field has been named in the QBE grid.

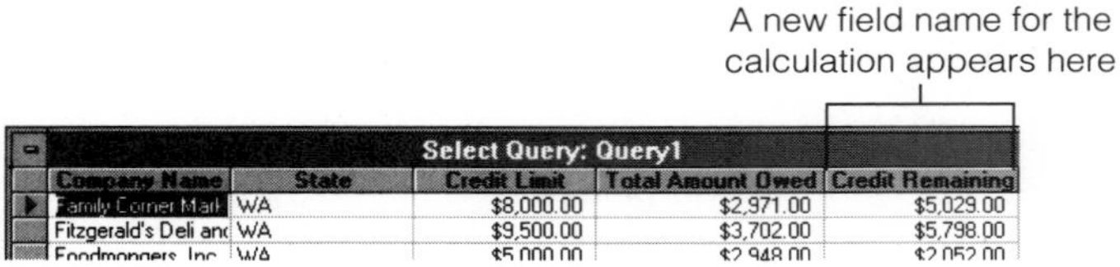

A new field name for the calculation appears here

Figure 8-17.
The dynaset of the query shown in Figure 8-16.

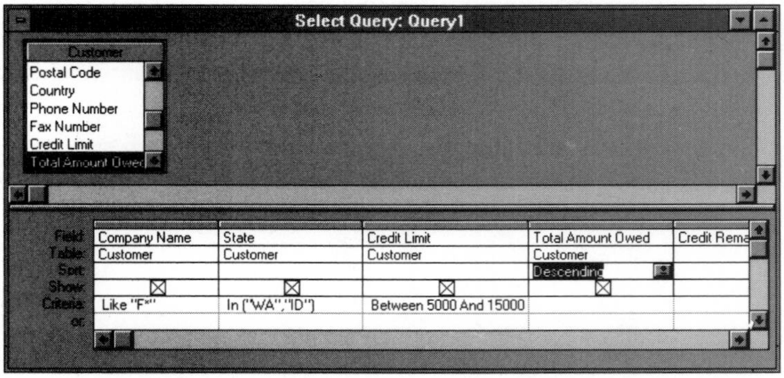

Figure 8-18.
A query with sorting criteria added.

As you can see in Figure 8-19, the query has selected all the customers in Washington and Idaho whose company name begins with F and who have credit limits between 5000 and 15000, and the query sorted the result according to who owes the most.

Company Name	State	Credit Limit	Total Amount Owed	Credit Remaining
Fitzgerald's Deli and	WA	$9,500.00	$3,702.00	$5,798.00
Family Corner Mark	WA	$8,000.00	$2,971.00	$5,029.00
Foodmongers, Inc	WA	$5,000.00	$2,948.00	$2,052.00

Figure 8-19.
The dynaset of the query shown in Figure 8-18.

You can also sort on multiple fields. Access honors your sorting criteria from left to right in the query's QBE grid. If you want to sort by Total Amount Owed and then by State, you should move the State field to the right of the Total Amount Owed field. The easiest way to do that is to select the State field by clicking the field selector box above the field name. You can then click the selector box again and drag the field to its new location. Once you save and close your query, you'll find the next time you open it in Design view that Access has moved all your sorted columns in sequence to the far left of the QBE grid.

Totals Queries

Sometimes you aren't interested in each and every detail row in your table. You'd rather see totals of different groups of data. For example, you might want the total sales to all customers in a particular state. Or, you might want to know the average of all sales for each month in the last year. To get these answers, you need a *totals query*. To calculate totals within any query, click the Totals button on the tool bar in Design view to open the Total line in the QBE grid, as shown in Figure 8-20 on the next page.

Totals Within Groups

When you first click the Totals button on the tool bar, Access displays *Group By* in the Total line for any fields you already have on the QBE grid. At this point the records in each field are grouped but not totaled. If you were to run the query at that point, you'd get one row in the dynaset for each set of unique values, but no totals. You can create totals by replacing Group By with some *totals functions* on the Total line.

Access provides nine different totals functions for your use. You can choose the one you want by typing its name on the Total line in the QBE grid or by selecting it from the drop-down list. The available functions are

SUM	Calculates the sum of all the values for this field in each group. You can specify this function only on number or currency columns.
AVG	Calculates the arithmetic average of all the values for this field in each group. You can specify this function only on number or currency columns. Access does not include any null values in the calculation.

(continued)

MIN	Returns the lowest value found in this column within each group. For numbers, returns the smallest value. For text, returns the lowest in collating sequence, without regard for case. Access ignores null values.
MAX	Returns the highest value found in this column within each group. For numbers, returns the largest value. For text, returns the highest in collating sequence, without regard for case. Access ignores null values.
COUNT	Returns the count of the rows in which the specified field is not a null value. You can also enter the special expression COUNT(∗) on the Field line to count all rows in each group, regardless of the existence of null values.
FIRST	Returns the first value in this field.
LAST	Returns the last value in this field.
STDEV	Calculates the statistical standard deviation of all the values for this field in each group. You can specify this function only on number or currency columns. If the group does not contain at least two rows, Access returns a null value.
VAR	Calculates the statistical variance of all the values for this field in each group. You can specify this function only on number or currency columns. If the group does not contain at least two rows, Access returns a null value.

Try working with a totals query now by first deleting the Company Name field from the query in Figure 8-18 and then clicking the Totals button on the tool bar. Then, in order to group the totals you create by state, keep *Group By* under the State

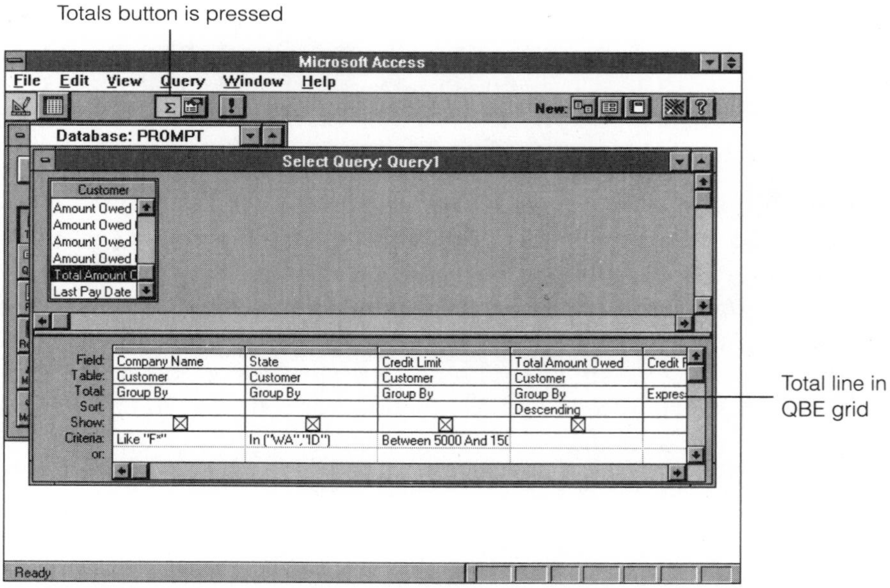

Figure 8-20.
The Totals button and the Total line in the QBE grid.

field. Next choose totals functions for the remaining fields, as follows: the Avg function for the Credit Limit field, the Sum function for the Total Amount Owed field, and the Avg function for the Credit Remaining Field. Change the name of the Credit Remaining field by preceding it with the word *Avg*. Remove all criteria from the Criteria line. Figure 8-21 shows these changes in the QBE grid. Figure 8-22 shows the results when you run the query.

On the drop-down list for the Total line in the QBE grid, you can also find an Expression setting. Choose this when you want to create an expression on the Field line that uses one or more of the total functions listed above. For example, you might want to calculate a value that reflects the range of values in the group, as in *MAX([Credit Limit]) – MIN([Credit Limit])*.

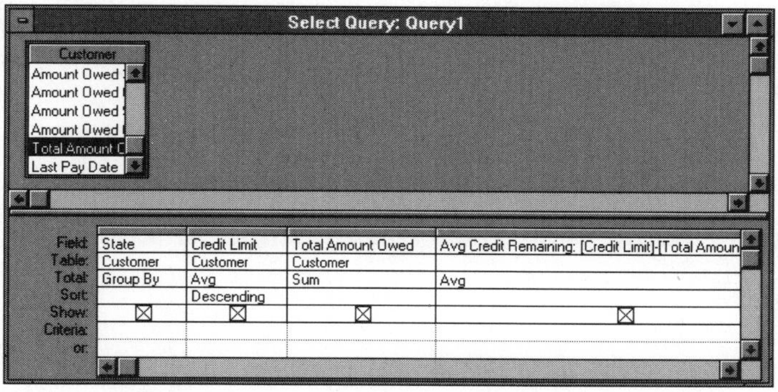

Figure 8-21.
The settings in the Total line for calculating a totals query.

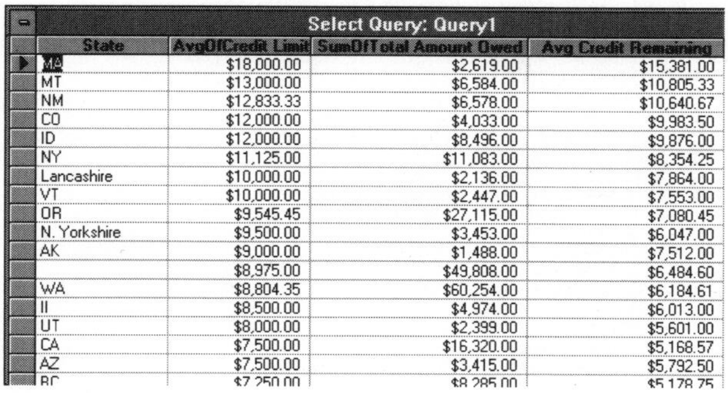

Select Query: Query1

State	AvgOfCredit Limit	SumOfTotal Amount Owed	Avg Credit Remaining
MA	$18,000.00	$2,619.00	$15,381.00
MT	$13,000.00	$6,584.00	$10,805.33
NM	$12,833.33	$6,578.00	$10,640.67
CO	$12,000.00	$4,033.00	$9,983.50
ID	$12,000.00	$8,496.00	$9,876.00
NY	$11,125.00	$11,083.00	$8,354.25
Lancashire	$10,000.00	$2,136.00	$7,864.00
VT	$10,000.00	$2,447.00	$7,553.00
OR	$9,545.45	$27,115.00	$7,080.45
N. Yorkshire	$9,500.00	$3,453.00	$6,047.00
AK	$9,000.00	$1,488.00	$7,512.00
	$8,975.00	$49,808.00	$6,484.60
WA	$8,804.35	$60,254.00	$6,184.61
Il	$8,500.00	$4,974.00	$6,013.00
UT	$8,000.00	$2,399.00	$5,601.00
CA	$7,500.00	$16,320.00	$5,168.57
AZ	$7,500.00	$3,415.00	$5,792.50
BC	$7,250.00	$8,285.00	$5,178.75

Figure 8-22.
The dynaset of the query shown in Figure 8-21.

Selecting Records to Form Groups

You might not want to include some records in the groups that form your totals query. For example, in both the Customer table in PROMPT and the Customers table in NWIND, there are customers from outside the United States. Using that data to calculate a total by State (or by Region in NWIND) doesn't make sense. That's why there is a blank value for the State field in Figure 8-22.

To filter out certain records from groups, you can add to the QBE grid the field or fields you want to use as filters. Then you need to choose the Where setting on the Total line, deselect that field's Show check box, and enter criteria that tell Access which records to exclude. In either the Customer table in PROMPT or the Customers table in NWIND, for example, you can narrow the selection to records of customers in the U.S. (to ensure you get valid groups by state) by dragging the Country field to the QBE grid. Then you must choose the Where setting on the Total row and deselect the Show check box. (Access will complain if you try to run a totals query while you display a field that doesn't have a Group By or a Total setting.) Finally you must enter *USA* on the Criteria line. See the example in Figure 8-23.

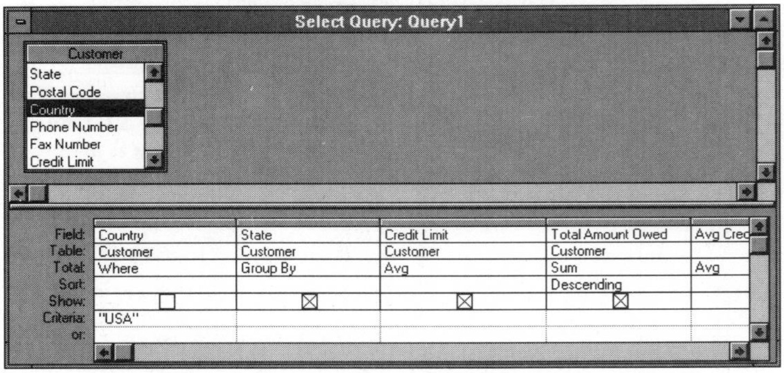

Figure 8-23.
The Country field is used to select the rows that will be included in groups.

Now when you run the query, you get totals only for customers in the United States. See the result in Figure 8-24.

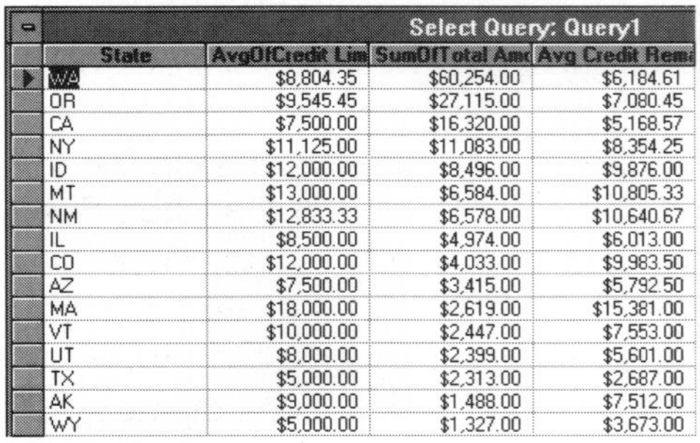
Select Query: Query1

State	AvgOfCredit Lim	SumOfTotal Amc	Avg Credit Rem
WA	$8,804.35	$60,254.00	$6,184.61
OR	$9,545.45	$27,115.00	$7,080.45
CA	$7,500.00	$16,320.00	$5,168.57
NY	$11,125.00	$11,083.00	$8,354.25
ID	$12,000.00	$8,496.00	$9,876.00
MT	$13,000.00	$6,584.00	$10,805.33
NM	$12,833.33	$6,578.00	$10,640.67
IL	$8,500.00	$4,974.00	$6,013.00
CO	$12,000.00	$4,033.00	$9,983.50
AZ	$7,500.00	$3,415.00	$5,792.50
MA	$18,000.00	$2,619.00	$15,381.00
VT	$10,000.00	$2,447.00	$7,553.00
UT	$8,000.00	$2,399.00	$5,601.00
TX	$5,000.00	$2,313.00	$2,687.00
AK	$9,000.00	$1,488.00	$7,512.00
WY	$5,000.00	$1,327.00	$3,673.00

Figure 8-24.
The dynaset of the query shown in Figure 8-23.

Selecting Specific Groups

You can also filter out groups of totals. To do that, enter criteria under any column that has a Group By setting, one of the nine Access total functions, or an Expression using the total functions. For example, you might want to find out which states had more than $10,000 remaining in average credit. To do that, you would keep the current settings and enter a criteria of >10000 in the Avg Credit Remaining column. See Figure 8-25.

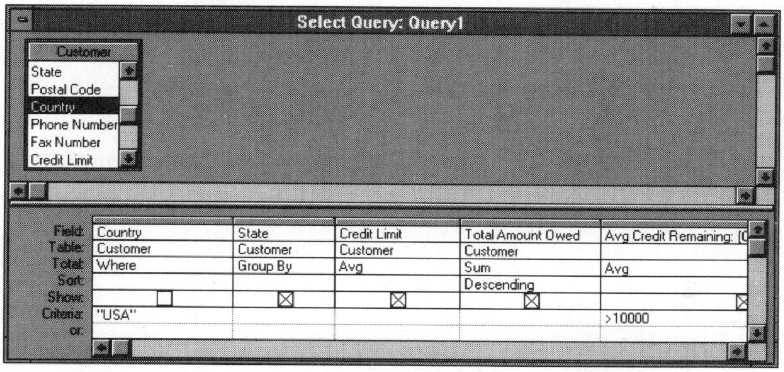

Figure 8-25.
A criteria setting in the Avg Credit Remaining field.

Using Query Parameters

Thus far, you have been entering selection criteria directly into the Query window in Design view. However, you don't have to decide at the time you design the query exactly what value you want Access to search for. Instead, you can include a parameter in the query, and Access will prompt you for the criteria before the query is run.

To set a parameter, you enter a name or phrase enclosed in brackets ([]) instead of entering a value on the Criteria line. What you enclose in brackets becomes the name by which Access knows your parameter. Access displays this name in a dialog box when you run the query, so it's a good idea to enter a phrase that describes what you want. You can enter several parameters in a single query, so each parameter name needs to be unique and informative.

You can adapt the query in Figure 8-23 so that Access will prompt for the state name criteria each time the query is run. In the State field, add the [Sum Customers in State:] parameter to the Criteria line. See Figure 8-26 on the next page.

For each parameter in a query, you can tell Access what data type to expect. Access uses this information to validate the value entered. For example, if you define a parameter as a number, Access won't accept alphabetic characters in the parameter value. By default, Access assigns the text data type to query parameters, which is fine for our example. If you need to change a parameter's data type, select the Parameters command from the Query menu to see the dialog box shown in Figure 8-27.

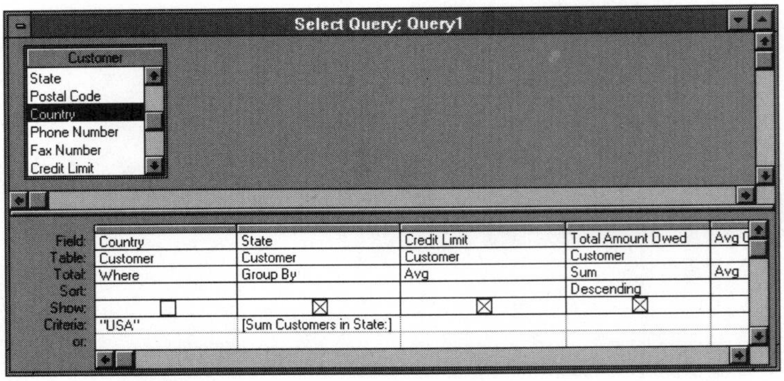

Figure 8-26.
A query parameter is set in the State field.

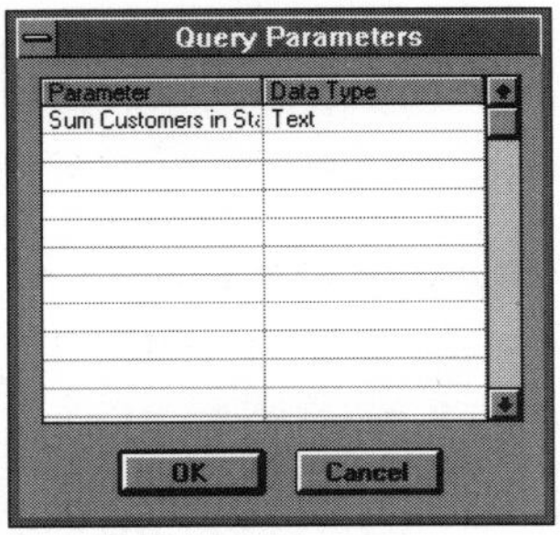

Figure 8-27.
The Query Parameters dialog box.

In this dialog box, enter each parameter name in the Parameter column, exactly as you entered it on the QBE grid but without the brackets. In the Data Type column, choose the appropriate data type from the drop-down list. Click the OK button when you have finished defining all your parameters.

When you run the query, Access prompts you for an appropriate value for each parameter, one at a time, with a dialog box such as the one shown in Figure 8-28. Since Access displays the "name" of the parameter that you provided on the QBE grid, you can see why naming the parameter with a phrase can help you enter the correct value later. In this case, *AZ* is typed in the Enter Parameter Value dialog box, and the dynaset is shown in Figure 8-29.

Figure 8-28.
The Enter Parameter Value dialog box.

Figure 8-29.
The dynaset of the query shown in Figure 8-26, when AZ is entered in the Enter Parameter Value dialog box.

Crosstab Queries

Microsoft Access supports a special type of totals query called a *crosstab query* that allows you to see calculated values in a spreadsheetlike format. For example, you can use this type of query to see total sales by month (in columns across) for each type of item (rows down) in the PROMPT Monthly Sales table. (In NWIND, you can total Order Amount by month (across) for each Customer ID (down) in the Orders table.)

To build a crosstab query, first select the table you want in the Database window and click the New Query button on the tool bar. Then select the Crosstab command from the Query menu. Access adds a Crosstab line to the QBE grid as shown in Figure 8-30 on the next page. Each field in a crosstab query can be a *Row Heading,* a *Column Heading,* the *Value* (calculated in the crosstab grid), or *Not Shown.* These choices represent the four possible settings for the Crosstab line in each field. For a crosstab query to work, you must specify at least one row heading, a single column heading, and a single value in your query. Each row heading and column heading must have Group By as the setting on the Total line. You must choose one of the available total functions or enter an expression that uses a total function for the column that contains the Value setting in your QBE grid.

As in other types of totals queries, you can include other fields to filter out values from the result. For these fields you should select the Where setting on the Total line, the Not Shown setting on the Crosstab line, and then enter your criteria. You can also enter criteria for any heading columns, and you can sort any of the fields.

To build the example crosstab query referred to above, one that shows total sales by month for each type of item, start by selecting the Monthly Sales table in the PROMPT Database window. Click the New Query button on the tool bar. Then choose the Crosstab command from the Query menu. Drag the Catalog Item ID field from the field list to the first field in the QBE grid. Fill in the column as shown in Figure 8-30 (with the Group By, Row Heading, and Ascending settings).

Crosstab Query: Query1
Monthly Sales
*
Catalog Item ID
Year
Month
Quantity sold
Total invoice a
Field: Catalog Item ID | Expr1: DateSerial([Year],[Month],1) | Total invoice amount
Table: Monthly Sales | | Monthly Sales
Total: Group By | Group By | Sum
Crosstab: Row Heading | Column Heading | Value
Sort: Ascending | Ascending
Criteria:
or:

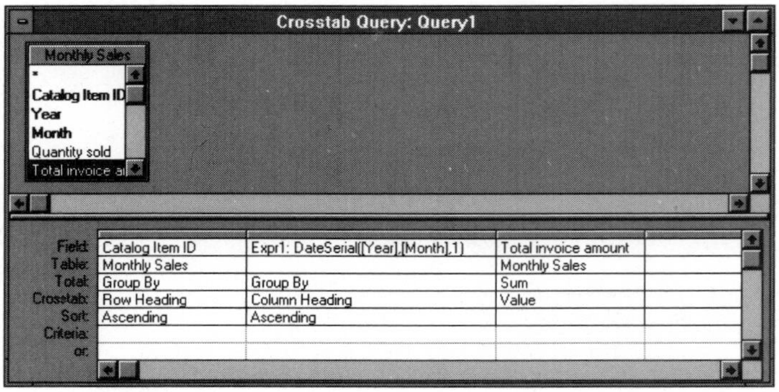

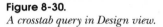

Figure 8-30.
A crosstab query in Design view.

To generate output in the form of columns of monthly sales you can create an expression that uses one of the Access functions. In the second field of the QBE grid, type *Expr1:DateSerial([Year],[Month],1)*. The DateSerial function creates a date/time value for the first day of the month. This is your column heading. Fill out the second column of your QBE grid, as shown in Figure 8-30 (with the Group By, Column Heading, and Ascending settings).

Finally, drag the Total Invoice Amount field to the third column in the QBE grid. This field will generate the values for the crosstab query. Use the Sum and Value settings.

Figure 8-31 shows you the dynaset of the query shown in Figure 8-30. Note that the DateSerial function has returned a short date format for the column headings.

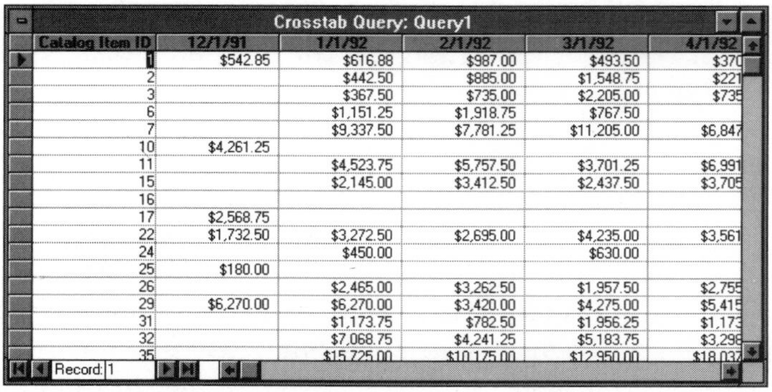

Crosstab Query: Query1
Catalog Item ID	12/1/91	1/1/92	2/1/92	3/1/92	4/1/92
1	$542.85	$616.88	$987.00	$493.50	$370
2		$442.50	$885.00	$1,548.75	$221
3		$367.50	$735.00	$2,205.00	$735
6		$1,151.25	$1,918.75	$767.50	
7		$9,337.50	$7,781.25	$11,205.00	$6,847
10	$4,261.25				
11		$4,523.75	$5,757.50	$3,701.25	$6,991
15		$2,145.00	$3,412.50	$2,437.50	$3,705
16					
17	$2,568.75				
22	$1,732.50	$3,272.50	$2,695.00	$4,235.00	$3,561
24		$450.00		$630.00	
25	$180.00				
26		$2,465.00	$3,262.50	$1,957.50	$2,755
29	$6,270.00	$6,270.00	$3,420.00	$4,275.00	$5,415
31		$1,173.75	$782.50	$1,956.25	$1,173
32		$7,068.75	$4,241.25	$5,183.75	$3,298
35		$15,725.00	$10,175.00	$12,950.00	$18,037
Record: 1

Figure 8-31.
The dynaset of the query shown in Figure 8-30.

You might prefer to see just the month name and year in the column headings. Because you converted Year and Month to a date value, you can now use another

Access function, the Format function, to display just the short month name and year. You enclose the DateSerial function within the Format function by typing *Expr1:Format(DateSerial([Year],[Month],1), "mmm yy")*. Figure 8-32 shows you the required format function. Notice that you originally asked for the dates in ascending order. That works when Access is working with the actual date values in the records, but not after you've reformatted them. If you run the query as is, you'll get Apr first, followed by Aug, and so on—the collating sequence of the displayed names, not the actual dates.

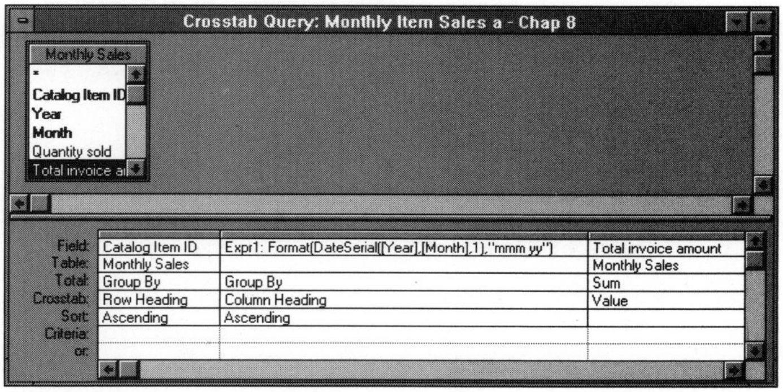

Figure 8-32.
A crosstab query with a customized heading.

Access provides a solution for that, too. You can specifically define the order of columns for any crosstab query by using the Query Properties dialog box. Choose the Properties button from the tool bar to see the window shown in Figure 8-33.

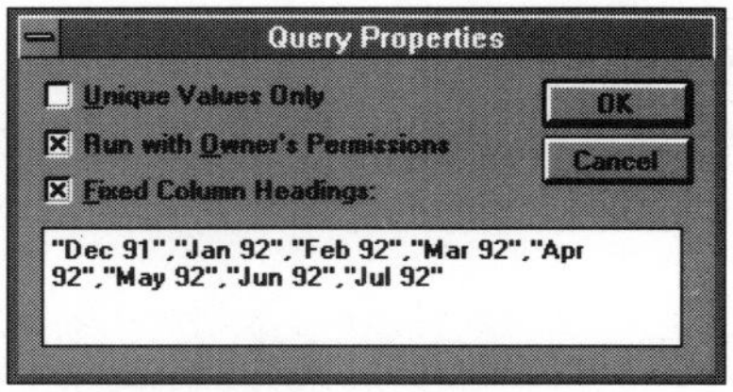

Figure 8-33.
The entries in the Query Properties dialog box that fix the order of column headings.

To control the order of columns displayed, check the Fixed Column Headings check box and enter the headings exactly as they are formatted and in the order you want. Be careful that you include all the column headings that match the result of the query. If you omit (or misspell) a column heading, Access won't show that column. When you run the query again with formatted column headings, you see the dynaset shown in Figure 8-34 on the next page.

Crosstab Query: Monthly Item Sales a - Chap 8					
Catalog Item ID	Dec 91	Jan 92	Feb 92	Mar 92	Apr 92
1	$542.85	$616.88	$987.00	$493.50	$370
2		$442.50	$885.00	$1,548.75	$221
3		$367.50	$735.00	$2,205.00	$735
6		$1,151.25	$1,918.75	$767.50	
7		$9,337.50	$7,781.25	$11,205.00	$6,847
10	$4,261.25				
11		$4,523.75	$5,757.50	$3,701.25	$6,991
15		$2,145.00	$3,412.50	$2,437.50	$3,705
16					
17	$2,568.75				
22	$1,732.50	$3,272.50	$2,695.00	$4,235.00	$3,561
24		$450.00		$630.00	
25	$180.00				
26		$2,465.00	$3,262.50	$1,957.50	$2,755
29	$6,270.00	$6,270.00	$3,420.00	$4,275.00	$5,415
31		$1,173.75	$782.50	$1,956.25	$1,173
32		$7,068.75	$4,241.25	$5,183.75	$3,298
35		$15,725.00	$10,175.00	$12,950.00	$18,037

Record: 1

Figure 8-34.
A crosstab query dynaset with custom headings, as defined in Figures 8-32 and 8-33.

Save this query as *Monthly Item Sales a–Chap 8*. You'll use it later in this chapter.

SEARCHING MULTIPLE TABLES

At this point, you've been through all the variations on a single theme—queries on a single table. It's easy to build on this knowledge to retrieve related information from many tables, and to place that information in a single view. You'll find this ability to select data from multiple tables most useful in designing forms and reports later in this book.

Try the following example in which you combine information about an order and about the customer who placed it. Start by bringing the PROMPT Database window to the front. Click the Query button on the left side of the Database window, and then click the New button to open up a new Query window in Design view. Access immediately opens an Add Table dialog box. This dialog box enables you to select tables and queries from which you can design a new query. Choose the Customer and Orders tables and then close the dialog box.

If you defined the relationships between your tables correctly, the top half of the Query window should look like the one shown in Figure 8-35. Access automatically links multiple tables in a query based on the relationship information you provided when you designed each table. Access shows you the links between tables as a line drawn from the primary key in one table to its matching field in the other table. If this line is missing, you can add it now by clicking the Customer ID field in the Customer table and dragging it to the Customer ID field in the Orders table.

In this example, you want all of the information from the Orders table and some of the information (company name, customer name, and address) from the Customer table. Click the asterisk (the special indicator for "all fields") at the top of the Orders table and drag it to the QBE grid. Find the Company Name, Customer Name, Address 1, Address 2, City, and State fields in the Customer table and drag them individually to the QBE grid. (If you haven't put data in the PROMPT database yet, you can create a similar multiple table query in NWIND with the Customers and Orders tables.) You can add criteria to any of the fields if you want.

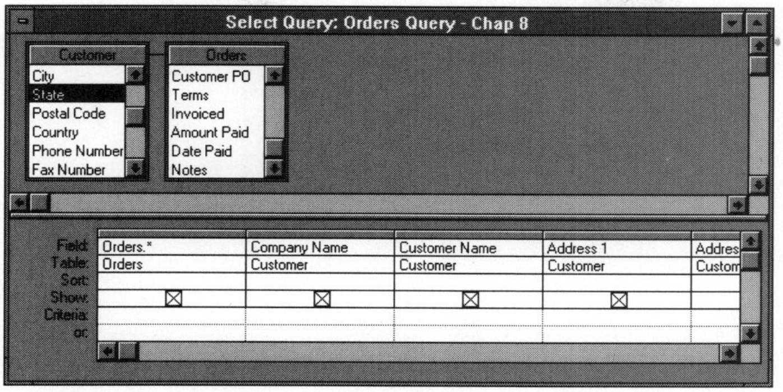

Figure 8-35.
A query that selects information from the Customer and Orders tables.

When you run your query, you see the dynaset shown in Figure 8-36. The fields from the Orders table appear first, left to right. You can scroll to the right to see the fields you added from the Customer table.

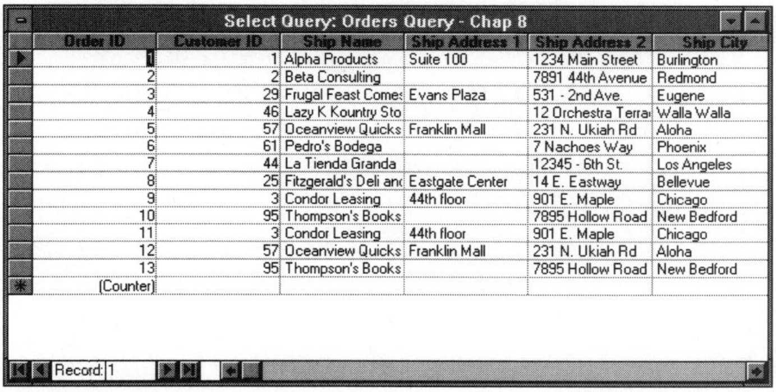

Figure 8-36.
The dynaset of the query shown in Figure 8-35.

As mentioned earlier, you can do many of the things with Query windows in Datasheet view that you can with Table windows in Datasheet view. To see customer information beside order information, you can select the Order ID, Customer ID, and SubTotal Cost fields and then choose the Freeze command from the Layout menu. This action will lock those fields at the left of the datasheet. You can then scroll to the right to bring the company name into view, as shown in Figure 8-37 on the next page.

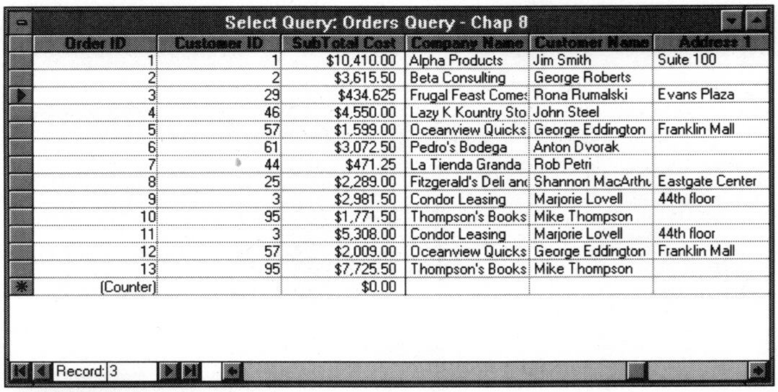

Order ID	Customer ID	SubTotal Cost	Company Name	Customer Name	Address 1
1	1	$10,410.00	Alpha Products	Jim Smith	Suite 100
2	2	$3,615.50	Beta Consulting	George Roberts	
3	29	$434.625	Frugal Feast Come:	Rona Rumalski	Evans Plaza
4	46	$4,550.00	Lazy K Kountry Sto	John Steel	
5	57	$1,599.00	Oceanview Quicks	George Eddington	Franklin Mall
6	61	$3,072.50	Pedro's Bodega	Anton Dvorak	
7	44	$471.25	La Tienda Granda	Rob Petri	
8	25	$2,289.00	Fitzgerald's Deli an	Shannon MacArthu	Eastgate Center
9	3	$2,981.50	Condor Leasing	Marjorie Lovell	44th floor
10	95	$1,771.50	Thompson's Books	Mike Thompson	
11	3	$5,308.00	Condor Leasing	Marjorie Lovell	44th floor
12	57	$2,009.00	Oceanview Quicks	George Eddington	Franklin Mall
13	95	$7,725.50	Thompson's Books	Mike Thompson	
(Counter)		$0.00			

Figure 8-37.
The Order ID, Customer ID, and SubTotal Cost fields are frozen at the left of this query in Datasheet view.

Save this query and name it *Orders Query–Chap 8.* You will use this query later in Chapter 19, "Designing the Prompt Computer Solutions Application," to design a form.

Outer Joins

Most queries that you create to request information from multiple tables will show results based on matching data in one or more tables. For example, the datasheet shown in Figure 8-36 will contain the names of customers who have orders in the Orders table—and will not contain the names of customers who don't. This type of query is called an *equi-join.* What if you want to see customers and orders and want to include customers who don't have any outstanding orders? You can get the information you need by creating an *outer join.*

To create an outer join, you must modify the join properties. Look at the Design view of the Orders Query–Chap 8 you created in the previous section. Double-click the join line between the two tables in the upper half of the Query window in Design view, as shown in Figure 8-38, to see the Join Properties dialog box, as shown in Figure 8-39.

The default setting in the Join Properties dialog box is option number 1—to include rows only where a match can be found in both tables. You can see that you have two additional options for this query: to see all customers and any orders that match, or to see all orders and any customers that match. If you have been entering data correctly, you shouldn't have orders for nonexistent customers. If you asked Microsoft Access to enforce referential integrity (see Chapter 5) when you defined the relationship between Customer and Orders, Access won't let you create any orders for nonexistent customers.

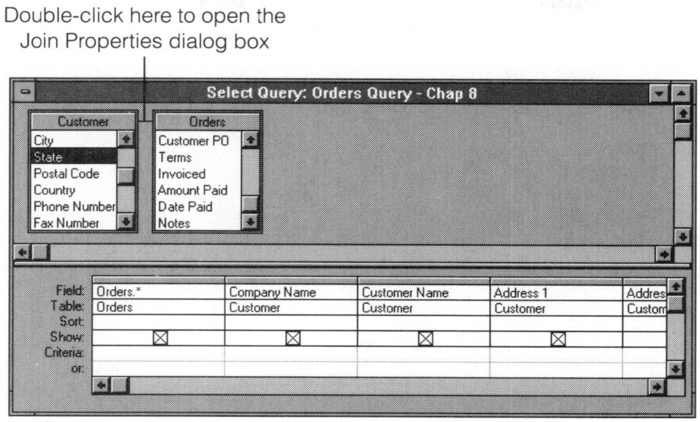

Double-click here to open the
Join Properties dialog box

Figure 8-38.
The join line in a query can be double-clicked to open the Join Properties dialog box.

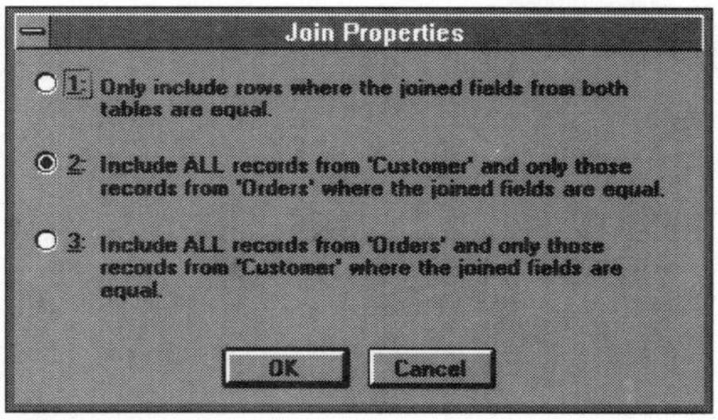

Figure 8-39.
The Join Properties dialog box with the second option selected.

Click option number 2 and then click the OK button in the dialog box. You should now see an arrow on the join line pointing from Customer to Orders, indicating you have asked for an outer join with all records from Customer regardless of match. See Figure 8-40 on the next page. When you run this query you should see a result similar to Figure 8-41. With the Order ID, Customer ID, and SubTotal Cost fields still frozen at the left of the Query window in Datasheet view, you can scroll until you can compare this data with the Company Name field. You can see that only a few customers have outstanding orders.

Using Multiple Tables in Total Queries

As you might suspect, you can also use multiple tables in a total or crosstab query. In Figure 8-32 and Figure 8-33, you built a crosstab query that you named Monthly Item Sales a–Chap 8. The query showed total sales by Catalog Item ID and month. However, Catalog Item ID isn't very informative—particularly if you want to use this

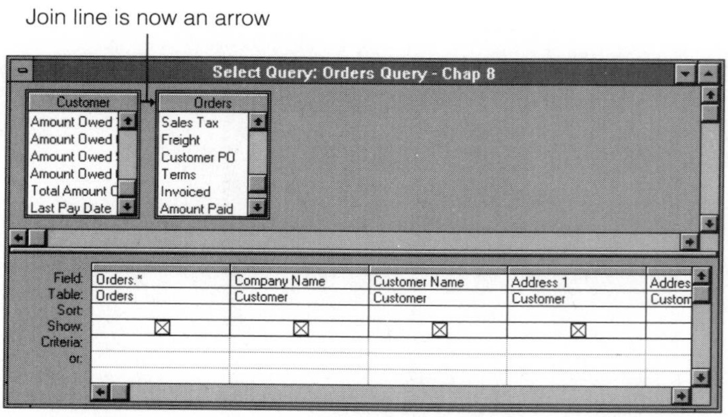

Join line is now an arrow

Figure 8-40.
The join line reflects an outer join that includes all records from the Customer table.

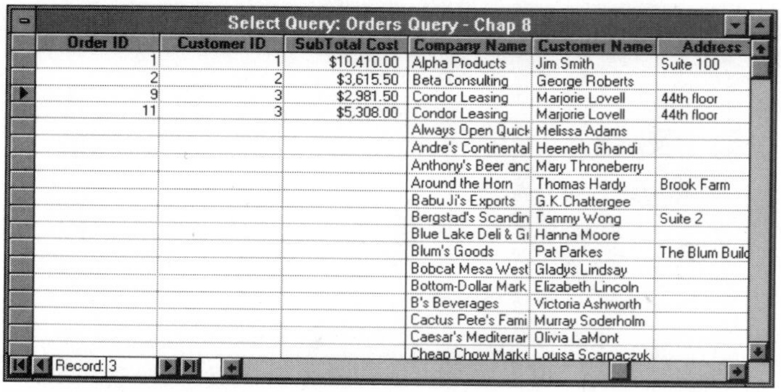

Figure 8-41.
The dynaset shows customers who have no orders in the Orders table.

query as the source for a report. The item description would be much more informative, but the item description is in another table.

Figure 8-42 shows you the crosstab query with the Catalog Items table added. Instead of using Catalog Item ID for the row heading, you can now use the Description field from the matching Catalog Items table instead. The settings in the field remain the same (Group By, Row Heading, and Ascending). Figure 8-43 shows you the result, with item descriptions instead of the Catalog Item ID. You should save this query and rename it *Monthly Item Sales—Chap 8.* You will use it later to create a report with a graph.

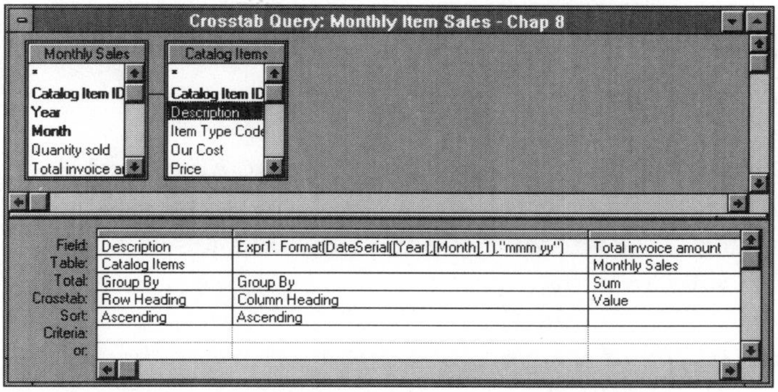

Figure 8-42.
A crosstab query that uses multiple tables.

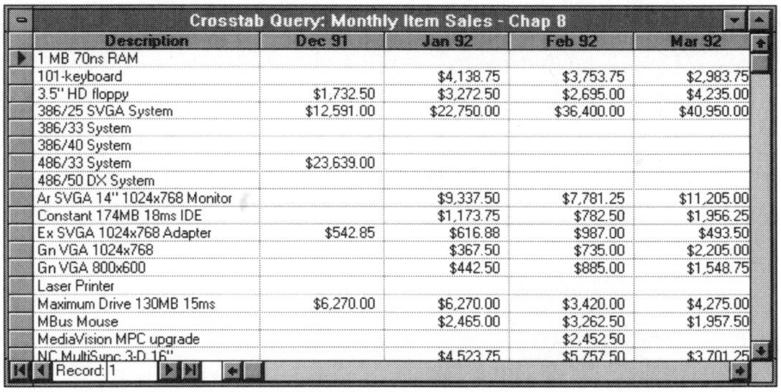
Crosstab Query: Monthly Item Sales - Chap 8

Description	Dec 91	Jan 92	Feb 92	Mar 92
1 MB 70ns RAM				
101-keyboard		$4,138.75	$3,753.75	$2,983.75
3.5" HD floppy	$1,732.50	$3,272.50	$2,695.00	$4,235.00
386/25 SVGA System	$12,591.00	$22,750.00	$36,400.00	$40,950.00
386/33 System				
386/40 System				
486/33 System	$23,639.00			
486/50 DX System				
Ar SVGA 14" 1024x768 Monitor		$9,337.50	$7,781.25	$11,205.00
Constant 174MB 18ms IDE		$1,173.75	$782.50	$1,956.25
Ex SVGA 1024x768 Adapter	$542.85	$616.88	$987.00	$493.50
Gn VGA 1024x768		$367.50	$735.00	$2,205.00
Gn VGA 800x600		$442.50	$885.00	$1,548.75
Laser Printer				
Maximum Drive 130MB 15ms	$6,270.00	$6,270.00	$3,420.00	$4,275.00
MBus Mouse		$2,465.00	$3,262.50	$1,957.50
MediaVision MPC upgrade			$2,452.50	
NC MultiSync 3-D 16"		$4,523.75	$5,757.50	$3,701.25

Record: 1

Figure 8-43.
The dynaset of the crosstab query shown in Figure 8-42.

LIMITATIONS ON USING SELECT QUERIES TO UPDATE DATA

The dynaset that Microsoft Access creates when you run a query looks and acts pretty much like a real table containing data. In fact, in most cases you can insert rows, delete rows, and update the information in a dynaset and Access will make the necessary changes to the underlying table or tables for you.

In some cases, however, Access won't be able to figure out what needs to be changed. Consider, for example, any calculated field. If you try to increase the amount in a field that is a result of multiplying data in the Quantity field times data in the Price field, Access can't know whether you mean to update the Quantity or the Price field. You can, however, change either the Price or Quantity field and then immediately see the change reflected in the calculated field.

In addition, Access won't accept any change that might potentially affect many rows in the underlying table. For that reason, you can't change any of the data in a totals query or crosstab query. Access can't update data in a Sum or Avg when the result might be based on the values in many records.

When working with a dynaset that is the result of a join, Access lets you update fields from the "many" side of a join, but not the "one" side. For example, one customer can have many orders. In a dynaset that is the result of a join between the Customer and Orders tables, you can update any fields that come from the Orders table, but you can't update any fields from the Customer table. If you try to change, for example, a customer name in one of the rows, Access would have to change the name in all of the order rows in the table that have the same customer. Another reason why Access can't accept this type of change is that it really can't figure out what you mean to do; do you just want to change the customer name in all the similar order records, or do you want to reassign this particular order to a different customer? To change the name, you must update the Customer table directly. To reassign the order, you must change the Customer ID in the Orders table, not the customer name.

In some cases you might find it useful to be able to update the "one" side of a relationship in a query. For example, it would be nice to be able to correct a customer's mailing address while entering a new order. You can do that using a special override option in a form. See Chapter 19, "Designing the Prompt Computer Solutions Application" for details.

Now that you understand the fundamentals of building select queries with Microsoft Access, you're ready to move on to updating sets of data with action queries in the next chapter.

9

Modifying Data with Action Queries

You learned in Chapter 7, "Using Datasheets," how to insert, update, or delete single rows of data within a datasheet. In Chapter 8, "Adding Power with Select Queries," you discovered that you can precisely select the data you want—even from multiple tables—using queries. Now you can take the concept of queries one step further and use *action queries* to change, insert, create, or delete sets of data in your database quickly and easily.

UPDATING GROUPS OF ROWS

It's easy enough to use a table or query in Datasheet view to find a single record in your database and change one value. But what if you want to change lots of similar records in the same way? Making changes to one record at a time could be very tedious.

Suppose in the Prompt Computer Solutions example that you've just found out that your major competition is raising its prices on video adapter cards by 12 percent. This sounds like a great opportunity to increase your profit margin, yet remain more than competitive, by raising your prices 10 percent.

It turns out that there are only six different video cards in the sample database, but imagine the size of the problem if there were dozens, and you had to calculate the 10 percent addition to price for each item and enter the new values one at a time. Why not let Microsoft Access do them all for you with a single query?

Testing with a Select Query

Before you create and run a query to update lots of records in your database, it's a good idea to create a select query first, using criteria that select the records you want to update. You'll see below that it's easy to convert this select query to an update query or other type of action query, after you're sure Access will be processing the records you want.

It turns out that all video cards in the sample database are listed in the Catalog Items table and have an Item Type Code of 008. You can use that code to select the rows you want to update. Figure 9-1 shows a select query that includes the Description field (to be doubly sure you have the rows you want), the Item Type Code field with a criteria setting of 008, and the Price field that you want to update. (See Chapter 8 if you need to review the process for creating select queries.)

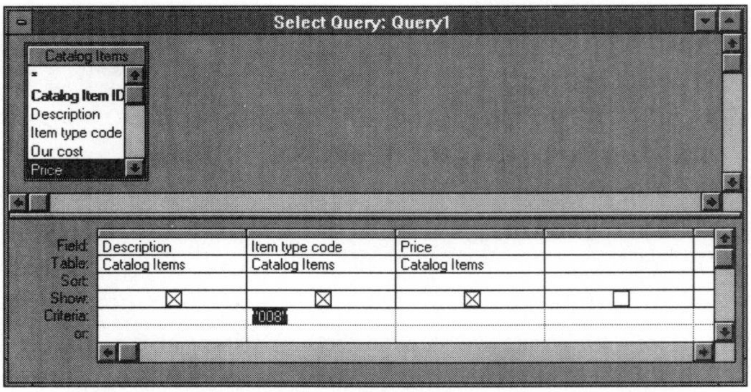

Figure 9-1.
A select query to show video card listings and prices.

When you run the query, you'll see the results shown in Figure 9-2, the video card records that you want to change.

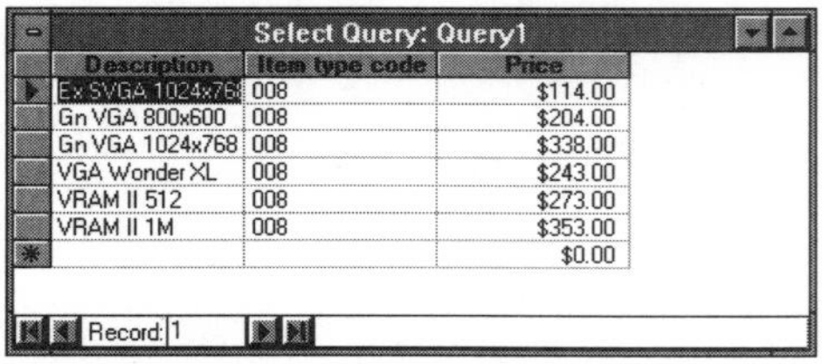

Figure 9-2.
The dynaset of the select query in Figure 9-1.

Converting a Select Query to an Update Query

Now you're ready to change the query so that it will update the table. When you first create a query, Microsoft Access creates a select query by default. Under the Query menu in Design view, as shown in Figure 9-3, you can find commands for the four types of action queries—Make Table, Update, Append, and Delete. Choose the Update command from this menu to convert the test select query to an update query.

When you convert your query to an update query, Access changes the title bar of your Query window in Design view and adds an Update To line in the QBE grid. You use this new line in the grid to specify how you want your data changed. In this case, you want to add 10 percent to the current Price values, so enter *[Price]*1.1* on the Update To line under the Price field, as shown in Figure 9-4.

Figure 9-3.
The Query menu.

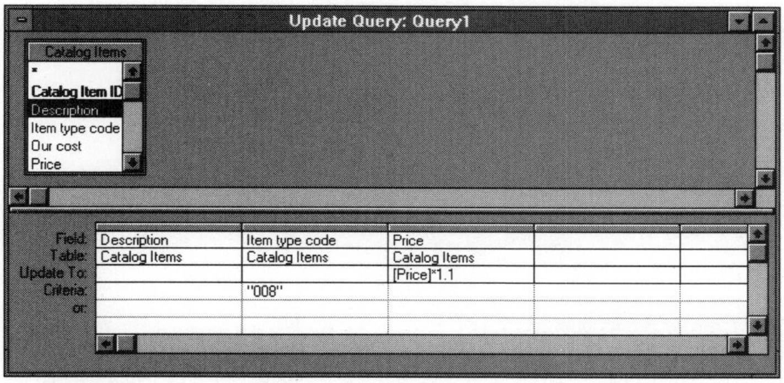

Figure 9-4.
An update query with its Update To setting.

Running Your Update Query

If you want to be completely safe, you should make a backup copy of your table before you run your update query. To do that, go to the Database window, select the table you're about to update, and choose the Copy command from the Edit menu. Then choose the Paste command from the Edit menu and give the copy of your table a different name when Access prompts you with a dialog box. Now you're ready to run your update query.

To run your query, choose the Run command from the Query menu or click the Run button on the tool bar. Access first scans your table to determine how many rows will change based on your selection criteria. You'll see a dialog box like the one shown in Figure 9-5 on the next page. You already know there are six records for video cards in the sample table, so this dialog box suggests that your update query is OK.

Figure 9-5.
The dialog box that confirms an update to a table.

To perform the updates, click the OK button in the dialog box. If you don't see the number of rows that you expect or if you're not sure that Access will be updating the correct records or fields, click the Cancel button to stop the query without updating. After the update query runs, you can check the table to confirm that Access made the changes you wanted. Figure 9-6 shows the result—new prices that are 10 percent higher for video cards.

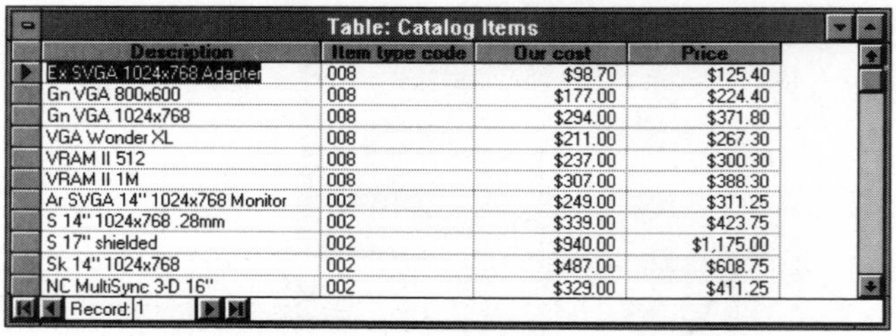

Description	Item type code	Our cost	Price
Ex SVGA 1024x768 Adapter	008	$98.70	$125.40
Gn VGA 800x600	008	$177.00	$224.40
Gn VGA 1024x768	008	$294.00	$371.80
VGA Wonder XL	008	$211.00	$267.30
VRAM II 512	008	$237.00	$300.30
VRAM II 1M	008	$307.00	$388.30
Ar SVGA 14" 1024x768 Monitor	002	$249.00	$311.25
S 14" 1024x768 .28mm	002	$339.00	$423.75
S 17" shielded	002	$940.00	$1,175.00
Sk 14" 1024x768	002	$487.00	$608.75
NC MultiSync 3-D 16"	002	$329.00	$411.25

Table: Catalog Items — Record: 1

Figure 9-6.
The updated data in the Catalog Items table.

If you think you might want to perform this update again, you can save your query and give it a name. In the Database window, Access distinguishes action queries from select queries by displaying an exclamation point before action query names. To run your action query again, select it in the Database window and click the Open button. When you run an action query from the Database window, Access shows you the action query confirmation dialog box shown in Figure 9-7. If you want to disable this extra confirmation, choose the Options command from the View menu and, in the General category, set Confirm Action Queries to No.

Figure 9-7.
The dialog box that confirms action queries.

Updating Multiple Fields

When you create an update query, you aren't limited to changing a single field at a time. You can ask Microsoft Access to update any or all of the fields in the record by including them on the QBE grid and by specifying an update formula. You can also update one field by using a formula that is based on a different field in the record.

When Access is about to update a record in your underlying table or query, it first makes a copy of the original record. Access applies the formulas you specify to the values in the original and places the result in the copy. It then updates your database by writing the updated copy to your table. Because updates are made to the copy from the original, you can, if you want, swap the values in a field named *A* and a field named *B* by specifying an Update To setting of [B] in the A field and an Update To setting of [A] in the B field. If Access were making changes directly to the original copy, you'd need a third field to swap values to because the first assignment of B to A would destroy the original value of A.

In the PROMPT database, the Customer table has fields for keeping track of amounts owed over several months. At the end of a month, after posting all payments, it would be useful to roll forward the amounts owed. As you might suspect, you can make the adjustment with a single update query.

For this example, look at three sample records that you added to the PROMPT Customer–Chap 6 table. The values for amount owed are shown in Figure 9-8. (Some of the columns are hidden.)

Company	Amount Owed Current	Amount Owed 30	Amount Owed 60	Amount Owed 90	Amount Owed Over
Alpha Prod	$1,197.00	$370.00	$263.00	$584.00	$33.00
Beta Const	$1,462.00	$765.00	$46.00	$87.00	$67.00
Condor Lea	$270.00	$513.00	$589.00	$210.00	$275.00
*	$0.00	$0.00	$0.00	$0.00	$0.00

Figure 9-8.
The amounts owed by three customers in the PROMPT Customer table.

To roll forward the amounts owed, you need to add the value in the Amount Owed 90 field to the value in the Amount Owed Over field, move the value in the Amount Owed 60 field to the Amount Owed 90 field, and so on. Finally the Amount Owed Current field should be set to zero, ready for the next month. To update these multiple fields in an update query, first create a new query based on the PROMPT Customer table. (See Chapter 8 if you need to review the process for creating queries.) Then drag the Company Name field to the QBE grid. Finally drag to the QBE grid the additional fields that are listed in Figure 9-9 on the next page and fill in the Update To line for each field as indicated. The Query window in Design view is shown, in part, in Figure 9-10.

Field	Update To
Amount Owed Current	0
Amount Owed 30	[Amount Owed Current]
Amount Owed 60	[Amount Owed 30]
Amount Owed 90	[Amount Owed 60]
Amount Owed Over	[Amount Owed Over]+[Amount Owed 90]

Figure 9-9.
Some fields and Update To settings of a query that updates multiple fields.

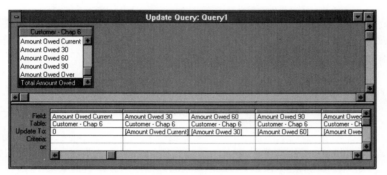

Figure 9-10.
The QBE grid, in part, of a query that updates multiple fields.

You can run the query and then check the result in the Customer–Chap 6 table in Datasheet view, as shown in Figure 9-11. You'll see that Access has updated the values correctly. As you can imagine, this is the type of query that you'll use many times in your databases.

Company	Amount Owed Current	Amount Owed 30	Amount Owed 60	Amount Owed 90	Amount Owed Over
Alpha Prod	$0.00	$1,197.00	$370.00	$263.00	$617.00
Beta Cons	$0.00	$1,462.00	$765.00	$46.00	$154.00
Condor Le	$0.00	$270.00	$513.00	$589.00	$485.00
	$0.00	$0.00	$0.00	$0.00	$0.00

Figure 9-11.
The Customer–Chap 6 table in Datasheet view after running the Update query shown in Figure 9-10.

DELETING GROUPS OF ROWS

You are not likely to keep forever all of the data you collect in your database. You will probably summarize some of your detailed information as time goes by and then delete the data you no longer need. You can remove sets of records from your database with a type of action query called a *delete query*.

Testing with a Select Query and Parameters

In the PROMPT database, there's a Monthly Sales History table. (At the end of this chapter, you'll learn how to summarize sales details into a Monthly Sales History at the end of each month.) The owners of Prompt Computer Solutions have decided that they only want to keep information about sales in the database for a couple of years. So, they need a query to selectively delete old data from this table.

This is clearly the kind of query that will be used over and over again. You can design the query to automatically calculate which year and month fields to delete based on the current system date. The query can also be designed with parameters so that a user can specify which data to delete at the time the query is run. With Microsoft Access there's no need to change the query design at each use.

As with update queries, it's a good idea to test which rows will be affected by a delete query by first building a select query to isolate these records. First make a copy of the PROMPT Monthly Sales table and name it *Monthly Sales–Chap 9*. Select the Monthly Sales–Chap 9 table in the PROMPT Database window and open a new Query window in Design view. (You can build a similar query in NWIND if you create a Monthly Sales table from data in Order Details and Products that uses Product ID instead of Catalog Item ID in its primary key.)

You need only the Year and Month fields on the QBE grid to perform the deletion, but it's useful to include the Catalog Item ID field and the Quantity Sold field in this select version of the query in order to check out the rows you will delete. To request that Access prompt you for Year and Month values, add parameters to the Criteria line in the QBE grid, as shown in Figure 9-12.

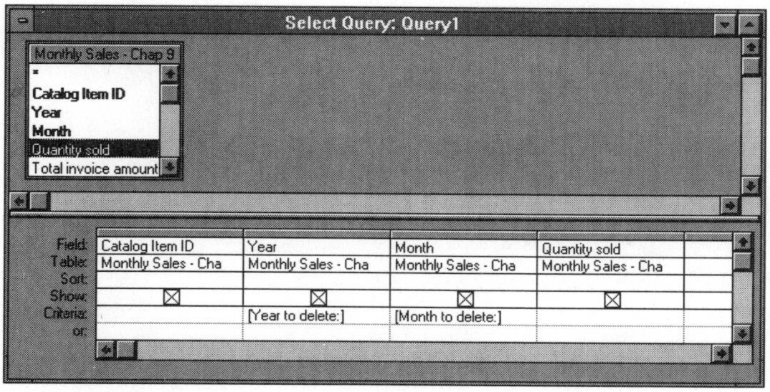

Figure 9-12.
A query to select monthly sales data to delete.

When you run this query, Access prompts you first for the Year and then for the Month, as shown in Figure 9-13. The entries in the dialog boxes in Figure 9-13 will test the query using December, 1991.

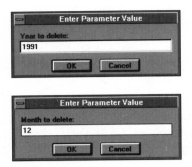

Figure 9-13.
The two Enter Parameter Value dialog boxes for the query in Figure 9-12, with entries that select records for 12/91.

Using the parameter values entered in Figure 9-13, Access creates the dynaset shown in Figure 9-14. Because the dynaset shows the rows you want to change, you can now convert the select query to a delete query and run it to remove these rows.

Catalog Item ID	Year	Month	Quantity sold
1	1991	12	4
10	1991	12	7
17	1991	12	5
22	1991	12	18
25	1991	12	12
29	1991	12	22
44	1991	12	9
48	1991	12	11
0	0	0	0

Figure 9-14.
The dynaset of the select query in Figure 9-12, with parameters set to 12/91.

Running Your Delete Query

Because you won't be able to retrieve any deleted rows, it's a good idea to make a backup copy of your table, especially if this is the first time you've ever run this delete query. Use the procedure noted previously in the section "Running Your Update Query" to make a copy of your table.

You can create a delete query from a select query by choosing the Delete command from the Query menu when your query is in Design view. (See Figure 9-3.) You don't have to make any further changes to choose the rows to delete. Simply choose Run from the Query menu or click the Run button on the tool bar to ask Access to delete the rows you specified. Because you included parameters in this query, you'll need to respond to the two dialog boxes shown in Figure 9-13. Access checks the rows to be deleted and displays the confirmation dialog box shown in Figure 9-15.

Figure 9-15.
A dialog box that confirms a deletion.

Click the OK button to complete deletion of the rows. Click the Cancel button if you're unsure about the rows that Access will delete.

INSERTING DATA FROM ANOTHER TABLE

Using an append query, you can copy a selected set of information and insert it into another table. (In the example at the end of this chapter, you will learn how to insert accumulated sales data into a Monthly Sales History table.) You can also use an append query to bring data from another source into your database—for example, a list of names and addresses purchased from a mailing list company—and then edit the data and insert it into an existing table. In Chapter 10 you'll learn how to import data from external sources.

Creating an Append Query

In Chapter 6 you began creating a Customer table for the PROMPT database called Customer–Chap 6. You entered just three records to the Customer–Chap 6 table at that time. Suppose you want to expand the PROMPT database to include some of the customer information from the sample NWIND database. You can append the NWIND data to the PROMPT Customer table easily. First copy the Customer–Chap 6 table and name your copy *Customer–Chap 9*. Then open the NWIND database and select the Customers table in the Database window. Click the New Query button on the tool bar, and choose the Append command from the Query menu. Access prompts you for the name of the table to which you wish to append the data. The dialog box is shown in Figure 9-16. In the dialog box click the Another Database option and type PROMPT.MDB in the File Name box. Click the down arrow next to the Table Name box and choose Customer–Chap 9 from the drop-down list of PROMPT tables. Click OK to close the dialog box.

The QBE grid for the append query is partially shown in Figure 9-17. Notice that Access shows you an Append To line. If all the fields in NWIND Customers exactly matched those in the PROMPT Customer table, you could simply move the shortcut asterisk field to the QBE grid to indicate you want to copy all the fields. Because some of the fields don't match, you have to move the ones you want one at a time.

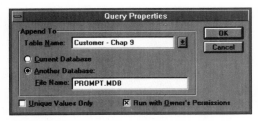

Figure 9-16.
The Query Properties dialog box that appears when the Append command is chosen.

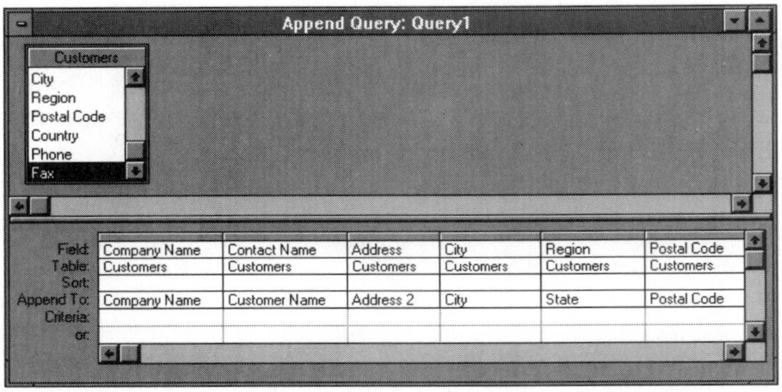

Figure 9-17.
An append query in Design view.

You don't need the Customer ID field from NWIND's Customers table because the Customer ID in the PROMPT Customer table is a counter field. Access automatically generates the next value for a counter field as it inserts new records into the table. Notice that when you move the Company Name field to the grid, Access automatically guesses that you want to move it to the field with the matching name in the PROMPT Customer table and fills that in for you on the Append To line. When you move the Contact Name field, you'll have to enter Customer Name on the Append To line or choose it from the drop-down list that appears when you click on the right end of that box in the QBE grid.

Other fields that you'll have to map to different names include the Address field from NWIND to the Address 2 field in PROMPT, also Region to State, Phone to Phone Number, and Fax to Fax Number. For fields that exist in PROMPT but not in NWIND, Microsoft Access will store the default value (if defined) for each of those fields as it copies new records into PROMPT.

You can also specify selection criteria in the QBE grid. You could, for example, copy only the rows for customers from a specific state by adding criteria in the Region column.

Running an Append Query

As with other action queries, you can run an append query as a select query first to be sure you will be copying the rows you want. However, Access doesn't retain the name mappings when you switch to a select query and back; you'll have to rebuild the mappings of field names between the two tables if you run the query as a select query before you run it as an append query. Although you can find and delete rows you append in error, you can save time if you make a backup of the receiving table first.

To run your completed append query, simply choose the Run command from the Query menu or click the Run button on the tool bar. Access displays a count of the new records, as shown in the dialog box in Figure 9-18.

Figure 9-18.
The dialog box that informs you of the results of an append query.

Click the OK button to append the new rows. Click the Cancel button if you're not sure you want Access to finish appending the new rows.

After you run this append query, open the Customer–Chap 9 table in the PROMPT database in Datasheet view. You should see a display similar to the one shown in Figure 9-19. The sample here includes rows that were originally in the PROMPT Customer–Chap 9 table followed by the customer information from NWIND.

Customer ID	Company Name	Customer Name	Address 1	Address 2	City
1	Alpha Products	Jim Smith		1234 Main Street	Burlington
2	Beta Consulting	George Roberts		7891 44th Avenue	Redmond
3	Condor Leasing	Marjorie Lovell		901 E. Maple	Chicago
4	Always Open Quick	Melissa Adams		77 Overpass Ave.	Provo
5	Andre's Continental	Heeneth Ghandi		P.O. Box 209	Bellingham
6	Anthony's Beer and	Mary Throneberry		33 Neptune Circle	Clifton Forge
7	Around the Horn	Thomas Hardy		Brook Farm	Colchester
8	Babu Ji's Exports	G.K.Chattergee		Box 29938	London
9	Bergstad's Scandin	Tammy Wong		41 S. Marlon St.	Seattle
10	Blue Lake Deli & Gr	Hanna Moore		210 Main St.	Port Townsend
11	Blum's Goods	Pat Parkes		The Blum Building	London
12	Bobcat Mesa West	Gladys Lindsay		213 E. Roy St.	Seattle

Table: Customer - Chap 9

Record: 1

Figure 9-19.
The PROMPT Customer–Chap 9 table with customer information appended from NWIND.

Append Query Limitation

You can't convert a total query into an append query. Microsoft Access doesn't allow you to append totals that are being calculated. You can, however, create a new table with totals and then append the records in that new table to another table. The example in the next section of this chapter shows this procedure.

CREATING A NEW TABLE WITH A QUERY

Sometimes you might like to save as a real table the data that you extract with a select query. If you find that you keep executing the same query over and over against data that isn't changing, it can be faster to access the data from a real table rather than from the query, particularly if the query must join several tables. Saving a query as a table is also useful for gathering summary information that you intend to keep long after you delete the detailed data on which the query is based. As noted in the previous section, if you want to update a summary table with data that must be totaled first, you have to create an intermediate table using a make-table query.

Creating a Make-Table Query

Assume that at the end of each year, you want to create and save a table for Prompt Computer Solutions that summarizes the sales for the year. The Monthly Sales–Chap 9 table contains the totals by month that must be totaled and saved in this summary. Just to make it interesting, you also need to pick up the Description field from the Catalog Items table. This is a good idea because you might want to keep the table of annual totals for a long time. Two or three years from now, Prompt Computer Solutions might no longer carry a particular item, and the description will have disappeared from the current Catalog Items table. A later query on this annual summary won't be able to retrieve a meaningful description unless the Description field is saved now.

Start by creating a query of the Monthly Sales–Chap 9 and Catalog Items tables. (See Chapter 8 if you need a review of the process for creating a query.) Click the Totals button on the tool bar or choose the Totals command from the View menu in order to total the information for an entire year. Drag the Catalog Item ID field from the Monthly Sales–Chap 9 table, the Description field from the Catalog Items table, and then the Year field, the Total Invoice Amount field, and the Total Cost field from the Monthly Sales–Chap 9 table to the QBE grid. Change the Total line under both the Total Invoice Amount field and the Total Cost field to Sum. See Figure 9-20. You can also give these two fields a new name; otherwise, Access will name them SumOfTotal Invoice Amount and SumOfTotal Cost in the resulting table. Enter the year you want to summarize on the Criteria line for the Year field. You can also create a parameter so that Access prompts you for the year value when you run the query. See Figures 9-12 and 9-13 for an example.

If you like, you can run this query to verify that you'll get the rows you want. To convert this select query to a make-table query, choose the Make Table command from the Query menu. Access shows you the dialog box in Figure 9-21. Type an appropriate name for the summary table you are creating, and click OK to close the dialog box.

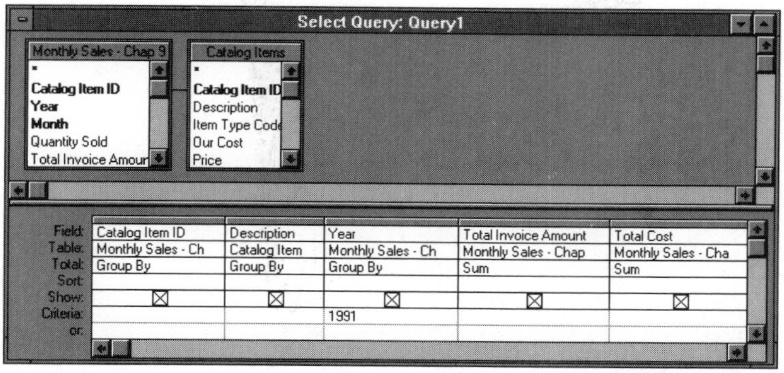

Figure 9-20.
The query that can be used to make a table of 1991 sales.

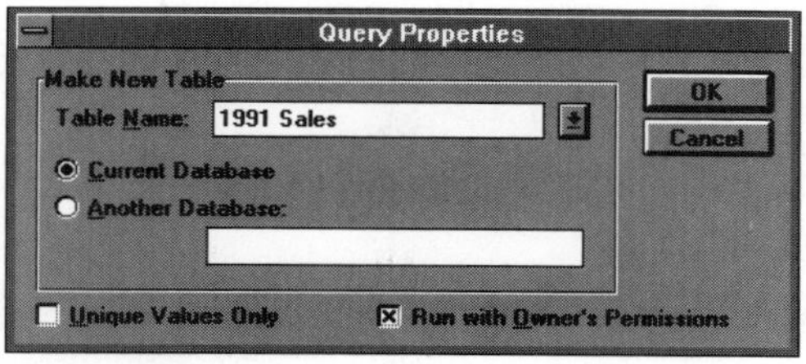

Figure 9-21.
The Query Properties dialog box for the Make Table command.

You can reopen this dialog box whenever the query is in Design view to change the name of the table you want to create by choosing the Query Properties command from the View menu.

Running a Make-Table Query

After you have set up your make-table query, you can run it by choosing Run from the Query menu or by clicking the Run button on the tool bar. Access runs the select portion of the query and displays a dialog box, as shown in Figure 9-22, to inform you how many rows you'll be creating in a new table.

Figure 9-22.
The dialog box that confirms the results of a make-table query.

Click the OK button to create your new table and insert the rows. Switch to the Database window and click the Table button to bring up the table list, and you should see your new table. Open the new table in Datasheet view to verify the information, as shown in Figure 9-23. You might want to switch to Design view to correct field names or define formatting information. Microsoft Access copies only basic field attributes when creating your new table.

Catalog Item ID	Description	Year	SumOfTotal invc	SumOfTotal cos
1	Ex SVGA 1024x768	1991	$542.85	$394.80
4	VGA Wonder XL	1991	$1,740.75	$1,266.00
10	Sk 14" 1024x768	1991	$4,261.25	$3,409.00
17	P P 9600 modem	1991	$2,568.75	$2,055.00
22	3.5" HD floppy	1991	$1,732.50	$1,386.00
25	Serial mouse	1991	$180.00	$144.00
29	Maxtor 130MB 15m	1991	$6,270.00	$5,016.00
44	386/25 SVGA Syst	1991	$12,591.00	$11,256.30
48	486/33 System	1991	$23,639.00	$18,734.10

Figure 9-23.
The results of the make-table query in Figure 9-20.

TROUBLESHOOTING ACTION QUERIES

Microsoft Access analyzes your action query request and the data you are about to change before committing changes to your database. When errors are identified, Access always gives you an opportunity to cancel the operation before proceeding with your action query.

Common Action Query Errors and Problems

There are three categories of errors that are identified (*trapped*) by Microsoft Access during the execution of an action query:

1. Duplicate Primary Keys. This category of error occurs if you attempt to append a record to a table or update a record in a table when the result is a duplicate primary key or a duplicate of a unique index key value. Access will not update or append those rows that would create duplicate values in primary keys or unique indexes. Before attempting to append the rows, you might have to change the primary key values in the source table to avoid the conflict.

2. Data Conversion Errors. This category of error occurs when you are appending data into an existing table and the data type of the receiving field does not match that of the sending field (and the data in the sending field cannot be transformed to the appropriate data type). For example, if you are appending a text field to an integer field, and the text field contains either alphabetic characters or a number string that is too

large for the integer field, the error will occur. You can also encounter a conversion error in an update query if you use a formula that attempts a calculation on a field that contains characters. For information on conversions and potential limitations, see Figure 6-16 in Chapter 6, ''Modifying the Database Design.''

3. Locked Records. This category of error occurs when you are running a delete query or update query on a table that you share with other users on a network. Access cannot update records that are in the process of being updated by others. You might want to wait and try again later to be sure your update or deletion occurs when no one else is using the affected records.

Another problem that occurs, though not an error as such, is that Access might truncate data being appended into text or memo fields when the data does not fit. Access does not warn you when this happens. You must be sure (especially with append queries) that the receiving text and memo fields have been defined as large enough to store the incoming data.

An Error Example

Earlier in this chapter, in the section called ''Inserting Data from Another Table,'' you saw how to append customer data from the NWIND database to the PROMPT database using an append query. At the time there were no problems with duplicate primary key values because the PROMPT Customer table was designed with a counter as the primary key. Also, the field data types and lengths matched.

But assume that the primary key (the Customer ID field) for the Customer–Chap 9 table in PROMPT is a 5-character text field just like the primary key in the Customers table in NWIND. And suppose you started with four records in the PROMPT Customer–Chap 9 table, as shown in Figure 9-24.

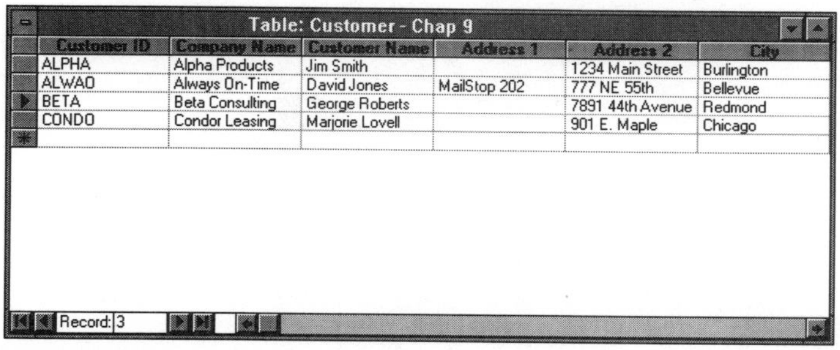

Customer ID	Company Name	Customer Name	Address 1	Address 2	City
ALPHA	Alpha Products	Jim Smith		1234 Main Street	Burlington
ALWAO	Always On-Time	David Jones	MailStop 202	777 NE 55th	Bellevue
BETA	Beta Consulting	George Roberts		7891 44th Avenue	Redmond
CONDO	Condor Leasing	Marjorie Lovell		901 E. Maple	Chicago

Record: 3

Figure 9-24.
The PROMPT Customer–Chap 9 table with a primary key (the Customer ID field) similar to the one in the NWIND Customers table.

Unlike the earlier append query, you'll need the Customer ID field from the Customer table in NWIND. Notice that there is a duplicate of one of the primary key values from the NWIND Customers table—ALWAO. In addition, imagine the data type of the Phone Number field in the PROMPT Customer–Chap 9 table had been changed from Text to Double. In NWIND you'll find that the phone numbers in the Customers table are really text fields with embedded parentheses and hyphens. Now if you try to append 91 records from the Customers table in NWIND to the Customer–Chap 9 table in PROMPT, Access displays the dialog box shown in Figure 9-25.

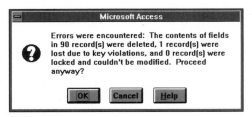

Figure 9-25.
The dialog box that declares there were action query errors.

The dialog box declares there's one record that won't be inserted; this error is the result of a duplicate primary key. Access also found 90 phone numbers in NWIND that can't be converted to a Long Integer data type. Since this table isn't shared on a network, there aren't any locking errors. When you see this dialog box, you can click the OK button to proceed with the changes that Access can make without errors. You might find it difficult, however, to track down all the records that will not be updated successfully. Click the Cancel button to abort the append query.

If you clicked the OK button you would see the result shown in Figure 9-26. There's an ALWAO record, but it's the one that was in the PROMPT Customer table before running the append query, not the new record from NWIND. In Figure 9-26 the first five columns are frozen and the datasheet is scrolled to reveal that none of the records appended from NWIND have telephone numbers.

Customer ID	Company Name	Customer Name	Address 1	Address 2	Phone Number
ALPHA	Alpha Products	Jim Smith		1234 Main Street	3125551212
ALWAO	Always On-Time	David Jones	MailStop 202	777 NE 55th	2068617978
ANDRC	Andre's Continental	Heeneth Ghandi		P.O. Box 209	
ANTHB	Anthony's Beer and	Mary Throneberry		33 Neptune Circle	
AROUT	Around the Horn	Thomas Hardy		Brook Farm	
BABUJ	Babu Ji's Exports	G.K.Chattergee		Box 29938	
BERGS	Bergstad's Scandin	Tammy Wong		41 S. Marlon St.	
BETA	Beta Consulting	George Roberts		7891 44th Avenue	2066781234
BLUEL	Blue Lake Deli & Gi	Hanna Moore		210 Main St.	
BLUMG	Blum's Goods	Pat Parkes		The Blum Building	
BOBCM	Bobcat Mesa West	Gladus Lindsau		213 E. Bou St.	

Table: Customer - Chap 9 — Record: 13

Figure 9-26.
The result of an append query after the errors declared in Figure 9-25 are accepted.

EXAMPLE: SUMMARIZING DETAILED SALES BY MONTH

Looking at individual action query examples is useful. However, real business problems are rarely as simple as a single query. To help you see some of the real potential of action queries, here's an example that shows how you might total some detailed sales figures and then append the result to a monthly history table.

Here's the problem statement: At the end of each month, Prompt Computer Solutions would like to total all the sales by item and save the result in a monthly sales total table. The first step is to build a query to calculate the totals and save the result in a temporary table. The second step is to insert (append) the calculated totals into a history table.

Building a Query That Will Total Sales

To build a query that will total sales, start by opening a new Query window in Design view and including the Orders, Order Items, and Catalog Items tables. If you defined the relationships between the tables correctly, you should see relationship lines between Orders and Order Items on the Order ID field and between Order Items and Catalog Items on the Catalog Item ID field. At this point you need to click the Totals button on the tool bar (or choose the Totals command from the View menu) to add the Total line to the QBE grid.

You need Catalog Item ID as a field on your grid, so drag that field from either the Order Items or Catalog Items table. Next you need a Year field, so extract the year from the Order Date field by using the Year function. This field is written *Year:Year([Order Date])*. Similarly, you can use the Month function on Order Date to get the month of the order. The month field is written *Month:Month([Order Date])*. Add parameters on the Criteria line to prompt for these two values when you run the query. Next drag the Quantity field from the Order Items table to the QBE grid. Set the Total line for the Quantity field to Sum. See Figure 9-27.

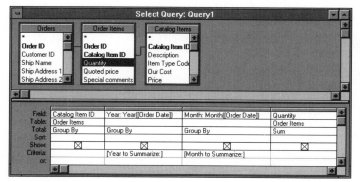

Figure 9-27.
The first four fields of the query that will generate monthly sales totals.

To get Total Invoice Amount, first create an expression that multiplies the Quantity field times the Quoted Price field (both from the Order Items table). The product is the invoice amount per item. You use the Sum function in the Total line to generate Total Invoice Amount from the per item invoice amounts. To get Total Cost, you need to create an expression that multiplies the Quantity field from the Order Items table by the Our Cost field from the Catalog Items table. When you're done you need to use the Sum function on the Total line to generate Total Cost from these costs per item. These fields on your QBE grid should look like the ones shown in Figure 9-28.

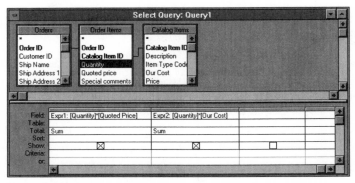

Figure 9-28.
The last two fields of the query that will generate monthly sales totals.

Because the two query parameters are to be compared to values calculated from a function, you should define the data types for these parameters so that Microsoft Access can successfully compare the values you supply with the values returned from the functions. The Year and Month functions both return the Integer data type, so you should use the Integer data type for the two parameters in the Query Parameters dialog box, as shown in Figure 9-29.

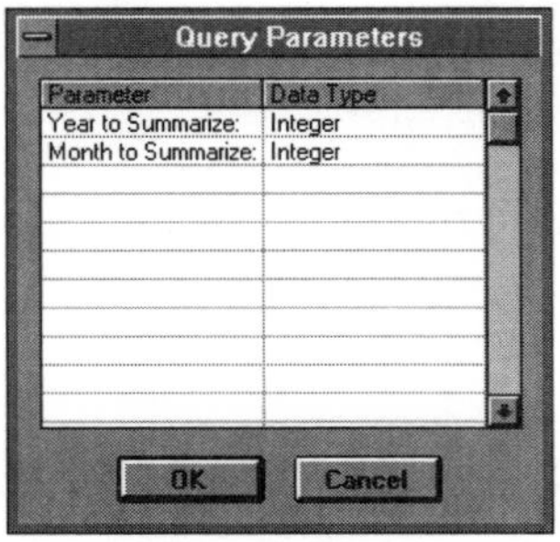

Figure 9-29.
The data type settings for the parameters in the Figure 9-27 query.

Catalog Item ID	Year	Month	SumOfQuantity	Expr1	Expr2
1	1992	6	1	$123.38	$98.70
7	1992	6	1	$311.25	$249.00
25	1992	6	1	$15.00	$12.00
26	1992	6	7	$507.50	$406.00
27	1992	6	1	$106.25	$85.00
32	1992	6	1	$471.25	$377.00
43	1992	6	3	$2,452.50	$1,962.00
44	1992	6	5	$10,146.00	$6,253.50
46	1992	6	1	$1,599.00	$1,430.70
47	1992	6	5	$7,995.00	$6,673.50
48	1992	6	1	$2,149.00	$1,703.10
49	1992	6	4	$10,396.00	$10,962.00
50	1992	6	4	$2,040.00	$1,908.00
51	1992	6	4	$200.00	$154.80

Record: 1

Figure 9-30.
A test of the monthly sales summary generated by the select query in Figures 9-27 and 9-28.

Before creating this working table for the first time, it's a good idea to run this as a select query (of the totals query type) in order to see if you're getting the results you expect. Use the month of June, 1992, for the prompts when you run the query. You can see the dynaset shown in Figure 9-30.

Change the select query to a make-table query by choosing the Make Table command from the Query menu. Access prompts you with a dialog box, as shown in Figure 9-31. Use One Month Total Sales as the name for this table and click OK.

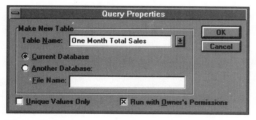

Figure 9-31.
The Query Properties dialog box for the make-table query in Figures 9-27 and 9-28.

After you set up this query, you'll probably run it every month. You could delete the One Month Total Sales table each time, but Access will take care of that for you. When you run the query in subsequent months, Access displays the dialog box shown in Figure 9-32, asking if you want to delete the table from the previous month. Click the Yes button to delete the old table before creating a new one.

Microsoft Access

Existing Table 'One Month Total Sales' will be deleted before running the query. Continue anyway?

Yes   No   Help

Figure 9-32.
The dialog box that gives you the option to delete an existing table.

When you run the make-table query, you should get one record for each different type of item that was sold during the month you requested. The dialog box in Figure 9-33 informs us that 14 different items were sold in June, 1992 (the month selected).

Figure 9-33.
The dialog box that confirms the rows inserted into a new table.

Appending Totals to a Monthly Sales History Table

Creating a table with monthly totals is only half the job. You couldn't create an append query to calculate the totals and insert them into the Monthly Sales History table because one of the limitations of append queries is that they do not allow you to calculate a total. So you created a temporary totals table first, but now you're ready to insert the newly calculated totals into the Monthly Sales History table.

Begin by selecting in the Database window the One Month Total Sales table that you created in the previous step. Then click the New Query button on the tool bar. Choose the Append command from the Query menu and enter *Monthly Sales History* in the dialog box, as shown in Figure 9-34.

Figure 9-34.
The Query Properties dialog box for an append query.

Next drag the individual fields from One Month Total Sales to the QBE grid. On the Append To line, type *Catalog Item ID* for the Catalog Item ID field, *Year* for the Year field, and *Month* for the Month field. Also on the Append To line, type the field name *Quantity Sold* for the SumOfQuantity field, type the field name *Total Invoice Amount* for the calculated expression Expr1 shown in Figure 9-28, and type the field name *Total Cost* for the expression Expr2 shown in Figure 9-28. Your append query should look like the query partially shown in Figure 9-35.

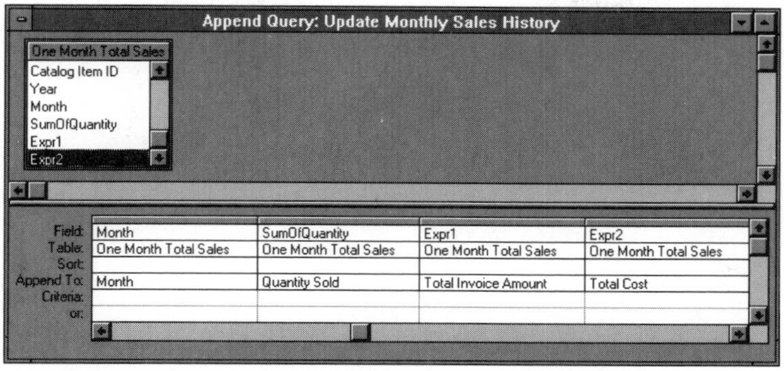

Figure 9-35.
The query that appends One Month Total Sales data to the Monthly Sales History table.

When you run this query, you should see all the rows generated in the Totals table appended (added) to the Monthly Sales History table.

At this point, you should have a reasonable understanding of how action queries can work for you. In the next chapter, you'll take a look at how you incorporate data from outside sources—text files, spreadsheets, other Microsoft Access databases, or data from other database management systems.

10

Importing, Attaching, and Exporting Data

Although you can use Microsoft Access as a self-contained database and application system, one of the primary strengths of the product (as its name implies) is that it allows you to work with many kinds of data in other databases, spreadsheets, or text files. In addition to using data in your local Microsoft Access database, you can *import* (copy in) or *attach* (connect to) data in other Access databases, dBASE files, Paradox files, FoxBase files, Btrieve files, and any other SQL database that supports the Open Database Connectivity (ODBC) standard. You can also export data from Access tables to database, spreadsheet, and text files of other applications.

A WORD ABOUT OPEN DATABASE CONNECTIVITY (ODBC)

If you look under the covers of Microsoft Access, you'll find that it uses a database language called *SQL* (*Structured Query Language*) to read, insert, update, and delete data. You can see the SQL that Access uses by choosing the SQL command from the View menu whenever you're viewing a Query window in Design view. SQL grew out of a relational database research project conducted by IBM in the 1970s. It has been adopted as an official standard for relational databases by organizations such as the American National Standards Institute (ANSI) and the International Standards Organization (ISO).

In an ideal world, any product "speaking" SQL should be able to "talk" to any other product that understands SQL. You should be able to build an application that can work with the data in several relational database management systems using the same database language. Although standards exist for SQL, the truth is that most software companies have implemented variations or extensions to the language to handle specific features in their products. Also, several products evolved before standards were well established, so the companies producing those products invented their own syntax that is different from the adopted standard. An SQL statement intended to be executed by Microsoft SQL Server might require modification before it can be executed by other databases that support SQL such as DB2 or Oracle or Rdb.

To solve this problem, several years ago a large group of influential hardware and software companies—more than 30 of them, including Microsoft—formed the SQL Access Group. Their goal was to define a common base SQL implementation that they could all use to "talk" to each other. They jointly developed something called the *Common Language Interface* or *CLI* for all the major variants of SQL, and these companies committed themselves to building support in their products that would allow any application using the CLI to work with their databases. About a dozen of these software companies jointly demonstrated this capability in early 1992.

In the meantime, Microsoft formalized the CLI for workstations and announced that all of its products—especially those designed for the Microsoft Windows operating system—would use this interface to access any SQL database. Microsoft has called this formalized interface the *Open Database Connectivity Standard,* or *ODBC.* In the spring of 1992, Microsoft announced that more than a dozen database and application software vendors had committed to provide ODBC support in their products by the end of 1992. Microsoft is providing the basic ODBC driver manager and the driver to translate ODBC SQL to the Microsoft SQL Server and is working jointly with several database vendors to develop drivers for other databases. The ODBC architecture is represented in Figure 10-1.

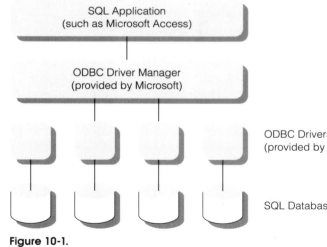

Figure 10-1.
The ODBC architecture.

Microsoft Access is one of Microsoft's first ODBC-compliant products. You have an option to install ODBC when you install Access on your computer. Once you add the drivers for the other SQL databases that you want to access, you can use Microsoft Access to build an application using data from any of these databases. See Appendix A for details on installing and managing ODBC drivers on your computer.

IMPORTING vs. ATTACHING DATABASE FILES

Because you have the choice of importing or attaching data from other databases, how can you know which type of access is best? Here are some guidelines.

Consider *importing* another database file when any of the following are true:

- The file you need is relatively small and is not changed frequently by users of the other database application.

- You don't need to share the data you create with users of the other database application.

- You are replacing the old database application and won't need to have the data in the old format any longer.

- You need the best performance while working with the data in the other database (because Access performs best with a local copy of the data in its native format).

On the other hand, you should consider *attaching* another database file when any of the following are true:

- The file is larger than the maximum capacity of a local Microsoft Access database (128 megabytes).

- The file is changed frequently by users of the other database application.

- You must share the file with users of the other database application on a network.

IMPORTING DATA

You can copy data from a number of different file formats to create a Microsoft Access table. In addition to copying data from a number of popular database file formats, Access can also create a table from data in a spreadsheet or text file.

Importing Databases

When you copy data from another database, Microsoft Access uses information stored by the source database system to convert or name objects in the target Access table. You can import database data not only from other Access databases but also from dBASE, Paradox, FoxBase, Btrieve, and—using ODBC—any SQL database that supports the ODBC standard.

Importing dBASE Files

To import a dBASE file, do the following:

1. Open the Microsoft Access database that you want to receive the dBASE file. If you already have that database open, switch to the Database window.

2. Choose the Import command from the File menu. Access opens the Import dialog box shown in Figure 10-2.

Figure 10-2.
The Import dialog box is used to pick a data source.

3. Select dBASE III or dBASE IV as appropriate in the Data Source list and click OK. Microsoft Access opens the Select File dialog box, from which you can pick the drive, directory, and name of the dBASE file that you want to import. See Figure 10-3.

4. Select a file and click Import in the Select File dialog box to import the dBASE file you've chosen. Microsoft Access opens a dialog box that informs you of the result of the import action, as shown in Figure 10-4.

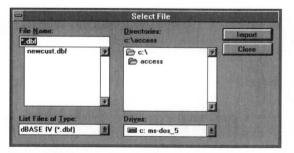

Figure 10-3.
The Select File dialog box is used to pick a file to import.

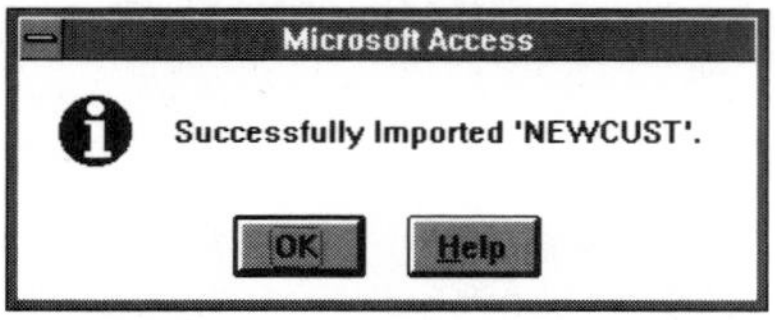

Figure 10-4.
A dialog box that indicates the result of an import action.

If the import was successful, you'll find a new table in your database with the name of the DBF file. If Access finds a duplicate name, it generates a new name by adding a unique integer to the end of the name. For example, if you are importing a file named NEWCUST.DBF and you already have tables named NewCust and NewCust1, Access creates a table named NEWCUST2.

5. Click the OK button to dismiss the dialog box that confirms the import action. Access returns you to the Select File dialog box. You can select a new file and click the Import button, or you can click the Close button to dismiss the Select File dialog box.

You will find a file named NEWCUST.DBF in the sample files you received with Microsoft Access. Follow the procedure described above to import this file into either PROMPT or NWIND. When you open the new table that Microsoft Access creates from this dBASE format data, you will see additional sample customer data, as shown in Figure 10-5.

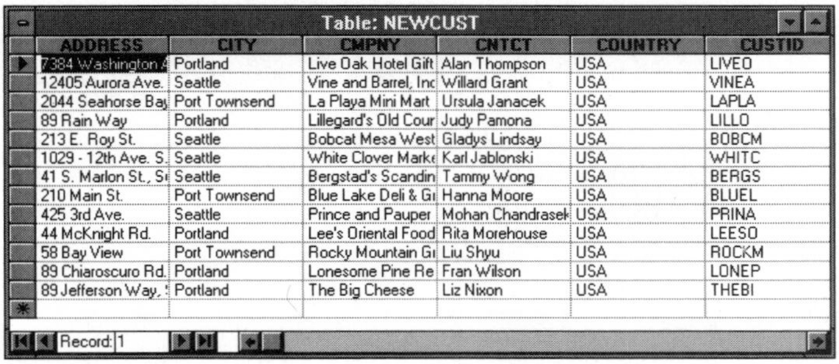
Table: NEWCUST

ADDRESS	CITY	CMPNY	CNTCT	COUNTRY	CUSTID
7384 Washington A	Portland	Live Oak Hotel Gift	Alan Thompson	USA	LIVEO
12405 Aurora Ave.	Seattle	Vine and Barrel, Inc	Willard Grant	USA	VINEA
2044 Seahorse Bay	Port Townsend	La Playa Mini Mart	Ursula Janacek	USA	LAPLA
89 Rain Way	Portland	Lillegard's Old Cour	Judy Pamona	USA	LILLO
213 E. Roy St.	Seattle	Bobcat Mesa West	Gladys Lindsay	USA	BOBCM
1029 - 12th Ave. S.	Seattle	White Clover Marke	Karl Jablonski	USA	WHITC
41 S. Marlon St., S	Seattle	Bergstad's Scandin	Tammy Wong	USA	BERGS
210 Main St.	Port Townsend	Blue Lake Deli & Gi	Hanna Moore	USA	BLUEL
425 3rd Ave.	Seattle	Prince and Pauper	Mohan Chandrasek	USA	PRINA
44 McKnight Rd.	Portland	Lee's Oriental Food	Rita Morehouse	USA	LEESO
58 Bay View	Port Townsend	Rocky Mountain Gi	Liu Shyu	USA	ROCKM
89 Chiaroscuro Rd.	Portland	Lonesome Pine Re	Fran Wilson	USA	LONEP
89 Jefferson Way,	Portland	The Big Cheese	Liz Nixon	USA	THEBI

Record: 1

Figure 10-5.
An imported dBASE file.

When you look at the Table window in Design view for a table imported from dBASE, you'll find that Microsoft Access converts data types, as shown in Figure 10-6 on the next page.

Original dBASE Data Type	Converted to Access Data Type
Character	Text
Numeric	Number, FieldSize property set to Double
Float	Number, FieldSize property set to Double
Logical	Yes/No
Date	Date/Time
Memo	Memo

Figure 10-6.
The dBASE-to-Access data type conversions.

Importing Paradox Files

The procedure for importing Paradox files is very similar to the procedure for importing dBASE files. To import a Paradox file, do the following:

1. Open the Microsoft Access database that you want to receive the Paradox file. If you already have that database open, switch to the Database window.

2. Choose the Import command from the File menu. Access opens the Import dialog box shown in Figure 10-2.

3. Select Paradox in the Data Source list and click OK. Microsoft Access opens a Select File dialog box similar to the one shown in Figure 10-3, from which you can pick the drive, directory, and name of the Paradox file that you want to import.

4. Select a file and click the Import button in the Select File dialog box to import the Paradox file you've chosen.

5. If the Paradox table is encrypted, Microsoft Access prompts you for the password, as shown in Figure 10-7. Type the correct password in the dialog box and click OK to proceed, or click Cancel to start over.

Figure 10-7.
The Password Required dialog box.

When you proceed, Microsoft Access responds with a dialog box, similar to the one shown in Figure 10-4, that indicates the result of the import action. If the import was successful, you'll find a new table in your database with the name of the DB file. If Access finds a duplicate name, it generates a new name by adding a unique integer to the end of the name. For example, if you are importing a file named NEWCUST.DB and you already have tables named NewCust and NewCust1, Access creates a table named NEWCUST2.

6. Click the OK button to dismiss the dialog box that confirms the import action. Access returns you to the Select File dialog box. You can select a new file and click the Import button, or you can click the Close button to dismiss the Select File dialog box.

When you look at a Table window in Design view the table imported from Paradox, you'll find that Access converts data types, as shown in Figure 10-8.

Original Paradox Data Type	Converted to Access Data Type
Alphanumeric	Text
Number	Number, FieldSize property set to Double
Short Number	Number, FieldSize property set to Integer
Currency	Number, FieldSize property set to Double
Date	Date/Time

Figure 10-8.
The Paradox-to-Access data type conversions.

Importing FoxBase Files

The procedure for importing FoxBase files is very similar to the procedure for importing dBASE files. To import a FoxBase file, do the following:

1. Open the Microsoft Access database that you want to receive the FoxBase file. If you already have that database open, switch to the Database window.

2. Choose the Import command from the File menu. Access opens the Import dialog box shown in Figure 10-2.

3. Select FoxPro 2.0 in the Data Source list and click OK. Microsoft Access opens a Select File dialog box similar to the one shown in Figure 10-3, from which you can pick the drive, directory, and name of the FoxBase file that you want to import.

4. Select a file and click the Import button in the Select File dialog box to import the FoxBase file you've chosen.

5. If the FoxBase table is encrypted, Microsoft Access prompts you for the password. The dialog box is similar to Figure 10-7. Type the correct password in the dialog box and click OK to proceed, or click the Cancel button to start over.

When you proceed, Microsoft Access opens a dialog box, similar to the one shown in Figure 10-4, that indicates the result of the import action. If the import was successful, you'll find a new table in your database with the name of the DBF file. If Access finds a duplicate name, it generates a new name by adding a unique integer to the end of the name. For example, if you are importing a file named NEWCUST.DBF and you already have tables named NewCust and NewCust1, Access creates a table named NEWCUST2.

6. Click OK to dismiss the dialog box that confirms the import action. Access returns you to the Select File dialog box. You can select a new file and click the Import button, or you can click the Close button to dismiss the Select File dialog box.

When you look at the Table window in Design view for a table imported from FoxBase, you'll find that Access converts data types, as shown in Figure 10-9.

Original FoxBase Data Type	*Converted to Access Data Type*
Character	Text
Numeric	Number, FieldSize property set to Integer
Float	Number, FieldSize property set to Double
Date	Date/Time
Logical	Yes/No
Memo	Memo

Figure 10-9.
The FoxBase-to-Access data type conversions.

Importing Btrieve Tables

To import a table from a Btrieve file, do the following:

1. Open the Microsoft Access database that you want to receive the Btrieve file. If you already have that database open, switch to the Database window.

2. Choose the Import command from the File menu. Access opens the Import dialog box shown in Figure 10-2.

3. Select Btrieve in the Data Source list and click OK. Microsoft Access opens a Select File dialog box similar to the one shown in Figure 10-3, from which you can pick the drive, directory, and the name of the Btrieve dictionary file containing the description of the tables you want to import. Click OK to open the dictionary. Microsoft Access shows you the list of tables in the dictionary file, as shown in Figure 10-10.

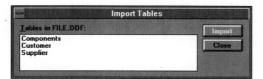

Figure 10-10.
The Import Table dialog box that is used to import a table from a selected Btrieve dictionary file.

4. From the list of tables in the dictionary file, select the name of the table you want to import. Click the Import button in the Import Tables dialog box to import the Btrieve table you've selected.

5. If the Btrieve table is password protected, Microsoft Access prompts you for the password with a dialog box similar to the one shown in Figure 10-7. Type the correct password in the dialog box and click OK to proceed, or click the Cancel button to start over.

   When you proceed, Microsoft Access responds with a dialog box, similar to the one shown in Figure 10-4, that indicates the result of the import action. If the import was successful, you'll find a new table in your database with the name of the Btrieve table. If Access finds a duplicate name, it generates a new name by adding a unique integer to the end of the name. For example, if you are importing a table named NewCust and you already have tables named NewCust and NewCust1, Access creates a table named NewCust2.

6. Click OK to dismiss the dialog box that confirms the import action. Access returns you to the Import Tables dialog box. You can select a new table and click the Import button, or you can click the Close button to dismiss the dialog box.

When you look at the Table window in Design view for a table imported from Btrieve, you'll find that Microsoft Access converts data types, as shown in Figure 10-11 on the next page.

Original Btrieve Data Type	Converted to Access Data Type
String, lstring, zstring	Text
Integer, 1-byte	Number, FieldSize property set to Byte
Integer, 2-byte	Number, FieldSize property set to Integer
Integer, 4-byte	Number, FieldSize property set to Long Integer
Float or bfloat, 4-byte	Number, FieldSize property set to Single
Float or bfloat, 8-byte	Number, FieldSize property set to Double
Decimal or Numeric	Number, FieldSize property set to Double
Money	Currency
Logical	Yes/No
Date or Time	Date/Time
Note	Memo
Lvar	OLE Object

Figure 10-11.
The Btrieve-to-Access data type conversions.

Importing SQL Tables

To import a table from another database system that supports ODBC SQL, you must first have the ODBC driver for that database installed on your computer. For details, see the *Microsoft Access User's Guide* and Appendix A of this book. Your computer must also be attached to the network that connects to the SQL server you want, and you must have a Login or User ID and password on that server. Check with your system administrator for information about correctly connecting to the SQL server from which you want to import data.

To import data from an SQL table, do the following:

1. Open the Microsoft Access database that you want to receive the SQL data. If you already have that database open, switch to the Database window.

2. Choose the Import command from the File menu. Access opens the Import dialog box shown in Figure 10-2.

3. Select SQL Database in the Data Source list and click OK. Access opens the SQL Data Sources dialog box shown in Figure 10-12, from which you can pick the name of the SQL server that contains the table you want to import. Select a server and click OK. Access then displays a Login dialog box for the SQL data source that you selected. See Figure 10-13.

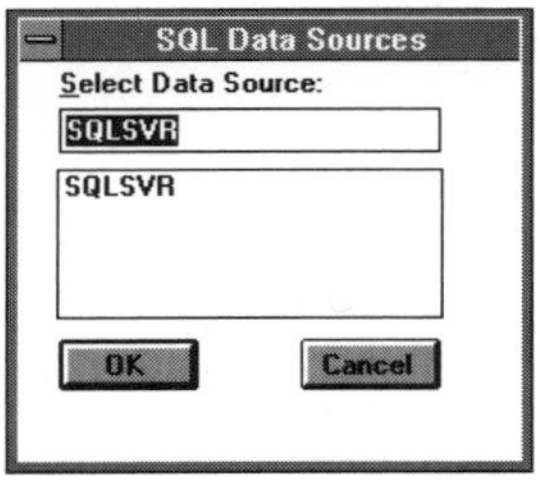

Figure 10-12.
The SQL Data Sources dialog box.

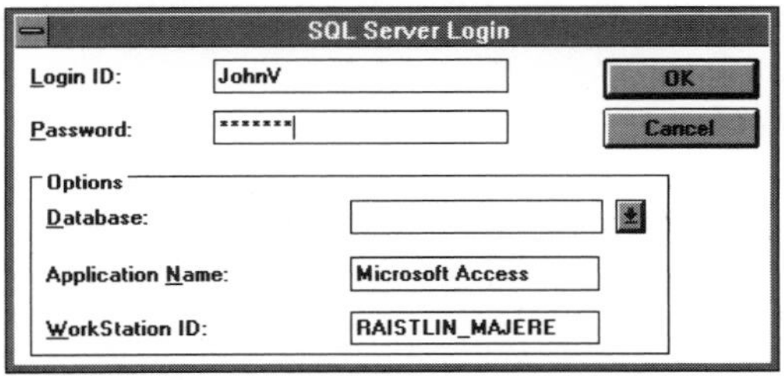

Figure 10-13.
A Login dialog box for an SQL data source.

4. Enter your Login or User ID and your password and click OK. When Access has connected you to the server successfully, you'll see a list of available tables in that server, as shown in Figure 10-14.

Figure 10-14.
A table list for an SQL data source.

5. From the list of tables in the server, select the one you want to import. Click the Import button in the Import Tables dialog box to import the SQL table you've selected.

6. Microsoft Access opens a dialog box, similar to the one shown in Figure 10-4, that indicates the result of the import action. If the import was successful, you'll find a new table in your database with the name of the SQL table. If Access finds a duplicate name, it generates a new name by

adding a unique integer to the end of the name. For example, if you are importing a table named newcust and you already have tables named NewCust and NewCust1, Access creates a table named newcust2.

7. Click OK to dismiss the dialog box that confirms the import action. Access returns you to the Import Tables dialog box. You can select a new table and click the Import button, or you can click the Close button to dismiss the dialog box.

In general, Microsoft Access converts SQL data types to Access data types as shown in Figure 10-15.

Original SQL Data Type	Converted to Access Data Type
CHAR[ACTER]	Text
VARCHAR	Memo
TINYINT	Numeric, FieldSize property set to Byte
SMALLINT	Numeric, FieldSize property set to Integer
INT	Numeric, FieldSize property set to Long Integer
REAL	Numeric, FieldSize property set to Single
FLOAT	Numeric, FieldSize property set to Double
DOUBLE	Numeric, FieldSize property set to Double
DATE	Date/Time
TIME	Date/Time
TIMESTAMP	Date/Time

Figure 10-15.
The SQL-to-Access data type conversions.

Importing Microsoft Access Objects

When the database from which you want to import data is another Microsoft Access database, you can import any of the six major types of Access objects: tables, queries, forms, reports, macros, or modules. To achieve the same result you can also open the source database, select the object you want, choose the Copy command from the Edit menu, open the target database, and choose the Paste command from the Edit menu. However, using the Import command allows you to copy several objects without having to switch back and forth between the two databases.

To import an object from another Microsoft Access database, do the following:

1. Open the Microsoft Access database that you want to receive the objects. If you already have that database open, switch to the Database window.

2. Choose the Import command from the File menu. Access opens the Import dialog box shown in Figure 10-2.

3. Select Microsoft Access in the Data Source list and click OK. Access opens a Select File dialog box similar to the one shown in Figure 10-3, from which you can select the drive, directory, and name of the MDB file containing the Access object that you want to import. Click OK.

4. Microsoft Access then opens the Import Objects dialog box shown in Figure 10-16. First select the object type and then select the specific object you want to import. When the object is a table, you can choose to import just the table structure (the table definition) or the structure *and* the stored data. Click Import to copy the object you selected to the current database.

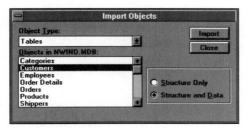

Figure 10-16.
The Import Objects dialog box.

5. Microsoft Access opens a dialog box, similar to the one shown in Figure 10-4, that indicates the result of the import action. If the import was successful, you'll find a new object in your database with the name of the object you selected. If Access finds a duplicate name, it generates a new name by adding a unique integer to the end of the name. For example, if you are importing a table named NewCust and you already have tables named NewCust and NewCust1, Access creates NewCust2. Because objects can refer to other objects by name within an Access database, you should carefully check preestablished name references to the new object if the object has to be renamed.

6. Click OK to dismiss the dialog box that confirms the import action. Access returns you to the Import Objects dialog box. You can select a new object and click the Import button, or you can click the Close button to dismiss the Import Objects dialog box.

Importing Spreadsheet Data

Microsoft Access allows you to import data from spreadsheet files created by Lotus 1-2-3, by 1-2-3 for Windows, and by Microsoft Excel version 2 and later. You can specify a portion of a spreadsheet or the entire spreadsheet file to import. (If you're working with a spreadsheet program that operates in the Microsoft Windows operating system and that supports Dynamic Data Exchange (DDE), you can also copy a single row or several rows of cells from a spreadsheet, and paste them into any Access table that has matching fields.) If the first row of cells contains names suitable for column names in the resulting Access table, you can ask Access to use these names for your fields.

Preparing a Spreadsheet

You can append a range of spreadsheet cells or a whole spreadsheet directly to an existing table. To append data, you must either supply matching field names or the columns must be in exactly the same sequence (and have the same data type) as fields in your target table. You create matching field names by entering them in the first row of your spreadsheet, as shown in Figure 10-17. If you don't provide column names, Access assigns a consecutive number to each field in the new table, starting with 1. You can open the Table window in Design view later to change these names.

If you're appending data to an existing table, the data types must match. Access can copy alphanumeric data into any Text or Memo field, numeric data into any Numeric or Currency field (as long as the FieldSize property is set large enough to contain the number value), and date or time data into any Date/Time field.

You can also import a spreadsheet to create a new table. (If you want to append a large spreadsheet but it doesn't exactly match your target table, it will be easier to

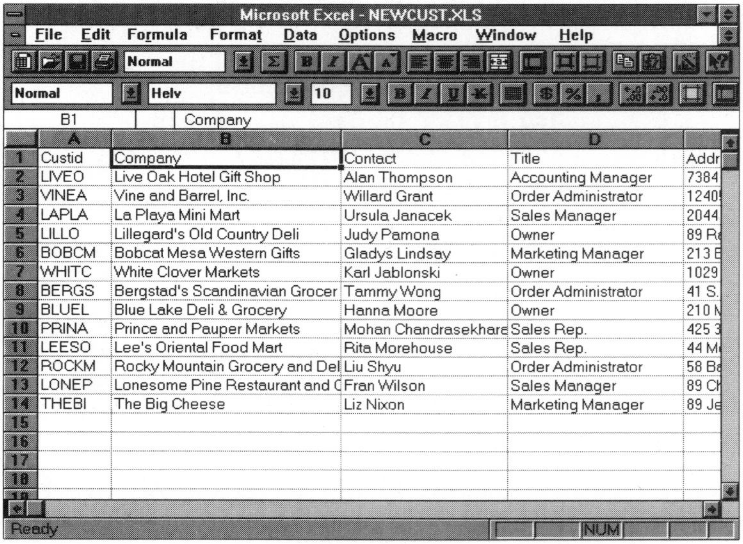

	A	B	C	D	
1	Custid	Company	Contact	Title	Addr
2	LIVEO	Live Oak Hotel Gift Shop	Alan Thompson	Accounting Manager	7384
3	VINEA	Vine and Barrel, Inc.	Willard Grant	Order Administrator	1240
4	LAPLA	La Playa Mini Mart	Ursula Janacek	Sales Manager	2044
5	LILLO	Lillegard's Old Country Deli	Judy Pamona	Owner	89 R
6	BOBCM	Bobcat Mesa Western Gifts	Gladys Lindsay	Marketing Manager	213 E
7	WHITC	White Clover Markets	Karl Jablonski	Owner	1029
8	BERGS	Bergstad's Scandinavian Grocer	Tammy Wong	Order Administrator	41 S.
9	BLUEL	Blue Lake Deli & Grocery	Hanna Moore	Owner	210 N
10	PRINA	Prince and Pauper Markets	Mohan Chandrasekhara	Sales Rep.	425 3
11	LEESO	Lee's Oriental Food Mart	Rita Morehouse	Sales Rep.	44 M
12	ROCKM	Rocky Mountain Grocery and Del	Liu Shyu	Order Administrator	58 B
13	LONEP	Lonesome Pine Restaurant and C	Fran Wilson	Sales Manager	89 C
14	THEBI	The Big Cheese	Liz Nixon	Marketing Manager	89 J
15					
16					
17					
18					

Figure 10-17.
A Microsoft Excel spreadsheet with field names entered in the first row.

import the entire spreadsheet as a new table and then use an append query to edit and move the data to the table you want to update.) Access can generate field names based on the names in the first row of the spreadsheet. You should also be aware that Access determines the data type for the fields in a new table from the values it finds in the first row of data being imported. When you import a spreadsheet to a new table, Access stores alphanumeric data as Text data type with an entry length of 255 characters, numeric data as Numeric with the FieldSize property set to Double, and any date or time data as Date/Time.

It might be worth your while to insert a single "dummy" row at the beginning of your spreadsheet with data values appropriate to the data type you want for the whole column. You can easily delete that row after you have imported the spreadsheet. For example, in the spreadsheet shown in Figure 10-18, suppose that the first entry in the Phone field is stored as a string of digits and that no value is specified in the first Credit Limit field. Access will interpret Phone as a Numeric data type and Credit Limit as a Text data type. The Credit Limit values in other records can be stored satisfactorily as text strings, but phone numbers in other records that have embedded parentheses and hyphens cannot be stored as numbers.

	G	H	I	J	K	L
1	Region	Zip	Country	Phone	Fax	Credit Limit
2	OR	97229	USA	5558946		
3	WA	98117	USA	(206) 555-3378	(206) 555-8202	$10,000.00
4	WA	98368	USA	(206) 555-8274		$7,000.00
5	OR	97219	USA	(503) 555-9573	(503) 555-5994	$12,000.00

Figure 10-18.
The initial entries in the Phone and Credit Limit columns in this Excel spreadsheet will generate the wrong data types for those fields when they are imported by Access.

Importing a Spreadsheet

If a spreadsheet's column names and their data types match fields in an existing Access table, you can import the spreadsheet rows and append them to the table. And of course you can import a spreadsheet to create a new table.

To import a spreadsheet into a Microsoft Access database, do the following:

1. Open the Microsoft Access database that you want to receive the spreadsheet. If you already have that database open, switch to the Database window.

2. Choose the Import command from the File menu. Access opens the Import dialog box shown in Figure 10-2.

3. Select the type of spreadsheet you want to import (Excel or Lotus 1-2-3) in the Data Source list and click the OK button. Microsoft Access opens a Select File dialog box similar to the one shown in Figure 10-3.

4. Select the name of the spreadsheet file that you want and click the Import button. Access opens the Import Spreadsheet Options dialog box shown in Figure 10-19.

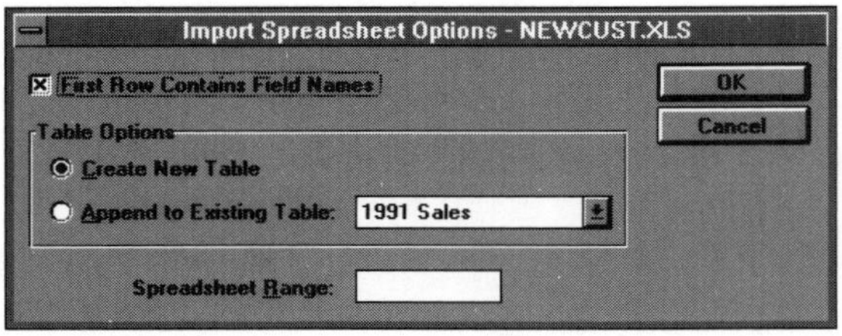

Figure 10-19.
The Import Spreadsheet Options dialog box.

5. Click the First Row Contains Field Names check box if you have placed names at the top of the columns in your spreadsheet. In the Table Options box you can choose to create a new table or to append data to an existing one. If you have included field names in your spreadsheet, the columns don't have to be in the same order as the fields in the table to which you want to append data. If you don't want to import the entire spreadsheet, specify the range of cells in the Spreadsheet Range box and be sure to include the field names row in the range if you have used field names in the spreadsheet. For example, if the upper left corner of the range you want is C9 and the lower right corner is R50, enter *C9:R50* or *C9..R50* in the range box. Click OK to start the import process.

6. Microsoft Access opens a dialog box, similar to the one shown in Figure 10-4, that indicates the result of the import action. If the import was successful and you had elected to create a table, you'll find a new table in your database with the name of the spreadsheet you selected. If Access finds a duplicate name, it generates a new name by adding a unique integer to the end of the name. For example, if you are importing a spreadsheet named NEWCUST and you already have tables named NewCust and NewCust1, Access creates a new table named NEWCUST2.

7. Click OK to dismiss the dialog box that confirms the import action. Access returns you to the Select File dialog box. You can select a new spreadsheet and click the Import button, or you can click the Close button to dismiss the Select File dialog box.

Fixing Errors

In the previous section, "Preparing a Spreadsheet," you learned that Microsoft Access determines data types for the fields in a new table based on the values it finds in the first row of data being imported from a spreadsheet. Figure 10-18 shows an example of spreadsheet data whose first row would generate wrong data types in a new Access table. The Numeric data type that Access would generate for the Phone field, based on the first entry, would not work for the remaining entries that have parentheses and hyphens in them.

If you were to import the data shown in Figure 10-18, Access would open an Import Results dialog box similar to the one shown in Figure 10-20.

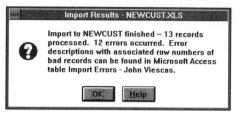

Figure 10-20.
An Import Results dialog box.

In any case, Access creates a table called Import Errors with your name in the title. That table contains a record for each error. Figure 10-21 shows the errors table that Access creates when you import the spreadsheet from Figure 10-18. Access creates this table even when you click Cancel in the Import Results dialog box, enabling you to see what needs to be corrected in the spreadsheet before you try again. Notice that the errors table lists not only the type of error but also the field and row in the spreadsheet where the error occurred. In this case, the second data row (the third row in the spreadsheet) and all subsequent entries in the Phone field are rejected for being text values. Also notice that when you append a spreadsheet to an existing table, you might also see rows rejected because of duplicate primary keys. Unless the primary key for your table is a Counter, the rows you are appending from the spreadsheet must contain the primary key fields, and the values in these fields must be unique.

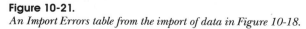

Figure 10-21.
An Import Errors table from the import of data in Figure 10-18.

If you look at the table that results from the import of the Figure 10-18 data, as shown in Figure 10-22, you find that no phone numbers appear in the second and subsequent records. If you were to look at the data type for Credit Limit in Design view, you would find that this data has been saved as the Text data type, not as the Number data type.

Region	Zip	Country	Phone	Fax	Credit Limit
OR	97229	USA	5558946		
WA	98117	USA		(206) 555-8202	10000
WA	98368	USA			7000
OR	97219	USA		(503) 555-5994	12000
WA	98124	USA			15000
WA	98124	USA		(206) 555-4115	9000
WA	98104	USA		(206) 555-8832	6500
WA	98368	USA		(206) 555-4247	8800
WA	98101	USA		(206) 555-6044	11000
OR	97229	USA		(503) 555-6655	18000
WA	98368	USA			13000
OR	97219	USA		(503) 555-9646	9500
OR	97201	USA			7600

Figure 10-22.
The errors that were created by importing the data shown in Figure 10-18.

Some errors you can correct in the Table window in Design view. For example, you can change the data type of Credit Limit to numeric, and because the text values in the second and subsequent rows are all valid numbers, Access can convert the data format correctly for all rows. See Figure 6-16 in Chapter 6 for a table of data conversion limitations. You have different choices for fixing the Phone field. You could either add the missing phone numbers in the Table window in Datasheet view, or you could delete and then reimport this table after correcting the numeric value in the first row in the spreadsheet.

Importing Text Files

You can import data from a text file into Microsoft Access even though, unlike spreadsheets, the data in a text file isn't broken up into columns and rows in an orderly way. You can make it possible for Access to understand the data in a text file by either including special characters to delimit the fields in each record (sometimes called a *delimited text file*) or by placing each field in the exact same location in each record (called a *fixed-width file*) and defining those field locations for Access.

Preparing Text Files

You might be able to import some text files into Microsoft Access without changing them, especially if the text file was created by another program using standard field delimiters. In most cases, you will have to modify the contents of the file or define the file for Access or do both before you can import it.

SETTING UP DELIMITED DATA: Microsoft Access needs some way to distinguish where a field starts and ends in each incoming text string. Access supports three standard separator characters: comma, tab, and space. When you use a comma as the separator (a very common technique), the comma (or the carriage return at the end of the record) indicates the end of each field, and the next field begins with the first nonblank character. The commas aren't part of the data. To include a comma within a text string as data, you must enclose all text strings in single or double quotes. If any of your text strings contain double quotes, you must enclose the strings in single quotes, and vice versa. Access accepts only a single or double quote (but not both) as a text delimiter, so any embedded quotes in a file that you want to import to Access must all be of the same type. In other words, you can't include a single quote in one field and a double quote in another field in the same file. Figure 10-23 shows you a sample comma-separated and double-quote-delimited text file.

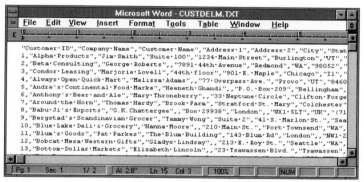

Figure 10-23.
A comma-separated text file.

Another common way to separate data is to use the tab character between fields. In fact, when you save a spreadsheet file as text from most spreadsheet programs, the program stores the columns with tabs between them. Figure 10-24 on the next page shows the NEWCUST spreadsheet from Microsoft Excel saved as text. Notice that Excel has added double quotes around text strings that include commas, but not in any other case.

By default, Microsoft Access assumes that fields in a delimited text file are separated by commas and that text strings are embedded in double quotes. If you want to import a file that is delimited differently, you can define a new *import/export specification* and then refer to it when you import the data.

To define an import/export specification, open your database and from the Database window choose the Imp/Exp Setup command from the File menu. Access opens the dialog box shown in Figure 10-25 on the next page. In this dialog box, {tab} was selected from the Field Separator list and the change was saved with a new Specification Name entry of TabDelim. In the next section, you'll learn how to use the Field Information area to define fields in a fixed-width file.

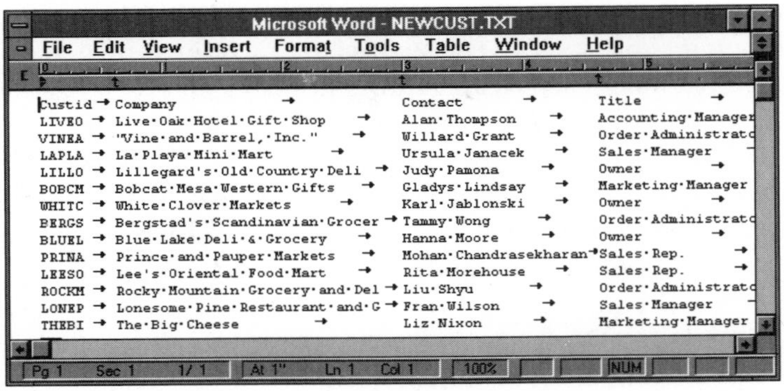

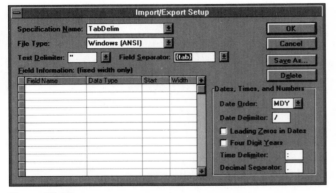

Figure 10-24.
A tab-separated text file.

Figure 10-25.
An Import/Export Setup dialog box that defines a tab-separated specification.

SETTING UP FIXED-WIDTH DATA: Microsoft Access can also import text files when the fields appear in fixed locations in each record in the file, but you must first define the locations for Access. You might encounter this type of file if you download a print output file from a host computer.

Figure 10-26 shows a sample fixed-width text file. Notice that each field begins in exactly the same location in all the records. To prepare this type of file for import, you must first remove any heading or summary lines from the file. The file must contain only records, with the data you want to import in fixed locations. You must also create an import/export specification that Access can use to determine the data type and location of each field in the records.

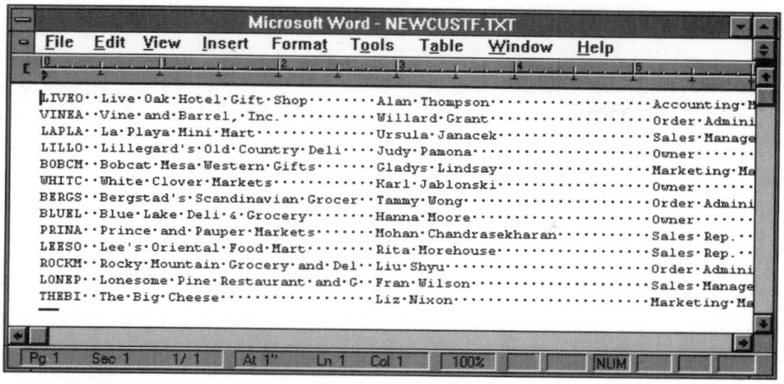

Figure 10-26.
A fixed-width text file.

To define an import/export specification, open your database or go to the Database window and then choose the Imp/Exp Setup command from the File menu. Access opens the Import/Export Setup dialog box. In the Import/Export Setup dialog box you can define each field in the file you want to import by filling in the Field Information area. You type the name you want to assign the field in the resulting table, and then you enter the data type, the starting location of the field data relative to the first character in each record, and the length of the field. See Figure 10-27. When you have finished defining a new specification, you can click Save As and type a name for the specification in the dialog box that opens. In Figure 10-27 the specification was saved as *NewCust in Fixed*.

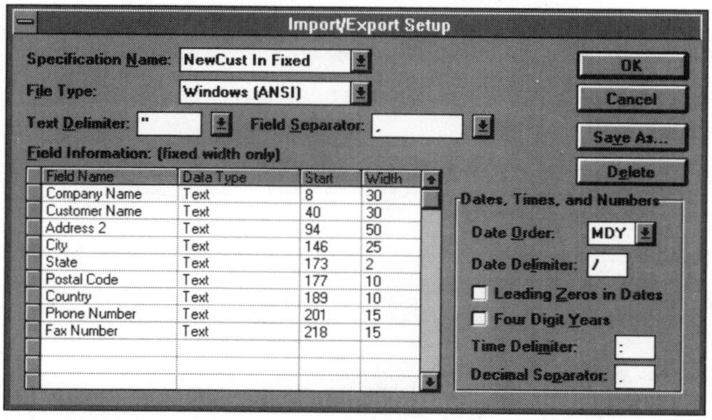

Figure 10-27.
An Import/Export Setup dialog box that defines a fixed-width specification.

In the Import/Export Setup dialog box, you can also indicate whether the text file was created using a program running under MS-DOS or under the Microsoft Windows operating system. For any file created with an application for Windows (such as Notepad), select the file type called *Windows (ANSI)*. For files created with an MS-DOS program (such as EDIT.COM or EDLIN.EXE), select the file type called *DOS or OS/2 (PC-8)*. For fixed-width files, you won't need to make a Text Delimiter selection or Field Separator selection; you use these options to define a specification for delimited files only. In the lower right corner of the Import/Export dialog box you can change the way Access recognizes date and time values and numeric fractions.

Importing a Text File

Before you can import a text file you will probably need to prepare the data or define the file for Microsoft Access, or do both. See "Preparing Text Files" above. Once that is done, you can import a text file into a Microsoft Access database by doing the following:

1. Open the Microsoft Access database that you want to receive the text data. If you already have that database open, switch to the Database window.

2. Choose the Import command from the File menu. Access opens the Import dialog box shown in Figure 10-2.

3. Select the type of text file you want to import, either Text (Delimited) or Text (Fixed Width), in the Data Source list and click OK. Access opens a Select File dialog box similar to the one shown in Figure 10-3.

4. Select the name of the text file that you want and click the Import button.

5. For delimited files, Access opens the Import Text Options dialog box shown in Figure 10-28. You can choose to create a new table or append a file to an existing table. Click the Options button to expand the dialog box, as shown in Figure 10-29. You can then select a specification name or define different delimiters and separators. Click the First Row Contains Field Names check box if the first record in your delimited text file contains field names.

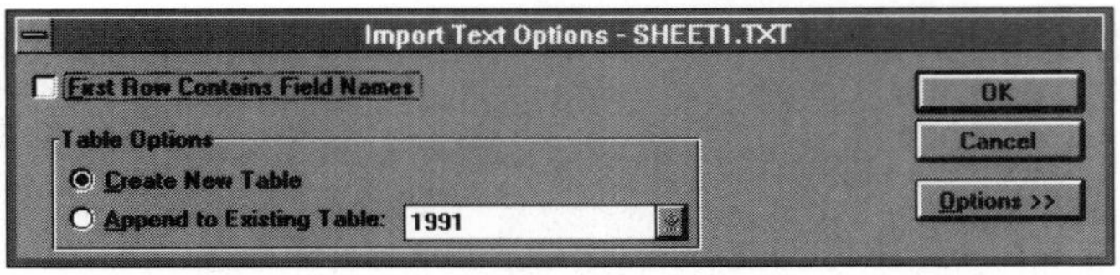

Figure 10-28.
The Import Text Options dialog box for delimited text files.

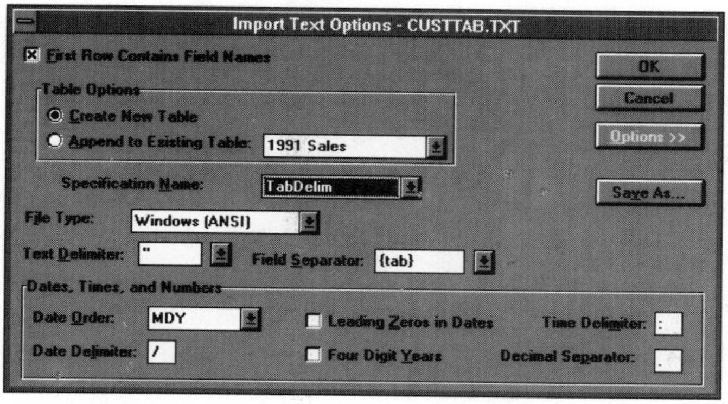

Figure 10-29.
The Import Text Options dialog box for delimited text files, after the Options button is clicked.

For fixed-width files, Access shows you the Import Text Options dialog box shown in Figure 10-30. You can choose to create a new table or append a file to an existing table. Choose the specification name you want Access to use from the drop-down list.

Click OK to start the import process.

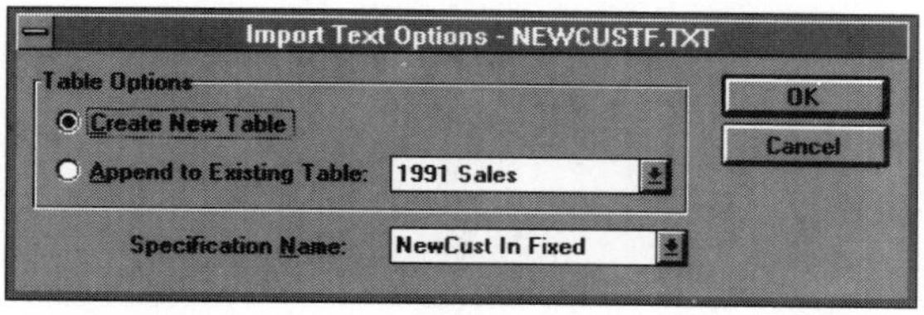

Figure 10-30.
The Import Text Options dialog box for fixed-width text files.

6. Microsoft Access opens a dialog box indicating the result of the import action. If the import was successful and you had elected to create a table, you'll find a new table in your database with the name of the text file you selected. If Access finds a duplicate name, it generates a new name by adding a unique integer to the end of the name. For example, if you are importing a text file named NEWCUST and you already have tables named NewCust and NewCust1, Access creates a new table named NEWCUST2.

7. Click the OK button to dismiss the import action dialog box. Access returns you to the Select File dialog box. You can select a new text file and click the Import button, or you can click the Close button to dismiss the Select File dialog box.

Fixing Errors

You can encounter errors importing text files. These errors are similar to those explained previously in the section called "Importing Spreadsheet Data." When you append a text file to an existing table, you might see rows rejected because of duplicate primary keys. Unless the primary key for your table is a Counter, the rows you are appending from the text file must contain the primary key fields, and the values in those fields must be unique. For delimited text files, Access determines the data type based on the fields in the first record being imported. If a number appears in a field in the first record that might later also contain text data, you need to enclose that number in quotes so that Access will use the Text data type for that field. If a number first appears without decimal places, Access uses the Number data type with the FieldSize property set to Integer. This setting will generate errors later if the numbers contain decimal places in other records.

Microsoft Access opens an error dialog box, similar to the one shown in Figure 10-20, that summarizes any errors found. You can click OK to complete the import with the errors noted, or you can click Cancel to abort the operation. As with spreadsheet errors, Access creates a table called Import Errors with your name appended to this title. The table contains a record for each error. Access creates this table even when you choose Cancel in the Import Results dialog box, enabling you to see what needs to be corrected before you try again. The errors table lists not only the type of error but also the column and row in the text file where the error occurred.

Some errors you can correct in the Table window in Design view. For example, you can change the data type of fields as long as the content of the fields can be converted to the new data type. See Figure 6-16 in Chapter 6 for data conversion limitations. With other errors you must either add missing data in the Datasheet view or delete and reimport the table after correcting the values in the text file that caused the errors originally.

Modifying Imported Tables

When you import data from an external source, Microsoft Access often has to use default data types or lengths that will accommodate the incoming data but which might not be correct for your needs. For example, Access assigns the maximum length of 255 characters to text data imported from a spreadsheet or text file. Even when the source of the data is another database, Access might choose numeric data types that can accept the data but that might not be correct. For example numeric data in dBASE might be of the type Integer, but Access stores all numeric data from dBASE with a FieldSize setting of Double.

Unless you are importing data from an SQL or Paradox database that has a primary key defined, Access does not define a primary key in the new table. Also, if you did not include field names from a text or spreadsheet file, you probably will want to enter meaningful names in the resulting table.

You can correctly specify most data types, change field names, and add a primary key in the Table window in Design view. For detailed information on modifying the Table window in Design view, see Chapter 6.

ATTACHING OTHER DATABASES

You can attach tables from other Microsoft Access databases—whether the other databases are local or on a network—and work with the data in them as if these tables were defined in your current Access database. If you want to work with data stored in another database format supported by Microsoft Access (dBASE, Paradox, Btrieve, or any SQL database that supports ODBC), you can attach the data directly as an alternative to importing it. In most cases, you can read data, insert new records, delete records, or change data just as though the attached file were a Microsoft Access table. This ability to attach data is especially important when you need to access data on a host computer or share data from your application with many other users.

Security Considerations

If you attempt to attach a file or table from another database system that is protected, Microsoft Access asks you for a password or Login information. If the security information you supply is correct and Access successfully attaches the secured data, Access stores the security information with the attached table entry so that you do not have to enter this information each time you (or your application) open the table. Although there is no way to directly access this information in your SYSTEM.MDB file from Microsoft Access, a knowledgeable person might be able to retrieve it by scanning the file with a dump utility. Therefore, if you have attached sensitive information to your Access database, for which you supplied security information, you should consider encrypting your database. Consult Chapter 25 in your *Microsoft Access User's Guide* for information about securing and encrypting your Microsoft Access database.

Performance Considerations

Microsoft Access always performs best when working with its own files on your local machine. If you attach tables or files from other databases, you might notice slower performance. And in particular you can expect slower performance if you connect to a table or file in another database over a network, even if the remote table is a Microsoft Access table.

When sharing data over a network, you should consider how you and other people can use the data in a way that maximizes performance. For example, you should use queries with shared data whenever possible to limit the amount of data you need at any one time. When inserting new data in a shared table, you should use a Microsoft Access form that is set only for data entry so that you don't have to access the entire table to add new data, as explained in Part IV of this book, "Using Forms."

You should set options so that records are not locked if you are only browsing through data. If you need to update data, your options should be set to lock only the records you are editing. When others are updating the data you are using, you'll occasionally notice that you cannot update a record. You can set options to limit the number of times Microsoft Access will retry an update to a locked record on your behalf and how long it will wait between retries. You can also control how often Access reviews updates made by other users to shared data. If this refresh interval is set very low, Access will be spending time performing this task repeatedly.

The original settings for Multiuser options are often appropriate when you share data over a network, so it's a good idea to consult your system administrator before making changes. If you need to alter the Multiuser options, you can choose the Options command from the View menu and select the Multiuser category at the bottom of the list. The Options dialog box, with the Multiuser category selected, is shown in Figure 10-31.

Figure 10-31.
The Options dialog box with the Multiuser category selected.

Attaching Microsoft Access Tables

To attach a table from another Microsoft Access database, do the following:

1. Open the Microsoft Access database to which you want to attach the table. If you already have that database open, switch to the Database window.

2. Choose the Attach Table command from the File menu. Access opens the Attach dialog box that lists the types of databases you can attach. See Figure 10-32.

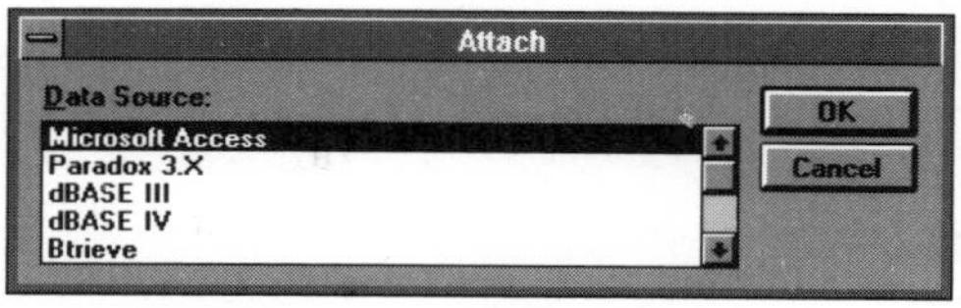

Figure 10-32.
The Attach dialog box.

3. Select Microsoft Access in the Data Source list and click the OK button. Access opens a Select Microsoft Access Database dialog box, similar to the dialog box shown in Figure 10-3, in which you can choose the drive, directory and name of the MDB file that contains the table you want to attach. If you are connecting over a network, you can select the logical drive that is assigned to the network server containing the database you want. If you aren't always connected to the remote server that contains the Access table you want, but you would like Access to automatically connect each time you open the table, type the fully qualified network name in the File Name box instead of choosing a logical drive. For example, on a Microsoft LAN Manager network you might enter a network location, such as *\\DBSVR\ACCESS\SHARED\NWIND.MDB*. Click OK.

4. Microsoft Access opens the Attach Tables dialog box, shown in Figure 10-33, that lists the tables available in the database you have chosen. Select the table you want and click the Attach button to connect the table you selected to the current database.

Figure 10-33.
The Attach Tables dialog box.

5. Microsoft Access opens a dialog box, similar to the one shown in Figure 10-4, that indicates the result of the attach action. If the attach action was successful, you'll find a new table in your database with the name of the table you selected. Access marks the icon for attached tables in the database window with an arrow as shown in Figure 10-34 on the next page. If Access finds a duplicate name, it generates a new name by adding a unique integer to the end of the name. For example, if you are attaching a table named NEWCUST and you already have tables named NewCust and NewCust1, Access creates a table named NEWCUST2.

Because objects such as forms, reports, macros, and modules might refer to this table by its original name, you should carefully check name references if Access has to rename an attached table.

Figure 10-34.
An arrow icon indicates an attached table in the Database window.

6. Click the OK button to dismiss the dialog box that confirms the attach action. Access returns you to the Attach Tables dialog box. You can select a new table and click the Attach button, or you can click the Close button to dismiss the Attach Tables dialog box.

Attaching dBASE, Paradox, and Btrieve Files

Attaching files from a foreign database is nearly as simple as attaching a Microsoft Access table. To attach a table from dBASE, Paradox, or Btrieve, do the following:

1. Open the Microsoft Access database to which you want to attach the table. If you already have that database open, switch to the Database window.

2. Choose the Attach Table command from the File menu. Access opens the Attach dialog box that lists the types of databases you can attach. See Figure 10-32.

3. Select dBASE III, dBASE IV, Paradox, or Btrieve, as appropriate, in the Data Source list and click OK. Access opens a Select File dialog box similar to the dialog box in Figure 10-3, in which you can choose the drive, directory, and name of the database file that you want to attach. If you are attaching a table from a Btrieve database, you'll select the dictionary file (a DDF file) at this time. If you are connecting over a network, select the logical drive that is assigned to the network server that contains the database you want. If you aren't always connected to the remote server that contains the file you want, but you would like Access to automati-

cally connect each time you open the attached file, enter the full network location in the File Name box instead of choosing a logical drive. For example, on a Microsoft LAN Manager network you might enter a network location such as *\\DBSVR\DBASE\SHARED\NEWCUST.DBF* for the NEWCUST file. Click the Attach button to attach the selected dBASE or Paradox file. Click OK to open the selected Btrieve dictionary file.

4. If you have chosen a dBASE file, Microsoft Access next prompts you to identify any index files (NDX or MDX files) that are associated with the file you want to attach. Access opens the Select Index Files dialog box shown in Figure 10-35. You must inform Access of all related indexes if you want the indexes updated properly any time you make a change to the dBASE file using Access. You must not move or delete these index files or the information file (an INF file) that Access builds when you attach the table or you will not be able to open the dBASE file from Access. You must also be sure that any dBASE applications always maintain these indexes. Access can't open an attached dBASE table if its indexes are not current.

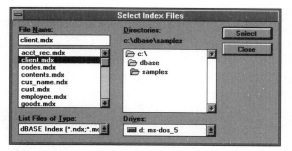

Figure 10-35.
The Select Index Files dialog box is used to associate index files with dBASE files you attach to your Access database.

Select the index files you need to associate with the dBASE file you are attaching. Click the Select button to add each index file to the information file one at a time. Click Close when you have selected all indexes.

5. If you are attaching a Btrieve table, Microsoft Access opens a Tables list box after you have selected a dictionary file in the Select File dialog box. The Tables list box shows the tables available in the dictionary you have chosen. Select the table you want and click the Attach button to connect the table you selected to the current database. This tables list is in a dialog box similar to the one shown in Figure 10-10.

6. If the file you selected requires a password to access it (because it's an encrypted Paradox file or password-protected Btrieve table), Microsoft Access next prompts you for the correct password. See Figure 10-7. Microsoft Access then opens a dialog box, similar to the one shown in Figure 10-4, that indicates the result of the attach action. If the attach action was successful, you'll find a new table in your database with the name of the file you selected. If Access finds a duplicate name, it generates a new name by adding a unique integer to the end of the name. For example, if you are attaching a file named NEWCUST and you already have tables named NewCust and NewCust1, Access creates a new table named NEWCUST2.

7. Click the OK button to dismiss the dialog box that confirms the attach action. Access returns you to the Select File dialog box (or in the case of Btrieve, to the Tables list box). You can select a new file and click the Attach button, or you can click the Close button to dismiss the dialog box.

Attaching SQL Tables

To attach a table from another database system that supports ODBC SQL, you must first have the ODBC driver for that database installed on your computer. For details, see Appendix D of the *Microsoft Access User's Guide* and Appendix A of this book. Your computer must also be attached to the network that connects to the SQL server you want, and you must have a Login or User ID and password on that server. Check with your system administrator for information about correctly connecting to the SQL server from which you want to attach a table.

To attach an SQL table, do the following:

1. Open the Microsoft Access database to which you want to attach an SQL table. If you already have that database open, switch to the Database window.

2. Choose the Attach Table command from the File menu. Access opens an Attach dialog box that lists the types of databases you can attach. See Figure 10-32.

3. Select SQL Database in the Data Source list and click the OK button. Microsoft Access opens an SQL Data Sources dialog box similar to the dialog box shown in Figure 10-12, in which you can pick the name of the SQL server that contains the table you want to attach. Click OK, and Access displays a Login dialog box for the SQL data source that you selected. See Figure 10-13.

4. Enter your Login or User ID and your password, and click OK. When Access has connected you to the server successfully, you'll see a list of available tables at that server, as shown in Figure 10-14.

5. From the list of tables in the server, select the one you want to attach. Click the Attach button in the Import Tables dialog box to attach the SQL table you've selected.

6. Access then opens a dialog box, similar to the one shown in Figure 10-4, that indicates the result of the attach action. If the attach action was successful, you'll find a new table in your database with the name of the SQL table. If Access finds a duplicate name, it generates a new name by adding a unique integer to the end of the name. For example, if you are attaching a table named newcust and you already have tables named NewCust and NewCust1, Access creates a new table named newcust2.

7. Click the OK button to dismiss the dialog box that confirms the attach action. Access returns you to the Import Tables dialog box. You can select a new table and click the Attach button, or you can click the Close button to dismiss the dialog box.

Modifying Attached Tables

You can make some changes to the definitions of attached tables to customize them for use in your Microsoft Access environment. When you attempt to open the Table window in Design view, Access opens a dialog box to warn you that you cannot modify some properties in an attached table. You can still click OK to open the attached table in Design view.

For an attached table, you can open the Table window in Design view to change the Format, Decimal Places, Caption, Default Value, Validation Rule, and Validation Text property settings for any field. You can set these properties to customize the way you look at, update, and validate data with Microsoft Access forms and reports. You can also give any attached table a new name for use within your Access database (although the table's original name remains unchanged in the source database) to help you identify the table better or to enable you to use the table with the queries, forms, and reports that you have already designed.

Changing a table's design in Microsoft Access has no effect on the original table in its source database. Notice, however, that if the design of the table in the source database changes, you will have to reattach the table to Access. You must also delete and reattach any table when your Login or your User ID or your password to access the source database changes.

EXPORTING DATA

You can export (copy) any object in an Access database to any other Access database. And you can also export data from Microsoft Access tables to spreadsheet files, other databases, or text files.

Exporting to Another Microsoft Access Database

Exporting objects from one Microsoft Access database to another works very much like importing Access objects. To export any object from an Access database to another Access database, do the following:

1. Open the Microsoft Access database from which you want to export the objects. If you already have that database open, switch to the Database window.

2. Choose the Export command from the File menu. Access opens the Export dialog box shown in Figure 10-36. Select Microsoft Access from the Data Destination list, and click OK.

Figure 10-36.
The Export dialog box.

3. Access opens the Select Microsoft Access Object dialog box shown in Figure 10-37. In this dialog box, you can select the object type and then the specific object you want to export. When the object is a table, you can choose to export just the table structure (the table definition) or the structure *and* the stored data. When you have selected the object you want, click OK.

Figure 10-37.
The Select Microsoft Access Object dialog box for exporting to another Access database.

4. Access opens the Export To File dialog box, shown in Figure 10-38, from which you can select the drive, directory, and name of the MDB file to which you want to export objects. Click OK.

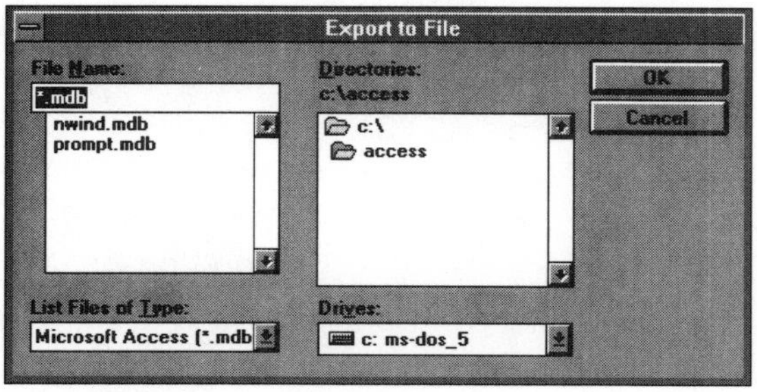

Figure 10-38.
The Export To File dialog box.

5. Next Microsoft Access shows you the Export dialog box shown in Figure 10-39, which asks you to enter a name for the object in the receiving database. You can leave the name as is or change it to meet your needs in the receiving database. Click OK to begin exporting the object.

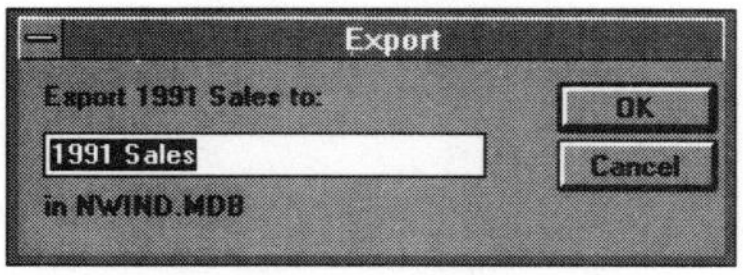

Figure 10-39.
A different Export dialog box is used to name an exported Access object.

6. If the export name you have chosen already exists in the target database, Microsoft Access warns you and asks you if you want to replace the existing object. Click OK to proceed or click the Cancel button to stop the export action. If the export was successful, you'll find a new object in the target database. Because objects can refer to other objects by name within an Access database, you should carefully check name references in the receiving database.

Exporting to a Spreadsheet, dBASE, Paradox, or FoxBase File

You can use the same procedure to export data from a table to a spreadsheet (Microsoft Excel or Lotus 1-2-3), dBASE, Paradox, or FoxBase file. If you want to export data selected by a query from a table or from multiple tables, change the select query to a make-table query (as explained in Chapter 8, "Adding Power with Select Queries") and create a temporary table containing the dynaset of the query. You can export the temporary table and then delete it.

1. Open the Microsoft Access database from which you want to export the data in a table. If you already have that database open, switch to the Database window.

2. Choose the Export command from the File menu. Access opens the Export dialog box. Select Excel, Lotus (WKS or WK1), dBASE III, dBASE IV, Paradox, or FoxBase from the Data Destination list, and click OK. See Figure 10-36.

3. Access opens the Select Microsoft Access Object dialog box, shown in Figure 10-40, from which you can select the table whose data you want to export. When you have selected the table you want, click OK.

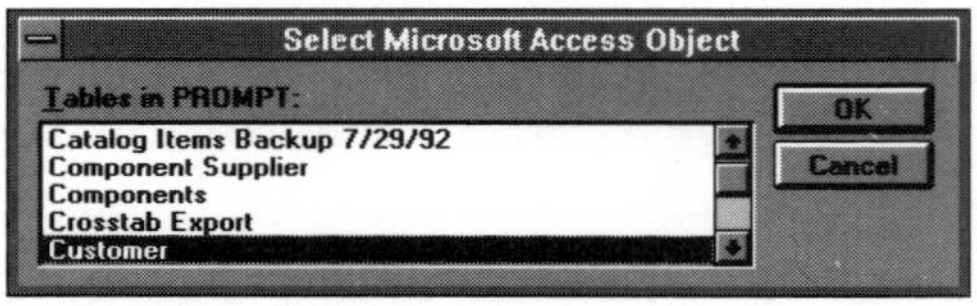

Figure 10-40.
The Select Microsoft Access Object dialog box for exporting data.

4. Microsoft Access opens the Export To File dialog box, from which you can select the drive, directory, and filename to which you want to export your data. Click OK to export your data to that file in the application format you have chosen. See Figure 10-38.

5. If the export was successful, you'll find a new file that you can use with your spreadsheet or other database program. Figure 10-41 shows you an Access table that has been exported to a Microsoft Excel spreadsheet. (It's the sample dBASE file that was imported into Microsoft Access in Figure 10-5.)

NOTE: *dBASE, Paradox, and FoxBase cannot support the 64-character field names available in Microsoft Access. Access truncates long field names when copying data to these files. If the truncated name results in a duplicate field name, Access reports an error and does not export your data. To correct this problem, you might have to make a temporary copy of your table, edit the field names in the temporary table to avoid duplicates, and retry the export using the temporary table. It's not a good idea to change the field names in your permanent table as you might cause errors in queries, forms and reports that use the table.*

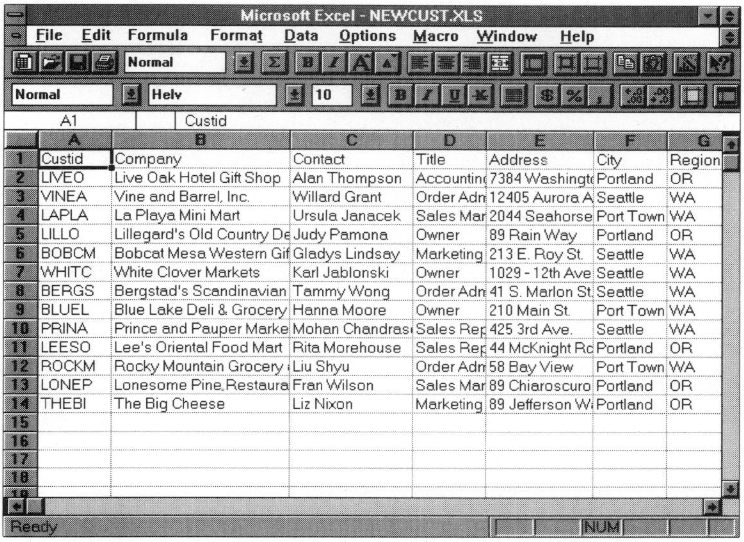

	A	B	C	D	E	F	G
1	Custid	Company	Contact	Title	Address	City	Region
2	LIVEO	Live Oak Hotel Gift Shop	Alan Thompson	Accountin	7384 Washingt	Portland	OR
3	VINEA	Vine and Barrel, Inc.	Willard Grant	Order Adr	12405 Aurora A	Seattle	WA
4	LAPLA	La Playa Mini Mart	Ursula Janacek	Sales Mar	2044 Seahorse	Port Town	WA
5	LILLO	Lillegard's Old Country De	Judy Pamona	Owner	89 Rain Way	Portland	OR
6	BOBCM	Bobcat Mesa Western Gif	Gladys Lindsay	Marketing	213 E. Roy St.	Seattle	WA
7	WHITC	White Clover Markets	Karl Jablonski	Owner	1029 - 12th Ave	Seattle	WA
8	BERGS	Bergstad's Scandinavian	Tammy Wong	Order Adr	41 S. Marlon St.	Seattle	WA
9	BLUEL	Blue Lake Deli & Grocery	Hanna Moore	Owner	210 Main St.	Port Town	WA
10	PRINA	Prince and Pauper Marke	Mohan Chandras	Sales Rep	425 3rd Ave.	Seattle	WA
11	LEESO	Lee's Oriental Food Mart	Rita Morehouse	Sales Rep	44 McKnight Rc	Portland	OR
12	ROCKM	Rocky Mountain Grocery	Liu Shyu	Order Adr	58 Bay View	Port Town	WA
13	LONEP	Lonesome Pine Restaura	Fran Wilson	Sales Mar	89 Chiaroscuro	Portland	OR
14	THEBI	The Big Cheese	Liz Nixon	Marketing	89 Jefferson W	Portland	OR
15							
16							
17							
18							

Figure 10-41.
An Access table exported to an Excel spreadsheet.

Exporting to a Text File

You can copy data from a Microsoft Access table to a text file in one of two formats: delimited or fixed width. You might find this procedure particularly useful for copying data from an Access table to a non-Windows word processor or text editor or for uploading the data to a host computer. If you want to export data selected by a query from part of a table or from multiple tables, you must change the select query to a make-table query (as explained in Chapter 8, "Adding Power with Select Queries"), and create a temporary table containing the dynaset of the query. You can export the temporary table and then delete it.

Before you export a table as a delimited text file, you need to decide what field separators and text delimiters you want Microsoft Access to use. By default, Access uses a comma to separate fields and encloses text data in double quotes. If you have previously defined an import/export specification with different options, you can choose it from the drop-down list box in the Export Text Options dialog box. You can also select different options at the time you export the table. When the Export Text Options dialog box opens, as shown in Figure 10-42 on the next page, you can click the Options button to expand the dialog box, as shown in Figure 10-43 on the next page.

To export a table in a fixed format, you must first define an import/export specification. To do this, first open the database from which you want to export data. While in the Database window, choose Imp/Exp Setup from the File menu.

Microsoft Access then opens the Import/Export Setup dialog box, which is shown in Figure 10-44.

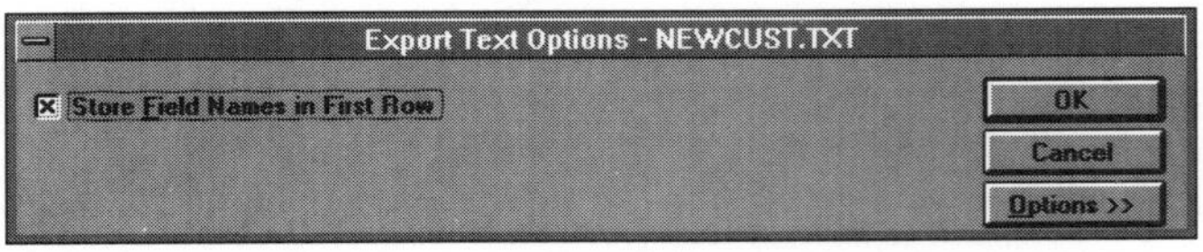

Figure 10-42.
The Export Text Options dialog box is used when you are exporting a delimited text file.

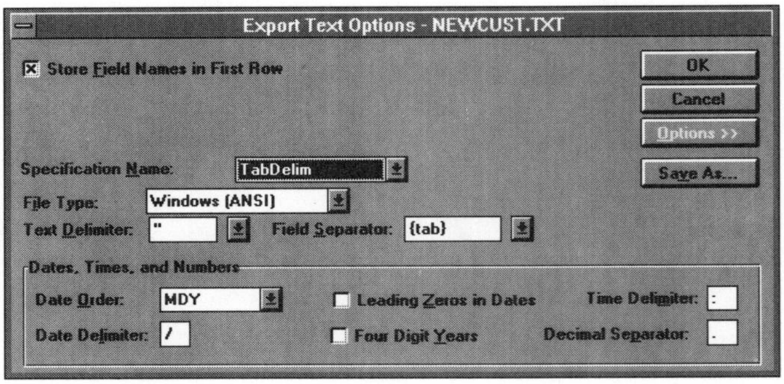

Figure 10-43.
The Export Text Options dialog box expands when the Options button is clicked.

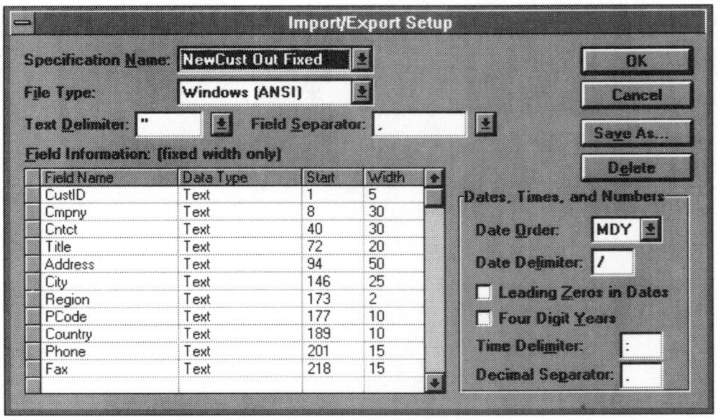

Figure 10-44.
The Import/Export Setup dialog box with settings for a fixed-width export specification.

Enter each field name from your table in the Field Name column. Define the data type of the source field in the next column. Specify the relative location where you would like the output data to begin (the first column in the resulting text file is 1) and the width of the field. Click the Save As button to open a dialog box in which you can name the new specification. You can now use this specification to create a fixed-width export text file.

To export the data from a Microsoft Access table to a text file, do the following:

1. Open the Microsoft Access database from which you want to export the data in a table. If you already have that database open, switch to the Database window.

2. Choose the Export command from the File menu. Access opens the Export dialog box. Select Text (Delimited) or Text (Fixed Width) as appropriate from the Data Destination list, and click OK. See Figure 10-36.

3. Access opens the Select Microsoft Access Object dialog box, shown in Figure 10-37, from which you can select the table whose data you want to export. When you have selected the table you want, click OK.

4. Microsoft Access opens the Export To File dialog box, from which you can select the drive, directory, and filename to which you want to export your data. When you have entered the filename you want, click OK. See Figure 10-38.

5. Microsoft Access next opens the Export Text Options dialog box similar to the one shown in Figure 10-42. If you are exporting in a fixed width format, select the Specification Name (as previously created in the Import/Export Setup dialog box shown in Figure 10-44). If you are exporting in a delimited format, use the default specification or click the Options button to define options, as shown in Figure 10-43. Click OK to begin exporting your data.

6. If the export was successful, you'll find a new file in the text format you selected.

Exporting to a Btrieve Table

Before you can export data to a Btrieve table, a dictionary file must exist into which Microsoft Access can define the output table. To export Access data to a Btrieve table, do the following:

1. Open the Microsoft Access database from which you want to export the data in a table. If you already have that database open, switch to the Database window.

2. Choose the Export command from the File menu. Access opens the Export dialog box. Select Btrieve from the Data Destination list, and click OK. See Figure 10-36.

3. Access opens the Select Microsoft Access Object dialog box, shown in Figure 10-37, from which you can select the table whose data you want to export. When you have selected the table you want, click OK.

4. Next Access opens the Export To File dialog box, from which you can select the drive and directory in which the dictionary file (a DDF file) is located. See Figure 10-45. When you have selected the file you want, click OK.

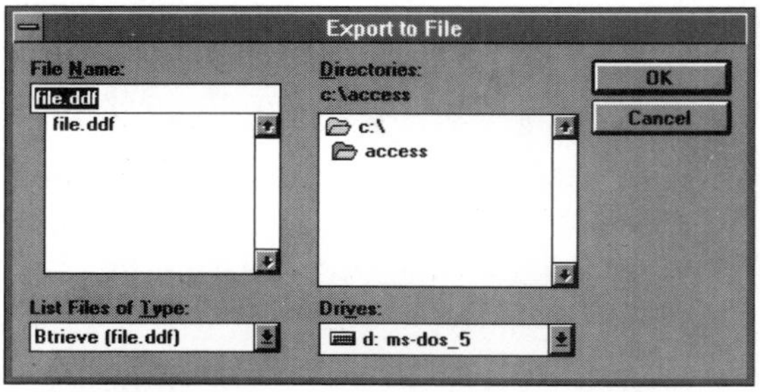

Figure 10-45.
The Export To File dialog box with a Btrieve dictionary file listed.

5. Access next prompts you for a name for the Btrieve table. Type the name and click OK to export the data in your table. See Figure 10-46.

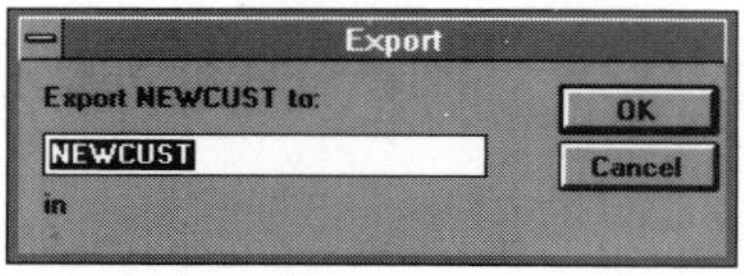

Figure 10-46.
The name of a table in the Btrieve dictionary, to which data will be exported.

6. If the export was successful, you'll find a new Btrieve table defined in the dictionary you selected.

Exporting to an SQL Table

You can export data from a Microsoft Access table to define a new table in any SQL database that supports the ODBC standard. To export data in an Access table to another database system that supports ODBC SQL, you must first have the ODBC driver for that database installed on your computer. For details, see Appendix D of the *Microsoft Access User's Guide*. Your computer must also be attached to the network that connects to the SQL server you want and you must have a Login or User ID and password on that server. Check with your system administrator for information about correctly connecting to the SQL server to which you want to export data.

To export data to an SQL table, do the following:

1. Open the Microsoft Access database from which you want to export your data. If you already have that database open, switch to the Database window.

2. Choose the Export command from the File menu. Access opens the Export dialog box. Select SQL Database in the Data Destination list and click OK. See Figure 10-36.

3. Access opens the Select Microsoft Access Object dialog box, as shown in Figure 10-40, from which you can select the table whose data you want to export. When you have selected the table you want, click OK.

4. Next Access asks you what name you want to give the new table on the server. The dialog box is similar to Figure 10-39. Type the name you want, and click OK.

5. Access opens a dialog box in which you can pick the name of the SQL server that will receive your data. This dialog box is similar to the one shown in Figure 10-12. Select the server name, and click OK.

6. Access displays a Login dialog box for the SQL data source that you selected. This dialog box is similar to the one shown in Figure 10-13. Enter your Login or User ID and your password and click OK to create a new table on the server containing your data.

Now you have all the information you need to import, attach, and export data using Microsoft Access. In the next part of this book, you'll learn the really interesting stuff—using forms. Forms are what make your data "come alive" in an Access application.

PART IV

USING FORMS

The next four chapters cover forms in Microsoft Access. First you'll learn about the uses and features of forms. Then you'll learn how to design and build forms that simplify the entry of data in your database.

Chapter 11 discusses the uses of forms and takes you on a tour of their major features.

Chapter 12 teaches you how to build a simple form from scratch and how to use a FormWizard to help you out. You'll also learn the basics of form creation by incorporating controls, such as command buttons, toggle buttons, check boxes, and combo boxes.

The next chapter, Chapter 13, shows you how to add custom touches to your forms. You'll learn about setting properties, adding calculated controls, and working with color and special effects.

Chapter 14, the last chapter in Part IV, explores advanced form design. There you'll learn about using queries with forms, linking subforms, adding OLE objects, and building form templates.

11

Form Basics

If you have worked through the book to this point, you should now understand all the mechanics of designing and building databases (and connecting to external ones), entering and viewing data in tables, and building queries. You need to understand tables and queries before you jump into forms because most forms you design will have an underlying table or dynaset.

This chapter focuses on the external aspects of forms—why forms are useful, what they look like, and how to use them. The tour will look at samples from the Northwind Traders database (NWIND) that is included with Microsoft Access. Later you'll learn how to design and build your own forms by working to create the database application for Prompt Computer Solutions.

USES OF FORMS

Forms are the primary interface between users and your Microsoft Access application. You can design forms for many different purposes:

- Displaying and editing data. This is the most common use of forms. Forms give you a way to customize the presentation of data in your database. You can also use forms to make it easier to change, add, or delete data in your database. You can set options in a form to make all or part of your data read-only, to fill in related information from other tables automatically, to calculate the values to be displayed, or to show or hide data based on either the value of other data in the record or the options chosen by the user of the form.

- Controlling application flow. You can design forms that work with macros to automate the display of certain data or the sequence of certain actions. You can create special controls on your form, called *command buttons,* that run a macro whenever the control is clicked. With macros, you can open other forms, run queries, restrict the data being displayed, execute a menu command, set values in records and on forms, display menus, print reports, and perform a host of other actions. You can also design a form so that macros are run when different events occur—for example, when someone opens the form, tabs to a specific control, clicks an option on the form, or changes data in the form. See Part VI of this book, "Creating an Application," for details on using macros with forms to automate your application.

■ Accepting input. You can design forms that are used only for entering new data into your database or for providing data values to help automate your application.

■ Displaying messages. Forms can provide information about how to use your application or about upcoming actions. Microsoft Access also gives you a MsgBox macro action that you can use to display information, warnings, or errors. See Chapter 18, "Adding Power with Macros," for details.

■ Printing information. Although you should design reports to print most information, you can also print information in forms. Because you can specify one set of options when Access displays a form and another set of options when Access prints a form, a form can serve a dual role. For example, you might set up a form with two sets of display headers and footers, one set for entering an order and another set for printing the customer invoice from the order.

THE TOOL BAR FOR THE FORM WINDOW IN FORM VIEW

It's useful to take a moment to look at the tool bar that Microsoft Access displays when you open a form. To open a form, first open the database you want, click the Form button in the Database window, select the form you want from the list, and click the Open button. Figure 11-1 shows the tool bar for the Form window in Form view.

Figure 11-1.
The tool bar for the Form window in Form view.

From left to right, the buttons are

  Design View button. Click this button to see the Form window in Design view.

  Form View button. This button appears pressed to indicate you are looking at a Form window in Form view.

  Datasheet View button. Click this button to see the Form window in Datasheet view, in which the data in the underlying table or query for the form is displayed.

 Print Preview button. You can print most forms and the data displayed in them. Click this button to see a preview of the printed page.

 Find button. Click this button to initiate a search for values in any field.

 Edit Filter/Sort button. You can restrict and sort the data you see in the form, much as you can specify selection criteria and sorting in a query. Click this button to create or edit a filter or sorting criteria.

 Apply Filter/Sort button. Click this button to apply any filter or sorting criteria you have created.

 Show All Records button. Click this button to remove any filter and display all records in an underlying table or query.

Undo button. Click this button to undo the last change you made to data in the table.

Help button. Click this button to access context-sensitive Help.

With one additional element on the tool bar, a drop-down list of fields, you can select a field name from the list to highlight the corresponding field in the current record. See Figure 11-2.

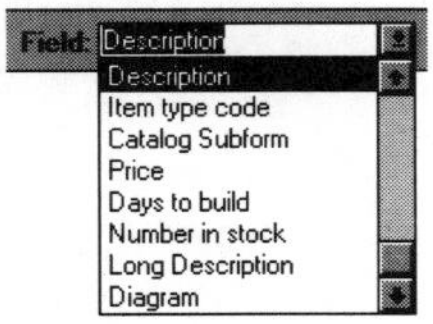

Figure 11-2.
The Field drop-down list box in the Form view tool bar.

A TOUR OF FORMS

The NWIND sample database included with the Microsoft Access software is full of interesting examples of forms. The rest of this chapter takes you on a tour of some of the major features of those forms. In the next chapter you will learn how to go about designing and building forms for the PROMPT database.

To start, open the NWIND database and click the Form button in the Database window to see the list of available forms.

Headers, Details, and Footers

You will normally place the information that you want to display from the underlying table or query in the detail section in the center of the Form window. You can add a header at the top or a footer at the bottom of the window to display information or controls that don't need to change with each different record.

An interesting form in NWIND that has both a header and a footer is Suppliers. Find the Suppliers form in the forms list in the Database window, select the form, and click the Open button to see a window similar to the one shown in Figure 11-3.

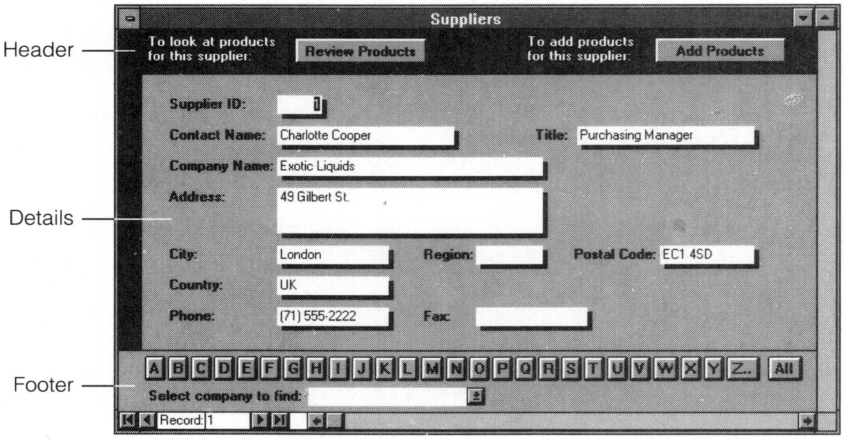

Figure 11-3.
The Suppliers form in NWIND, with a header, details, and a footer.

The black bar across the top of the window is the header for this form. Inside this header you can see some instructions and two command buttons that are used to activate other forms. At the bottom is a gray panel with command buttons for the letters of the alphabet. This panel is the footer for the form. At the bottom left corner of the form is the record number box that you saw in tables and queries in Datasheet view. Click the arrow button immediately to the right of the record number and you should see the next supplier record in the detail section of the form. Notice that the header and footer don't change.

If you click the B command button in the footer, you should see details of the first company whose name begins with the letter B. The way this form is designed, each letter command button actually applies a filter to show you only suppliers with a company name starting with the letter you select. Click the All button to make all the supplier records available again in the form.

Multiple-Page Forms

When you have a lot of information from each record to display in a form, you can design a *multiple-page form*. Open the Employees form in NWIND to see an example. When you open the form, you'll see the first page of the employee data for the first employee. You can use the record number box and buttons in the lower left corner to move through the records, viewing the first page of information for each employee. Figure 11-4 shows you the first page from the seventh employee record (Jonathan King). To see the second page of information for any employee, use the scroll bar at the right side of the form or press PgDn. See Figure 11-5. Notice that this form has a header, but no footer. As you view different forms, the black bar at the top of the form (with the employee's name) doesn't move. This name display on the header is actually a calculated field resulting from concatenating the First Name field and the Last Name field in the record.

Use scroll bar to see additional pages of this record

Use record number box to see other records

Figure 11-4.
The first page of a record in the multiple-page Employees form.

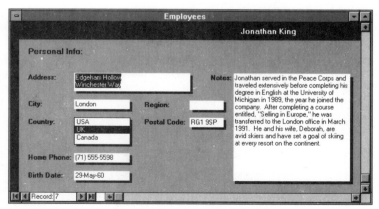

Figure 11-5.
The second page of a record.

231

Continuous Forms

You can create another type of form that is useful for browsing through a list of records when each record has just a few data fields. This form is a *continuous form*. Rather than showing you only a single record at a time, continuous forms display formatted records back-to-back, in the manner of a datasheet.

The Sales Totals form in NWIND is a continuous form. See Figure 11-6. You can use the vertical scroll bar to move through the record display, or you can click the record number box and buttons in the lower left corner to move from record to record. As you might guess, the records you see in this form are from a totals query that joins information from the Employees and Orders tables.

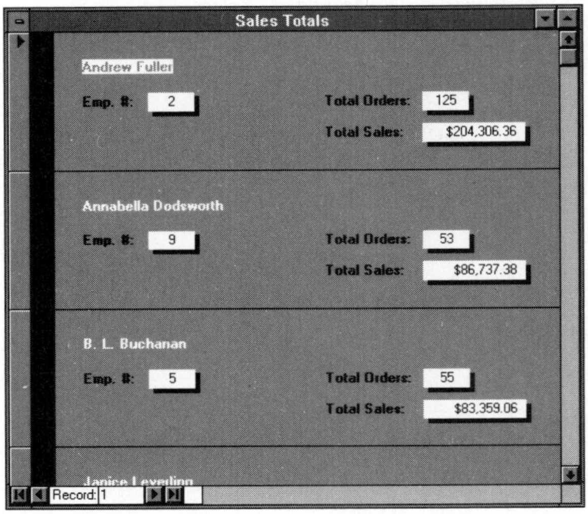

Figure 11-6.
The Sales Totals form is a continuous form.

Subforms

A good example of a *subform* is the Orders form of NWIND. See Figure 11-7. Although the Orders form looks much like a single display panel, the part of the window that looks more like a datasheet than a form is actually a subform embedded in the Orders form. The main part of the form displays information from a query that joins the Customers, Employees, and Orders tables. The information in the subform comes from a query on the Order Details and Products tables.

Although this form looks pretty complicated, it really isn't all that difficult to build. Because the NWIND database is well designed, it doesn't take much effort to build the two queries that extract information from five different tables. Most of the work of creating the form goes into selecting and placing the controls that display

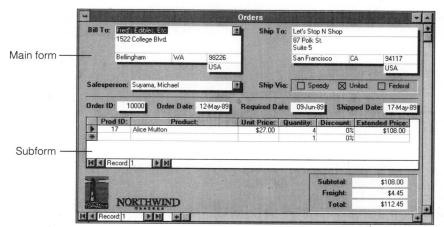

Figure 11-7.
The Orders form with products listed on an embedded subform.

the data. To link a subform with a main form, you have to set only two properties that tell Access which linking fields to use. In Chapter 14, "Advanced Form Design," you'll build and link a form with a subform.

Modal Forms

As you add functionality to your application, you'll find situations in which you need to get some data or convey some important information before Microsoft Access can proceed. Access provides you with a special type of form—a *modal form*—that requires a response before you can continue working in the application. A sample modal form is the Print Reports dialog box in the NWIND database, as shown in Figure 11-8. This dialog box normally opens when you choose the Print Reports

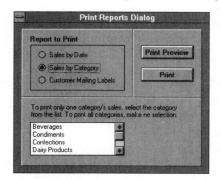

Figure 11-8.
The Print Reports dialog box is a modal form.

option on the NWIND Main Switchboard form, but you can also open the form on which the dialog box is based directly from the Database window. You'll notice that as long as this dialog box is open, you can't select any other window or menu that you can see on the screen. So in order to proceed, you must either select the type of report and click a button or close the Print Reports dialog box by double-clicking the Control-menu box in the upper left corner.

This form might not look exactly like the one shown in Figure 11-8 when you first open it. Click the Sales by Category option button to see the category list at the bottom of the form. As you might suspect, when you click one of the option buttons, a simple macro runs that makes the category list visible if you select Sales by Category. Chapter 19, "Designing the Prompt Computer Solutions Application," shows you how to build a similar form.

Special Controls

The information on a form is contained in *controls*. The most common control you'll use on a form is a simple text box. A text box can display data from an underlying table or query, or it can display data calculated on the form itself. You've probably noticed that there are lots of special controls, elements on the forms that allow you to choose between several values or to see additional content. You can also use special controls to trigger a macro. These special controls are discussed below.

Option Buttons, Check Boxes, Toggles, and Option Groups

Whenever the data you're displaying can have only two or three valid values, you can use special controls such as option buttons, check boxes, and toggles to see or set the value you want in the field. For example, when there are two values, as in the case of a simple Yes/No field, you can use a check box to graphically display the value in the field; a box that's checked means the value is "Yes," and a box that's unchecked means the value is "No."

To provide a graphical choice between more than two values, you can group any of these special controls. In a group, only one of the controls can be "Yes." For example, the Ship Via group shown in Figure 11-9 is from the Orders form in the NWIND database. This is an option group consisting of three check boxes. Because there are only three valid shipping methods in this application, the option group can show which shipping method is in effect for the current order. As you'll read in more detail later, Microsoft Access uses the relative numeric value of the control to determine the value in the underlying field.

Figure 11-9.
An option group.

In the Print Reports dialog box shown in Figure 11-8, an option group is used in a slightly different way. When you click one of the option buttons in this group, you're setting a value. You'll notice that when you click the Sales by Category option button, a list of categories appears in the lower part of the form. This list appears because a macro tests the value set by the option button and triggers the display of the category list whenever the value corresponds to the second button in the option group. Later, when you click either the Print or the Print Preview command button on the form, a macro again tests this value to determine which report to run for you.

List Boxes and Combo Boxes

The list of categories discussed above is another special control called a list box. See the detail shown in Figure 11-10. A list box can show a list of values you entered when you designed the control, a list of values from an SQL statement or field in a table or query, or a list of field names from a table or query. In the example shown in Figure 11-10, the list includes the set of names from the Category Name field of the Categories table.

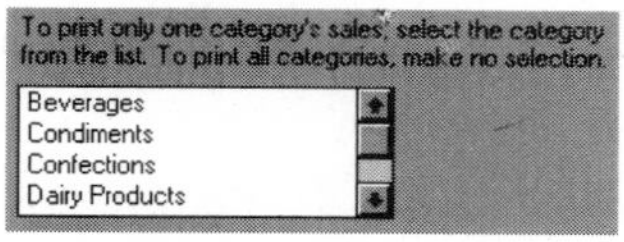

To print only one category's sales, select the category from the list. To print all categories, make no selection.

Beverages
Condiments
Confections
Dairy Products

Figure 11-10.
A list box.

When you select a category from the list, you set the value of the control. If the control represents a field in the underlying table or query, you update that field. In this example, the control is tested by the macro that runs the Sales by Category report to see if the report should be restricted to a category chosen by you from the list. A list box like this one can actually use data from more than one field. You can, for example, display the more meaningful name of the Category field in the list, but set a value of the related Category ID in the control when the name is selected.

Combo boxes are similar to list boxes. The major difference is that a combo box has a text box and a drop-down list. One advantage of the combo box is that it requires space for only one of the values in the underlying list. The Salesperson field on the Orders form in NWIND is set using a combo box. See Figure 11-11 on the next page. The combo box actually has two columns—the Employee Name and the Employee ID (which you can't see). When you select a name, the combo box sets the Employee ID in the underlying field in the record—a very useful feature.

OLE Objects

You've probably noticed pictures in several places in the NWIND forms. There's one on the Employees form. There's another on the Categories form. Both of these pictures are embedded in fields within database tables using the technology called *object*

Figure 11-11.
An open combo box.

linking and embedding or *OLE*. The logo in the lower left corner of the Orders form is a picture that Microsoft Access has stored as part of the form. See the section titled ''Working with Objects'' in Chapter 14.

The control you use to display pictures or any other OLE object is called an *object frame*. A bound object frame control is used to display OLE objects that are stored in fields in a table. An unbound object frame control is used to display an object that is not stored in a table. Again, see the section titled ''Working with Objects'' in Chapter 14.

When you include an object frame control on a form and bind the object frame control to an OLE object in the database, you can edit that object by selecting it and choosing the command at the bottom of the Edit menu that starts the object's application. See Figure 11-12. If the object is a picture, graph, or spreadsheet, you can see the object in the object frame control, and you can activate its application by double-clicking the object itself. If the object is a sound, you can hear it by double-clicking the object frame control.

Figure 11-12 shows you one of the pictures from the NWIND Category table that is bound in an object frame control in the Categories form. When you select the picture and choose the Edit command or double-click the picture, Microsoft Access starts the Paintbrush application in which the picture was created. Paintbrush starts with the picture file open and ready to edit, as shown in Figure 11-13. You can update the picture using any of the Paintbrush tools. You can paste in a different picture by copying a picture to the Clipboard and choosing the Paste From command from Paintbrush's Edit menu. Finally, when you're done with your changes, choose the Update command from the File menu in Paintbrush, and then choose the Exit And Return To Access command, also from Paintbrush's File menu.

Command Buttons

Although you can get a lot of work done by entering and reviewing data on individual forms, you can also link many forms together to create a complete database

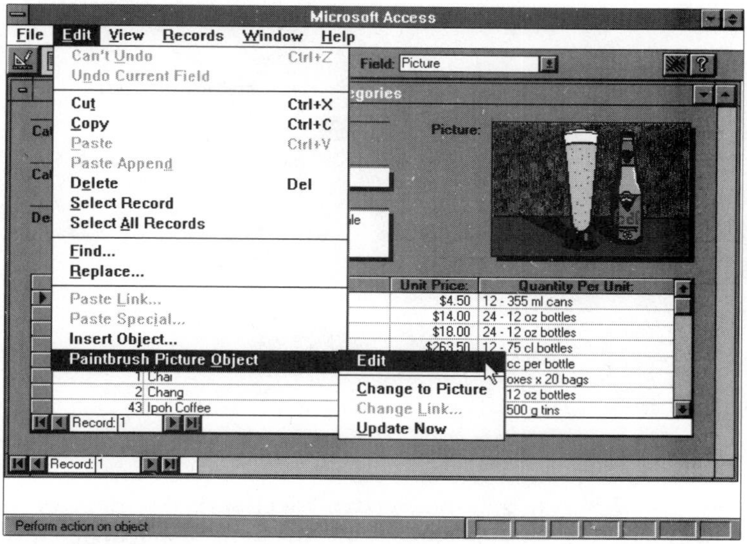

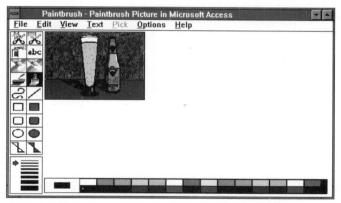

Figure 11-12.
An OLE object has been selected on a form, and the object can be edited by choosing the Edit command at the bottom of the Edit menu.

Figure 11-13.
The OLE object from Figure 11-12, in its original application and ready for editing.

application using command buttons. In the Northwind Traders sample database, for example, most of the sample forms are tied to the Main Switchboard form, as shown in Figure 11-14 on the next page, from which command buttons launch various functions in the application.

The advantage of command buttons is really quite simple; they offer an easy way to trigger a macro. The macro might do nothing more than open another form, print a report, or run an action query to update many records in your database. In

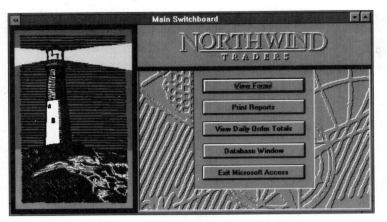

Figure 11-14.
The command buttons on the Main Switchboard form.

all, there are more than 40 different actions you can specify with a Microsoft Access macro. As you'll see by the time you get to the end of this book, you can easily build a fairly complex application using forms, reports, and macros.

MOVING AROUND IN FORMS AND WORKING WITH DATA

The rest of this chapter shows you how to move around and work with data on the various types of forms that were discussed in the first half of this chapter.

Viewing Data

If you've read through Chapter 7, "Using Datasheets," and have followed along in this chapter with the form examples, you already have a pretty good idea of how to view data and move around in forms. There are a few subtle differences between datasheets and forms that are usually determined by how the form was designed. You can use the Categories form in NWIND to explore how forms work.

To get to the Categories form, first open the NWIND sample database. Next click the Form button in the Database window. Select the Categories form from the list, and click the Open button to see the form shown in Figure 11-15.

Moving Around

The way you move around in a form depends in part on the form design. For example, the Categories form contains a subform. To move back and forth between the form and the subform you would use the Ctrl-Tab and Ctrl-Shift-Tab key combinations.

The subform itself is a datasheet, and you move around in it as you would move around in any datasheet. The window for this subform is wide enough to display all

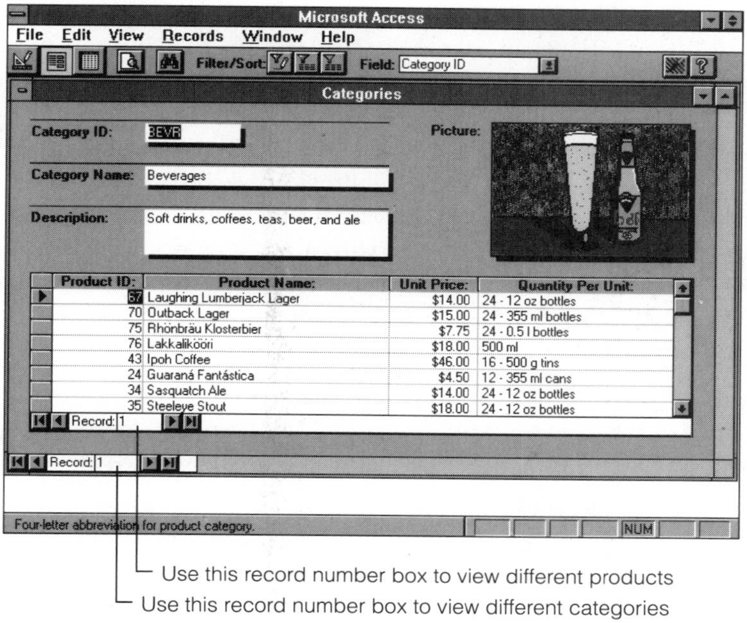

Use this record number box to view different products
Use this record number box to view different categories

Figure 11-15.
The Categories form.

of the fields in the datasheet, but if some columns couldn't be displayed, you would see a horizontal scroll bar at the bottom that you could use to move the display left or right. On this subform you can use the vertical scroll bar at the right to move the display up or down. The subform can be toggled between two different views—Datasheet view (its current state) and Form view. If you want to see the Form view of the subform, click in any of the fields in the subform datasheet (to ensure that the focus is on the subform), and then open the View menu. You'll notice that the Subform Datasheet command is checked. This command is a toggle. If you choose the Subform Datasheet command, the subform will change to look like the one shown in Figure 11-16. Choose the Subform Datasheet command (which is no longer checked) from the View menu again to restore the datasheet display.

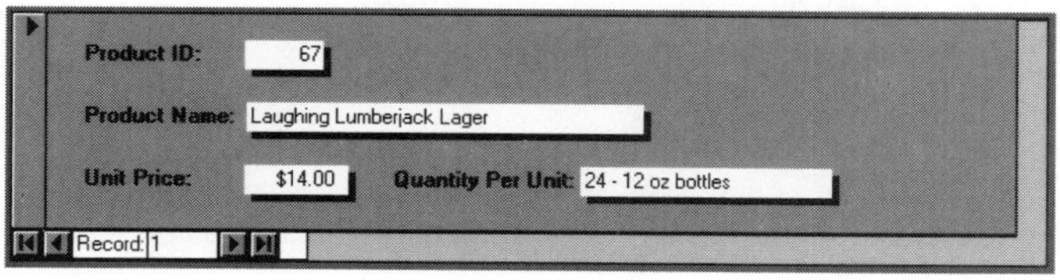

Figure 11-16.
The Categories subform in Form view.

In the Categories form you view different records by using one of two record number boxes. To change to the next category, use the main form's record number box; to see different products within a category, use the subform's record number box. See Figure 11-15.

Using your keyboard, you can also choose the Go To command from the Records menu to move to the First, Last, Next, or Previous records in the main form or subform. To select a different field you can choose a field from the Field drop-down list on the tool bar. (See Figure 11-2.) You can also select any field you can see on the form by clicking anywhere in that field. To use the Go To command or Field drop-down list you must first move to the form or subform, depending on which set of records you want to traverse.

Keyboard Shortcuts

If you are typing in new data, you might find it easier to use the keyboard rather than your mouse to move around on the form. Some of the keyboard shortcuts are listed in Figures 11-17 and 11-18.

Keys	Movement in Fields and Records
Tab	Moves to the next field
Shift-Tab	Moves to the previous field
Home	Moves to the first field of the current record
End	Moves to the last field of the current record
Up Arrow	Moves to the current field of the previous record
Down Arrow	Moves to the current field of the next record
Ctrl-Up Arrow	Moves to the current field of the first record
Ctrl-Down Arrow	Moves to the current field of the last record
Ctrl-Home	Moves to the first field of the first record
Ctrl-End	Moves to the last field of the last record
Ctrl-Tab	If on a subform, moves to the next field on the main form. If the subform is the last field in tab sequence on the main form, moves to the first field on the next main record.
Ctrl-Shift-Tab	If on a subform, moves to the previous field on the main form. If the subform is the first field in tab sequence on the main form, moves to the last field on the previous main record.
Ctrl-Shift-Home	Moves to the first field on the main form
F5	Moves to record selection box

Figure 11-17.
The keyboard shortcuts for moving in fields and records.

Keys	Action in a List or Combo Box
F4 or Alt-Down Arrow	Opens a drop-down list
Down Arrow	Moves down one line
Up Arrow	Moves up one line
Page Down	Moves down to next group of lines
Page Up	Moves up to next group of lines
Tab	Exits the box

Figure 11-18.
The keyboard shortcuts for actions in a list box or combo box.

Adding Records and Changing Data

You will probably design most forms so that you can insert new records, change field values, or delete records in Form view or Datasheet view. The following sections explain procedures for adding new records and changing data.

Adding a New Record

The procedure for entering a new record varies depending on the design of the form. With a form that's been designed for data entry only, you open the form and type data into the (usually empty) data fields. Sometimes forms of this type open with default values in the fields or with data that's been entered by a macro. Another type of form displays data and allows you to add new records as well. Choose the Data Entry command from the Records menu to shift the form into data-entry mode. See Figure 11-19 on the next page. When you have finished entering new records, you can choose the Show All Records command from the Records menu to return to normal data display.

There's also a "blank" row at the end of the normal data display that you can use to enter new rows. You can jump to the blank row to begin adding a new record by choosing the Go To command from the Records menu and then clicking New on the submenu, or by pressing Ctrl-+. Microsoft Access places the cursor in the first position of the first field when you start a new record. As soon as you begin typing, Access changes the indicator on the record selector (if your form shows the record selector) to the pencil icon to indicate that updates are in progress. Press Tab to move to the next field.

If you violate a field's validation rule, Access notifies you as soon as you attempt to leave the field. You must provide a correct value before you can move to another field. Press Shift-Enter at any point in the record or press Tab in the last field in the record to save your new record to the database. If you want to cancel the new record, press Esc twice.

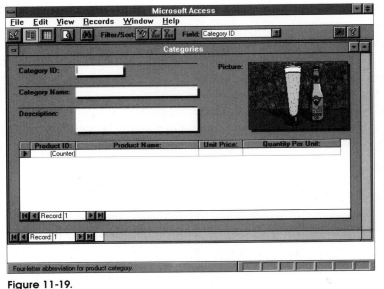

Figure 11-19.
The Categories form in data-entry mode.

If you are adding a new record to a form such as Categories, you'll encounter a special case. You'll notice when you tab to the picture that you can't type anything in it. This is because the field in the underlying table is an OLE object. To enter data in this type of field in a new record, you must create the object in an application that supports OLE before you can store the data in Access. To do this, select the Picture field and choose the Insert Object command from the Edit menu. Access displays the dialog box shown in Figure 11-20. Select the object type you want (in this case, Paintbrush Picture), and click OK. Access starts the Paintbrush application for you with a link established to the graphic so that whatever you design in Paintbrush can be embedded in the field in the table.

Try adding a new record to the Categories form. Open the form, choose the Go To command from the Records menu, and click New on the submenu. You should see a screen similar to the one shown in Figure 11-19. You can start adding a new category for paper products with a category ID of PAPR. Follow the procedure discussed above to create a new picture.

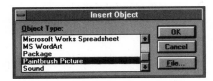

Figure 11-20.
The Insert Object dialog box.

To begin adding products in the Paper Products category, tab into the subform datasheet. Because the Product ID is a Counter (and the table's Primary Key), Microsoft Access will create a new key value using the next available number in the Products table. Enter a product name, a unit price, and a quantity per unit. See Figure 11-21. When you tab out of the last field or press Shift-Enter, Access adds the new product for you and assigns a Product ID. Access also automatically inserts the linking information required between the record in the main form and the new record in the subform. Here, Access adds a Category ID of PAPR to the new record in the Products table.

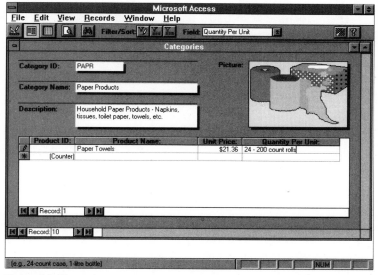

Figure 11-21.
The addition of new products in the new PAPR category of the Categories form.

Changing and Deleting Data

If your form permits updates, you can easily change or delete existing data in the underlying table or query. If the form is designed to be used in Datasheet view, you can use the same techniques you learned in Chapter 7 to work with your data.

In Form view, your data might appear in one of several formats. If the form is designed to be used in single form view, you can see the data from only one record at a time in the form. If the form is designed as a continuous form, you might be able to see data from more than one record at a time.

As with datasheets, you must select a field on the form in order to change the data in the field. To select a field on the form, either tab to the field or click in the field with the mouse. Once you have selected a field, you can change the data in it using the same techniques for working with data in a datasheet. You can type over individual characters, replace a sequence of characters, or copy and paste data from one field to another.

You might find that you can't tab into or select some fields on a form. When you design a form, you can set the properties of controls on the form so that a user can't select the field. These properties prevent users from changing fields you don't want updated, such as calculated values or fields from the "one" side of a query. You can also set the tab order to control the sequence of field selection when you use Tab or Shift-Tab to move around the form. See the following two chapters for details.

Deleting a record in single form view or continuous form view is different from deleting a record in a datasheet. First you must select the record as you would select a record in a datasheet. If the form is designed with record selectors, simply click the record selector to select the row. If the form does not have a record selector, choose the Select Record command from the Edit menu. To delete a selected record, press the Del key or choose the Delete command from the Edit menu.

Performing a Simple Search

You can use Access's Find capability in a form just as you would in a datasheet. First select the field. Then choose the Find command from the Edit menu or click the Find button on the tool bar to open the Find dialog box you saw in Chapter 7, Figure 7-24. You can enter search criteria exactly as you would for a datasheet. Note that on a form you can also perform a search on any control that you can select, including controls that are calculated.

Adding a Filter to a Form

One of Access's most powerful features in a form is its ability to further restrict or sort the information displayed in the form without your having to create a new query. This restriction is accomplished with a filter that you define while you are using the form. When you apply the filter, you will see only the data that matches the criteria you enter. You can apply a filter only to the records in a main form, not to the records in any subform.

To begin defining a new filter, click the Edit Filter/Sort button on the tool bar or choose the Edit Filter/Sort command from the Records menu. Open the Categories form and click the Edit Filter/Sort button now. Microsoft Access opens a Filter window as shown in Figure 11-22.

The Filter window looks similar to a Query window. In the top part of the window is the Categories field list for the table or query that provides data for the form. You can use the field list to select field names to place on the QBE grid. You can enter selection criteria exactly as you would for a query. You can also sort selected fields in ascending or descending alphabetic order. In the example in Figure 11-22, the category names are being restricted to those that begin with the letter S.

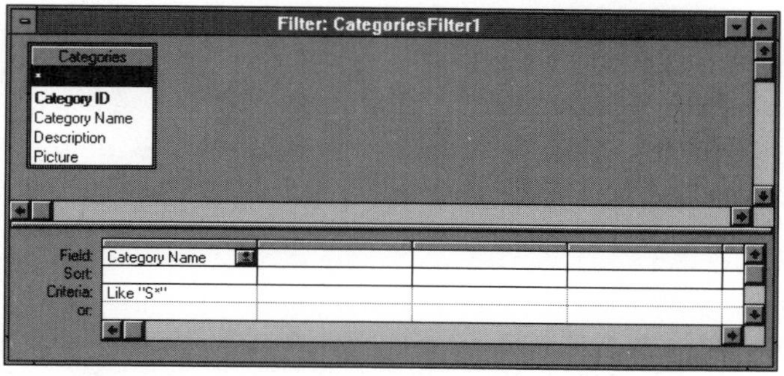

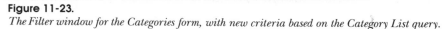

Figure 11-22.
The Filter window for the Categories form.

When you have finished defining your filter, close the Filter window. To apply your filter, click the Apply Filter/Sort button on the tool bar or choose the Apply Filter/Sort command from the Records menu. To turn off the filter, click the Show All Records button on the tool bar or choose the Show All Records command from the Records menu.

If you find you are often using the same filter with your form, you can save the filter as a query and give it a name. Open the Filter window and create the filter. Choose the Save As Query command from the File menu and type in a name for the query when prompted by Access. You can also load an existing query definition to use as a filter. Open the Filter window and choose the Load From Query command from the File menu. Access presents you with a list of valid select queries (those that are based on the same table or tables as the form you are using). In this case, there's a Category List query that sorts the category records in ascending order by Category Name rather than Category ID as in the form. If you select Category List from the list of valid select queries, the query will replace the existing field and criteria in the Filter window with the information shown in Figure 11-23.

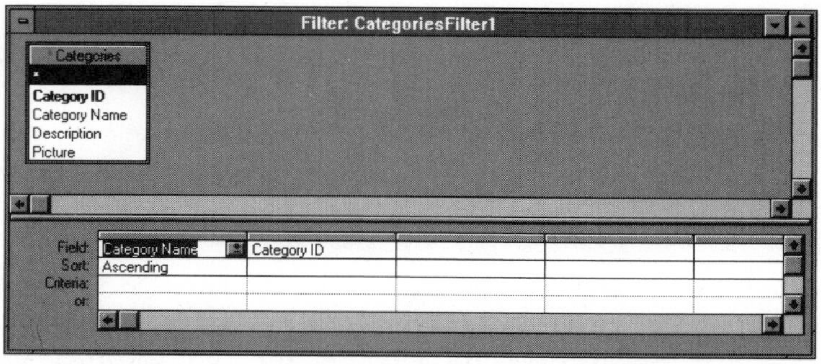

Figure 11-23.
The Filter window for the Categories form, with new criteria based on the Category List query.

Printing from a Form

You can use a form to print information from your table. When you design the form, you can specify different header and footer information for the printed version. You can also specify which controls are visible. For example, you might define some grid lines that are visible on the printed form but not on the screen.

An interesting form to print in NWIND is the Suppliers form. Open the form and then click the Print Preview button on the tool bar, or choose the Print Preview command from the File menu. You probably won't be able to read any of the data unless you have a large screen. Click the Zoom button and scroll to the top of the first page. You should see a screen that looks like the one shown in Figure 11-24. Notice that the form headers and footers that you saw in Figure 11-3 do not appear in the printed version.

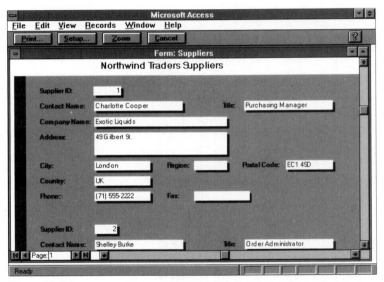

Figure 11-24.
The Suppliers Form window "zoomed" in Print Preview.

You can use the scroll bars to move around on the page. Use the page number box in the lower left corner of the form in the same way you'd use the record number box on a form or datasheet. Click the Zoom button again to see the entire page on the screen.

Click the Setup button to customize the way the form prints. The Print Setup dialog box is shown in Figure 11-25. At the top of the dialog box you can pick the printer you want to use. Click the Options button to open the Options dialog box for the printer you have chosen. See Chapter 7, "Using Datasheets," for details on choosing printer options.

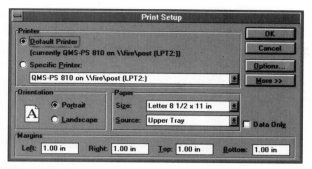

Figure 11-25.
The Print Setup dialog box for forms.

Just below the Printer selection box, you can set options to print in Portrait mode (vertically) or Landscape mode (horizontally). In the box to the right, you can specify the size of paper you have loaded in your printer and the location of the paper tray (if your printer supports multiple trays). Finally, to the right of that area is a useful check box you can use to ask Microsoft Access to print only the data on the form and not any of the labels or other controls.

Click the More button to see additional options, as shown in Figure 11-26. When you click the More button, Access opens the margin and layout option sections at the bottom of the dialog box. If the data on your form displays in a fairly narrow width, you can ask Access to stack the data from the form either horizontally or vertically across the page. If you enter the settings shown in Figure 11-26 for the Suppliers form, you'll see the supplier data printed horizontally across the paper, three suppliers to a row and two rows on each page.

Figure 11-26.
The Print Setup dialog box expands when you click the More button.

You should now have a good understanding of how forms work and of many of the design elements you can include when you build forms. Now on to the fun part—building your first form in Chapter 12.

12

Building a Form

From the perspective of daily use, forms are the most important objects you'll build in your Microsoft Access application; forms are what users see and work with every time they run your application. This chapter shows you how to design and build forms in Access. You'll learn how to work with the Forms window in Design view to build basic forms from a single table. You'll also learn how to use a FormWizard to simplify the form creation process. The last section of this chapter shows you how to use some of the special forms controls to simplify data entry in your forms.

FORMS AND OBJECT-ORIENTED PROGRAMMING

Microsoft Access was not designed as a full object-oriented programming facility, but it does have many characteristics found in object-oriented application development systems. Before you dive into building forms, it's useful to examine how Access implements objects and actions, particularly if you come from the world of procedural application development.

In classic procedural application development, the data that you need for the application is clearly distinct from the programs you write to work on the data and from the results produced by your programs. Each program works independently on the data and generally has little structural connection with other programs in the system. An order-entry program might accept input from a clerk and write the order out to the application files. Later a billing program is run to collect the orders and print invoices. Another characteristic of procedural systems is that events must occur in a specific order and cannot be executed out of sequence. A procedural system has difficulty looking up supplier or price information while in the middle of processing an order.

In contrast, all objects in an object-oriented system are defined in terms of a subject and an action on that subject. Objects can contain other objects as subjects. When an object defines a new action on another object, it inherits the attributes and properties of the other object and expands on the object's definition. Microsoft Access queries define actions on tables, and the queries then become new logical tables (or dynasets). You can define a query on another query with the same effect. Forms further define actions on tables or queries, and the fields you include in forms initially inherit the underlying properties, such as formatting and validation rules, of the fields in the source tables or queries.

Within a Microsoft Access database, you can interrelate application objects and data. For example, you can set an initial macro (more about that in Chapter 18, "Adding Power with Macros") that prepares your application to run. That macro (called AUTOEXEC) will usually open a starting form in your application. Your starting form might act on some of the data in your database or might offer controls that open other forms, print reports, or close the application.

Figure 12-1 shows you the conceptual architecture of a Microsoft Access application. In addition to operating on tables or queries in your database, forms can contain other forms. These subforms can, in turn, define actions on other tables, queries, or forms and can trigger additional macro actions. As you'll learn when you read about advanced form design and create an application, macro actions can be triggered in many different ways. The most obvious way to trigger a macro action is by clicking a command button on a form. But you can also define a macro action so that it executes when an event occurs, such as someone clicking on a field, changing the data in a field, adding or deleting a row, or simply moving to a new row in the underlying table or query.

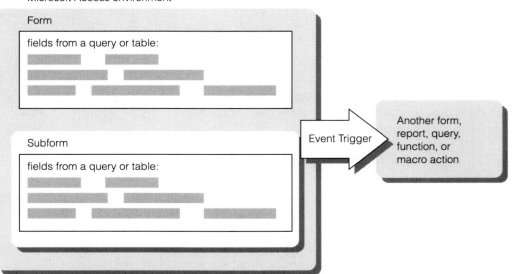

Figure 12-1.
The relationship of objects in Microsoft Access.

In the last chapter in this book, you'll build a sophisticated form to enter and review orders for Prompt Computer Solutions. You'll also define many macro actions on the form that are triggered by events. Figure 12-2 shows you just a few of those actions and events. For example, there's a command button to print the invoice for the order currently shown on the form. When the invoice prints, another action sets an indicator in the order to show that you've printed the invoice for this order. Whenever you add, change, or delete an order item, macro actions are triggered that automatically recalculate the sales tax and total amount of the order. Even a small detail like changing the state the customer lives in triggers a macro action to determine a new sales tax percentage and calculate a new order total amount.

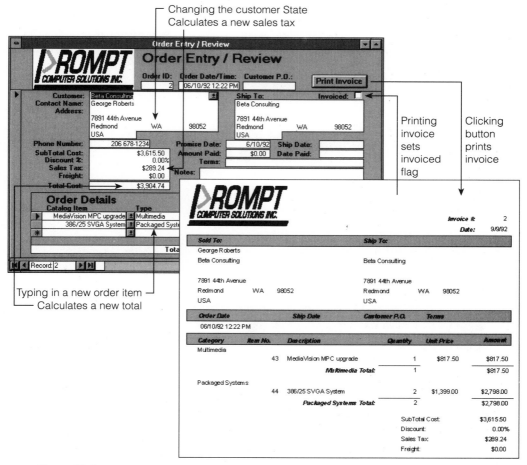

Figure 12-2.
The Microsoft Access environment in action.

Object-oriented systems are not particularly sensitive to a required sequence of events. So an operator entering an order in Access can minimize the order-entry form and start a search in a products table for pricing information or start a search in a customer table for a customer's credit history without ending the order. You might provide a simpler way for the operator to do this in your application by means of a command button or other selection on the order-entry form.

THE TOOL BAR FOR THE FORM WINDOW IN DESIGN VIEW

Microsoft Access provides you with a custom tool bar to use as you design forms. Figure 12-3 shows you the tool bar for the Form window in Design view.

Figure 12-3.
The tool bar for the Form window in Design view.

From left to right, the buttons are

 Design View button. This button appears pressed to indicate you are in Design view.

 Form View button. Click this button to see the Form view. While you are building a form you can click here to see what your changes will look like after you save the form.

 Datasheet View button. Click this button to see a datasheet containing the data in the underlying table or query for the form.

 Print Preview button. You can print most forms and the data displayed in them. Click this button to see a preview of the printed page.

 Properties button. Click this button to show or hide the property sheet. You can define properties for the form as a whole, for each section in the form, and for any control on the form.

 Field List button. Click this button to show or hide the list of fields available in the underlying table or query. You can drag and drop fields from the list into your form design.

 Palette button. Click this button to show or hide the palette. Use the palette to set the appearance and color of the form and controls.

 Font box. When you select a control that contains text or data, you can use this box to select a font that will be used in the control.

Font Size box. When you select a control that contains text or data, you can use this box to select a font size that will be used in the control.

(continued)

252

Bold button. Click this button to make the text in the selected control bold. Click the button again to make the text normal.

 Italic button. Click this button to make the text in the selected control italic. Click the button again to make the text normal.

 Underline button. Click this button to underline the text in the selected control. Click the button again to make the text normal.

 Align-Left button. Click this button to align the text in the selected control flush left.

 Center button. Click this button to center the text in the selected control.

 Align-Right button. Click this button to align the text in the selected control flush right.

 General Alignment button (the default). Click this button to display text left aligned and numbers and dates right aligned in the selected control.

Undo button. Click this button to undo the last change you made to the design.

Help button. Click this button to open context-sensitive Help.

STARTING FROM SCRATCH—A SIMPLE INPUT FORM

To start, you'll learn how to create a simple form that enters and displays data in the Supplier table in the PROMPT database. (If you haven't built PROMPT using Appendix B or copied it from CompuServe as explained in the Introduction, you can build a similar form from the Suppliers table in NWIND.) Later you'll learn how to create a form using a powerful FormWizard.

Starting to Design a New Form

To begin building a new form, open your database and select in the Database window the table or query that you want to use in the form. Click the New Form button on the tool bar, and Microsoft Access opens up the New Form dialog box shown in Figure 12-4 on the next page.

Notice that Microsoft Access shows you the name of the table or query that you selected in the Database window in the combo box at the top of the New Form dialog box. If you want to select a different table or query, you can open the combo box to see a list of all the tables and queries in your database. So that you understand all of the components that go into designing a form, you'll build this first form without the aid of a FormWizard. Click the Blank Form button to open up a new Form window in Design view.

Figure 12-4.
The New Form dialog box.

Working with Design Tools

When you start building a new form, Microsoft Access opens the Form window in Design view and with it several design tools, as shown in Figure 12-5. In the sample screen shown here, the Form window is in the background, the toolbox is in the lower left corner, the field list is at the upper center, and the property sheet for the form is in the lower right. If you've experimented with forms in Design view before and moved some of the overlay windows around, Access opens them where you last left them on the screen.

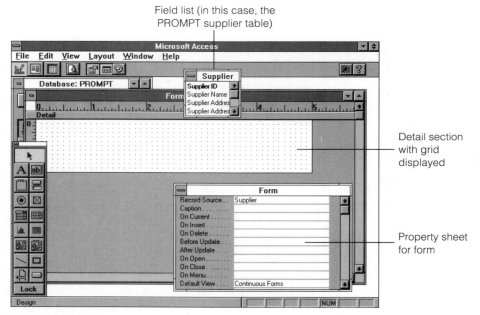

Figure 12-5.
The Form window in Design view.

Microsoft Access starts with a form that has only a white detail section. You can grab the edge of the detail section with your mouse pointer and drag the edge to make the detail section larger or smaller. You can fill the detail section with a grid of dots by choosing the Grid command from the View menu. If you want to add headers and footers, choose the Form Hdr/Ftr command from the Layout menu.

The detail section starts out at 5 inches wide by 1 inch high. The "inch" gradations that you can see on the rulers are relative to the size and resolution of your screen. On a standard VGA 640 × 480 screen, the full screen is approximately 6.5 inches wide by 5 inches high. By default, Access sets the grid at 10 dots per inch horizontally and 12 dots per inch vertically. You can change the density of the grid dots by altering the Grid X and Grid Y settings in the form's property sheet.

The number you enter in Grid X and Grid Y tells Microsoft Access how many intervals per measure of unit you want in the design grid. You can provide a number from 1 (coarsest) through 64 (finest). You set the unit of measure you want using the Measurement field in the International category of Windows' Control Panel. Your unit of measure is inches if the Measurement setting is English, and centimeters if the Measurement setting is Metric.

For example, if your unit of measurement is inches and you specify a Grid X of 10, Access divides the grid horizontally into .10-inch increments. When your measurement is in inches and you set the Grid X and Grid Y values at 16 or less, Access shows you the grid intersection points as dots on the design grid. In centimeters, you can see the grid dots when you choose a setting of 6 or less. If you set a finer grid, Access won't show you the intersection dots, but you can still use the grid to line up controls.

The sections that follow in this chapter describe some of the tools that you can use to design a form.

The Toolbox

The toolbox is the "command center" of form design. See Figure 12-6 on the next page. If you don't see the toolbox in the form's Design view, choose the Toolbox command from the View menu. You can move the toolbox around on your screen by dragging its top bar. You can close the toolbox by double-clicking the control menu box in the upper left corner of the toolbox or by choosing the Toolbox command again from the View menu.

The toolbox contains buttons for all the controls you can use to design your form. When you want to place a particular control on your form, click the control in the toolbox. When you move the mouse pointer over the form your mouse pointer turns into an icon that represents the tool you've chosen. Position the mouse pointer where you want the control and click the left mouse button to put the selected control on your form. If you want to bind a field in the underlying table or query to the control you have selected, find the field in the field list, and then drag the field to the form.

Figure 12-6.
The toolbox.

Left to right, top to bottom, the tools in the toolbox are

 Pointer tool. This is the default tool. Use this tool to select, size, move, and edit controls.

Label tool. Use this tool to create label controls that contain fixed text information on your form. By default, most controls have a label control attached to them. You can use this tool to create stand-alone labels for headings and instructions on your form.

 Text box tool. Use this tool to create text box controls for displaying text, numbers, dates, times, and memo fields on your form. You can bind a text box to one of the fields in the underlying table or query. If you allow a text box that is bound to a field to be updated, you can change the value (in the field in the underlying table or query) by entering a new value in the text box. You can also use a text box to calculate values using expressions.

 Option group tool. Use this tool to create option group controls that contain one or more toggle buttons, option buttons, or check boxes. (See below.) You can assign a separate numeric value to each button or box you include in the group. When you have more than one button or box in a group, you can select only one button or box at a time, and the value assigned to that selected button or box becomes the value for the option group. You can pick one of the buttons or boxes in the group as the default value for the group. If you bind the option group to a field in the underlying query or table, you can set a new value in the field by selecting a button or box in the group.

 Toggle button tool. Use this tool to create a toggle button control that holds an On/Off, True/False, or Yes/No value. When you click a toggle button, its value becomes −1 (to represent *on, true,* or *yes*), and the button appears pressed. Click the button again and its value becomes 0 (to represent *off, false,* or *no*). You can include a toggle button in an option group and assign to the button a unique numeric value. If you create a group with multiple toggle buttons, any previously clicked toggle button, option button, or check box will turn *off* when you click a new toggle button *on*.

(continued)

256

Option button tool. Use this tool to create an option button control (also sometimes called a radio button control) that holds an On/Off, True/False, or Yes/No value. When you click an option button, its value becomes −1 (to represent *on, true,* or *yes*) and a filled circle appears in the center of the button. Click the button again and its value becomes 0 (to represent *off, false,* or *no*). You can include an option button in an option group and assign to the button a unique numeric value. If you create a group with multiple option buttons, any previously clicked toggle button, option button, or check box turns *off* when you click a new option button *on.*

Check box tool. Use this tool to create a check box control that holds an On/Off, True/False, or Yes/No value. When you click a check box, its value becomes −1 (to represent *on, true,* or *yes*) and an *X* appears in the box. Click the check box again and its value becomes 0 (to represent *off, false,* or *no*) and the *X* disappears from the box. You can include a check box in an option group and assign to the check box a unique numeric value. If you create a group with multiple check boxes, any previously clicked toggle button, option button, or check box turns *off* when you click a new check box *on.*

Combo box tool. Use this tool to create a combo box control that contains a list of potential values for the control and an editable text box. To create the list, you can enter the values in the Row Source property of the combo box. You can also specify a table or a query as the source of the values in the list. Microsoft Access displays the currently selected value in the text box. When you click the down arrow at the right end of the box, Access shows you the values in the list. Choose a new value in the list to reset the value in the control. If the control is bound to a field, you can change the value in the field by choosing a new value in the list.

List box tool. Use this tool to create a list box control that contains a list of potential values for the control. To create the list, you can enter the values in the Row Source property of the list box. You can also specify a table or a query as the source of the values in the list. List boxes are always open, and Microsoft Access highlights the currently selected value in the list box. Select a new value in the list to reset the value in the control. If the control is bound to a field, you can change the value in the field by choosing a new value in the list.

Graph tool. Use this tool to add a Microsoft Graph object to your form. You can link the graph to a table or to a query, or you can import data to the graph from another source. Placing this tool on a form activates a Graph-Wizard to assist you in designing the graph. See Chapter 14, "Advanced Form Design," for details.

Subform tool. Use this tool to embed another form in the current form. You can use the subform to show data from a table or query related to the data on the outer form. Microsoft Access maintains the link between the two forms for you. See Chapter 14 for details.

(continued)

Unbound object frame tool. Use this tool to add an object from another application that supports object linking and embedding (OLE) to your form. The object becomes part of your form, not part of the data from the underlying table or query. You can add pictures, sounds, graphs, or slides to enhance your form. See Chapter 14 for details.

 Bound object frame tool. Use this tool to make available on your form an OLE object from your underlying data. Microsoft Access can display most pictures and graphs directly on your form. For other objects, Access displays the icon of the linking application. For example, if the object is a sound object created in Sound Recorder, you'll see a microphone icon on your form. See Chapter 14 for details.

 Line tool. Use this tool to add lines to your form to enhance its appearance. See the next chapter for details.

 Rectangle tool. Use this tool to add filled or empty rectangles to your form to enhance your form's appearance. See the next chapter for details.

Page break tool. Use this tool to add a page break between multiple pages on your form.

Command button tool. Use this tool to create a command button control that can activate a macro or an Access Basic function. See "Linking Forms with Command Buttons" in Chapter 14 for details.

Tool lock. Click this button to keep the currently selected tool active after placing a control on the form. When the tool lock is off, the currently selected tool is deselected after placing a control on the form. The Tool Lock button is useful if you plan to create several controls with the same tool—for example, a series of check boxes in an option group.

The Field List

Use the field list in conjunction with the toolbox to place bound controls (controls linked to fields in a table or query) on your form. You can open the field list by clicking the Field List button on the tool bar or by choosing the Field List command from the View menu. Microsoft Access shows you the name of the underlying table or query in the window title bar, as shown in Figure 12-7. You can drag the edges of the window to resize the field list so that you can see any long field names. You can also drag the title bar to move the field list out of the way. Use the scroll bar on the right to move through the list of available names.

Figure 12-7.
A field list.

To use the field list to place a control for a field on your form, first choose the tool you want. (The default tool is for a text box control.) Then drag the field you want and drop it into position on the form. If you choose a control that's inappropriate for the data type, Microsoft Access selects the default control for the data type. For example, if you choose anything but a bound object frame control for an OLE Object, Access creates a bound object frame for you anyway. If you try to drag and drop a field using the graph, subform, unbound object frame, line, rectangle, or page break tools, Access creates a text box or bound object frame control instead.

The Property Sheet

The form, each section on the form (header, detail, footer), and every control on the form has a list of properties associated with it, and these properties are set on the property sheet. The kinds of properties you can specify vary depending on the object. To open the property sheet, click the Properties button on the tool bar or choose the Properties command from the View menu. A window will open that is similar to the window shown in Figure 12-8.

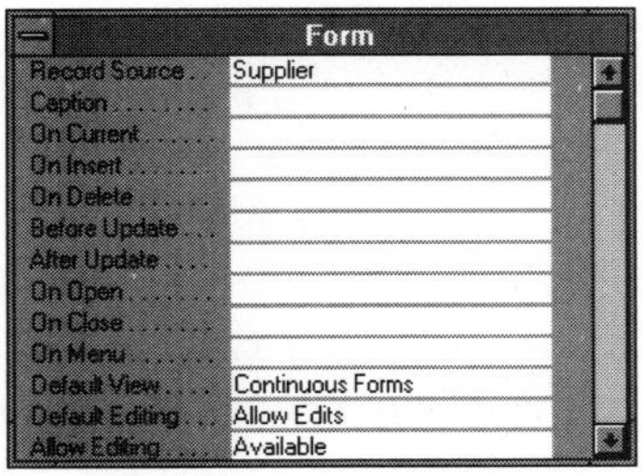

Figure 12-8.
A property sheet for a form.

You can drag the title bar of the property sheet to move the window around on your screen. You can also drag the edges of the window to resize the property sheet so that you can see more of the longer property settings. When you select a property that has a list of valid values, a down arrow button appears to the right of the field. This button opens a drop-down list of the values. For properties that can have a very long value setting, you can use Shift-F2 to open a *Zoom box*. The Zoom box provides an expanded text box for entering or viewing an entry.

The Palette

The palette provides a quick and easy way to alter the appearance and color of a control by allowing you to click options rather than set properties. The palette is also handy for setting background colors for sections of the form. To open the palette shown in Figure 12-9, click the Palette button on the tool bar or choose the Palette command from the View menu.

Figure 12-9.
The palette.

Depending on the object you select, some of the palette options might not be available. For example, you can't set text color on a bound object frame control. Nor can you set fill or border colors on a toggle button, because these areas are always set to raised gray on a toggle button. If you have the property sheet open at the same time as the palette, and the property sheet is scrolled so that you can see the properties that the palette sets, you can watch the settings in the property sheet change as you click different options in the palette.

Building a Simple Input Form for the Supplier Table

Here's where you actually create a simple input form for the Supplier table in PROMPT (or for the Suppliers table in NWIND). If you haven't done so already, go to the Database window, open the tables list, select the Supplier table, and click the New Form button on the tool bar. Choose the Blank Form option in the New Form dialog box. You'll see the Form window in Design view and a set of design tools, as shown in Figure 12-5. If necessary, open the toolbox, field list, and property sheet by clicking the appropriate buttons on the tool bar. In the blank form for Supplier, drag the bottom of the detail section down to give yourself some room to work.

Because you'll be using default text boxes, you don't need to pick a tool from the toolbox. If you'd like to practice, though, click the text box tool and then the Lock Tool button in the toolbox before dragging fields from the field list. In this way you can drag fields one at a time to the details section of the form.

An even quicker way to place several successive fields on the form is to highlight the first field you want, scroll down until you can see the last field you want, and then hold down the Shift key while you click the last field. This procedure selects all the fields in between the first and last field you selected. You can now click any of the highlighted fields and drag them as a group to the details section of the form.

Follow this procedure to drag the Supplier ID through the Supplier Fax fields from the field list to the detail section. Your result should look something like Figure 12-10.

When you position the field icon that you're dragging from the field list, you should be aware that the point where you release your mouse button is the upper left corner of the new text box in the detail section of the form. For default text boxes, Microsoft Access attaches a label using the field's caption value (or field name if you didn't specify a caption value when you designed the field) 1 inch to the left of the text box. (The position of the attached label depends on the Windows display mode. In VGA mode, attached labels appear about 1 inch to the left of the text box.) So, you should leave room to the left of the icon for Access to place the control labels. If you don't leave room, the labels will overlap the text boxes.

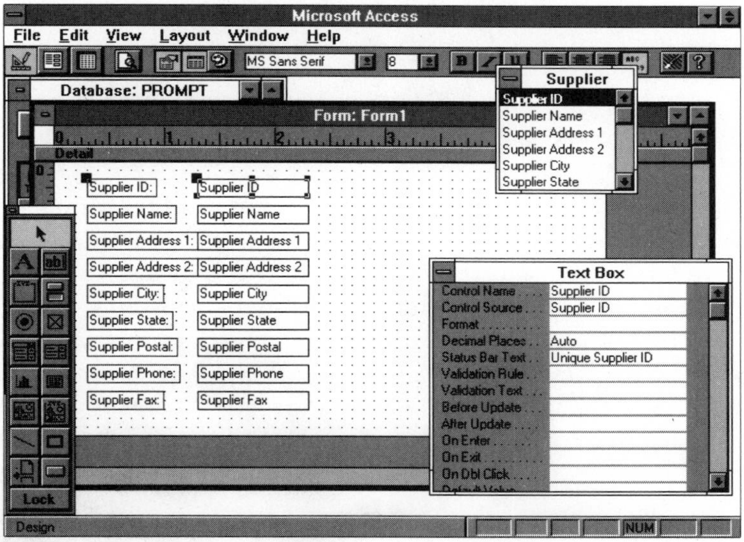

Figure 12-10.
The text box controls that are created on a form when you drag-and-drop fields from the Supplier list.

Moving and Sizing Controls

By default, Microsoft Access creates text boxes that are 1 inch wide and that have a label 1 inch to the left of the text box. For some of the fields, 1 inch is larger than necessary to display the field value—especially using the default font size of 8. For other fields, the text box isn't large enough. You probably also want to adjust the location of some of the controls.

To change a control's size or location, you usually need to select the control first. Be sure the tool lock is off and that you have selected the pointer tool. Click the control you want to resize or move, and you'll see the moving and sizing *handles* appear around the control. In Figure 12-10 the Supplier ID text box is selected. The handles are small boxes that appear at each corner of the control. If the control is wide enough or high enough, Microsoft Access gives you additional handles in the center of the sides of the control.

To change the size of a control, you can use the sizing handles on the sides, in either of the lower corners, or in the upper right corner. When you place your mouse pointer over one of these sizing handles, the pointer turns into a double arrow, as shown in Figure 12-11. Drag the edge of the control to a new size. You can practice on the Supplier form by shortening the Supplier ID text box until it's 0.5 inch long. The name and address fields need to be stretched until they are about 1.75 inches long. You can also adjust the state, postal code, and phone number fields.

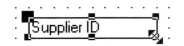

Figure 12-11.
The mouse pointer shaped like a double arrow can drag a handle of a selected control to size the control.

You can move a control whether it's currently selected or not. To move a control that is not currently selected, you can click anywhere in the control and drag it to a new location. After you have selected a control, you can grab and move it by placing your mouse pointer anywhere along the edge of the control between handles. When you do that, the mouse pointer turns into a flat hand, as shown in Figure 12-12. When you see the flat hand, drag the control to a new location. Microsoft Access shows you a shadow outline as you move the control to help you locate it. When a control has an attached label, moving the control or the label moves both together.

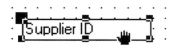

Figure 12-12.
The mouse pointer shaped like a hand can "grab" the edge of a selected control to move the control.

You can position a control and its label independently by grabbing the control by the larger square handle in the upper left corner. When you position your mouse pointer over this handle, the pointer turns into a hand with a pointing finger, as shown in Figure 12-13. Drag the control to a new location relative to its label. You can remove a label from its control by selecting the label and pressing Del. If you want to create a label that is independent of a control, you can use the label tool.

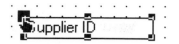

Figure 12-13.
The mouse pointer shaped like a pointing finger can drag the large handle of a selected control to move the control independent of its label.

Setting Text Box Properties

The next thing you might want to do is adjust some of the text box properties. Figure 12-14 shows you the property sheet for the Supplier ID control. Because Supplier ID in both PROMPT and NWIND is a counter, you should change this control to prevent it from being selected on the form; Microsoft Access always controls the value of counter fields. To prevent the selection of a control, set the control's Enabled property to No. But Access shades a control that isn't enabled and that isn't locked. Set the Locked property to Yes to indicate you won't be updating this control. The control will not be shaded, and you will not be able to tab to it or select it on the form in Form view.

Text Box	
Control Name	Supplier ID
Control Source . . .	Supplier ID
Format	
Decimal Places . .	Auto
Status Bar Text . .	Unique Supplier ID
Validation Rule . .	
Validation Text . .	
Before Update . . .	
After Update	
On Enter	
On Exit	
On Dbl Click	
Default Value	
Visible	Yes
Display When . . .	Always
Enabled	No
Locked	Yes
Scroll Bars	None
Can Grow	No
Can Shrink	No
Left	1.3 in
Top	0.17 in
Width	1 in
Height	0.17 in
Special Effect . . .	Color

Figure 12-14.
The property sheet for the Supplier ID text box control.

If you specify a Format, Decimal Places, Validation Rule, Validation Text, or Default Value setting when you define a field in a table, Microsoft Access automatically copies those settings into any text box that is bound to the field. The Status Bar Text property derives its value from the Description setting you entered for the field. In Figure 12-14 you can see properties labeled Before Update, After Update, On Enter, On Exit, and On Dbl Click; by entering macros as values here you can make certain events trigger certain actions, as explained in Chapter 18, "Adding Power with Macros." Other properties on this property sheet can be set to customize your form, as will be explained in Chapter 13.

Setting Label Properties

You can also set separate properties for the labels attached to controls. Click in the label for Supplier ID to see a property sheet, as shown in Figure 12-15. Microsoft Access copies the caption property from the fields to the caption property in the associated control label. In Figure 12-15 the caption was changed to *Supplier No.* from *Supplier ID*.

Label	
Control Name	Text8
Caption	Supplier No.
Visible	Yes
Display When	Always
Left	0.3 in
Top	0.17 in
Width	0.63 in
Height	0.17 in
Special Effect	Color
Back Style	Normal
Back Color	16777215
Border Style	Clear
Border Color	0
Border Width	Hairline
ForeColor	0
Font Name	MS Sans Serif
Font Size	8
Font Weight	Normal
Font Italic	No
Font Underline	No
Text Align	General

Figure 12-15.
The property sheet for the label of the Supplier ID control.

Notice also that you can correct the caption inside a label by first selecting the label, then moving the mouse pointer inside the label until the pointer changes into an I-beam pointer, and then clicking again to set the insertion point inside the label text. You can delete unwanted characters, and you can type in new information. When you have finished correcting the control labels, you might find that the controls are either too large or too small to adequately display the new names. You can change settings in the property sheet to adjust the size of a label, or you can select the control and use the control's handles to fix the size and alignment.

Setting Form Properties

Click anywhere outside the detail section of the form or choose the Select Form command from the Edit menu, and you will cause the open Property window to display the property sheet for the entire form, as shown in Figure 12-16. In Figure 12-16 the Caption is set to *Supplier–Chap 12*. This value will be displayed on the Form window's title bar in Form view or in Datasheet view.

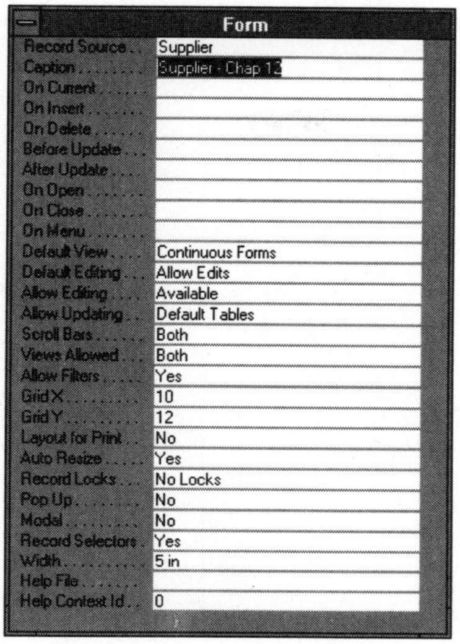

Figure 12-16.
The property sheet for the Supplier–Chap 12 form.

The properties from On Current through On Menu on the property sheet can be set to macros. The events associated with the properties can trigger macro actions, as explained in Chapter 18.

More than halfway down the list of properties, you can see the Grid X and Grid Y properties that control the density of dots on the grid. The defaults are 10 dots per inch across (X), and 12 dots per inch down (Y). If you decide to use the Snap To Grid command from the Layout menu to help you line up controls on your form, you might want to refine the granularity of the grid to give you greater control over where you place objects on the form.

Checking Your Design Results

When you've finished working on this form in Design view, it might look something like the one shown in Figure 12-17 on the next page. To make the fields on the form stand out, you can click in the detail section and then open the palette by clicking the Palette button or by choosing the Palette command from the View menu. In the palette, set Fill to a dark gray color, as shown in Figure 12-17.

Click the Form View button on the tool bar to see your form. It will be similar to the form shown in Figure 12-18 on the next page. Notice that the captions of some of the labels have been changed. You should have four records from the PROMPT Supplier table: AAA Computer Supply, Best Computer Wholesale, Computer Wholesale, Inc., and Lovell Electronics Supply. Microsoft Access assigns consecutive numbers from 1 through 4 in the Supplier No. field. You can scroll to the bottom of the form and experiment with entering data for a new supplier record. Save this form as *Supplier–Chap 12.*

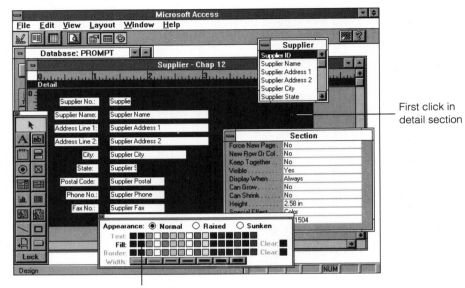

First click in detail section

Then click here to fill detail section with dark gray color

Figure 12-17.
The finished Supplier–Chap 12 form in Design view.

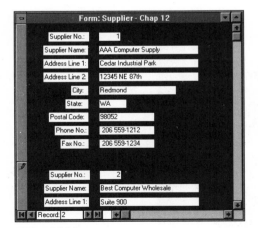

Figure 12-18.
The Supplier–Chap 12 form in Form view.

WORKING WITH FORMWIZARDS

The second form you'll build in this chapter is a bit more complex, so it might be a good idea to use a FormWizard to get started. For this form, use the Components table in PROMPT. (If you want to follow along in NWIND, use the Products table.)

Creating the Components Form with a FormWizard

Start by selecting the Components table in the PROMPT Database window. Then click the New Form button on the tool bar. A dialog box opens, similar to the one shown in Figure 12-4. If you click the FormWizards button, Microsoft Access opens the dialog box shown in Figure 12-19.

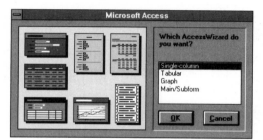

Figure 12-19.
The Microsoft AccessWizard dialog box.

As you can see, you have four choices in this dialog box: Single-column, Tabular, Graph, and Main/Subform. You'll read about most of these choices in Chapter 14 on advanced form design. For this example, select Single-column and click OK. Access opens the dialog box shown in Figure 12-20. You can select any field in the Available Fields list box and click the single right arrow button to copy that field to the

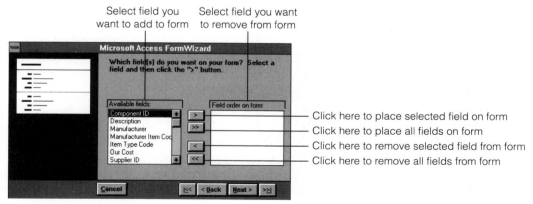

Figure 12-20.
The FormWizard dialog box for choosing fields.

Field Order On Form list box. You can click the double right arrow button to copy all available fields to the Field Order On Form list box. If you copy a field in error, you can select the field in the Field Order On Form list box and click the single left arrow button to remove the field from the list. You can remove all fields and start over by clicking the double left arrow button. For this example, click the double right arrow button to copy all the fields from the Components table to the new form.

Click the Next button to move on to the next screen. If you want to skip the next screen, you can click the button to the right of Next to go directly to the following step. Click the Cancel button to stop creating your form.

After all the fields from the Components table are added to the form, click the Next button. Since you're working with the single-column format, Access opens a dialog box in which you can select the "look" for your form, as shown in Figure 12-21. The nice thing about this dialog box is that Access shows you a sample of what each selection looks like in the picture on the left. You can try them all to see the effect and decide which one you like best. In this example, pick Standard and click the Next button to go on to the last dialog box.

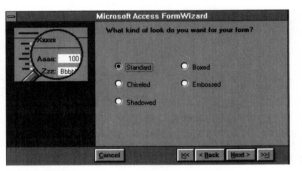

Figure 12-21.
The FormWizard dialog box for choosing the "look" of your form.

In the final dialog box, the FormWizard asks you for a title for your form. Type in an appropriate title like *Components–Chap 12* and click the Open button to see the finished form in Form view, or click the Design button to open the new form in Design view. The finished form is shown in Figure 12-22.

If you're curious about what the Tabular format looks like, you can start a new form on the Components table and click the FormWizard button. Select Tabular in the first dialog box and click OK, copy all the fields in the second dialog box to the new form, and select Boxed for your form look. For a title, type *Components–Tabular*, and open the new form in Form view. It should look something like the one shown in Figure 12-23. Close this form when you've finished looking at it.

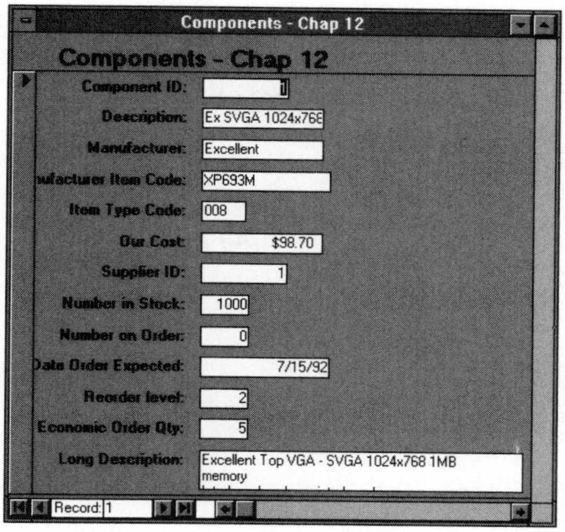

Figure 12-22.
The Components–Chap 12 form in a single-column format.

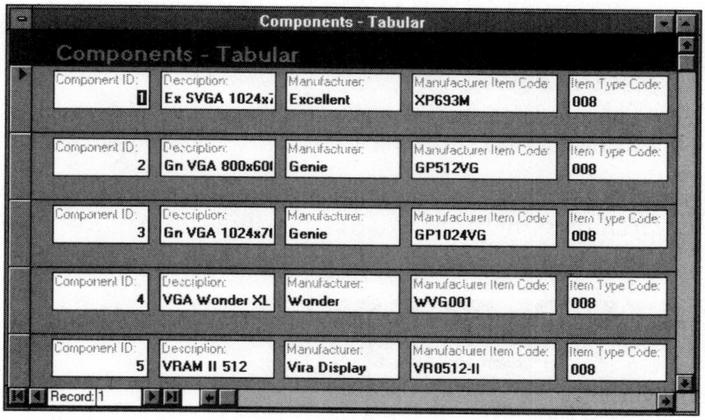

Figure 12-23.
The Components form in a tabular format.

Modifying the Components–Chap 12 Form

The FormWizard took care of some of the work, but you still have to improve the appearance and usability of this form. The FormWizard adjusted the control display lengths, but they're still not perfect. Description and Long Description need to be larger. Several other controls could be shorter. Also, you could make better use of the space on the form if you moved some of the fields into a second column.

Open the Components–Chap 12 form in Design view. To make things easier to see, click in the detail section, open the palette, and temporarily set the fill of the

269

detail section to white. To help align controls, click outside the detail section so that the form is selected (or choose the Select Form command from the View menu), and set both Grid X and Grid Y on the form's property sheet to 16. Be sure the Grid command is checked on the View menu. Move controls around until the form looks similar to the one shown in Figure 12-24. If you want to use this form in later exercises, place the Item Type Code control in the upper right corner of the form, and reserve a fairly open space on the right half of the form for the Supplier ID control.

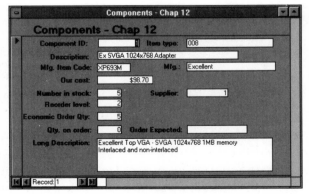

Figure 12-24.
The modified Components–Chap 12 form in Design view.

Change the detail section background color back to light gray and switch to Form view. Your form should look something like the one shown in Figure 12-25. Save your work.

Figure 12-25.
The modified Components–Chap 12 form in Form view.

SIMPLIFYING DATA INPUT IN A FORM

One drawback to working with a relational database is that often you are dealing with information stored in multiple tables. That's not a problem when you're using a query to join data together, but multiple tables can be confusing if you're entering new data. Microsoft Access provides some great ways to show information from related tables, to make data input much simpler.

Combo Boxes and List Boxes

In Chapter 11, "Form Basics," you saw that you can use a list box or a combo box to present a list of potential values for a control. To create the list, you can type the values in the Row Source property of the list box or combo box. You can also specify a table or a query as the source of the values in the list. Microsoft Access displays the currently selected value in the text box portion of the combo box or as a highlighted selection in the list.

Creating a Combo Box to Display Item Type

To see how a combo box works, you can replace the Item Type Code text box control with a combo box in the Components–Chap 12 form. Open the Components–Chap 12 form that you saved previously. Change to Design view. (If you're using NWIND for this exercise, you can experiment with the Category ID control in the Products form that is linked to the Categories table.) First select the Item Type Code text box control and press the Del key to remove the text box control from the form. Next choose the combo box tool in the toolbox and then drag the Item Type Code from the field list to the form. Your result should look something like Figure 12-26.

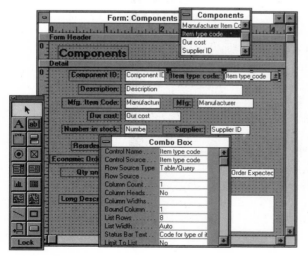

Figure 12-26.
A combo box has been created for the Item Type Code control.

Codes don't mean much to the people who read a form, but for efficiency you need a code to identify components in the Components table, not a description. In the next section you'll learn how to use a combo box not only to display a description on the form but actually to store a code in the underlying table.

Creating a Valid List of Item Types

Because you're going to display the code description in the Item Type Code combo box instead of the code itself, change the label text to read *Item type:* instead of *Item Type Code:*, the original label. Also stretch the combo box control until it is large enough to display the text.

Next you need to tell Microsoft Access where to get the information to display the item type description instead of the code. If you still have the Item Type Code combo box selected, you should see its properties in the property sheet. If you don't see the property sheet, click the Properties button on the tool bar. The property sheet is shown in Figure 12-27.

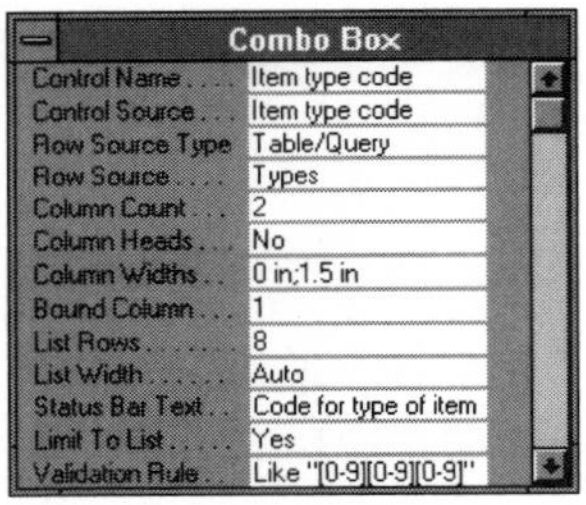

Figure 12-27.
The property sheet settings for displaying Item Type descriptions in the Item Type Code combo box.

Be sure the Row Source Type property in the property sheet for the Item Type Code combo box is set to Table/Query. For the Row Source property, enter the name of the table where the item type descriptions are located—Types. If you look at the Types table in Design view, you can see that Item Type Code is the first field and Type Description is the second field. Set Column Count to 2 in the property sheet for the Item Type Code combo box to indicate you want to use both fields. Later if you're building a similar combo box from a table that doesn't have the columns you want at the beginning, you can always create a query that selects the rows you want and refer to that query in the combo box's Row Source property.

You don't need column headings, so leave that property set to No. You don't want to show the code (the first column), but you do want to show the related description (the second column). To do that, set the Column Widths property to a display width of 0 for the first column. Then enter an appropriate display width for the description in the second column. Separate the width specifications with a semicolon, as shown in Figure 12-27.

272

You do want the Item Type Code to be taken from the first column in the Types table. So set the Bound Column property to 1. You can modify the List Rows property to control the size of the combo box when it opens. Because you know the Types table contains 17 entries (see Appendix B), you might try 8 as your starting number in List Rows. Finally, you don't want to be able to enter values that aren't in the Types table, so set the Limit To List property to Yes.

Now when you open the form in Form view, it should look like the one shown in Figure 12-28. Notice that Item Type now shows meaningful descriptions instead of numbers, yet the type you choose from the list will set the correct type code in the record.

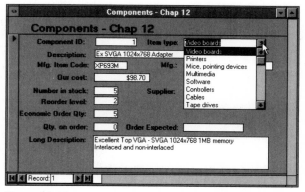

Figure 12-28.
The finished Item Type combo box.

You'll find that Microsoft Access sets the alignment of the data displayed in a combo box according to the data type of the Bound Column. If the Bound Column is a number, the data will be right aligned, even though the actual data displayed is a text description. To correct the alignment, set the Text Align property to fit the data you want displayed—usually right aligned for numbers and left aligned for text.

Toggles, Check Boxes, and Option Buttons

If the list of values you want to display contains only a few values and those values are not likely to change, Microsoft Access has a few other controls that simplify data entry and display. Users can select from several choices with toggle buttons, check boxes, or option buttons. You can assign a separate numeric value to each button or check box you include in the group. When you have more than one button or check box in a group, you can select only one button or check box at a time, and the value assigned to the selected button or check box becomes the value for the option group. You can choose one of the buttons or check boxes in the group as the default value for the group. If you bind the option group to a field in the underlying table or query, selecting a button or check box sets a new value in the field.

Because there are only four suppliers in PROMPT (as listed in Appendix B), it might be reasonable to represent the suppliers on a form as an option group. This works especially well because the Supplier ID is a counter that can be set directly by a numeric value, which is the result of selecting a button or check box in an option group. (You can also try this exercise with the Supplier ID control for the Products form in NWIND, although there are many more than four suppliers in NWIND.) As you did earlier when you replaced an item type code with a list of item types, here you are replacing a relatively meaningless code with something recognizable.

Continue working in the Components–Chap 12 form in Design view. To change the Supplier ID control on the Components–Chap 12 form, first delete the Supplier ID text box control. Next choose the option group tool and then drag the Supplier ID field from the field list onto the form in the open space you left on the right side of the form. Stretch the group box so that it is large enough to contain four option buttons and associated labels.

Next choose the option button tool and click the tool lock button so you can use the option button tool more than once. Place four option buttons inside the option group control in a column down the left side of the group box. Select the option buttons (not their labels) one by one and look at the Option Button property sheet. Microsoft Access should set the Option Value property for each button for you, using the consecutive numbers 1 through 4. Finally click on the label for each option button and type in the name of each of the four supplier companies, so that

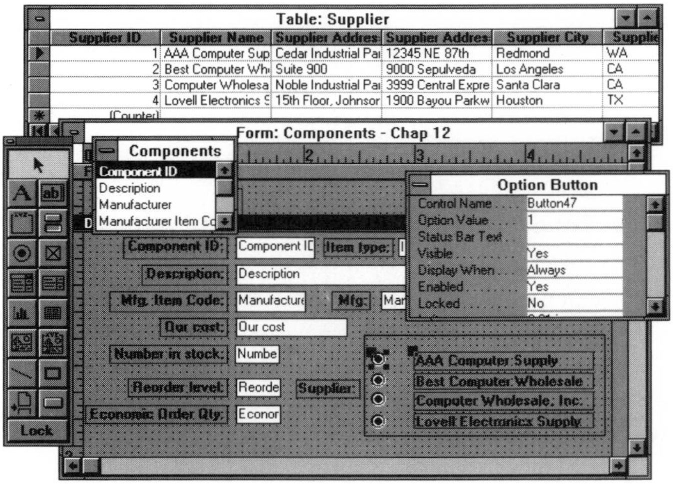

Figure 12-29.
The Components–Chap 12 form with an option group control for supplier names.

their Supplier ID numbers match the Option Values in the option buttons. You can find the supplier names and ID numbers by opening the Supplier table in the PROMPT database. You might also want to correct the label for the option group itself to say *Supplier* instead of *Supplier ID*. Your form in Design view should now look like the one shown in Figure 12-29.

Click the Form View button to see the result. Your form should look like the one shown in Figure 12-30. You can test the Supplier option group by clicking one of the buttons and then switching to the Datasheet view for the form. You'll find that the Supplier ID field in the record is set to the relative number of the option button you clicked.

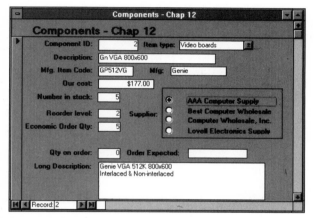

Figure 12-30.
The Components–Chap 12 form in Form view.

Another common use for a large group of option or toggle buttons is to create a row of controls labeled with each letter of the alphabet. As you saw in Chapter 11, "Form Basics," the Suppliers form in NWIND uses this technique.

By now, you should be getting a feel for the process of designing and building forms. In the next chapter you'll learn how to customize the appearance of your forms.

13

Customizing Forms

In the previous chapter you learned how to create a basic form, both by building it from scratch and by using a FormWizard. In this chapter you'll look at ways you can refine your form's appearance and operation.

ALIGNING AND SIZING

In Chapter 12 you built a form from the Components table, as shown in Figure 13-1. Copy this form and rename it *Components—Chap 13*. Change the caption property of the label in the form's header to *Components—Chap 13*. This form looks pretty good, but in truth, the labels and fields are out of alignment and different sizes. If you've just thrown the form together to help you enter some data (as you did to create a simple Supplier input form in Chapter 12), it probably doesn't matter if the form's appearance isn't perfect. But if you've designed this form to be used continuously in an application you're building, it's worth making the extra effort to polish the form's design. Otherwise, users will suffer eyestrain and fatigue.

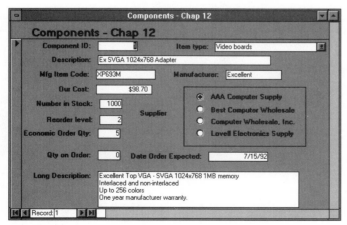

Figure 13-1.
The Components—Chap 12 form that was created in Chapter 12.

To check out the alignment and relative size of controls on your form, you can open the property sheet in Design view and click various controls. For example, Figure 13-2 shows the property sheets for the Number in Stock and Reorder Level controls. You can see by looking at the values for the Left property (the distance from the left edge of the form) that the Number in Stock control is a little bit closer to the left margin and a little less wide than the Reorder Level control.

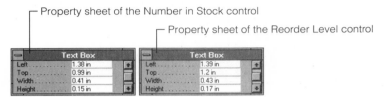

Figure 13-2.
The properties that define the placement and size of the Number in Stock and Reorder Level controls.

Now, you could go around the form and adjust controls so that they fit your data. Then you could painstakingly enter numbers in the Left property to get all controls in a column to line up exactly, and set the Top property (defining the distance from the top of the form section) for controls that you want to appear in a row. You could also adjust the values for the Width and Height properties so that controls and labels are the same width and height where appropriate. Fortunately, there are easier ways to fix all of these problems.

Sizing Controls to Fit Content

One of the first things you can do with this form is be sure all the boxes you have drawn are the right size to display your data. Open in Design view the Components–Chap 13 form you created in Chapter 12 and fill the grid with white. Microsoft Access has a command that automatically sizes label controls to fit around the text you have typed in them. This command also ensures that text, combo, and list boxes are tall enough to display your data in the font size you've chosen.

Because you built all controls and labels on this form using the same font, it makes sense to resize them all at once. First choose the Select All command from the Edit menu to highlight all controls on your form. If you want to size a specific group of labels or controls, select the first one with your mouse pointer, and then hold down the Shift key as you select each control or label you want. You can also drag the mouse pointer across your form (as long as you don't start the drag over a control!), and the mouse pointer will delineate a selection box. Any controls that are inside the selection box when you release the mouse button will be selected. When you have the controls that you want selected, choose the Size To Fit command from the Layout menu. The result on the design grid should look something like Figure 13-3.

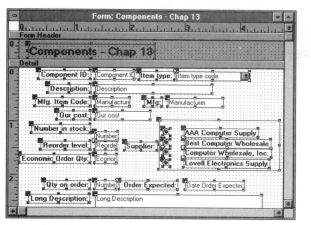

Figure 13-3.
The Components–Chap 13 form after you select the controls and choose the Size To Fit command.

"Snapping" Controls to the Grid

Next it's a good idea to verify that all your controls are spaced evenly down the form. One way to do this is to take advantage of the grid. You can adjust the density of the grid using the Grid X and Grid Y properties of the form. Be sure that your property sheet is open and then choose the Select Form command from the Edit menu. Also be sure that the Grid command in the View menu has a check mark in front of it.

In this example, set the values for the Grid X and Grid Y properties to 16 (.0625 inch between grid points). This works well for the default MS Sans Serif font in 8 point size because the "sized to fit" text boxes will be 0.17 inches high. You can place these text boxes every .25 inch (four grid points) down the form and leave adequate space between the controls.

Turn on the Snap To Grid command in the Layout menu. You can see a check mark next to this command when Snap To Grid is active. Now grab each control and position it vertically every .25 inch (every fourth grid point) down the grid. When you release the mouse button, you will see the upper left corner of the control "snap" to the nearest grid point. As you saw in Chapter 12, "Building a Form," Microsoft Access moves a control and its label as a unit. So, if you have previously moved the label up or down independently of the attached control, you might need to use the positioning handle in the upper left corner of the control or its label to get them in line horizontally.

If you're having difficulty moving the controls to the nearest quarter inch, you can try setting Grid X to 8 or 4. Don't worry about vertical alignment yet. You'll take care of that shortly. When you're done, your results might look something like the ones shown in Figure 13-4 on the next page.

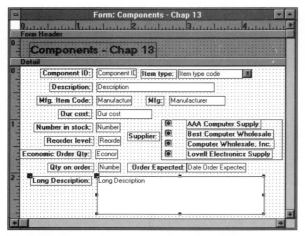

Figure 13-4.
The Components–Chap 13 form after you "snap" the controls to the grid vertically.

Lining Up Controls

You have your controls spaced evenly down the form, but they probably look a little jagged left to right. That's easy to fix. First select all the labels down the far left column. Do this by clicking the first label (not its associated control) and then pressing the Shift key. Hold down the Shift key as you click all of the remaining labels down the column. When you have them all selected, your design grid should look something like Figure 13-5. Note that Microsoft Access also shows you the positioning

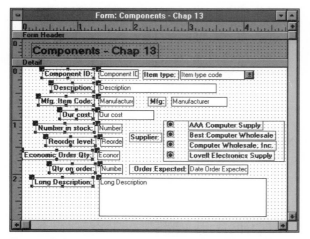

Figure 13-5.
A column of labels is selected.

handle for all the related controls but not the sizing handles on the controls. In this way you see the related control, but you know that you have selected only the labels.

The labels will look best if their right edges align. You have two choices at this point. If you turn off the Snap To Grid command, you can have Access line up all the labels with the label whose right edge is farthest to the right, even if that edge is between dots on the grid. If you leave on Snap To Grid, you can have Access line up the labels with the label farthest to the right, and then snap the entire group to the nearest grid point.

When you're ready to line up the selected controls on your form, choose the Align command from the Layout menu. This command opens up a submenu, as shown in Figure 13-6. Choose the Right command from the submenu and click inside the grid to see results similar to the ones shown in Figure 13-7.

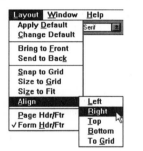

Figure 13-6.
The Align command and its submenu.

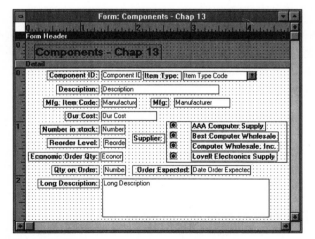

Figure 13-7.
The labels from Figure 13-5 are right aligned.

To complete alignment of the Components form, use the Align submenu commands (Figure 13-6) to do the following:

1. Select the Item Type, Mfg, and Order Expected labels (not the controls) and align them using the Right command.

2. Turn the Snap To Grid command on if you had previously turned it off. You are about to start lining up controls, and it will be easier to do final length adjustments later if the ends of controls align on a grid point.

3. Select the Component ID, Description, Mfg. Item Code, Our Cost, Number in Stock, Reorder Level, Economic Order Qty, Qty on order, and Long Description controls (not the labels) and align them using the Left command.

4. Select the Item Type, Mfg, the Supplier option group, and Order Expected controls. Do not include the Description and Long Description controls in this group. Align the group using the Right command.

5. Select the Component ID and Item Type labels *and* controls and align them using the Top command.

6. Select the Description label and control and align them using the Top command.

7. Select the Mfg. Item Code and Mfg labels *and* controls and align them using the Top command.

8. Select the Our Cost control and label and the Supplier option group (but not its label) and align them using the Top command.

9. Select the Number in stock control and its label, and the label for the Supplier option group and align them using the Top command.

10. Select the Qty on order and Order Expected labels *and* controls and align them using the Top command.

11. Use the Top command to individually align the remaining controls and their labels.

When you've completed these steps, your result should look something like the one shown in Figure 13-8.

Making Control Length Adjustments

You have a couple of long controls (Description and Long Description) that stretch most of the way across the form. You lined up their left edges, but it would be nice if their right edges also lined up with the items in the second column on the form. You can do that by adjusting the Width property for the two controls.

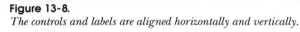

Figure 13-8.
The controls and labels are aligned horizontally and vertically.

To figure out what adjustment you need (if any), first take a look at the Left and Width properties of the Item Type Code control's property sheet. See Figure 13-9. In this example, the Item Type Code combo box starts 3.02 inches from the left edge of the form and is 1.6 inches long. This means that the right edge is 4.62 inches away from the left edge of the form. Next take a look at the Left and Width properties of the Long Description text box. You don't want to move this text box from its location 1.37 inches from the left edge because it's lined up with the other controls in that column. Left plus Width should equal 4.62 inches to line up the edge of Description with Item Type Code. So, you need to change the Description control's Width property to 3.25 inches (4.62 minus 1.37) to achieve the desired result. You should make a similar adjustment to the Width property for the Long Description control.

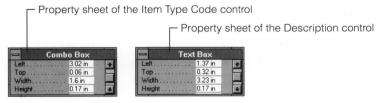

Property sheet of the Item Type Code control

Property sheet of the Description control

Figure 13-9.
The values for the Left and Width properties can be compared and adjusted to align the right edges of two controls.

As a final touch, you should adjust controls in a column to the same length where it makes sense to do so. For example, you could make the Component ID and Mfg. Item Code controls the same length (about 0.6 inches works well). Similarly, the

Number in Stock, Reorder Level, Economic Order Qty, and Qty on Order controls can be the same length. If you decide to make Item Type, Mfg, and Order Expected the same length, you might have to realign them right.

When you're all done, fill the grid with light gray. Then switch to Form view and move the form to the upper left corner of your screen. Choose the Size to Fit Form command from the Window menu to resize the Form window to show only the controls. (Notice that you must move the form to the top left of your screen before choosing this command because the Size To Fit Form command expands a form only to the right and down.) Your result should look something like Figure 13-10. Choose the Save command from the File menu to save your design changes.

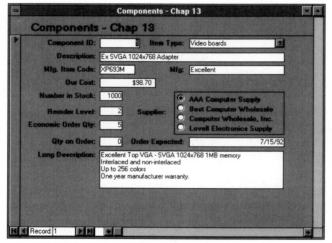

Figure 13-10.
The Components - Chap 13 form with controls aligned and sized.

SPECIAL EFFECTS

When you first built the Components form using a FormWizard and asked for Standard format, the Wizard automatically added one special effect—a gray background color. In this section you'll learn about a few more enhancements you can make to your form's design.

Lines and Rectangles

Microsoft Access comes with two drawing tools that you can use to enhance the appearance of your forms. Lines can be added to visually separate parts of your form. Rectangles are useful for surrounding and setting off a group of controls.

On the Components–Chap 13 form, it might be helpful to separate the primary information about component type and description at the top of the form from the rest of the information. To make room to add a line under this information, you need to move Mfg. Item Code, Mfg, and all the controls below them down two grid points. The easiest way to do this is to switch to Design view and use the pointer tool to highlight all the affected controls and labels, and then move them as a group. Start by clicking just above and to the right of the Mfg control and then dragging to the lower left corner of the form until the selection box surrounds all the controls you want to move. Release your mouse button, and Access will have selected all the controls that were inside the selection box. Grab a handle on any of the controls and slide the whole selection box down two grid points. You might have to drag the bottom margin of the detail area downward to provide room to do this.

Next select the line tool from the toolbox. To draw your line, click the left side of the form, about one row below the Description label, and drag across to the right edge. If the line isn't exactly straight, you can drag the right end up or down to adjust it. Click the third Width button in the palette window to make the line a little thicker. You should now have something that looks similar to Figure 13-11.

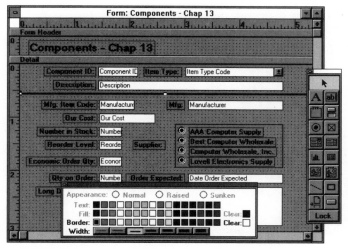

Figure 13-11.
The line tool is used to draw a line on a form, and the palette is used to adjust line width.

You can add emphasis to the Supplier option group by drawing a rectangle around it. To do this, you might first need to move the Supplier option group down and to the left a bit. The idea is to make the top and right edges of the new rectangle line up where the top and right edges of the option group used to be. Select the option group (if necessary) and move it down and to the left one point on the grid. Select the Supplier label and drag it until it's again lined up with the Reorder Level control. Now select the rectangle tool, click where you want to place one corner of the rectangle, and drag to the intended location of the opposite corner. When you draw a rectangle around the Supplier option group, the Supplier control will look similar to Figure 13-12 on the next page.

Figure 13-12.
A rectangle with a white fill is created, and it covers the option group.

The Supplier group is covered up because the default color for the interior of the rectangle is white, not clear. Whenever you overlap one control with another, Access places the last defined control on top. You have two choices with the rectangle selected. You can click the Clear box on the Fill row in the palette to make the rectangle clear and allow the Supplier group to show through; or you can choose the Send To Back command from the Layout menu and effect the change shown in Figure 13-13.

Figure 13-13.
The rectangle has been sent to the back of the option group control.

Now you can switch to Form view and choose the Size To Fit Form command from the Window menu. (Remember, the form must be in the upper left of the Access window before it can be properly sized.) Your Components form should now look similar to the one shown in Figure 13-14. Now is a good time to save your result.

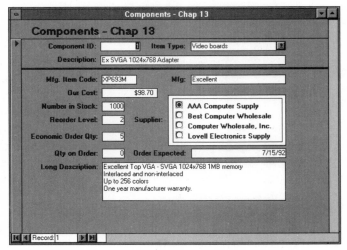

Figure 13-14.
The Components–Chap 13 form with a line and a rectangle added.

Color and Raised Effect

The FormWizard added a light gray color to the background of the form for you. You can do additional things with color and special effects to highlight objects on your form. For example, you can make the Supplier option group appear to "float" on the form.

First switch to Design view and select the rectangle behind the Supplier option group. (It might take a bit of practice to select the rectangle instead of the group.) Next open the palette and click the medium dark gray color in the second box of the Fill line. Your form will look similar to the one shown in Figure 13-15.

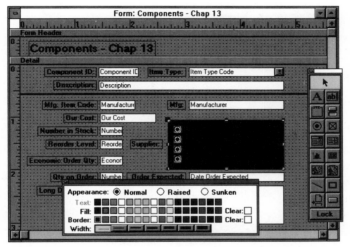

Figure 13-15.
The rectangle is filled with a dark gray color.

Because the default fill attribute for the option group is Clear, the dark gray color of the rectangle behind the group shows through. Because you're using black letters for the option names, you need to make the option group lighter to improve readability. You could make the Supplier group light gray or white if you like. Access also provides a couple of interesting special effects. Select the Supplier option group. (Again, selecting the option group and not the rectangle might be difficult, but you can keep the property sheet open nearby to verify that you've selected the group.) Click the light gray fill color and then click the Clear checkbox (so that the checkbox is no longer selected). Now click the Raised option button in the palette, as shown in Figure 13-16 on the next page.

Switch to Form view to see the result of your work. The Supplier option group now appears to "float" in the dark gray rectangle on the form. See Figure 13-17 on the next page.

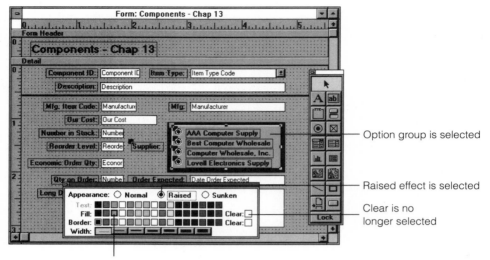

Option group is selected

Raised effect is selected

Clear is no longer selected

Light gray is selected

Figure 13-16.
The Supplier option group is lighter and appears raised.

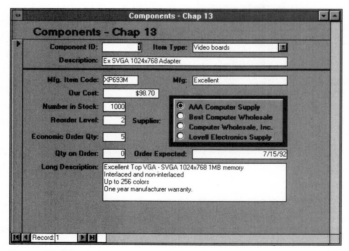

Figure 13-17.
A "floating" Supplier option group.

Fonts

Another way you can enhance the appearance of your forms is by varying the fonts and font sizes you use. When you select any control or label that can display text or data, Microsoft Access adds font, font size, and font attribute buttons to the tool bar to make it easy to change how that control or label looks. Simply click the down arrow next to the Font box to open a list of all the available fonts, as shown in Figure 13-18. Choose the font you want for the selected control or label.

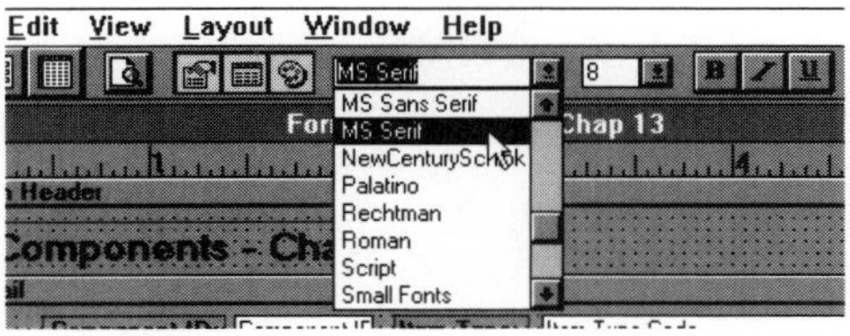

Figure 13-18.
An open list in the Font box.

In this case, it might be interesting to add some character to the label in the form header. Select the label in the form header and change the font from the MS Sans Serif font to MS Serif. Open the Font-size combo box next to the Font combo box and select a size of 18 points. Click the Italic button to add an italic tilt. You might find that you must resize the text box in order to display the large content. Use a text box handle to resize it, or choose the Size to Fit command from the Layout menu. When you're done, your result will look similar to the one shown in Figure 13-19.

You should note that a form with too many different fonts or font sizes will look busy and jumbled. In general, you should choose only two or three fonts per form. Use one font and size for most data in controls and labels. Make the label text bold or colored for emphasis. Choose a second font for headers and perhaps a third for information you include on the form.

Figure 13-19.
The header label Components–Chap 13 *with new font, font-size, and italic settings.*

SETTING CONTROL PROPERTIES

Microsoft Access gives you several additional properties for each control to allow you to customize the way your form works. These properties affect format, scroll bars, and enabling or locking.

Format

In the property sheet of each text box, combo box, and list box, you can find two properties that you can set to determine how Access displays your data on the form. These properties are Format and Decimal Places. See Figure 13-20 on the next page.

Access copies these properties from the definition of the fields in the underlying table. If you haven't specified a format in the field definition, Access chooses a default format depending on the data type of the field bound to the control. You can customize the appearance of your data by choosing a format setting from the list that you can open on the Format line of the control's property sheet or by entering a custom set of formatting characters. The following sections show you the format settings and formatting characters available for each data type.

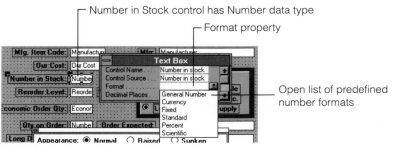

Figure 13-20.
The format list for the Number in Stock control, a Number data type.

Numbers and Currency

If you don't specify a Format property for a control that displays a number or currency value, Microsoft Access displays numbers in a General Number format and currency in a Currency format. You can choose from six format settings, as shown in Figure 13-21.

Number/ Currency Format	Description
General Number	Displays numbers as entered or stored with up to 15 significant digits. When the number contains more than 15 significant digits, first rounds decimal places, and then uses exponential format for very large or very small numbers (more than 15 digits to right or left of decimal point). Displays the same as Currency format for currency numbers.
Currency	Displays numeric data according to the Currency setting in the International section within the Control Panel of the Windows operating system. In the U.S., uses a leading dollar sign, maintains two decimal places (rounded), and encloses negative numbers in parentheses.
Fixed	Displays numbers without thousands separator and with two decimal places.

Figure 13-21. *(continued)*
The formats for the Number and Currency data types.

Figure 13-21. *continued*

Number/ Currency Format	Description
Standard	Same as Fixed but with thousands separator.
Percent	Multiplies value by 100, displays two decimal places, and adds a trailing percent sign.
Scientific	Displays numbers in scientific (exponential) notation.

You can also create your own custom format. You can specify a different display format for Access to use depending on whether the numeric value is positive, negative, zero, or Null by providing up to four format specifications in the Format property. The specifications should be separated by semicolons. When you enter two specifications, Access uses the first for all non-negative numbers and the second for negative numbers. When you provide three specifications, Access uses the third specification to display numbers with a value of zero. Provide the fourth specification to indicate how you want Null values handled.

To create a custom number format, use the formatting characters shown in Figure 13-22. Notice that you can include text strings in the format and specify a color to use to display the number on the screen.

Formatting Characters	Usage
decimal separator	Use to indicate where you want Access to place the decimal point. Use the decimal separator defined in the International section of Windows' Control Panel. In the U.S., the separator is a period (.).
thousand separator	Use to indicate placement of the thousands separator character that is defined in the International section of Windows' Control Panel. In the U.S., the separator is a comma (,).
0	Use to indicate digit display. If no digit exists in the number in this position, Access displays a zero.
#	Use to indicate digit display. If no digit exists in the number in this position, Access displays a blank.
− + $ ( ) space	Use these characters anywhere you want in your format string.
"*text*"	Use quotation marks to embed any text you want displayed.
\	Use to always display the immediately following character (the same as including a single character in double quotes).
!	Use to force left alignment.

Figure 13-22. *(continued)*

The formatting characters for the Number and Currency data types.

Figure 13-22. *continued*

Formatting Characters	Usage
*	Use to generate the immediately following character as a fill character. Access normally displays formatted data right aligned and filled with blanks to the left.
%	Use to multiply the value by 100 and include a trailing percent sign.
E– or e–	Use to generate scientific notation and display a minus sign preceding negative exponents. It must be used with other characters, as in 0.00E–00.
E+ or e+	Use to generate scientific notation and display a minus sign preceding negative exponents and a plus sign preceding positive exponents. It must be used with other characters, as in 0.00E+00.
[color]	Use brackets to display the text in the color specified. Valid color names are Black, Blue, Green, Cyan, Red, Magenta, Yellow, and White. It must be used with other characters, as in 0.00[Red].

For example, if you want to display a number with two decimal places and comma separators when positive, surrounded by parentheses and shown in red when negative, "Zero" when zero, and "Not Entered" when null, specify

#,##0.00;(#,##0.00)[Red];"Zero";"Not Entered"

Text

If you don't specify a Format property for a control that displays a text value, Access displays the data in the control left aligned. You can also specify a custom format with one or two entries separated by a semicolon. If you include a second format specification, Access uses that specification to show null values. Notice that when you specify formatting for text, Access uses right alignment. Figure 13-23 lists the formatting characters applicable to character strings.

Formatting Characters	Usage
@	Use to display any available character or a space in this position.
&	Use to display any available character in this position.
<	Use to display all characters in lowercase.

Figure 13-23.   *(continued)*
The formatting characters for the Text data type.

Figure 13-23. *continued*

Formatting Characters	Usage
>	Use to display all characters in uppercase.
− + $ ( ) space	Use these characters anywhere you want in your format string.
"text"	Use quotation marks to embed any text you want displayed.
\	Use to always display the immediately following character (the same as including a single character in double quotes).
!	Use to force left alignment. It also forces placeholders to fill left to right instead of right to left.
*	Use to generate the immediately following character as a fill character. Access normally displays formatted data right aligned and filled with blanks to the left. It must be used with other characters, as in >*#.
[*color*]	Use brackets to display the text in the color specified. Valid color names are Black, Blue, Green, Cyan, Red, Magenta, Yellow, and White. It must be used with other characters, as in >[Red].

For example, if you want to display a six-character text part number with a hyphen between the second and third characters, left aligned, specify *!@@-@@@@*

Date/Time

If you don't specify a Format property for a control that displays a date/time value, Microsoft Access displays the date/time in the General Date format. You can also choose one of seven format settings, as shown in Figure 13-24.

Date/Time Format	Description
General Date	Displays the date as numbers separated by the date separator character. Displays the time as hours and minutes separated by the time separator character and followed by an AM/PM indicator. If the date/time value has no time part, Access displays the date only. If the date/time value has no date part, Access displays the time only. Example: 3/15/93 06:17 PM.
Long Date	Displays the date according to the Long Date format in the International section of Windows' Control Panel. Example: Monday, March 15, 1993.
Medium Date	Displays the date as dd-mmm-yy. Example: 15-Mar-93.

Figure 13-24. *(continued)*
The formats for the Date/Time data type.

Figure 13-24. *continued*

Date/Time Format	Description
Short Date	Displays the date according to the Short Date format in the International section of Windows' Control Panel. Example: 3/15/93.
Long Time	Displays the time according to the Time format in the International section of Windows' Control Panel. Example: 6:17:12 PM.
Medium Time	Displays the time as hours and minutes separated by the time separator character and followed by an AM/PM indicator. Example: 06:17 PM.
Short Time	Displays the time as hours and minutes separated by the time separator character using a 24-hour clock. Example: 18:17.

You can also specify a custom format with one or two entries separated by semicolons. If you include a second format specification, Access uses that specification to show null values. Figure 13-25 lists the formatting characters applicable to Date/Time data.

Formatting Characters	Usage
time separator	Use to show Access where to separate hours, minutes, and seconds. Use the time separator defined in the International section of Windows' Control Panel. In the U.S., the separator is a colon (:).
date separator	Use to show Access where to separate days, months, and years. Use the date separator defined in the International section of Windows' Control Panel. In the U.S., the separator is a slash (/).
c	Use to display General Date format.
d	Use to display day of the month as one or two digits, as needed.
dd	Use to display day of the month as two digits.
ddd	Use to display day of the week as three-letter abbreviation (Saturday = Sat).
dddd	Use to display day of the week fully spelled out.
ddddd	Use to display Short Date format.
dddddd	Use to display Long Date format.

Figure 13-25.   *(continued)*
The formatting characters for the Date/Time data type.

Figure 13-25. *continued*

Formatting Characters	Usage
w	Use to display a number for day of the week (Sunday = 1).
ww	Use to display week of the year (1–53).
m	Use to display month as a one or two-digit number, as needed.
mm	Use to display month as a two-digit number.
mmm	Use to display name of the month as a three-letter abbreviation (March = Mar).
mmmm	Use to display name of the month fully spelled out.
q	Use to display the calendar quarter number (1–4).
y	Use to display day of the year (1–366).
yy	Use to display last two digits of the year.
yyyy	Use to display the full year value (within the range of 0100–9999).
h	Use to display the hour as one or two digits, as needed.
hh	Use to display the hour as two digits.
n	Use to display the minutes as one or two digits, as needed.
nn	Use to display minutes as two digits.
s	Use to display seconds as one or two digits, as needed.
ss	Use to display seconds as two digits.
ttttt	Use to display Long Time format.
AM/PM or am/pm	Use to display twelve-hour clock values with trailing AM or PM, as appropriate.
A/P or a/p	Use to display twelve-hour clock values with trailing A or P, as appropriate.
AMPM	Use to display twelve-hour clock values using forenoon/afternoon indicators as specified in the International section of Windows' Control Panel.
– + $ ( ) space	Use these characters anywhere you want in your format string.
"*text*"	Use quotation marks to embed any text you want displayed.
\	Use to always display the immediately following character (the same as including a single character in double quotes).
!	Use to force left alignment.
*	Use to generate the immediately following character as a fill character. Access normally displays formatted data right aligned and filled with blanks to the left. It must be used with other characters, as in A/P*#.

(continued)

Figure 13-25. *continued*

Formatting Characters	Usage
[*color*]	Use brackets to display the text in the color specified. Valid color names are Black, Blue, Green, Cyan, Red, Magenta, Yellow, and White. It must be used with other characters, as in ddddd[Red].

For example, to display a date as full month name, day, and year (as in December 20, 1992) with a color of cyan, specify *mmmm dd, yyyy[Cyan]*

Yes/No

You can choose from one of three standard formats—Yes/No, True/False, On/Off—to display Yes/No data type values. See Figure 13-26. Of the three, the Yes/No format is the default. As you have seen earlier, it's often more useful to display Yes/No values in a check box or an option button rather than in a text box.

Yes/No Format	Description
Yes/No	Displays 0 as No and any nonzero value as Yes.
True/False	Displays 0 as False and any nonzero value as True.
On/Off	Displays 0 as Off and any nonzero value as On.

Figure 13-26.
The formats for the Yes/No data types.

To format the data in the Components form's controls, you might want to set the Format and Decimal Places properties as indicated in Figure 13-27. The Components form in Form view will then look similar to the one shown in Figure 13-28.

Control	Data Type	Format	Decimal Places
Our Cost	Currency	Currency	
Number in Stock	Number	Standard	0
Reorder Level	Number	Standard	0
Economic Order Qty	Number	Standard	0
Qty on Order	Number	Standard	0
Date Order Expected	Date/Time	Long Date	

Figure 13-27.
The settings for the Format and Decimal Places properties of some Components–Chap 13 form controls.

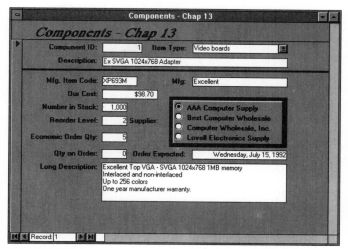

Figure 13-28.
The Components–Chap 13 form with control formats specified.

Scroll Bars

When you have a control that can contain a long data string (for example, the Long Description control on the Components form), it's a good idea to provide a scroll bar in the control to make it easy to scan through all the data. This scroll bar appears whenever you select the control. If you don't add a scroll bar, you have to use arrow keys to move down and up through the data.

To add a scroll bar, first open the Components–Chap 13 form in Design view. Select the Long Description control and open the property sheet. Then set the Scroll Bars property to Vertical. If you open the Components form in Form view and tab to (or click inside of) the Long Description text box, the vertical scroll bar will appear, as shown in Figure 13-29 on the next page.

Enabling and Locking

You might not want users of your form to select or update certain controls. You can set these conditions with the Enabled and Locked properties. For example, because the Component ID control on the Components–Chap 13 form is a counter and Access always provides its value, it's a good idea to set Enabled to No (so that no one can select it) and Locked to Yes (so that no one can update it). Figure 13-30 on the next page shows the effects of the Enabled and Locked property settings.

297

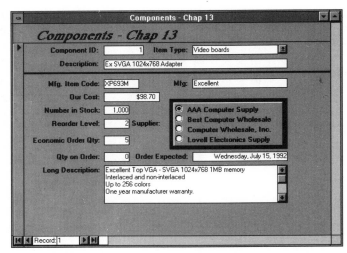

Figure 13-29.
The Long Description control with a scroll bar.

Enabled	Locked	Description
Yes	Yes	Control can have the focus. Data displays normally and can be copied but not changed.
No	No	Control can't have the focus. Control and data appear dimmed.
Yes	No	Control can have the focus. Data displays normally and can be copied and changed.
No	Yes	Control can't have the focus. Data displays normally but can't be copied or changed.

Figure 13-30.
The combinations of settings for the Enabled and Locked properties.

SETTING FORM PROPERTIES

There are a number of properties for the form itself that you can use to control its appearance and how it works.

Default View and Views Allowed

When the FormWizard built the original form for you, it set the Default View property for the form to Single Form. This is the view you'll see first whenever you open the form. Notice that with Single Form set, you can see only one record at a time. You have to use the record number box or the Go To command on the Records menu to move to another record. If you set Default View for the form to Continuous Forms, you can see multiple records on a short form, and use the right scroll bar to move down through the records. Because one record's data in Components really fills the form, the Single Form setting is probably the best choice.

With another property, Views Allowed, you can control whether or not a user can change to a Datasheet view of the form. The default setting is Both, meaning that a user can use the tool bar or the View menu to switch back and forth between views. If you're designing a form to be used in an application, you will usually want to eliminate either Form or Datasheet view. In this case, set the Views Allowed property to Form; you should see the Datasheet button on the tool bar become gray when you switch to Form view.

Setting Tab Order

After the FormWizard built the form, you moved several controls around and changed Item Type to a combo box and Supplier to an option group. As you design a form, Access sets up the tab order for the controls in the order in which the controls are defined. You can determine the tab order you want, however. Choose the Tab Order command from the Edit menu to see the Tab Order dialog box, as shown in Figure 13-31.

Figure 13-31.
The Tab Order dialog box.

As you can see, the Item Type Code control is near the bottom of the list in Figure 13-31, even though you defined it at the top of the form. Click the Auto Order button to reorder the tab order of controls so that it corresponds to the arrangement of controls on the form, from left to right and top to bottom. You can make additional adjustments to the list (such as moving the Supplier option group to last in the list) by clicking the selector button for a control to highlight it, and then clicking the selector button again and dragging the control to the location you want in the list. Click OK to save your changes to the tab order list.

Setting Record Selectors and Scroll Bars

Because this form displays one record at a time, it might not be all that useful to show the record selector on the left side of the form. You have also designed the form to show all the data in a single window, so a scroll bar down the right side of the window really isn't necessary. You probably should keep the scroll bar on the bottom of the form because that contains the record number box. To make these changes, set the form's Record Selectors property on the form property sheet to No and the Scroll Bars property to Horizontal Only. Your result should look something like the one shown in Figure 13-32.

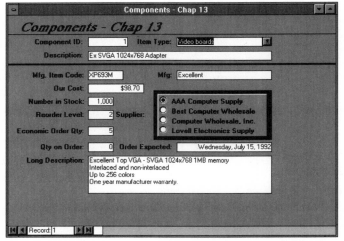

Figure 13-32.
The Components—Chap 13 form without a record selector or right scroll bar.

Creating a Pop-Up Form

You might occasionally want to design a form that stays in view on top of all other forms even when it doesn't have the focus. You might have noticed that the toolbox, property sheet, field list, and palette in Design view all have this characteristic. These are called *pop-up forms*. You make the Components form a pop-up form by setting the Pop Up property to Yes. Figure 13-33 shows you the Components—Chap 13 form as a pop-up form in front of the Database window that has the focus. Be sure to set the Pop Up property back to No.

Controlling Editing

You can set several properties on forms to control whether data on the form can be updated or whether data in the underlying tables can change. These properties and their settings are shown in the table that follows.

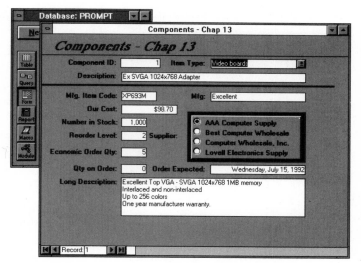

Figure 13-33.
The Components—Chap 13 form as a pop-up form in front of the Database window that has the focus.

DefaultEditing   Determines whether a user can update controls on the form, including controls that are not bound to fields. The possible settings are

     Allow Edits   Lets you update data in any controls.

     Read Only   Disallows any updating, including unbound controls.

     Data Entry   Sets the form for appending records only. You cannot display existing records.

AllowEditing   Determines whether the Editing Allowed command on the Records menu is enabled. The Editing Allowed command allows users to update data even if the Default Editing property is set to Read Only. The possible settings are

     Available   Enables the Editing Allowed command on the Records menu.

     Not Available   Disables the Editing Allowed command on the Records menu.

AllowFilters   Determines whether a user can see selected records by applying filter and sorting criteria or can see all records by choosing the Show All Records command on the Records menu. If you set the DefaultEditing property to Data Entry and you set the AllowFilters property to No, the user can only enter new data with this form and cannot change the form to view other existing records. The valid settings for the AllowFilters property are Yes and No.

AllowUpdating   Determines which, if any, fields in tables you can update through this form. The possible settings are

     Default Tables   Allows you to change information only in underlying tables or queries of the form. If the underlying object is a single table, you

(continued)

can change all fields. If the underlying object is a query, you can change only fields in the table on the "many" side of the join. See Chapter 8, "Adding Power with Select Queries," for details on update rules for joined tables.

Any Tables — Allows you to update any field in any underlying table or query. Access does not enforce rules for updating joined tables when you choose this option. Use this option with care. See Chapter 19, "Designing the Prompt Computer Solutions Application," for an example.

No — Does not allow you to update any fields in tables, although you can update unbound controls.

SETTING CONTROL DEFAULTS

You can use the Apply Default and Change Default commands on the Layout menu to apply and change the defaults for the various controls you can use on your form. If you've placed a control on your form and modified the control but you don't like the way it turned out, you can restore the control to the default property settings by selecting the control and choosing Apply Default. If you want to change the default property settings for a type of control, select a control of that type, set the control's properties to the desired default values, and then choose the Change Default command from the Layout menu. The settings of the currently selected control will become the default settings for any subsequent definitions of that type of control on your form.

For example, you might want all labels to have a white background and blue text. Place a label on your form and set the label's text to blue and the background to white using the palette. Choose the Change Default command while this label is selected. Any new labels you place on the form will have the new settings.

You can also create a special form called Normal to define new defaults for all your controls. To do this, open a new blank form, place controls on the form for which you want to define global defaults, modify the controls to your liking, and save the form with the name *Normal*. The Normal form becomes your *form template*. Any new control that you place on a form (except for forms where you have already changed the default for one or more controls) will use the new property settings you defined for that control type on the Normal form.

SETTING FORM DESIGN OPTIONS

You can also customize the way you work with forms in Design view by setting the Form & Report Design options. Choose the Options command from the View menu and select the Form & Report Design category. You'll see the dialog box shown in Figure 13-34.

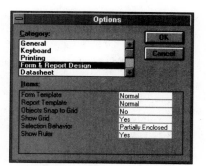

Figure 13-34.
The Form & Report Design options.

Notice that with these options you can change the name of your form template from Normal to something else. You can also set whether the Snap To Grid command is on and whether you can see the grid and ruler. You can set Selection Behavior to Fully Enclosed so that any selection box you draw on the grid must fully enclose a control in order to select it. With Partially Enclosed, only part of a control must be inside a selection box for the control to be selected.

Now you should be really comfortable with designing forms and adding special touches to make your forms more attractive and usable. In the next chapter you'll learn about "power forms": using queries with data from multiple tables in forms, building forms within forms, adding pictures and graphs, and doing simple form linking with command buttons.

14
Advanced Form Design

In the last two chapters you learned how to design a form that works with data in a table. Although you saw how to display some data from another table by using a combo box or a list box, you haven't learned how to consolidate in a form the information from multiple tables. In this chapter you'll find out how to

- Create a form using a query that joins multiple tables

- Embed a *subform* in a *main form* so you can work with related data from two tables or queries at the same time

- Enhance forms with pictures or graphs

- Link two related forms together with a simple command button

BASING A FORM ON A QUERY

In Chapter 8 you learned how to bring together data from multiple tables using queries. The result you get when you run a select query—a dynaset—contains all the information you need, but it's in the unadorned Datasheet view format. Forms enable you to present this data in a more attractive and meaningful way. And in the same way as you can update data in queries, you can also update data using a form that is based on a query.

A Many-to-One Form

As you have discovered in the past few chapters, it's really easy to design a form that allows you to view and update the data from a single table. You also learned how to include selected single fields from related tables using a list or combo box. But what if you would like to see more information from the related tables? The best way to do this is to design a query based on the two (or more) related tables and use that query as the basis of your form.

Most of the time when you create a query with two or more tables, you're working with one-to-many relationships between the tables. As you learned earlier, Microsoft Access lets you update data in the table that is on the "many" side of the relationship. So, when you base a form on a query, you can update the fields in the form that come from the "many" table. Because the primary purpose of the form is to search and update records in the "many" side of the relationship while reviewing information on the "one" side, this is called a *many-to-one* form.

For example, in the last two chapters you created and customized a form to view and update data from the Components table in PROMPT. (Or you created a form to work with data from the Products table in NWIND.) You created an option group to deal with setting the Supplier ID on the assumption that there are four suppliers and there won't ever be any others. This was probably a bad assumption, but it provided an interesting exercise for learning how to build option groups.

Suppose instead that there will ultimately be dozens of suppliers. You could simply add a combo box to display the Supplier Name to help set the Supplier ID correctly for each component. However, you want to use this form for more than just data entry. If you're using the Components form to search for items low in stock, it would be nice to have the supplier address and phone number handy when you find a component you need to reorder. You could base your form on a query that selects information from the Components and Supplier tables. Every supplier might produce many components but each component has just one supplier. You will be building a many-to-one form.

Designing a Many-to-One Query

First you must design a query that contains the fields you need. Open a new Query window and add the Components and Supplier field lists using the Add Table command from the Query menu. You should see a relationship line from Supplier ID in the Supplier field list to Supplier ID in Components. If you don't, you need to close the Query window and go back to the Database window, choose the Relationships command from the Edit menu and add the proper one-to-many relationship between Supplier and Components, and then open a new Query window and add the Components and Supplier field lists.

Because you want to be able to update all fields in Components, drag the special "all fields" indicator (*) from the Components field list to the QBE grid. From Supplier, you need Supplier Name, the two Supplier Address fields, Supplier City, Supplier State, Supplier Postal, and Supplier Phone Number. Do not include Supplier ID from Supplier; you want to be able to update the Supplier ID field, but only in the Components table. If you include Supplier ID from Supplier, it might confuse you later as you design the form.

You should end up with a query that looks like the one shown in Figure 14-1. Save this query as *Components and Suppliers–Chap 14.*

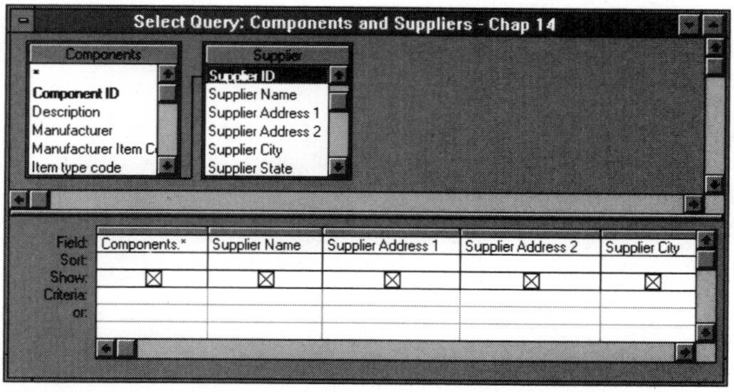

Figure 14-1.
The Components and Suppliers–Chap 14 query in Design view.

Designing a Many-to-One Form

Next make a copy of the Components–Chap 13 form you created earlier. Name your copy *Display/Add Components–Chap 14*. Open this form in Design view. Change the caption of the label at the top of the form to *Components–Chap 14*. In the property sheet for the form, change the caption to *Components and Suppliers–Chap 14*, and change the Record Source setting from Components (the table) to *Components and Suppliers–Chap 14* (the query), as shown in Figure 14-2.

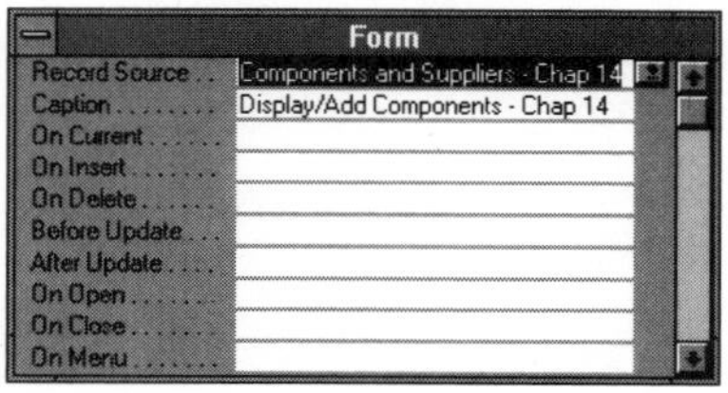

Figure 14-2.
The form's Record Source setting has been changed to the new Components and Suppliers–Chap 14 query.

Now you need to delete the old Supplier option group and replace it with a combo box for Supplier ID and text boxes for Supplier Address 1, Supplier Address 2, Supplier City, Supplier State, Supplier Postal, and Supplier Phone. As shown in Figure 14-3 on the next page, you can leave the shaded rectangle to provide emphasis for the Supplier data. Use the technique you learned earlier for building the combo box for Item Type (see the section in Chapter 12 called "Creating a Combo Box to Display Item Type") to display Supplier Name in the Supplier ID control box. With this technique you tie the Supplier ID display to the Supplier ID and Description columns from the Supplier table. Then you hide the first column (Supplier ID). The appropriate settings for the combo box property sheet are shown in Figure 14-3 on the next page.

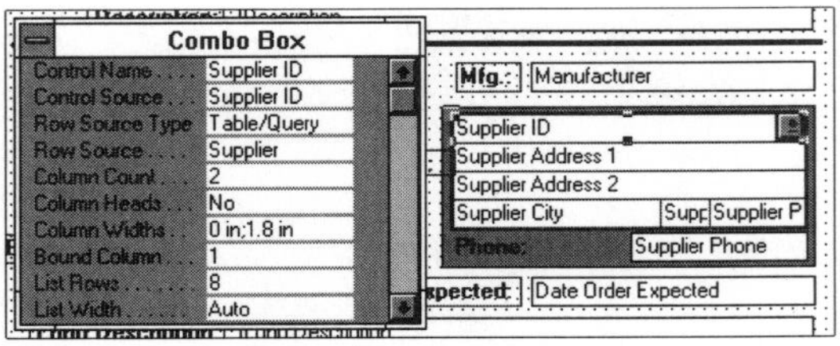

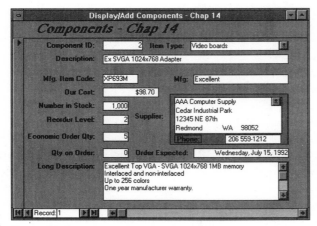

Figure 14-3.
The new Supplier controls and the property sheet for Supplier ID.

You can't update any of the fields in the Supplier table from this form. If you try to make such a change, Microsoft Access alerts you by playing Windows' default beep. To avoid the error alert, set the Enabled property to No and the Locked property to Yes for the Supplier Address, City, State, Postal, and Phone fields. With these settings, you won't be able to tab to or select any of these fields. For the Supplier ID control, be sure to leave the Enabled property set to Yes and the Locked property set to No so that you can update that field.

The results of these changes in Form view are shown in Figure 14-4. When you find the component you want, you can immediately see the relevant supplier name, address, and phone information. You can also update the Supplier ID in Components by opening the combo box and selecting a new Supplier Name. Notice that because the underlying Supplier ID is a number, you have to set the Text Align property of the Supplier ID control to Left if you want to see the text value for Supplier Name correctly aligned with the Supplier Address.

Figure 14-4.
The Components form is now a Components/Suppliers many-to-one form.

If you're curious how to end up with a white box and no lines for the supplier information (as shown in Figure 14-4), you can use combo and text boxes with no border. (Check Clear in the Border setting on the palette.) To create the outline around the supplier information, you can add a clear rectangle behind the fields. Finally, you can carefully enter settings for the Left, Top, Width, and Height properties so that the text boxes all touch each other and appear as a single display area.

Save this form as *Display/Add Components–Chap 14*. You'll use it again later in this chapter.

A Form on a Joined Crosstab Query

At the end of Chapter 8, in the section called "Crosstab Queries," you built a crosstab query to display sales totals by catalog item and month. The resulting query in Datasheet view was interesting, but not very usable. You could convert the query to a Make Table query and export the result to a spreadsheet program to format or graph the data. But why do that when you can format and graph the crosstab query data directly with a form?

Designing the Crosstab Query

Imagine that at the end of each year, you copy the monthly sales data to a sales summary for the year. In this example you will create a crosstab query called *1992 Sales Crosstab–Chap 14* that displays and formats the data in a form. Start with the Monthly Item Sales–Chap 8 crosstab query from Chapter 8. Use the Add Table command on the Query menu to add the Types field list to the Query window. Drag the Type Description field to the QBE grid. Set its crosstab line to Row Heading and its Sort line to Ascending. In the expression for the date, you can remove the "yy" formatting characters because you're only going to select 1992 data. The expression reads *Expr1: Format(DateSerial([Year],[Month],1), "mmm")*. See Figure 14-5.

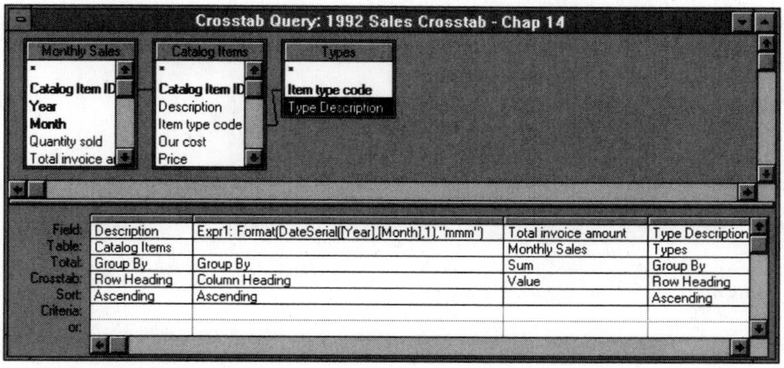

Figure 14-5.
The 1992 Sales Crosstab–Chap 14 query in Design view, first three fields.

For interest, also drag the Our Cost and Price fields from the Catalog Items field list to the QBE grid. Set their Total lines to Group By and their Crosstab lines to Row Heading. Drag the Year field from the Monthly Sales field list to the QBE grid, set the Total line to Where, and add 1992 to the Criteria line. See Figure 14-6. Finally, remove the Fixed Column Headings for the crosstab query by choosing the Query Properties commands from the View menu and turning off the Fixed Column Headings check box. You'll use the form design to set the months in the order you want.

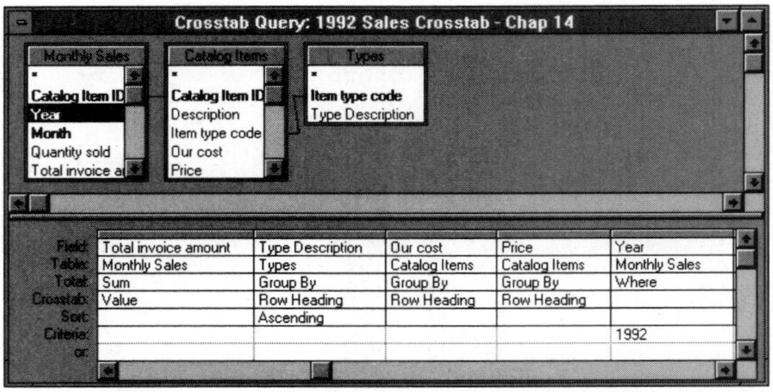

Figure 14-6.
The 1992 Sales Crosstab–Chap 14 query in Design view, last four fields.

When you run the query shown in Figure 14-6, you should get a dynaset similar to the one shown in Figure 14-7. Save this query as *1992 Sales Crosstab–Chap 14*. Now you're ready to build the form to handle this data.

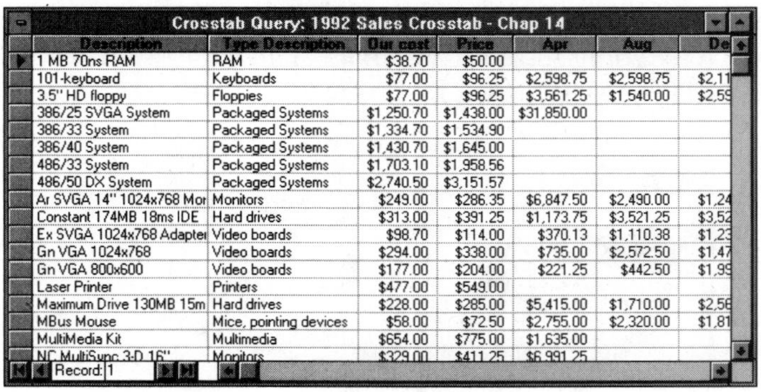

Figure 14-7.
The 1992 Sales Crosstab–Chap 14 query in Datasheet view.

Designing the Crosstab Form

Create a new form based on the crosstab query you just designed. The easiest way to get started is to use the FormWizard. Select the single-column design and the standard format. When the FormWizard shows you the list of fields you can place on the form, you should see the fields you added to the 1992 Sales Crosstab–Chap 14 Crosstab query, and a list of months in alphabetic sequence. If you choose the fields in calendar sequence, the FormWizard will place them on the form for you in that order. Choose the standard look, and title this new form *1992 Sales by Month and Quarter–Chap 14.*

After you have the basic form built by the FormWizard, you can create four columns of numbers on the form, one for each calendar quarter, as shown in Figure 14-8. Add column labels to enhance the appearance of your form. Because you only want to view data in this form, it's a good idea to set the properties on the form property sheet to the following settings: Default Editing property to Read Only, Allow Editing property to Unavailable, and Allow Updating property to No Tables. You can set the Default View property to Single Form (sales totals for one item at a time) or to Continuous.

When you switch to Form view, you can see the result, as shown in Figure 14-9. (You might need to view another record to see numbers in all the text boxes.)

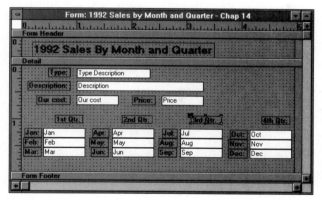

Figure 14-8.
A form based on the 1992 Sales Crosstab–Chap 14 query.

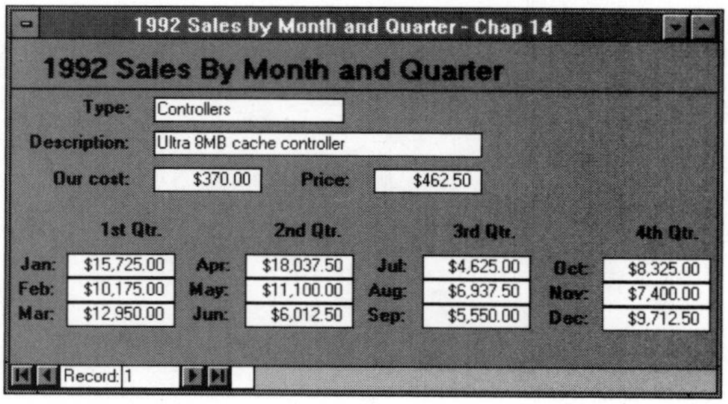

Figure 14-9.
The Form view of the form shown in Figure 14-8.

The form in this example is a single form view with no vertical scroll bars. You can click down to the subsequent records by using the buttons in the record number box.

Adding Calculated Values

The form shown in Figure 14-9 is a much more interesting view of the crosstab dynaset than the query's Datasheet view, but even here you've only begun to tap the capabilities of Microsoft Access. For example, you can add some totals for each quarter and a grand total for the year. To generate totals, you add some text boxes that aren't bound to any fields in the query. Simply select the text box tool from the toolbox, and then click in the form where you want to place the upper left corner of the text box control. Set each total control's Format property to Currency.

You can display the results of any calculated expression in an unbound control by adding the expression to the control's property sheet. Simply enter the expression you want preceded by an equal sign (=) in the Control Source property. You can also select the control, click in the text box area, and then type the expression directly. Figure 14-10 shows you the quarterly and annual totals added to the form in Design view. You can see the simple addition formula for the first quarter in the text box property sheet: *=[Jan]+[Feb]+[Mar]*. The controls for the quarterly totals were named *Q1, Q2, Q3,* and *Q4* respectively so that those names could be used to calculate the annual total.

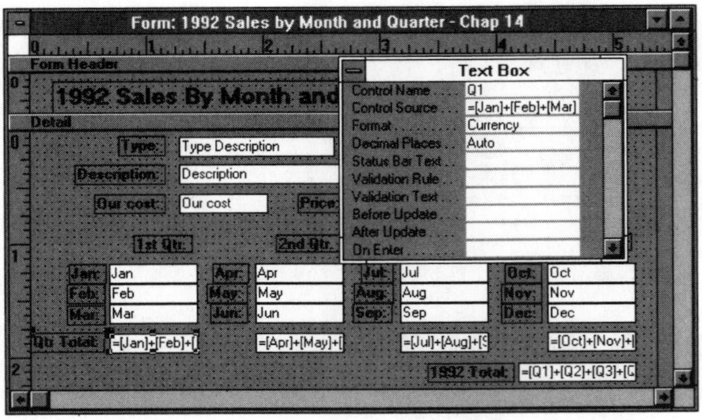

Figure 14-10.
The text boxes that calculate totals on the sales form.

Figure 14-11 shows you the form in Form view. Later in this chapter you'll make this form really interesting by adding a graph of the month-to-month sales totals.

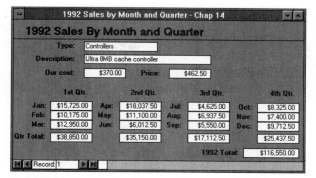

Figure 14-11.
The Form view of the form shown in Figure 14-10.

CREATING SUBFORMS

If you want to show data from several tables and you want to be able to update the data in more than one of the tables, you probably need something more complex than a standard form. In the PROMPT database, the company's products are listed in the Catalog Items table. Since Prompt Computer Solutions sells assembled systems, there's also a separate Components table of component parts.

There's another table, called Item Components, that forms a link between Catalog Items and Components. Item Components lists the components in each assembled system. Catalog Items is related one-to-many to Item Components (because an assembled system can be made up of many components). The Components table is also related one-to-many to Item Components (because a component—for example, a disk drive—might be included in several system configurations).

You could create a single form to display Catalog Items and the related components, but you'd be limited by the fact that you could update only the "many" side of the relationship. In other words, you could add components to an existing system, but you couldn't create new system configurations. To be able to both define new systems *and* add components, you could create a form with another form embedded: a *main* form to handle Catalog Items and a *sub* form to handle Item Components. When you build such a form-subform, Microsoft Access allows you to create a link to keep the two forms synchronized; you see on the Item Components subform only those components that belong to the Catalog Item displayed on the main form.

Designing the Subform Source

You can embed forms within forms several layers deep. You should always start with the innermost form and work outward. So begin by deciding on the source of data for the subform.

In the problem stated above, you want to create or update rows in the Item Components table to create, modify, or destroy links between systems in Catalog Items and parts in Components. Also, you'll want to modify the display; Item Components only contains two linking fields and a quantity—not very useful information to display on a form. You need to include in the subform the Components table so that you can display component descriptions, and you need to include the Types table so that you can show the kind of component you're adding.

Start by opening a new query. Use the Add Table command on the Query menu to add the Item Components, Components, and Types field lists to the Query window. You want to be able to update all the fields in Item Components, so copy them to the QBE grid. You will set Component ID to display the Description field from the Components table, so you don't need to add Description to the QBE grid, but instead add the Our Cost field from the Components table so that you can calculate the total cost of the components in an unbound text box. Add Type Description from the Types table so that you can also display the related component type without resorting to a combo or list box. Your query should look similar to the one shown in Figure 14-12.

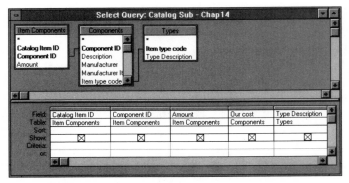

Figure 14-12.
A query for updating the Item Components table from a subform.

If you check the relationships between these tables, you'll find that the Item Components table is the only table that can be updated. The Types table is related one-to-many to the Components table; if you included only Types and Components in this query, you could update any Components field. However, Components is related one-to-many to Item Components. As a result, you can update only the fields in Item Components in this query. Save the query and name it *Catalog Sub–Chap 14* so that you can use it as you design the subform.

Designing the Subform

It would be nice to display the component name, type, amount, and cost in a Datasheet view with multiple lines that you could scroll through to see all the parts that belong to a particular assembled computer system. You can't display a form header or footer in Datasheet view. In this example, you can build a form that looks and acts like a datasheet but also has a customized header and a footer for displaying a calculated total. Start by opening a new form based on the Catalog Sub–Chap 14 query you just created. Try creating the form without using the FormWizard.

Figure 14-13 shows you the design for the subform. If you line up controls of equal height in a row in the detail section, then size the section so that it shows only those controls, and finally set the Default View property of the form to Continuous Forms, the form will look like a datasheet when you switch to Form view. At the same time, in Design view you can add a header and a footer by choosing the Form Hdr/Ftr command from the Layout menu. Notice that this form includes in the footer a total of cost multiplied by amount for all the rows on the form—another use of a calculation in an unbound control.

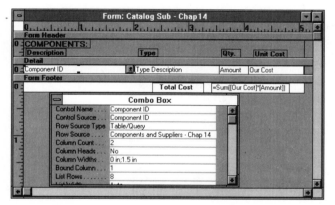

Figure 14-13.
The Catalog Sub–Chap 14 form that will eventually be embedded as a subform.

If you're curious, you can open this Catalog Sub–Chap 14 form in Form view. Because you haven't yet limited Catalog Item ID by embedding this form as a subform, you'll get all the components for all catalog items and a grand total cost at the bottom, as shown in Figure 14-14 on the next page. Notice that this form looks like a Datasheet view even though it's really a Form view, with a header, footer, and embedded combo box.

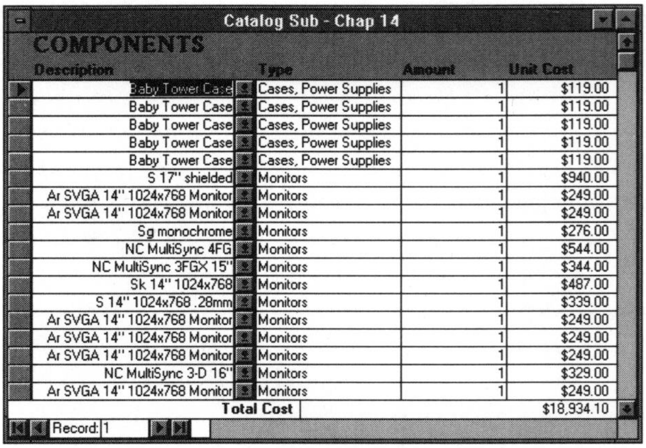

Figure 14-14.
The Catalog Sub–Chap 14 form in Form view.

Choosing the Main Form Source

Now it's time to move on to the Main form. First you need a table or query as the source of the form. You want to be able to view, update, add, and delete certain catalog items so you can use the Catalog Items table as the source. However, your principal concern is assembled systems, not all catalog items. By creating a Catalog Items query instead of using the Catalog Items table as the source of your form, you can sort the catalog items based on Item Type Code and ensure that assembled systems appear first in the form. Figure 14-15 shows you the query you need. An easy way to create your query is to drag all Catalog Item fields at once to the QBE grid (using *) and then add the Item Type Code field with the Show box unchecked to specify your sort criteria. Save the query and name it *Catalog Main–Chap 14* to use in your main form.

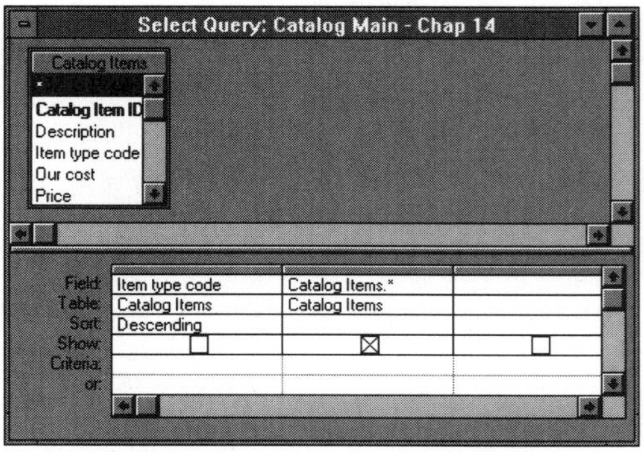

Figure 14-15.
A query for updating the Catalog Items table from a main form.

Creating the Main Form

Building the form for Catalog Items is fairly straightforward. In fact, you can select the Catalog Main–Chap 14 query and use a FormWizard to build the basic form in both single-column and shadowed formats. If you decide to use these formats, you must be careful when you move controls around, because the shadow boxes behind the controls are actually separate rectangle controls. The best way to drag and move the shadow and the control together is to drag the pointer to create a selection box around both and move them as a group.

Look at the design shown in Figure 14-16. The Catalog Item ID field has been placed in the form header because it's a counter that Microsoft Access maintains. You can also change Item Type Code to a combo box based on the Type description to make it easy to choose the code for a catalog item.

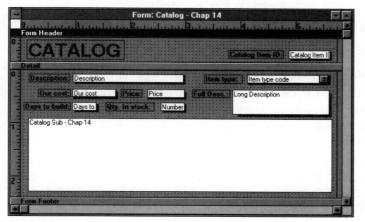

Figure 14-16.
The Catalog–Chap 14 form in Design view.

To create a place for the subform, click the subform tool and then click in the detail section of the form. The subform you designed earlier is about 5 or 5½ inches wide. Knowing that dimension helps you size the subform control on the main form. You can also add the subform to the main form by moving the Form window in Design view to the side so that you can see the Database window; click Forms in the Database window, click the Catalog Sub–Chap 14 subform, and drag and drop it onto the open Catalog Main–Chap 14 form. See Figure 14-17 on the next page. When you do this, Microsoft Access sizes the width of the subform control based on the width of the subform. With the subform in place, you should make the subform control high enough to display four or five rows of content—perhaps 1¼ inches high. You can further adjust the size of the subform later after you see how it looks in Form view.

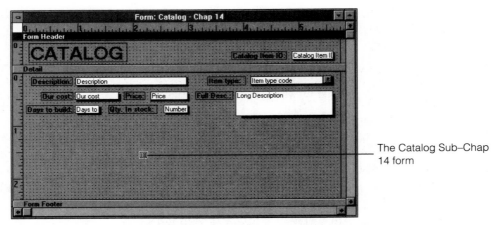

The Catalog Sub–Chap 14 form

Figure 14-17.
The Catalog Sub–Chap 14 form is being dragged to the Catalog Main–Chap 14 form, where it will appear as a subform.

Linking Main and Subform

To link the main and subform together, you need to set three properties for the subform control. The property sheet is shown in Figure 14-18. If you used the subform tool to create an unbound subform control, you need to enter the name of the form you want to use as a subform for the Source Object property. The name in this case is Catalog Sub–Chap 14. If you dragged and dropped the subform onto the form, Microsoft Access set the Source Object name for you. In the Link Master Fields property, you must enter the name of the control on the main form whose value determines what Access displays on the subform; in this case, it's the *Catalog Item ID* field from the Catalog Items table. Likewise, type the name of the linking field on the subform in Link Child Fields. The linking field also happens to be named *Catalog Item ID*, but the linking field is on the subform and originates in the Item Components table.

Subform/Subreport	
Control Name	Catalog Sub - Chap 14
Source Object . . .	Catalog Sub - Chap 14
Link Child Fields . .	Catalog Item ID
Link Master Fields	Catalog Item ID
Status Bar Text .	
Visible	Yes
Display When . . .	Always
Enabled	Yes
Locked	No
Can Grow	Yes

Figure 14-18.
The property sheet for the subform control in the Catalog form.

NOTE: *If the source of the main form and the subform is a table (not a query), and you have defined a relationship between the two tables, Access automatically generates the link properties (Link Master Fields and Link Child Fields) for you using the related fields when you drag and drop the subform onto the main form. Access also automatically links a subform to a main form when the main form is based on a table and there's a field on the subform with the same name as the primary key of the main form's source table.*

When you're finished, click the Form view button on the tool bar to see the completed form, as shown in Figure 14-19. If you see a partial row displayed on the subform, return to Design view and adjust the height of the subform control. Save your form and name it *Catalog–Chap 14*. Next you will make your form more interesting using pictures.

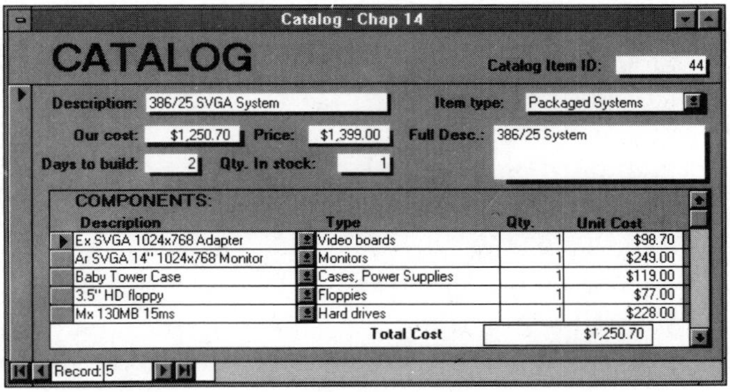

Figure 14-19.
The Catalog—Chap 14 form with subform.

By the way, you can also use a FormWizard to create a form/subform for you. When you do that, the FormWizard creates a single column form for the main form and a Datasheet view of the subform. In this case, because you did some special designing of the subform, making the Datasheet view inappropriate, you only used the FormWizard to create the main form.

WORKING WITH OBJECTS

Microsoft Access makes it easy to work with objects created by any application that supports Object Linking and Embedding (OLE). One way you can enhance a form is to add pictures to the form design. Many of the forms in NWIND are designed with pictures. In this section you'll add a logo to the Catalog–Chap 14 form.

Adding an Unbound Picture

Start by opening up the heading of the form and making room on the left side about 1 inch high by 2 inches wide. Select the unbound object frame tool in the toolbox and place the unbound object frame control in the upper left corner of the form. Microsoft Access responds with an Insert Object dialog box, as shown in Figure 14-20, to ask you what type of object you would like to insert on the form.

Figure 14-20.
The Insert Object dialog box.

You can choose from any drawing application that supports OLE—including Microsoft Draw, Microsoft WordArt, Microsoft Paintbrush, and Microsoft Power-Point. Select an application such as Paintbrush and click OK to start the application to create a new picture. If you already have the object saved as a file, click File to open a dialog box to choose the drive, directory, and filename. Access automatically lists file types compatible with the OLE application you have chosen. If you specify a file, Access copies it directly into the unbound object frame control. If you open the application, you use it to create your drawing. Choose Update from that application's file menu to store your work back on your form. Then exit the application.

This example will use a sample logo for Prompt Computer Solutions that was scanned in from a letterhead and then sized as small, medium, and large bitmap (BMP) files compatible with Paintbrush. The result is shown in Figure 14-21.

Figure 14-21.
A picture object is embedded in an unbound object frame control, and its properties are set.

For the Scaling property, you have three choices. Clip (the default) leaves the picture the original size, places the picture in the upper left corner of the control, and clips the picture on the bottom and right if it's too large to fit. Scale shrinks or enlarges the picture horizontally and vertically to fit the control, and distorts the proportion of your picture if the control doesn't match the original picture proportions. Zoom shrinks or enlarges your picture, but maintains aspect ratio. In this case, the Zoom setting was chosen to shrink the picture slightly without distortion.

Now when you open the form in Form view, you can see a logo at the top, as shown in Figure 14-22.

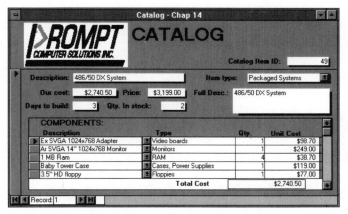

Figure 14-22.
The Catalog form with an embedded picture (a logo).

Adding a Bound Picture

If you look at the Catalog Items table in Design view, you'll notice that there's a field called Diagram that is an OLE object in each record. This field stores a picture of each major item in the catalog. The picture can be displayed on the screen or printed in fliers that are mailed to customers. If you want to be able to update all the Diagram objects in the Catalog Items table from your Catalog–Chap 14 form, you need to add a bound object frame control to the Catalog–Chap 14 form.

Open the Catalog–Chap 14 form's window in Design view. Drag the bottom border down to enlarge the Catalog–Chap 14 form. Clear some space on the right side of the form by moving the Item Type and Full Description fields to the left. Click the bound object frame tool, and then click the Diagram field in the field list and drag the field to the form. Size the bound object frame control about 1½ inches square. See Figure 14-23 on the next page.

It's easy to replace a picture in the bound object frame control. If you have PowerPoint or a similar graphics program, you can probably find a clip art graphic of a personal computer to try out as a replacement. Or, you can scan in and size any crisp black and white picture and save it as a bitmap file. Switch to Form view, select the picture control, and choose the Insert Object command from the Edit menu. You'll see an Insert Object dialog box, as shown in Figure 14-20. Choose an object type and click OK to open the related application, or click the File button in the dialog box to copy directly in a picture file.

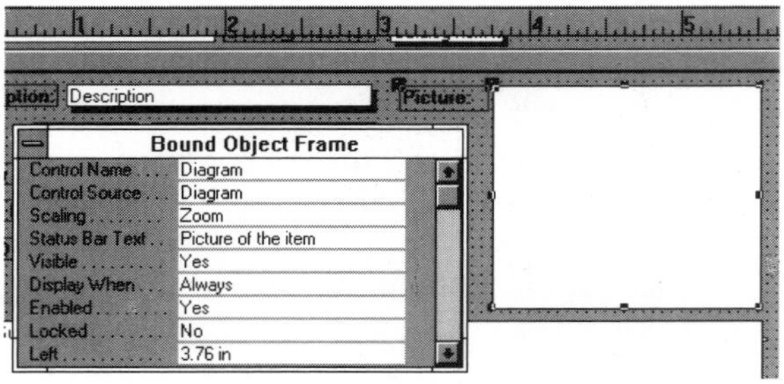

Figure 14-23.
A bound object frame control and its property sheet.

In this example a PC graphic was found in a PowerPoint clip art file, pasted into Paintbrush, and saved as a bitmap file. Then it was inserted into the picture control or the Catalog–Chap 14 form in Form view. The result is shown in Figure 14-24.

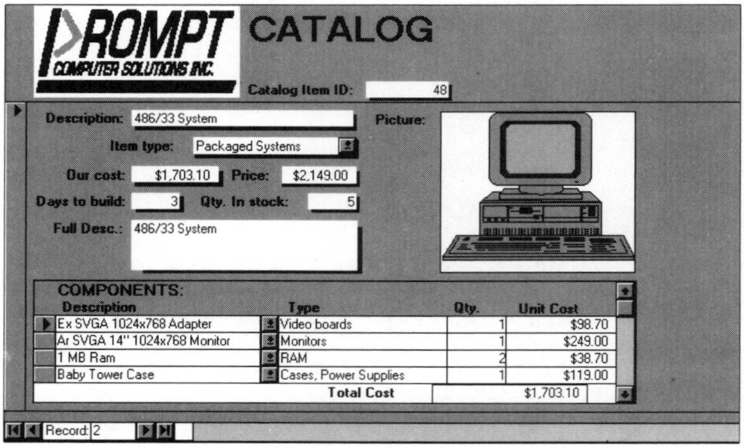

Figure 14-24.
The Catalog–Chap 14 form with a new picture object, in Form view.

Using Graphs

Graphs are another kind of object you can embed in a form. Go back to the crosstab form you created earlier in this chapter, 1992 Sales by Month and Quarter–Chap 14. Open a space in the upper right corner of the form by moving the monthly totals down and stacking the other fields on the left. The result is shown in Figure 14-25.

Now click the graph tool in the toolbox and place a graph control in the new blank space on your form. Microsoft Access responds with a GraphWizard dialog box, as shown in Figure 14-26.

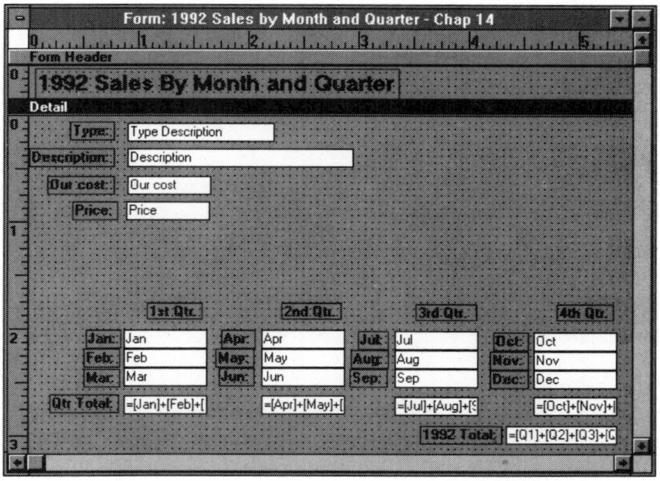

Figure 14-25.

The controls on this form are rearranged to make room for a graph in the upper right.

Figure 14-26.

The first GraphWizard screen.

The GraphWizard Screens are similar to those you'll see if you choose the Graph option on the FormWizard. In fact, one good way to create a graph is to use the Graph option on the FormWizard to create a new form that has only the graph you want. You can then cut and paste the result to any form or report.

To use the GraphWizard shown in Figure 14-26, you must first choose the source for the graph. In our example, you want to graph the monthly sales data on the existing form, so you choose the same crosstab query that you used to create the form, 1992 Sales Crosstab–Chap 14. You can pick the graph type you want by clicking its picture. For this example, choose a filled-in line chart (the button on the upper left), and click Next.

Then the GraphWizard asks you for the fields you want to graph and include as labels. See Figure 14-27. Choose the Description field (which will serve as your link back to the form) and each of the month totals. Be sure to pick the month totals one at a time in calendar sequence so that they show up in the right order on the chart, and then click Next. In the next dialog box, the GraphWizard asks you which fields to use as labels on the chart. Again, choose all the month fields in calendar sequence but not the Description field. Click Next.

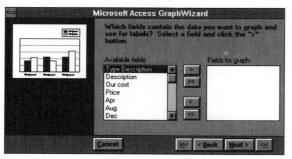

Figure 14-27.
The GraphWizard screen in which you choose fields to graph.

The GraphWizard will ask you whether you want to link the graph to the form. Click Yes to see the dialog box shown in Figure 14-28. Click the Description field on both sides and then click the <=> button in the center of the GraphWizard screen to move Description to the Link(s) area. If you do not link your graph to the form, your graph will reflect unfiltered data and will remain constant for each record on the form in Form view.

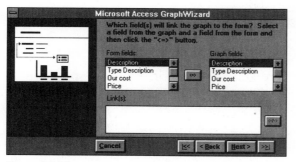

Figure 14-28.
The GraphWizard screen that links graph data to form data.

Click the Next button to see the final GraphWizard screen so that you can title your graph. Then click the Design button in the screen to see the result shown in Figure 14-29.

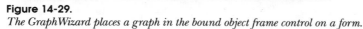

Figure 14-29.
The GraphWizard places a graph in the bound object frame control on a form.

Change to Form view to see the records and their related sales charts, as shown in Figure 14-30. Each time you move to a new record, Microsoft Access links to the Microsoft Graph program to produce a new chart on the form, which takes a few seconds. You can see that Access approaches the capability of many spreadsheet programs, linking data directly from your database into useful charts that you can view and print.

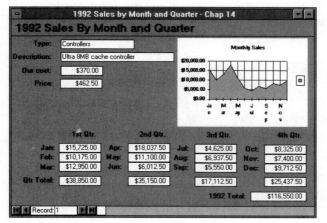

Figure 14-30.
The form in Form view with the linked graph.

LINKING FORMS WITH COMMAND BUTTONS

One of the most exciting features of Access is its ability to trigger macros by events on forms. Suppose you are working in the Catalog–Chap 14 form, listing new systems. Every time you realize that you're missing a new Component, you don't have to go to the Database window, find the Display/Add Components–Chap 14 form that you designed earlier, create your new component, and then switch back to the Catalog–Chap 14 form. Microsoft Access provides an easy way to open the Display/Add Components–Chap 14 form directly from the Catalog–Chap 14 form. You can create a command button in your form in Design view that uses a macro to open another form.

Creating a Macro

If you've looked at any of the form or control property sheets in any detail, you've probably noticed several properties with names like *On Insert, Before Update, On Close,* and the like. These properties refer to events for which you can define actions that you want Microsoft Access to execute when the event happens. For example, selecting a control, clicking a button, and making a menu choice are events to which Access can respond.

You can define most of the actions you'll ever need with a macro. (And if you need to do something really tricky, Microsoft Access gives you the option of writing code with Access Basic.) Macros give you more than 40 different actions you can use as responses to events. To define a simple macro, go to the Database window, click the Macro button, and then click the New button. Microsoft Access opens a Macro window, as shown in Figure 14-31.

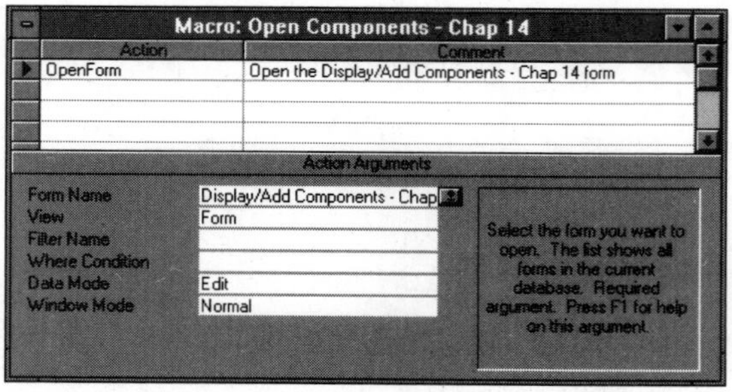

Figure 14-31.
The Macro window.

The Macro window looks a lot like the Table window in Design view and works in much the same way. You enter action names and comments in the top part of the window and use F6 to jump down to the bottom part of the window to set arguments for each action. When you choose an action at the top of the window, Access asks for the appropriate arguments at the bottom of the window. You don't even have to remember the names of all the actions. If you click in the action column, Access shows you a drop-down list button. Click that button to open the list of available actions.

It's time to try creating your own macro now. Your macro will open the Display/Add Components–Chap 14 form you created previously.

Open a new Macro window. In the Action column select the OpenForm action. Press F6 to move to the bottom of the window. On the Form Name line, select Display/Add Components–Chap 14 from the drop-down list. Now all you have to do is save your macro. Choose the Save As command from the File menu, and name your macro *Open Components–Chap 14.*

Adding a Command Button

It's easy to create a command button for your newly created macro. Open the Catalog–Chap 14 form in Design view. Select the command button tool in the toolbox and place a button in the header of the form. Size the button to be about 1 inch long. In the property sheet for the command button, type the button name, *Open Components,* on the Caption line. The result is shown in Figure 14-32.

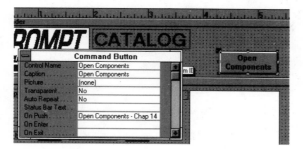

Figure 14-32.
An Open Components command button is added to the Catalog–Chap 14 form.

Also in the property sheet for the command button, you will find an On Push property. Type *Open Components–Chap 14* as the setting for On Push. Now when you "push" this new button on the Catalog–Chap 14 form, you will run the Open Components macro. Save the Catalog–Chap 14 form and open it in Form view. Click the Open Components button, and you should see the Display/Add Components–Chap 14 form pop up conveniently on top, as shown in Figure 14-33 on the next page. (You can also create a command button on a form and link it to a macro by selecting the macro in the Database window and dragging and dropping it onto your form in Design view.)

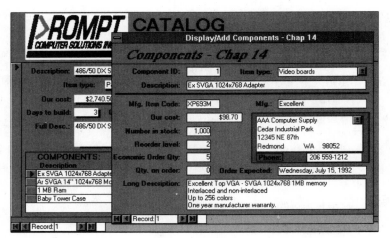

Figure 14-33.
The Display/Add Components–Chap 14 form opens when the new Open Components button is pressed.

This is the last chapter on forms. You'll learn a few more design tricks when you start to build an application using macros in the last part of this book. Now you can learn about reports in the next few chapters.

PART V

BUILDING REPORTS

The three chapters in Part V discuss the Microsoft Access report facilities. First you'll learn about the features of reports and how to use them. Then you will learn how to construct both simple and complex reports.

Chapter 15 discusses how you can use reports and takes you on a tour of the major report features. You'll also learn how to set up and print reports.

Chapter 16 teaches you how to build a simple report from scratch and how to use a ReportWizard to automate report building tasks.

The last chapter in this part, Chapter 17, explores advanced report design. Topics covered include sorting and grouping data, calculating values, and embedding graphics and subreports.

15
Report Basics

Previously you learned that you can format and print tables and queries in Datasheet view. You can use this technique to produce a printed copy of simple lists of information. Later you found that you could use forms not only to view and modify data, but also to print data—including data from several tables. However, because the major focus of forms is to allow you to view single records or small groups of related records displayed on screen in an attractive way, forms aren't the best way to print and summarize large sets of data in your database.

This chapter explores the external aspects of reports—why you should use a report instead of other methods of printing data and what features reports offer. Because you aren't building any reports for Prompt Computer Solutions yet, this chapter uses examples you can readily find in the sample NWIND database that you received with Microsoft Access. After you understand what you can do with reports, you'll look at the process of building reports for Prompt in the following two chapters.

USES FOR REPORTS

Reports are the best way to create a printed copy of information extracted or calculated from data in your database. Reports have two principal advantages over other methods of printing data:

- Reports can compare, summarize, and subtotal large sets of data.

- Reports can be created to produce attractive invoices, purchase orders, mailing labels, presentation materials, and other output you might need to efficiently conduct business.

Reports are designed to group data, to present each grouping separately, and to perform calculations. They work as follows:

- You can define up to 10 grouping criteria to separate levels of detail.

- You can define separate headers and footers for each group.

- You can perform complex calculations not only within a group or set of rows but also across groups.

- In addition to page headers and footers, you can define a header and footer for the entire report.

As with forms, you can embed pictures or graphs in any section of a report. You can also embed subreports or subforms within report sections.

A TOUR OF REPORTS

You can take a tour of reports by exploring many of the features designed into the samples in NWIND. A good place to start is the Percentages of Sales report. Open the NWIND database and click the Report button in the Database window. Scroll down the list of reports in the Database window until you see the Percentages of Sales report, as shown in Figure 15-1. Double-click that report (or select it and click the Preview button) to see Print Preview—a view of how the report will look when printed.

Figure 15-1.
The report list in the Database window.

The Percentages of Sales report is based on the Employee Sales by Country query, which brings together information from the Employees, Orders, and Order Details tables. You'll be prompted for two parameters: a beginning date and an ending date. For this exercise, enter *January 1, 1991* and *December 31, 1991* (or enter *1/1/91* and *12/31/91*) when prompted by the Enter Parameter Value dialog boxes.

When the Percentages of Sales report opens in Print Preview, you'll see a tool bar at the top of the Microsoft Access window, as shown in Figure 15-2, and a view of the report in the Report: Percentages of Sales window, as shown in Figure 15-3.

The Tool Bar for Print Preview

When you open a report in Print Preview, Microsoft Access displays a tool bar with four buttons, as shown in Figure 15-2. Click the Print button to send the report to your printer. Click the Setup button to specify printer and alignment options.

Figure 15-2.
The tool bar for Print Preview.

Use the Zoom button or click inside the report itself to switch between a full-page view and a close-up view of your report. By default, Access shows you the upper left corner of the first page of the report in close-up view when you open the report. Click Cancel to close Print Preview and return to the window from which you started the preview. As you'll see later in the chapter, if you enter Print Preview from a Report window in Design view, Cancel returns you to the Report window in Design view. In this case, if you click Cancel, you'll return to the Database window.

More About Print Preview

Maximize the window in Print Preview so that it's easy to see a large portion of the Percentages of Sales report at one time. You should be able to use the vertical and horizontal scroll bars to position the report so that you can see most of the top half of the first page, as shown in Figure 15-3. You can also use the arrow keys to move the page left, right, up, and down.

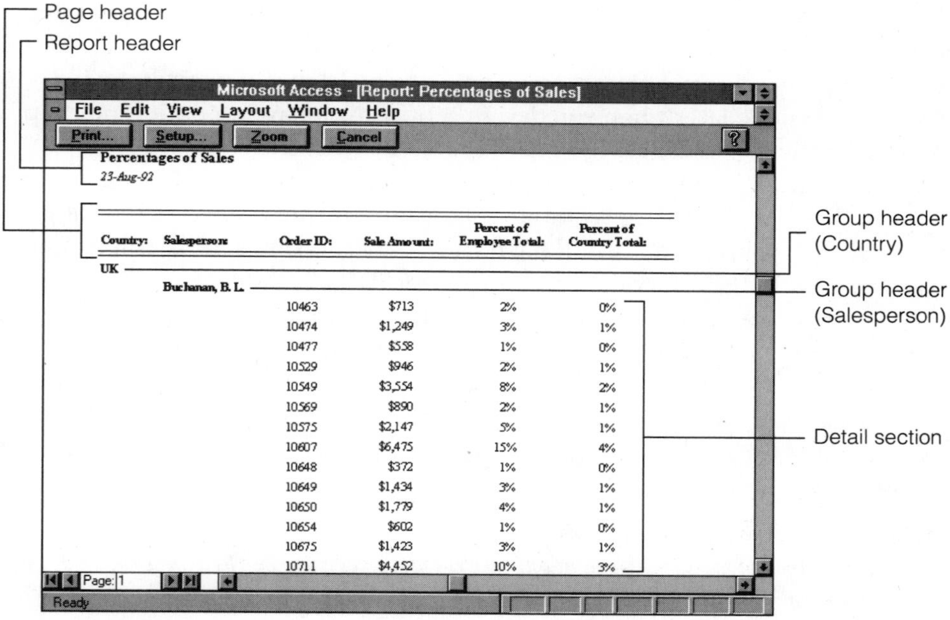

Page header
Report header
Group header (Country)
Group header (Salesperson)
Detail section

Microsoft Access - [Report: Percentages of Sales]

File   Edit   View   Layout   Window   Help

Print...   Setup...   Zoom   Cancel

Percentages of Sales
23-Aug-92

Country:	Salesperson:	Order ID:	Sale Amount:	Percent of Employee Total:	Percent of Country Total:
UK					
	Buchanan, B. L.				
		10463	$713	2%	0%
		10474	$1,249	3%	1%
		10477	$558	1%	0%
		10529	$946	2%	1%
		10549	$3,554	8%	2%
		10569	$890	2%	1%
		10575	$2,147	5%	1%
		10607	$6,475	15%	4%
		10648	$372	1%	0%
		10649	$1,434	3%	1%
		10650	$1,779	4%	1%
		10654	$602	1%	0%
		10675	$1,423	3%	1%
		10711	$4,452	10%	3%

Page: 1

Ready

Figure 15-3.
The NWIND Percentages of Sales report in Print Preview.

To view other pages of the report, you use the page number box at the bottom left of the window, as shown in Figure 15-4. To move forward one page at a time, click the arrow button immediately to the right of the page number box. You can also click the page number (or press F5 to select the page number), change the number, and press Enter to skip to the page you want. As you might guess, the left arrow button moves you backward one page, and the two arrows on either end of the page number box move you to the first or last page in the report. You can also move to the bottom of a page by pressing Ctrl-down arrow, to the top of the page by pressing Ctrl-up arrow, to the left margin of the page by pressing Home or Ctrl-left arrow, and to the right margin of the page by pressing End or Ctrl-right arrow. Pressing Ctrl-Home moves you to the upper left corner of the page, and pressing Ctrl-End moves you to the lower right corner of the page.

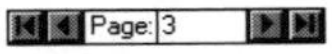

Figure 15-4.
The page number box in a Report window in Print Preview.

Headers, Details, Footers, and Groups

Although the Percentages of Sales report shown in Figure 15-3 appears simple at first glance, it actually contains a lot of information. On the first page you can see a report header that provides a title for the overall report and also displays the date on which you open the report. Below that is a page header that you'll see at the top of every page. As you'll see later when you design reports, you have an option not to print this header on the page that also displays the report header.

Next is a simple group header that Microsoft Access prints each time the country changes. This first page begins with data for salespeople in the United Kingdom. Below that is the group header you'll see for each salesperson. The salesperson name field is calculated in the query on which the report is based by concatenating the last name field, a comma, and the first name field from the Employees table. You could also perform this calculation in the report rather than in the query.

Below the salesperson header, Microsoft Access prints the detail information, one line for each row in the dynaset formed by the query. Also in the detail section, Access calculates for each order the percentage it represents of total sales by the salesperson as well as the percentage it represents of total sales in the country.

> **CAUTION:** *If you are working in a report with many pages, moving to the bottom, top, or back one page in the report might take a long time. Press Esc to cancel your page movement request. Access leaves you on the last page it attempted to format.*

On the fourth page of the Percentages of Sales report (although the page number might vary slightly depending on the printer you are using), you can see the group footer for one of the salespeople, the group footer for the country, and the next country and salesperson group headers, as shown in Figure 15-5. Notice that the salesperson footer contains the salesperson's total sales figure and the percentage this represents of sales within the country. In the country footer, Microsoft Access has calculated the total country sales and the percentage this represents of the grand total sales (which you'll see on the last page). The report continues with data for the first salesperson in the USA. At the bottom of the page is a page number, which is the content of the page footer.

Country:	Salesperson:	Order ID:	Sale Amount:	Percent of Employee Total:	Percent of Country Total:	
		10791	$1,830	4%	1%	
		10794	$315	1%	0%	
		10804	$2,278	5%	1%	
		10822	$238	1%	0%	
		10833	$907	2%	1%	
	Total for Suyama, Michael:		$44,271		26%	— Group footer (Salesperson)
Total for UK:			$172,511			— Group footer (Country)
Percent UK is of Grand Total:			27%			
USA						
	Callahan, Linda					
		10435	$632	1%	0%	
		10437	$393	1%	0%	
		10443	$517	1%	0%	
		10450	$425	1%	0%	

Figure 15-5.
The NWIND Percentages of Sales report has subtotals and percentage calculations in group footers.

If you skip to the last page of the report (about page 12), you can see the total and percentage calculations for USA sales and the grand total sales for the report, as shown in Figure 15-6. The grand total is the content of the report footer.

Country:	Salesperson:	Order ID:	Sale Amount:	Percent of Employee Total:	Percent of Country Total:	
Total for USA:			$455,878			
Percent USA is of Grand Total:			73%			
Grand Total:			$628,389			— Report footer

Figure 15-6.
The NWIND Percentages of Sales report has the grand total calculation in the report footer.

Reports Within Reports

Just as you can embed subforms within forms, you can also embed subreports (or subforms) within reports. Sometimes you might find it useful to calculate summary information in one report and also include the information in a report that shows detailed information. You don't have to define the summary report twice; simply include it as a subreport within the detail report. Microsoft Access automatically links the summary information with the related details.

You can see an example of this use of a subreport in the Sales by Year report and the Sales by Year Subreport in NWIND. Open the Sales by Year Subreport in Design view by selecting the subreport in the Database window and clicking the Design button, as shown in Figure 15-7. The Report window in Design view is shown in Figure 15-8.

Figure 15-7.
The Sales by Year Subreport is opened in Design view.

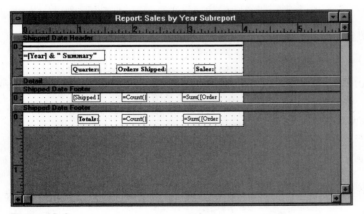

Figure 15-8.
The Report window for the Sales by Year Subreport, in Design view.

Notice that there isn't a detail section on this report. You can see one header for the column titles and two footers—one footer for the quarter totals (the footer repeats once for each quarter) and another footer for the year total. Because this report is intended to be embedded in another report, there are no report or page headers or footers. When the Sales by Year report is opened, the subreport will appear, as shown in Figure 15-9.

1991 Summary

Quarter:	Orders Shipped:	Sales:
1	93	$111,191
2	93	$155,131
3	105	$172,016
4	135	$190,052
Totals:	426	$628,390

Figure 15-9.
The data for 1991 on the Sales by Year Subreport.

Now run the Sales by Year report. Access prompts you for a beginning and ending date. If you enter *1/1/91* through *12/31/91*, you'll see the first page of the report, as shown in Figure 15-10. There's a report header to provide a title and run date. Within the group header for the year, you can see the embedded subreport, followed by the column headings for the subsequent detail.

Sales by Year
23-Aug-92

1991 Summary

Quarter:	Orders Shipped:	Sales:
1	93	$111,191
2	93	$155,131
3	105	$172,016
4	135	$190,052
Totals:	426	$628,390

Details

Year:	Shipped Date:	Orders Shipped:	Sales:
1991	01-Jan-91	10428	$192
		10426	$338
	04-Jan-91	10429	$1,441
		10431	$1,892
		10432	$485
		10435	$632
	07-Jan-91	10439	$1,078

Figure 15-10.
The Sales by Year report with the embedded subreport.

You can see another interesting feature in reports in the detail lines. Notice that there are two order entries for the January 1, 1991 date and four order entries for the January 4, 1991 date. But these dates are not repeated in the Shipped Date column, and neither is 1991 repeated in the Year column. Microsoft Access lets you set an option for detail lines to avoid printing duplicate values. In contrast, if you were looking at this data in a regular datasheet or a form, you would see the value 1991 repeated seven times, the value 01-Jan-91 repeated twice, and 04-Jan-91 repeated four times.

Another good use for embedding one report within another is to display several groups of data that are related many-to-many. In NWIND, there's a Sales Summaries report that contains no detail, only two subreports. These subreports summarize 1991 sales both by salesperson and by item category. Without subreports, it would be difficult to bring this information together because of the many-to-many relationship between the data—a salesperson can sell items in many categories, and a category can contain items sold by many different salespeople.

Objects in Reports

As with forms, you can embed OLE (Object Linking and Embedding) objects in reports. The objects embedded in or linked to reports are usually either pictures or charts. You can embed a picture or a chart as an unbound object in the report itself, or you can link a picture or a chart as a bound object from data in your database.

The Catalog report in the NWIND database has both unbound and bound objects. When you open the Catalog report in Print Preview, you can see the Northwind Traders logo (a lighthouse) embedded in the report title as an unbound Microsoft Draw object. (See Figure 15-11.) This drawing is actually a part of the report design.

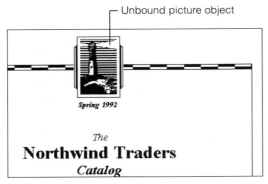

Figure 15-11.
An unbound object embedded in the Catalog report.

If you skip forward to page 3 of the report, you can see a picture displayed on the form, as shown in Figure 15-12. This picture is a bound Paintbrush object from the Categories table.

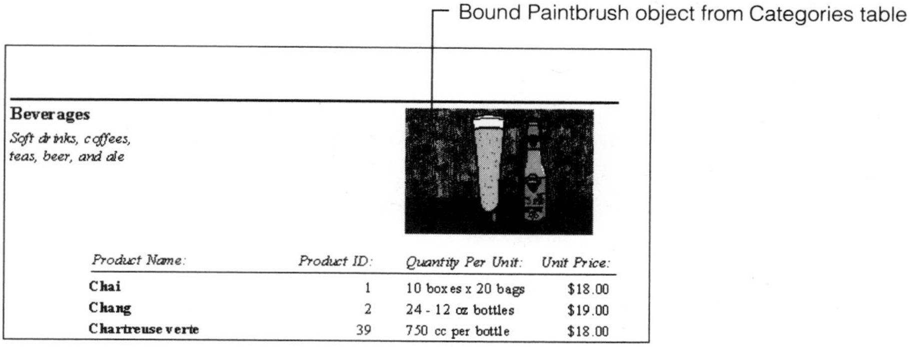

┌─ Bound Paintbrush object from Categories table

Figure 15-12.
A bound object linked to the Catalog report.

PRINTING REPORTS

Previously you learned the basics of viewing a report in Print Preview. Here are a few more tips and details about setting up reports for printing.

Print Setup

When you decide you want to print a report, you might first want to check its appearance and then change the printer setup. Open the Sales by Year report you looked at earlier; select the report in the Database window and click the Preview button to run the report. Enter *1/1/91* and *12/31/91* as the beginning and ending dates when you are prompted. After Microsoft Access shows you the report, click the Zoom button and then maximize the window to see the full-page view, as shown in Figure 15-13 on the next page. You can see that the report does not occupy a lot of space on the page. You might be able to increase the amount of data per page by asking Access to print data in several columns. To do that, you need to modify some parameters in the Print Setup dialog box.

You can open the Print Setup dialog box by clicking the Setup button in the Print Preview tool bar. You can also define the printer setup for a report by selecting the report in the Database window and choosing the Print Setup command from the File menu. Microsoft Access shows you a dialog box similar to the one shown in Figure 15-14 on the next page. You can expand the dialog box by clicking the More button. The expanded dialog box is shown in Figure 15-15 on page 341.

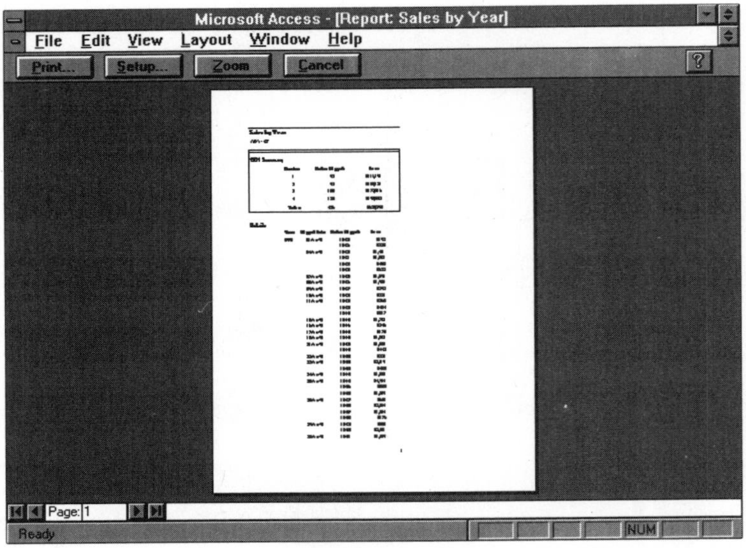

Figure 15-13.
The full-page Sales by Year report in Print Preview.

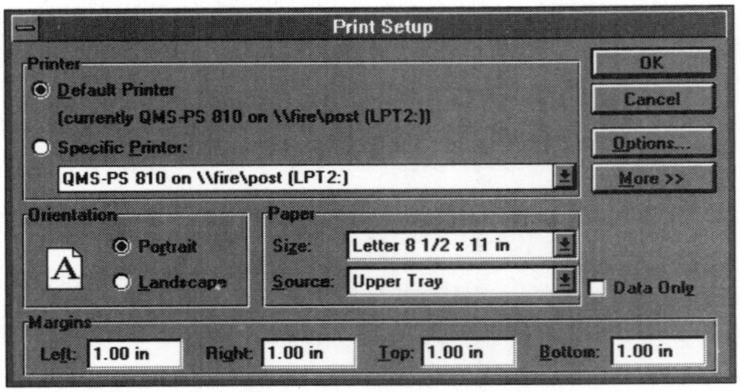

Figure 15-14.
The Print Setup dialog box.

To print the Sales by Year report in two columns, change the printer's orientation from Portrait (up and down the page) to Landscape (across the page). Set Items Across to *2* and set Column Spacing to *0.5 in*. Indicate to Access that you want the detail information arranged vertically on the page to retain the original sequence of the printing in two columns. Figure 15-15 shows the correct settings.

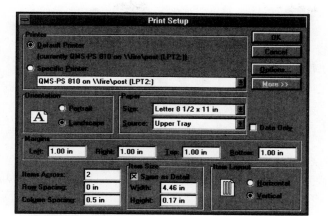

Figure 15-15.
The expanded Print Setup dialog box, with settings to print the Sales by Year report in two columns.

When you enter the settings shown in Figure 15-15, your report in Print Preview will look like the one shown in Figure 15-16.

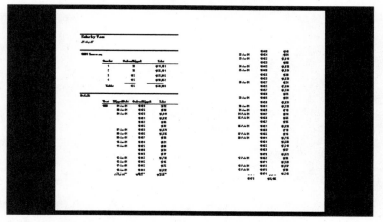

Figure 15-16.
The Sales by Year report displayed in Landscape orientation and in two columns.

That covers the fundamentals of reports and how to view them and set them up for printing. The next two chapters show you how to design and build reports for your application.

16

Constructing a Report

Constructing a report is very similar to building a form. In this chapter you'll apply many of the techniques you used in working with forms, and you'll learn how to apply some of the unique features reports offer. After a quick tour of the report design facilities, you'll build a simple report for Prompt Computer Solutions, and then use a ReportWizard to create the same report. The next chapter shows you how to apply advanced techniques to report design.

STARTING FROM SCRATCH—A SIMPLE REPORT

In this section you'll build a relatively simple report as you tour the report design facilities. Because you are most likely to use reports to look at the "big picture," you'll usually design a query that brings together data from several related tables as the basis for your reports.

The report you'll build uses the Catalog Items and Types table in the PROMPT database. (If you prefer to work with the NWIND database that comes with Microsoft Access, build a report using the Products and Categories tables.)

Designing the Report Query

To construct a report for PROMPT, most of the data you need is in the Catalog Items table whose fields are Catalog Item ID, Description, Item Type Code, Our Cost, Price, and Long Description. It would be interesting to add the Item Type Description and also to calculate the total stock on hand and the average cost by item type. You could include a combo box on the report to extract the Item Type Description from the Types table, but it's more efficient to include that information in a query that provides the data for the report rather than to include the information in the report directly.

Similarly, you'll discover that it's easier to define a complex calculation once in a query and use the data from that query for the summaries in your report rather than enter the calculation several times for multiple groups in the report. You can also use the query to create text fields that concatenate several fields from your table—for example, to concatenate first name and last name or to concatenate city, state, and zip code.

Figure 16-1 shows the query you'll need for this first report. To create the query, go to the Database window, select the Catalog Items table, and click the New Query button on the tool bar. Use the Add Table command from the Query menu to add the Types table to the query. Drag all the fields from the Catalog Items table and the Type Description field from the Types table to the QBE grid. Save the query and name it *Catalog Items for Report–Chap 16*. (In the PROMPT sample database, you can find the query named *Category Items for Report*.)

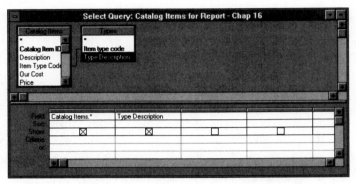

Figure 16-1.
A query that selects catalog item data for a report.

Starting to Design a New Report

Now you're ready to start constructing a report. Select in the Database window the query you just built and then click the New Report button on the tool bar. Microsoft Access displays the dialog box shown in Figure 16-2.

Figure 16-2.
The New Report dialog box.

Microsoft Access shows you the name of the query you just selected in the combo box at the top of the dialog box. (If you want to select a different table or query, you can open the drop-down list to see a list of all the tables and queries in your database, and select another.) You'll use ReportWizards later in this chapter to create a report. For now, click the Blank Report button to open up a new Report window in Design view.

Working with Design Elements

When you open a blank report, Microsoft Access shows you a Report window in Design view similar to the one shown in Figure 16-3. The tool bar for the Report window is at the top of the Microsoft Access window. As with forms design, the Report window itself is in the background (but on top of the Database window) with the field list, property sheet, and toolbox open to assist you as you build your report. (If necessary, you can use the Field List, Properties, and Toolbox commands on the View menu to open these windows.)

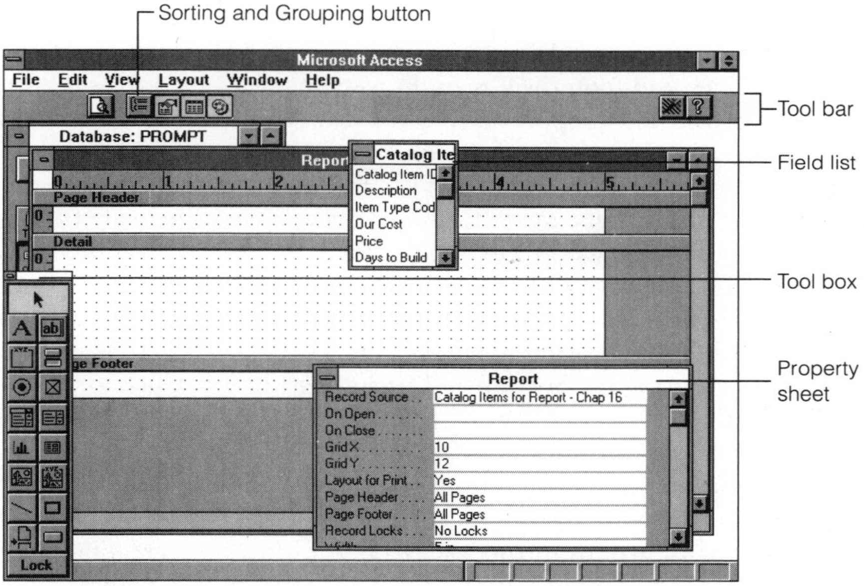

Figure 16-3.
The Report window in Design view.

NOTE: *The tool bar for the Report window in Design view is very similar to the tool bar for the Form window in Design view. See Chapter 11, "Form Basics," for a detailed description of most tool bar buttons. Similarly, the field list, property sheet, toolbox, and palette are similar to the elements you used in building forms. See Chapter 12, "Building a Form," for a detailed description of their use.*

On the blank report, Access starts you out with page header and footer sections and a 5 inch wide by 1 inch high detail section in the center. The rulers at the top and left of the Report window help you plan space on the printed page. If you plan to have 0.5-inch side margins, you can design the body of the report up to 7.5 inches wide for a normal 8.5-by-11-inch page. The space you can use vertically depends on how large you design your headers and footers and how large you define the top and bottom margins. As with forms, you can drag the edge of any section to make the section larger or smaller. Notice that the width of all sections must be the same, so if you change the width of one section, Access changes the width of all other sections to match.

Within each section you can see an initial design grid that has 10 dots per inch horizontally and 12 dots per inch vertically. If you're working in centimeters, Access divides the grid into 5 dots per centimeter both vertically and horizontally. You can change these settings using the Grid X and Grid Y properties on the report property sheet. (If the dots are not visible in your Report window, choose the Grid command from the View menu. If the Grid command is checked and you still can't see the dots, try resetting the Grid X and Grid Y properties on the property sheet.)

The page header and footer will print in your report at the top and bottom of each page. You can also add a report header that prints once at the beginning of the report and a footer that prints once at the end of the report. To add these sections, choose the Report Hdr/Ftr command from the Layout menu. You can use the Page Hdr/Ftr command on this same menu to add or remove the page header and footer sections. You'll learn how to add group headers and footers later in this chapter.

Sorting and Grouping

One way in which reports are different from forms is that you can group information for display on reports using the Sorting and Grouping window. Click on the Sorting and Grouping button on the tool bar (Figure 16-3) to open the Sorting and Grouping window, as shown in Figure 16-4. In this window, you can define up to 10 fields or expressions that you will use to form groups on the report. The first item on the list determines the main group, and subsequent items define groups within groups. (You saw this nesting of groups in the last chapter, within the Percentages of Sales report in NWIND; there was a main group for each country and a subgroup within that main group for each salesperson in that country.)

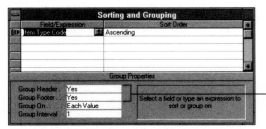

Set these to Yes to see a header and a footer in the report

Figure 16-4.
The Sorting and Grouping window.

In the simple report you're creating for Catalog Items, you need to group data by Item Type Code so that you can calculate a total of items on hand and an average cost by item type. If you click in the first row of the Field/Expression column, a down arrow appears in the right corner. Click this arrow (or press Alt-down arrow) to open up the list of fields from the underlying table or query. Select the Item Type Code field to place it in the Field/Expression column. The Field/Expression column can also be used to enter an expression based on any field in the underlying query or table. By default, Microsoft Access sorts each grouping value in ascending order. If you like you can change that to descending order by choosing Descending from the drop-down list that appears when you click in the Sort Order field.

You need a place to put header information for each group (at least for the Type Description field) and a footer for the calculated fields (total and average). To add those sections, change the settings for Group Header and Group Footer to Yes in the Sorting and Grouping window, as shown in Figure 16-4. When you do that, Microsoft Access will add those sections to the Report window for you. You'll look at using the Group On and and Group Interval properties in the next chapter. For now, leave them set to their default values. Click the Sorting and Grouping button on the tool bar to close the Sorting and Grouping window.

Constructing a Simple Report for Catalog Items

Now you're ready to finish building an inventory report based on the Catalog Item table. First save your report as *Inventory Report–Chap 16*. Perform the following steps to construct a report similar to the one shown in Figure 16-5 on the next page.

1. Place a label control on the page header and type *Catalog Item Inventory* as the label caption. Select the label control and then, from the tool bar, select the Arial font in 18-point bold. You'll have to resize the label control so that the text fits.

2. Click the text box control, and then click and drag the Type Description field from the field list to the Item Type Code header. Use Arial 10-point bold for the label and control. Change the caption in the label to *Category:* from *Type Description.*

3. You'll need some column labels in the Item Type Code header. The easiest way to create them is to open up the detail section to give yourself some room, select the label control and click Lock on the toolbox, and then drag-and-drop the fields Catalog Item ID, Description, Our Cost, and Number in Stock from the field list to the detail section. Click the Lock button on the toolbox and then click the Pointer tool. Select the label for Catalog Item ID and then choose the Cut command from the Edit menu (or press Ctrl-X) to separate the label from the control and place the label on the clipboard. Choose the Paste command from the Edit menu (or press Ctrl-V) to paste the label into the upper left corner

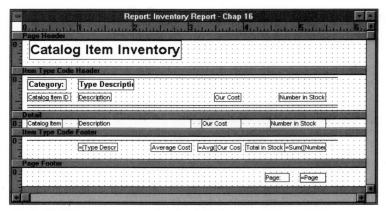

Figure 16-5.
The Report window in Design view for the Inventory Report–Chap 16 report.

of the detail section. You can now drag the label independently in the Item Type Code header section. (The mouse pointer must be a full hand rather than a single finger to be able to drag a label between sections.) Notice that if you try to move the label before you separate it from the control to which it's attached, the control moves with it. Now separate the labels from the Description, Our Cost, and Number in Stock controls, and move the labels to the Item Type Code header section of the report.

4. Line up the column labels in the Item Type Code header, placing Catalog Item ID near the left margin, Description about 1.2 inches from the left margin, Our Cost about 3.5 inches from the left margin, and Number in Stock about 4.75 inches from the left margin. You can set these distances in the Left property of each label's property sheet. Now is a good time to line up the tops of the labels. Select all four labels using the pointer tool to drag a selection box around them. Then choose the Align Top command from the Layout menu.

5. You can enhance the appearance of the report by placing a line across the top of the Item Type Code header and a double line across the bottom of the Item Type Code header. Click the line tool in the toolbox, and drag your lines across the report.

6. Line up the controls for Catalog Item ID, Description, Our Cost, and Number in Stock under their respective headers. The controls for Catalog Item ID, Our Cost, and Number in Stock can be made smaller. You'll need to make the Description control about 2 inches wide.

7. The depth of the detail section on a report determines the spacing between lines on the report. You don't need any space between report lines, so make the detail section smaller until it's only as high as the row of controls for displaying your data.

8. Now add a line across the top of the Item Type Code footer and three unbound text boxes below the line.

9. Delete the label from the first text box, and then select the text box control. Go to the property sheet for the control, and then type =*[Type Description]* & " -- " as the setting for the Control Source property. With this setting, the item category will be displayed in the footer, concatenated with two dashes. Line up this control under the Description control.

10. Change the caption in the label of the second text box to read *Average Cost*. In the Control Source property of the second text box, enter the formula =*Avg([Our Cost])*. This formula calculates the average of all the cost values within the group. Set the Format property to currency so that the average will be preceded by a dollar sign. Line up this control under the Our Cost control.

11. Change the caption in the label of the third text box to read *Total in Stock*. In the Control Source property of the third text box, enter the formula =*Sum([Number in Stock])*. This formula calculates the total of all the in-stock values within the group. Line up this control under the Number in Stock column.

12. Finally create an unbound text box in a corner of the Page Footer section. Type *Page:* as the caption of the label and enter the formula =*Page* in the Control Source property of the text box. Page is a system variable that contains the current page number.

When you've finished, click the Print Preview button on the tool bar to see your results, as shown in Figure 16-6 on the next page. Note that in this figure, the detail lines are sorted in ascending order based on the Catalog Item ID field. You can change the Sort Order setting to Descending in the Sorting and Grouping box to see the components with the highest Catalog Item ID numbers first. You can also modify the Catalog Items for the Report–Chap 16 query so that the detail lines are in the sequence you want.

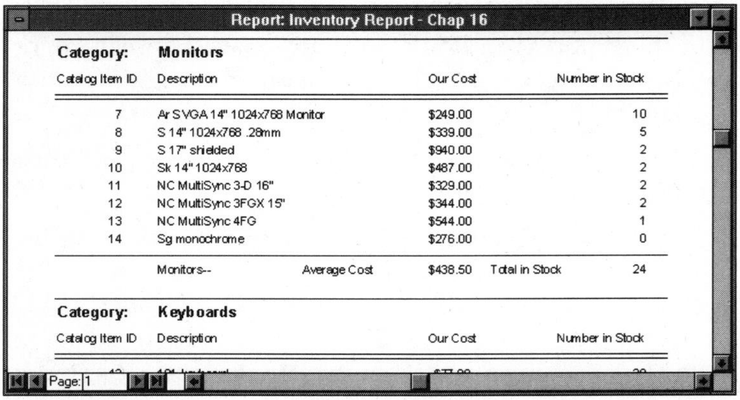

Figure 16-6.
The Inventory Report–Chap 16 report.

WORKING WITH REPORTWIZARDS

Similar to the FormWizards you used to create forms are the ReportWizards that Microsoft Access provides to assist you in constructing reports. To practice using a Report-Wizard, you can build the Inventory Report–Chap 16 report again. Open the Database window, click the Query button, and select the Catalog Items for Report–Chap 16 query you built earlier. Click the New Report button on the tool bar and click the ReportWizards button in the first dialog box.

Choosing a Report Type

The Microsoft Access ReportWizard gives you three major report format options, as shown in Figure 16-7. These format options are

Single-Column	This report is very similar in format to the single-column form you saw in Chapter 12, ''Building a Form.'' The ReportWizard builds a simple report header and footer and displays in a column the data from fields you select. Labels are placed to the left of the column.
Groups/Totals	This report displays in a single row across the report the data from fields you select. The ReportWizard provides subtotals for all numeric fields within each group of fields you select. You'll use this ReportWizard in the next section to duplicate the Catalog Item Inventory report.
Mailing Label	This ReportWizard lets you select name and address fields and format them to print mailing labels. You can choose from a number of popular label types. The ReportWizard will size your labels correctly.

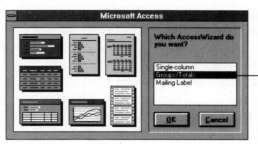

Select this option to create a
Catalog Items Inventory report

Figure 16-7.
The Microsoft Access ReportWizard dialog box.

Because the report you built earlier included a group and subtotals, select the Groups/Totals option in the Microsoft ReportWizard dialog box shown in Figure 16-7, and click OK.

Specifying Parameters for a Groups/Totals Report

The next dialog box the ReportWizard shows you will allow you to select the fields you want in your report. See Figure 16-8. You can select all available fields in the sequence in which they appear in the underlying query or report by clicking the double right arrow button. If you want to pick only some of the fields or if you want to choose the order in which the fields appear on the report, select one field at a time in the list box on the left, and click the single right arrow button to move the field into the list box on the right. If you make a mistake, you can select from the list box on the right the field you placed in the report in error, and then click the single left arrow to remove the field from the list box. Click the double left arrow to remove all selected fields from the right list box and start over.

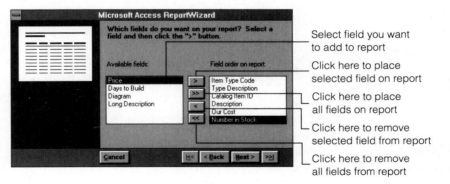

Select field you want
to add to report

Click here to place
selected field on report

Click here to place
all fields on report

Click here to remove
selected field from report

Click here to remove
all fields from report

Figure 16-8.
The ReportWizard dialog box for selecting fields.

To create a Catalog Item Inventory report, you should select Item Type Code. You also want to display the Type Description, Catalog Item ID, Description, Our Cost, and Number in Stock fields in that order. When you have finished selecting fields, click the Next button to go on to the next step.

In the next ReportWizard dialog box, shown in Figure 16-9, the ReportWizard asks you which fields you want to use for grouping records. You can select up to three fields. The ReportWizard doesn't allow you to enter an expression as a grouping value—something you can do when you build a report "from scratch." If you want to use an expression as a grouping value in a ReportWizard, you have to include that expression in the underlying query. For this report, you should select Item Type Code as the field by which you want to group records, as shown in Figure 16-9. Click the Next button to go on to the next step.

In the next ReportWizard dialog box, shown in Figure 16-10, the ReportWizard asks you to specify how you want to group data in each grouping field you selected.

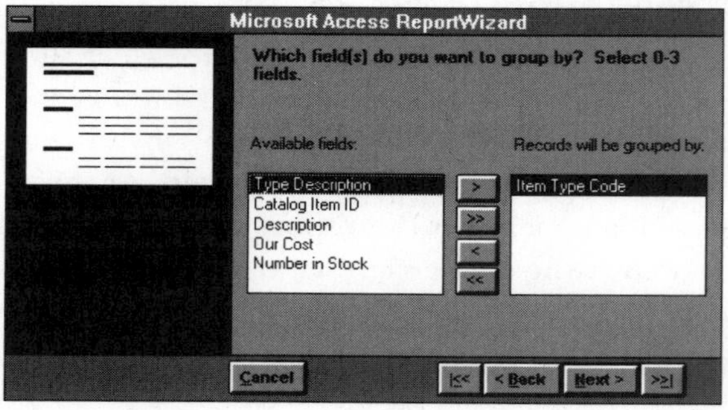

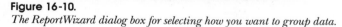

Figure 16-9.
The ReportWizard dialog box for selecting the fields by which you want to group.

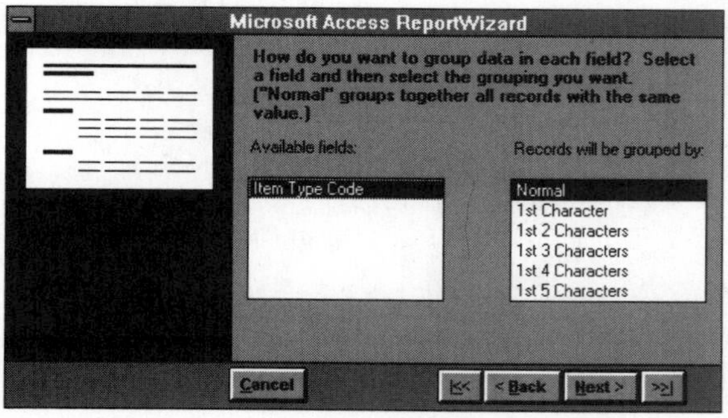

Figure 16-10.
The ReportWizard dialog box for selecting how you want to group data.

For text fields, you can group by the entire field or by one to five of the leading characters. For date/time fields, you can group by individual values or by year, quarter, month, week, day, hour, or minute. For numeric fields, you can group by individual values or by 10, 50, 100, 500, 1000, and so on up to 500,000 unit increments. The Item Type Code field, although it contains numbers, is actually a text field. Select the Normal grouping to create a new group for each unique Item Type Code field. Click the Next button to see a dialog box that asks you to pick any additional fields to determine sorting within the detail section of the report, as shown in Figure 16-11. You can select Catalog Item ID, and then click Next.

Figure 16-11.
The ReportWizard dialog box for selecting the fields by which you want to sort.

The next-to-last ReportWizard dialog box is shown in Figure 16-12. It lets you choose from three formatting styles. When you click any of the option buttons, the ReportWizard shows you a sample of that report style in the display box to the left of the dialog box. The Executive style is a crisp format with lines dividing sections. The Presentation style highlights column labels with white letters on black boxes. The Ledger style surrounds all data in boxes, in the style of a spreadsheet. Check the Executive option button and then click the Next button.

Figure 16-12.
The ReportWizard dialog box for selecting a formatting style.

In the final ReportWizard dialog box, which is shown in Figure 16-13, you can type a report title. You can also ask the ReportWizard to attempt to fit all fields on one page.

Figure 16-13.
The ReportWizard dialog box for selecting a title.

If you are using the ReportWizard to start the design for a complex report with many fields, selecting the Fit All Fields On One Page option causes the Report-Wizard to lay the fields one on top of another in a single row. You might find it difficult to sort out the overlapped fields when you customize the resulting designs in Design view. If you do not check the Fit All Fields On One Page check box, the ReportWizard places only the fields that fit across your report, starting with the first field in your list. You can add fields when you customize the design by using the toolbox and the field list. In the case of the Catalog Item Inventory report, you have only a few fields, so you should ask the ReportWizard to attempt to fit all fields on a single page.

Viewing the ReportWizard Result

Click the Design button in the final ReportWizard dialog box (Figure 16-13) to create the report and display the result in Design view. Click the Print Preview button to create the report and display the finished product, as shown in Figure 16-14.

You can see that it's easy to change to Design view to modify a few minor items (such as changing the cost total to an average and deleting the total that the Report-Wizard created of Catalog Item ID) to obtain a result nearly identical to the report you constructed earlier. You can save this report as *Inventory Wizard–Chap 16*. As you might imagine, ReportWizards are a good way to get a head start on more complex report designs.

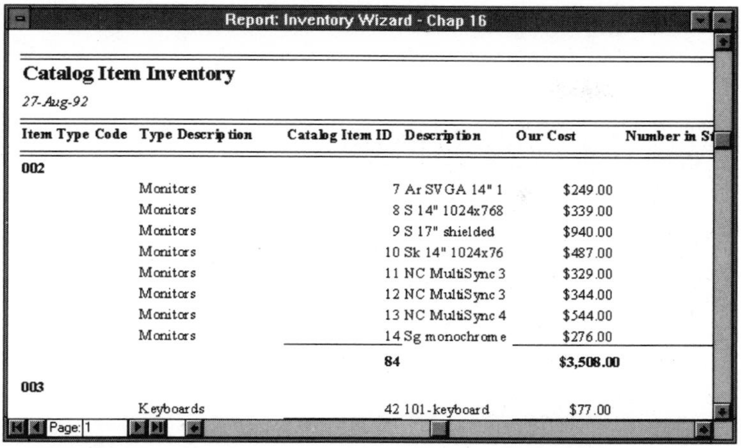

Catalog Item Inventory

27-Aug-92

Item Type Code	Type Description	Catalog Item ID	Description	Our Cost	Number in St
002					
	Monitors	7	Ar SVGA 14" 1	$249.00	
	Monitors	8	S 14" 1024x768	$339.00	
	Monitors	9	S 17" shielded	$940.00	
	Monitors	10	Sk 14" 1024x76	$487.00	
	Monitors	11	NC MultiSync 3	$329.00	
	Monitors	12	NC MultiSync 3	$344.00	
	Monitors	13	NC MultiSync 4	$544.00	
	Monitors	14	Sg monochrome	$276.00	
		84		$3,508.00	
003					
	Keyboards	42	101-keyboard	$77.00	

Page:1

Figure 16-14.
The Catalog Item Inventory report as created by the ReportWizard.

You should now feel comfortable with constructing reports. In the next chapter, you'll learn how to build a complex report with a subreport and embedded pictures—the Prompt Computer Solutions customer invoice.

17

Advanced
Report Design

In the last chapter you learned how to create a relatively simple report with a single subtotal level. You also saw how a ReportWizard can assist you in constructing a new report. This chapter shows you how to

- Design a report with multiple subtotal groups
- Add complex calculations to your report
- Display or hide information based on a condition
- Embed a report within another report
- Add pictures to enhance your report

To learn how to work with these features, you'll build an Invoice report for the PROMPT database. (If you are not using PROMPT, you can see some of the same features described here in the Invoice report of the NWIND database.)

CREATING THE INVOICE QUERY

As noted in the previous chapter, because reports tend to bring together information from many different tables, you are most likely to begin constructing a report by designing a query to retrieve the data you need for the report. For this example, you need information from the Catalog Items, Customer, Order Items, Orders, and Types tables in the PROMPT database. Open a new Query window in Design view and add these tables to the query. The top of the Query window should look similar to the one shown in Figure 17-1. If you don't see relationship lines between the tables, Microsoft Access won't be able to automatically relate the information for you. You can add missing relationship lines by dragging and dropping related fields from one table to another. Add the fields listed in Figure 17-2 to the QBE grid of this query. Drag and drop the * from the Orders field list to the QBE grid to create the Orders.* field.

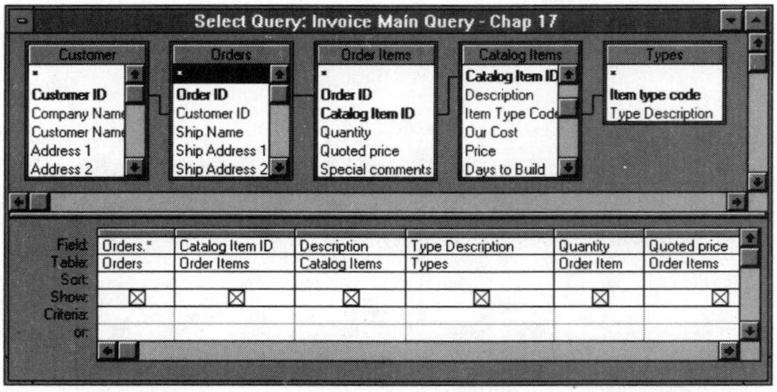

Figure 17-1.
The main query for the Invoice report.

Field	Source Table
Description	Catalog Items
Company Name	Customer
Customer Name	Customer
Address 1	Customer
Address 2	Customer
City	Customer
State	Customer
Postal Code	Customer
Country	Customer
Catalog Item ID	Order Items
Quantity	Order Items
Quoted price	Order Items
Orders.*	Orders
Type Description	Types
Item type code	Types

Figure 17-2.
The fields in the Invoice Main Query–Chap 17.

Save the query and name it *Invoice Main Query–Chap 17.* You can find this query in the PROMPT sample database in the Microsoft Access form on CompuServe named "Invoice Main Query." (You'll build another query for a subreport later.) Select this query in the Database window and click the New Report button on the tool bar. Click the Blank Report button in the New Report dialog box to open the Report window in Design view. (Because there are so many fields on this report, it is easier to build the report without a ReportWizard.)

DEFINING GROUPS

The first thing you need to do is define the sorting and grouping criteria for the report. Click the Sorting and Grouping button on the tool bar to open the Sorting and Grouping window. Because you might decide to print several invoices in one print run, you should start with a group based on the Order ID field. Select Yes for both the Group Header and Group Footer properties. Notice that when you set Group Header or Group Footer to Yes for any field or expression in the Sorting and Grouping window, Access shows you a grouping symbol on the row selector for that line. Assume that your largest customers have also asked for a subtotal by item type in the report, so add a group for the Type Description field and also set the Group Header and Group Footer to Yes. (You could use the Item Type Code field for this group, but it would be nice to have these category descriptions sorted alphabetically using the Type Description field.) Finally you should sort the Description field within each detail group alphabetically. You could have specified this sorting on the Invoice Main Query–Chap 17, but it's just as easy to perform the sort here. Your result should look something like Figure 17-3.

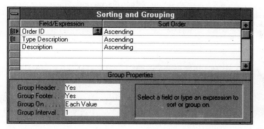

Figure 17-3.
The sorting and grouping settings for the Invoice report.

SETTING GROUP RANGES BY DATA TYPE

For each field or expression at the top of the Sorting and Grouping window, you can define Group On and Group Interval properties. Normally, you want to start a new grouping of data whenever the value of your field or expression changes. You can, however, specify that a new grouping starts based on a range of values. The kind of range you can specify varies depending on the data type of the field or expression.

For text grouping fields, you can ask Microsoft Access to start a new group based on a change in value of one or more leading characters in the string. For example, you could create a new group based on a change in the first letter of the field, rather than on a change anywhere in the field, to create one group per letter of the alphabet—a group of items beginning with *A*, a group of items beginning with *B*, and so on. To group on a prefix, set the Group On property to Prefix Characters. Set the Group Interval property to the number of leading characters you want to determine each group.

For numbers, you can choose to set the Group On property to Interval. When you select this setting, you can enter a setting for the Group Interval property that will cluster multiple values within a range. Microsoft Access calculates ranges from 0. For example, if you choose 10 as the interval value, you'll see groups for the values –20 through –11, –10 through –1, 0 through 9, 10 through 19, 20 through 29, and so on.

For date/time fields, you can set the Group On property to calendar or time subdivisions and multiples of those subdivisions, such as Year, Qtr, Month, Week, Day, Hour, and Minute. Include a setting for the Group Interval property if you want to group on a multiple of the subdivision—for example, set Group On to Year and Group Interval to 2 if you want groupings for every two years.

> **NOTE:** *When you create groupings in which the Group Interval property is set to something other than Each Value, Microsoft Access sorts only the grouping value, not the individual values within each group. If you want the detail items within the group sorted, you must include a separate sort specification for that field. For example, if you group on the first two letters of a Name field and also want the names within each group sorted, you must enter* Name *as the field in the Sorting and Grouping window with* Sort Order = Ascending, Group On = Prefix Characters, *and* Group Interval = 2, *and then you must enter the* Name *field again with* Sort Order = Ascending *and* Group On = Each Value.

CREATING THE BASIC INVOICE REPORT

Now that you have defined the groups, you're ready to start building the report. Before you go further, choose the Save As command from the File menu, and save the report as *Invoice–Chap 17*. You can create the basic report by performing the following steps. Refer to Figure 17-4 to see the results of the steps described.

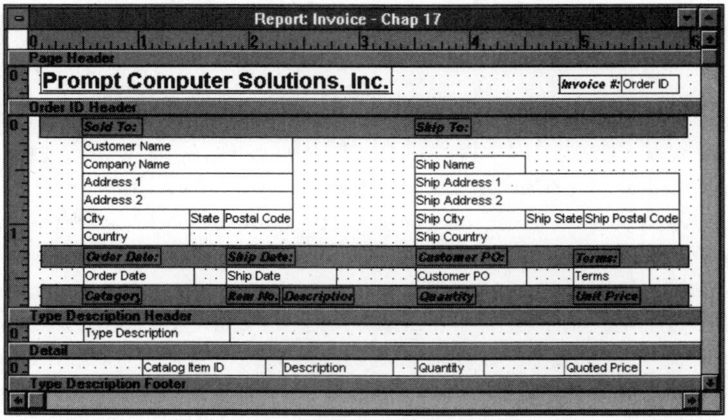

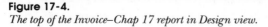

Figure 17-4.
The top of the Invoice–Chap 17 report in Design view.

1. Place a label in the page header and type *Prompt Computer Solutions, Inc.* Select the label to see the full Report window tool bar. Set the font to Arial and choose a font size of 14 points from the tool bar. Click the Bold and Underline buttons to add emphasis. Choose the Size To Fit command from the Layout menu to expand the label to fit your text. Drag the right border of the design area to widen the report to about 6 inches. Drag the Order ID field to the page header near the right margin, and then select the control's label and change it to read *Invoice #.* Make the label bold and italic.

2. Move from the page header section to the Order ID header section. Expand the Order ID header section to give yourself at least 2 vertical inches of working space. At the top of the Order ID header section, add a rectangle about 0.2 inches high and extend it to almost the width of the report. Open the palette. Be sure the rectangle's border is black, and set its fill color to light gray. Create two labels, one reading *Sold To:* and the other *Ship To:*, and place them on the rectangle, as shown in Figure 17-4. Make their text bold italic, and select the Clear check box on the Fill line of the palette for both of these labels.

3. Under *Sold To:* add text box controls (but delete their labels) for the Customer Name, Company Name, Address 1, Address 2, City, State, Postal Code, and Country fields. Add shipping name and address field text box controls (but delete their labels) under the *Ship To:* label.

4. Select the rectangle you created at the top of the Order ID header section, and choose the Copy command from the Edit menu to copy the rectangle to the Windows clipboard. Choose the Paste command from the Edit menu to paste a copy of the rectangle and position it below the name and address fields. Choose the Paste command from the Edit menu again to create a second copy of the rectangle. Drag the second copy of the rectangle a little lower in the header section than the first copy of the rectangle.

5. Drag the Order Date, Ship Date, Customer PO, and Terms fields to the Order ID header section. Position them below the second gray rectangle. Grab the move handle in the upper left corner of each label and place the label in the second gray rectangle, above its corresponding text box. Change the titles in the labels to bold italic for emphasis. In the palette, select the Clear check box on the Fill line for these labels.

6. Drag the Type Description field to the Type Description header section. Select its label and choose the Cut command on the Edit menu to disconnect the label from the control. Choose the Paste command on

the Edit menu to paste the label into the detail section (although the label won't be connected to the control any more), and then move this label to the third gray rectangle in the Order ID header section and change its caption to read *Category* in bold italic. In the palette, select the Clear check box on the Fill line. Position the Type Description text box immediately under the category label and at the very top of the Type Description header section. Widen the Type Description text box. Shrink the Type Description header section to include no space around the control.

7. Drag the Catalog Item ID, Description, Quantity, and Quoted Price fields to the detail section of the report. Separate each label (using the Cut and Paste commands) and place the labels above their respective controls on the third gray rectangle you created in the Order ID header section. Change the Catalog Item ID caption to *Item No.* Change the Quoted Price caption to *Unit Price.* Leave some room at the right end to add one more control later in this exercise. Change the titles in the labels to bold italic for emphasis. In the palette, select the Clear check box on the Fill line for these labels.

8. Next scroll down in the Report window until you can see the Type Description and Order ID footer sections. Close up the Type Description footer section to zero height for now; you'll add some controls to show totals here later. Drag the SubTotal Cost, Discount, Sales Tax, and Freight fields to the Order ID footer, in a column to the right. Your result should look something like the one shown in Figure 17-5. Because you want to force a new page at the end of each invoice, add a page break control in the lower left corner of the Order ID footer section.

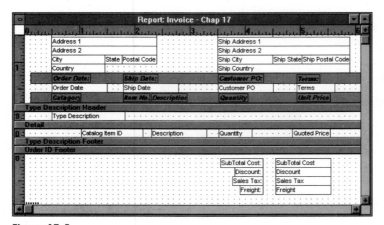

Figure 17-5.
The bottom portion of the Invoice–Chap 17 report in Design view.

When you click the Print Preview button on the tool bar, your result should look something like the one shown in Figure 17-6.

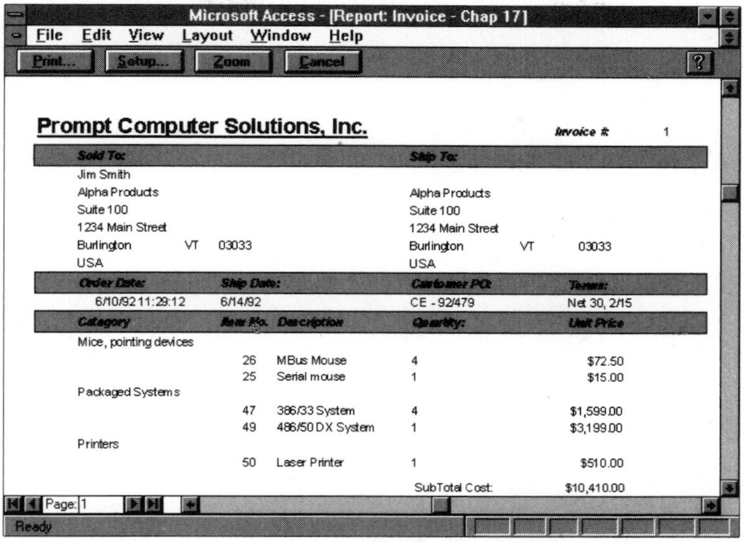

Figure 17-6.
The Invoice–Chap 17 report in Print Preview.

UNDERSTANDING SECTION AND REPORT PROPERTIES

You have probably noticed that Microsoft Access has a property sheet for each section in the Report window in Design view. There's also a property sheet for the report as a whole. You don't need to change any of these properties at this time, but the following sections of the book explain the available property settings.

Section Properties

Click in the blank area of any group section or detail section of a report, and Access shows you a property sheet, as shown in Figure 17-7.

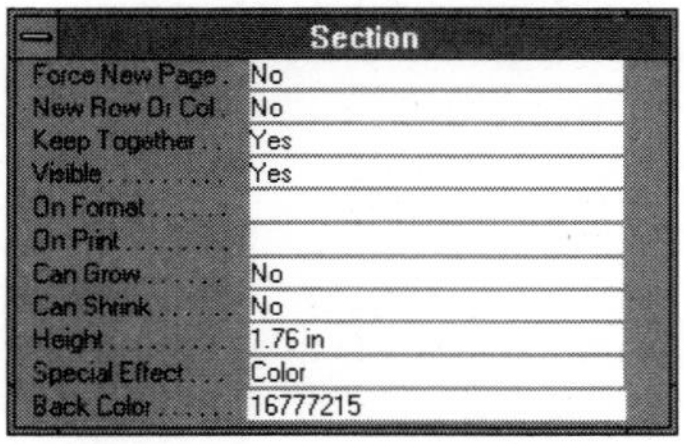

Figure 17-7.
A property sheet for a report section.

The available properties and their uses are described below:

Force New Page   Set this property to Yes to force this section to print at the top of a new page.

New Row Or Col   When you use Print Setup to format your report with more than one column (vertical) or more than one row (horizontal) of sections, you can set this property to Before Section, After Section, or Before & After to force Access to produce the section again at the top or bottom (or both) of a new column or row. This property is useful to force headers to print again at the top of each column on a multiple column report.

Keep Together   Set this property to No to allow Access to flow a section across page boundaries. The default setting Yes tells Access to attempt to keep all lines within a section together on a page. In this case, leaving this property set to Yes in the detail section property sheet means that Access will attempt to keep all detail lines for a given Type Description together on one page.

Visible   Set this property to Yes to make the section visible, or No to make the section invisible. This is a handy property to set from a macro while Access formats and prints your report. You can make sections disappear depending on data values in the report. See Chapter 18, "Adding Power with Macros," for details.

On Format   Enter the name of a macro or module function you want Access to execute when it begins formatting this section. See Chapter 18 for details.

On Print   Enter the name of a macro or module function you want Access to execute when it begins printing this section or displays the section in Print Preview. See Chapter 18 for details.

Can Grow   Microsoft Access sets this value to Yes automatically when you include any control in the section that also has its Can Grow property set to Yes. This allows the section to expand to accommodate controls that might expand because you are using the controls to display memo fields or long text strings. You can design a control to display one line, but you should allow the control to expand to display more lines of text as needed.

Can Shrink   This property is similar to Can Grow. You can set it to Yes to allow the section to become smaller if controls in the section become smaller to accommodate less text. You'll use Can Shrink later in this chapter to make the space occupied by a control disappear when the control contains no data.

The remaining properties in the property sheet (Height, Special Effect, Back Color) control how the section looks. Whenever you adjust the height of the section by dragging its lower border, Microsoft Access resets the section's Height property. You can set the Special Effect and Back Color properties using the palette.

For page and report headers and footers, you have only the Visible, On Format, On Print, Height, Special Effect, and Back Color properties available.

Report Properties

If you choose the Select Report command from the Edit menu or click beyond the right edge of the design area, Microsoft Access shows you the report properties in the property sheet, as shown in Figure 17-8.

Report	
Record Source	Invoice Main Query - Chap 17
On Open	
On Close	
Grid X	10
Grid Y	12
Layout for Print	Yes
Page Header	All Pages
Page Footer	All Pages
Record Locks	No Locks
Width	6.42 in
Help File	
Help Context Id	0

Figure 17-8.
The property sheet for a report.

The available properties and their uses are described below:

Record Source	This setting is the name of the table or query that provides the data for your report.
On Open	Enter the name of a macro or module function you want Access to execute when it begins printing this report or displaying the report in Print Preview. See Chapter 18, "Adding Power with Macros," for details.
On Close	Enter the name of a macro or module function you want Access to execute when you close Print Preview or when Access has finished sending the report to your printer or to Print Manager in Microsoft Windows. See Chapter 18 for details.
Grid X, Grid Y	Specify the number of horizontal (X) or vertical (Y) divisions per inch or centimeters for the dots in the report design area. When you are using inches (because Measurement is set to English in the International section of the Control Panel in Windows), you can see the dots whenever you choose a value of 16 or less for both X and Y. In centimeters (Measurement is set to Metric), you can see the dots when you choose values of 6 or less.
Layout for Print	When this property is set to Yes, you can choose from TrueType and printer fonts in your design. When set to No, you have TrueType and screen fonts available.
Page Header	This property controls whether the page header appears on all pages. You can choose not to print the page header on the first and last pages if these pages contain a report header or footer.

(continued)

Page Footer	This property controls whether the page footer appears on all pages. You can choose not to print the page footer on the first and last pages if these pages contain a report header or footer.
Record Locks	You should set this property to Yes if the data for your report is on a server shared by others and you want to be sure no one can update the records you need in the report until Access creates all the pages in the report. You should not set this property to Yes for a report you plan to use in Print Preview because you will be locking out other users for the entire time that you are viewing the report on your screen.
Width	This property is set automatically by Access when you stretch the width of the report on the design grid.
Help File, Help Context ID	You can create custom help text using the Microsoft Windows Help Compiler provided in the Microsoft Windows Software Development Kit. See the development kit documentation for details.

USING CALCULATED VALUES

Some of the true power of reports comes from the ability to perform both simple and complex calculations on the data from your underlying table or query. Microsoft Access also provides dozens of built-in functions that you can use to work with your data or to add information to your report. The following sections show you samples of the types of calculations you can perform.

Adding Print Date and Page Numbers

One of the most common pieces of information you might add to a report is the date you prepared the report. You will probably also want to add page numbers. For dates, Microsoft Access provides two built-in functions that you can use to add the current date and time to your report. The Date() function returns the current system date as a date/time variable with no time component. The Now() function returns the current system date and time as a date/time variable.

To add the current date to your report, create an unbound text box control, and set its Control Source property to *=Date()*. Then, in the Format property box, choose a date/time setting. Go back to the report and type a meaningful caption for the label. You can see an example in Figure 17-9. The result in print preview is shown in Figure 17-10.

To add a page number, refer to the Page property for the report. You can't see this property in any of the property sheets because it is maintained automatically by Microsoft Access. You can reset the value of the Page property in a macro or function that you activate from an appropriate report property. For example, you might want to define a macro for the On Format property of the Order ID header section to set the page number back to 1 each time Access starts to print an invoice for a different order. See Chapter 18, "Adding Power with Macros," for details.

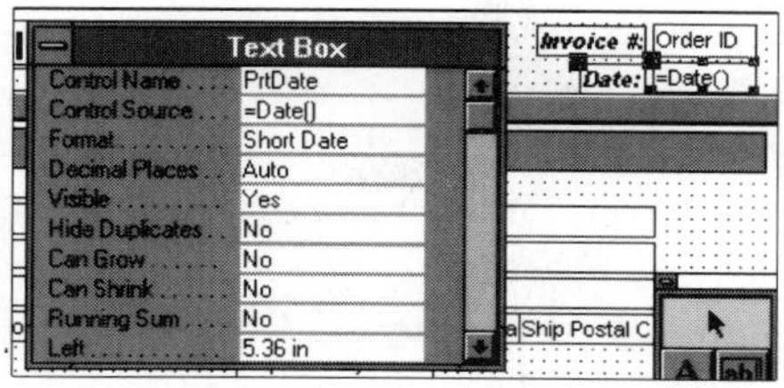

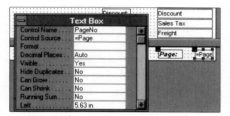

Figure 17-9.
The Date() function is used to add the date to a report.

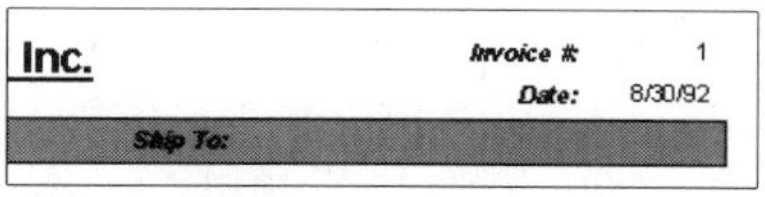

Figure 17-10.
The current date is displayed on the Invoice–Chap 17 report in Print Preview.

To add the current page number to your report (in this example, in the page footer section), create an unbound text box control, and set its Control Source property to *=Page* as shown in Figure 17-11.

Figure 17-11.
The Page property is used to add page numbers to a report.

Arithmetic Calculations

Another common task is to calculate extended values from detail values in your tables. You might remember from the exercise in which you designed your database tables in Chapter 4 that it is usually redundant and wasteful of storage space to define in your tables fields that you calculate from other fields. (The one time that this is acceptable is when saving the calculated value greatly improves performance in parts of your application; for example, in the PROMPT database there's an extended subtotal in the Orders table so that you don't have to fetch all the Order Items in an order when you want to know only the total amount due for the order.)

Calculation on a Detail Line

Notice that the Order Items table contains a Quantity field and a Quoted Price field but not a calculation of the extended amount (quantity times price). Your customers probably want to see that value on the invoice, so you need to calculate that value in your report. Remember there's some room at the right side of the detail section in the Invoice–Chap 17 report. Create an unbound text box control and place it there. Cut and paste the control's label, and move the label onto the last gray title bar in the Order ID header section. Change the label's caption to *Amount*, select the label, format it in bold italic, and select the Clear check box on the Fill line of the palette. Choose the Size To Fit command from the Layout menu to size the label.

The calculation of the extended amount will be the content of the new unbound text box control. To refer to the name of any control in a calculation expression, simply type the name of the control enclosed in brackets. You can add arithmetic operators and parentheses to create complex calculations. You can also reference any of the many built-in functions or any of the functions you define yourself in a module. Because you want to multiply the value in the Quantity control by the value in the Quoted Price control, enter *=[Quantity]*[Quoted Price]* in the Control Source property of the Text Box property sheet. (See Figure 17-12.) Set the Format property to Currency to display the number correctly.

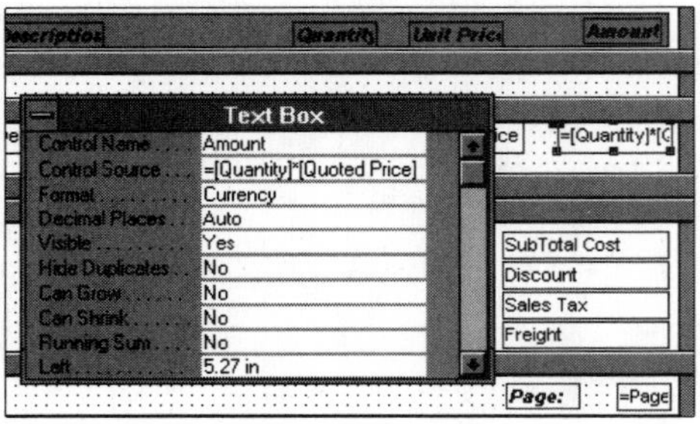

Figure 17-12.
An arithmetic calculation is set as the source of a control.

Figure 17-13 shows you the result in Print Preview. You can see that Microsoft Access has performed the required calculation on each line and displayed the result.

Total Across a Group

Another common task on a report is to add values across a group. You already learned how to do that for uncalculated values in the previous chapter using the built-in Sum function. You can also use the Sum function to add calculated values. You might think that you can use the name of the unbound control (in this case, [Amount]) with the Sum function to get a total of the extended amounts listed in the Amount control. However, Microsoft Access doesn't actually store the calculated values in the control, so Sum([Amount]) would be trying to add nothing. To get the sum of calculated values, you need to repeat the calculation formula as the parameter for the Sum function.

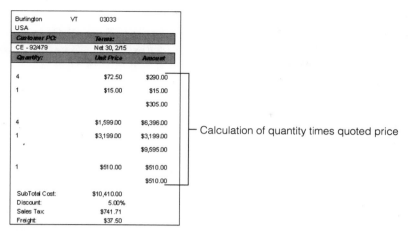

Figure 17-13.
The calculation is displayed in the Amount column of the report in Print Preview.

For example, to calculate the subtotal number of items ordered and the subtotal amount for each, you can add unbound text boxes to the Type Description footer section under the Quantity and Amount columns. (You'll first need to drag down the Order ID footer section.) Enter *=Sum([Quantity])* in the Control Source property box for the first text box and *=Sum([Quantity]*[Quoted Price])* in the Control Source property box for the second text box, as shown in Figure 17-14. Delete the labels bound to these text box controls and set the Format property of the second text box control to Currency. You might also want to add a line control immediately above each text box to indicate that you are displaying a total.

Notice the interesting new property for controls on reports—Running Sum. You can set this property to ask Microsoft Access not to reset totals at the end of a group. If you set the Running Sum property to Over Group, Access accumulates the

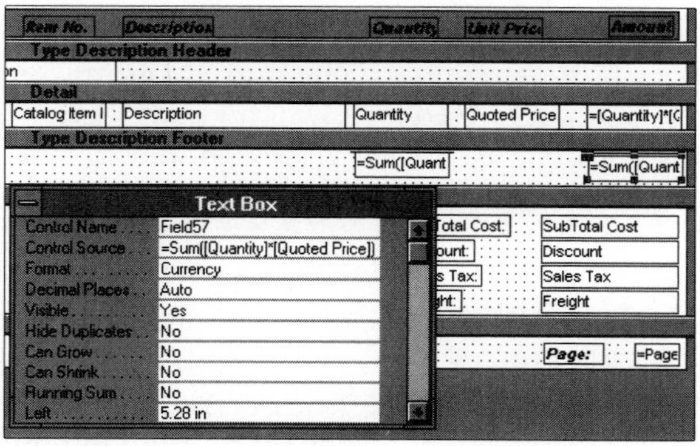

Figure 17-14.
A sum of calculated values is set as the source of a control.

total over all groups at this level until a new group value is encountered at the next higher level. In this case, you could total quantity or amount over all types and display that incremental total in the Type Description footer section. The total would reset to 0 with every new Order ID. You can also set the Running Sum property to Over All, which allows you to accumulate a total and not have it reset. You could, for example, show the total amount accumulated to the current point for all previous types within orders.

Creating a Grand Total

In the Order ID footer section, you placed the calculated subtotal from the Orders table along with other fields for discount percent, sales tax, and freight charges. You should create a grand total for these items at the bottom of the report. To do this, make some space below the Freight text box control to add an unbound text box control labeled Total Due. The formula for the calculation used by this control is a bit complicated because it uses the Discount field that contains a percentage by which the subtotal must be reduced. You could type

[SubTotal] − ([SubTotal] * [Discount])

to multiply the percentage by the subtotal and then subtract that amount from the subtotal. Or you could type

[SubTotal] * (1 − [Discount])

to subtract the percentage from 1 and then multiply the result by the subtotal. Either formula yields the correct result.

A problem that is introduced when you multiply or divide currency values by another value is that the result might have more than two decimal places. To ensure that you get the correct result when you add a series of calculated currency values, you should always multiply the result by 100 and truncate it using CLng (convert to long integer function) and then divide by 100 and use the CCur (convert to currency) function to round the result to the nearest penny and store it as a currency value. You need to use this function in the discount calculation before you add the Sales Tax and Freight values. The formula you need is shown in Figure 17-15.

After you finish setting up the calculations, Print Preview should yield a result similar to the one shown in Figure 17-16.

Concatenating Text Strings

You can add labels to your report to provide descriptive information. Sometimes, it's useful to combine descriptive text with a value from a text field in the underlying query or table or to combine multiple text fields in one control. In Figure 17-17, you can see descriptive labels (created by a single text box control) on the subtotal lines.

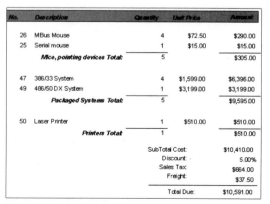

Figure 17-15.
A grand total calculation (using the CLng and CCur functions) is set as the source of a control.

Item No.	Description	Quantity	Unit Price	Amount
26	MBus Mouse	4	$72.50	$290.00
25	Serial mouse	1	$15.00	$15.00
		5		$305.00
47	386/33 System	4	$1,599.00	$6,396.00
49	486/50 DX System	1	$3,199.00	$3,199.00
		5		$9,595.00
50	Laser Printer	1	$510.00	$510.00
		1		$510.00

SubTotal Cost:	$10,410.00
Discount:	5.00%
Sales Tax:	$741.71
Freight:	$37.50
Total Due:	$10,668.71

Figure 17-16.
The grand total (Total Due) is displayed in the report in Print Preview.

No.	Description	Quantity	Unit Price	Amount
26	MBus Mouse	4	$72.50	$290.00
25	Serial mouse	1	$15.00	$15.00
	Mice, pointing devices Total:	5		$305.00
47	386/33 System	4	$1,599.00	$6,396.00
49	486/50 DX System	1	$3,199.00	$3,199.00
	Packaged Systems Total:	5		$9,595.00
50	Laser Printer	1	$510.00	$510.00
	Printers Total:	1		$510.00

SubTotal Cost:	$10,410.00
Discount:	5.00%
Sales Tax:	$664.00
Freight:	$37.50
Total Due:	$10,591.00

Figure 17-17.
The descriptive labels on the subtotal line are concatenations of a text field and a string.

These labels concatenate the information from the Type Description field followed by the word *Total*, as shown in Figure 17-18. Certainly you could define a text box followed by a label to create the same display. The advantage of a single control is that you don't have to worry about lining up two controls or setting the font characteristics twice.

Figure 17-18 shows the concatenation as a setting of the Control Source property. The special character & (ampersand) indicates a concatenation operation between two text strings. To get the proper spacing between the descriptions, set the text box control's Text Align property to Right.

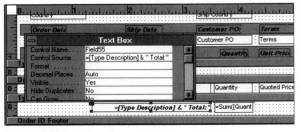

Figure 17-18.
A text field and a string are concatenated as the source of a control.

Microsoft Access provides an alternative syntax for concatenating text string variables. You can include any control name inside the double quotation marks that delimit a string as long as you type the pipe character (¦) before and after the name of the control you want inserted in the string. On the Invoice–Chap 17 report, it would be nice to display City, State, and Postal Code as a single string, with a comma separating City and State. To do this, delete the City, State, and Postal Code text boxes, insert an unbound text box control, and delete the bound label control. Figure 17-19 shows you the alternative syntax for combining these three fields.

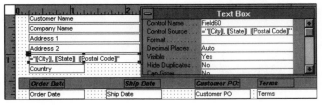

Figure 17-19.
A concatenation of three text fields is set as the source of a control.

When you look at the report in Print Preview, you can see the city, state, and zip code placed together as a single string, as shown in Figure 17-20. One advantage of concatenating address fields in this way is that Access automatically adjusts the position of the state name relative to the length of the city name. Using the separate field method, you'd have to show the state always in a fixed location.

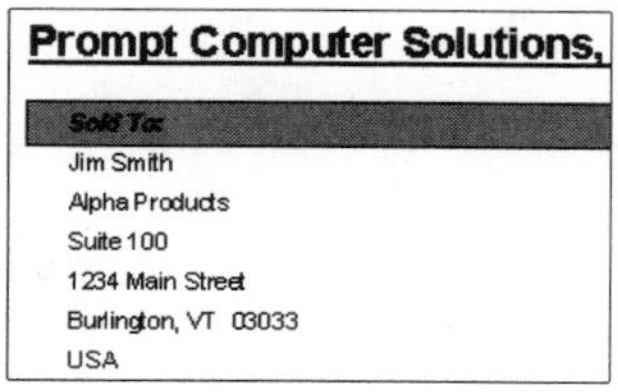

Figure 17-20.
The City, State, and Postal Code fields displayed as a single string in Print Preview.

Conditional Data Display

Sometimes you don't want to show certain fields on your report, depending on their value or the value of other controls. For example, on the Invoice–Chap 17 report you might not want to display the Discount field to all your customers if only some customers receive discounts. Microsoft Access provides a conditional testing function called *Immediate If* (*IIF*) that returns one of two values depending on whether a test is true or false. You provide to the function in the first parameter the condition you want tested, in the second parameter the value you want returned if the test is true, and in the third parameter the value you want returned if the test is false.

You can now display the Discount control conditionally using the IIF function. You will also use some of the calculated values previously discussed to change the Discount control so that it displays the dollar amount of the discount as well as the percentage. The first step is to delete the Discount control from your report and add in its place an unbound text box control with no label. You need to size this text box to about 2 inches wide because it will include a label, the percent value, and the calculated amount when the discount value is greater than 0. Figure 17-21 shows how to position this control.

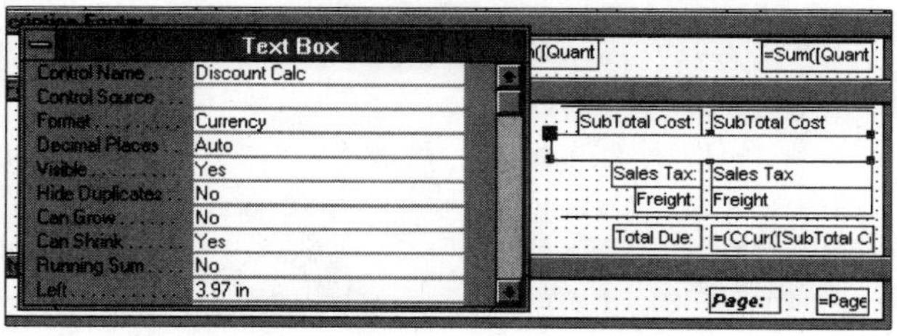

Figure 17-21.
The position of the Discount control that will display conditionally.

The formula you need to enter is quite long and complex, so it would be a good idea to open the Zoom edit window from the property sheet. To do so, click inside the Control Source property box for the unbound text box control you just added, and press Shift-F2. Access opens a Zoom box, as shown in Figure 17-22.

Figure 17-22.
A conditional display statement is set as the source of a control.

Enter *=IIF(* to start the formula in the Zoom window. In this case, you want to test whether the value in the Discount field is 0, so enter *[Discount]=0* as the first parameter, followed by a comma. If the value in the Discount field is 0, you don't want to display anything at all. Enter quotation marks as shown, with no intervening space, to set no display in the second parameter. Enter a second comma and a quotation mark. When the value in the Discount field is not 0, you want to display a label, the value in the Discount field as a percent, some spaces to separate the values, and the Discount expressed in dollars and cents. These displays are connected by using the concatenation symbol in your formula. Your label is created by entering the word *Discount,* a colon, some spaces, and another quotation mark. There's another built-in function called *Format* that returns a value formatted according to a format name or string; *Format([Discount],"Percent")* works to return the discount as a percentage. Enter *&*, several spaces enclosed in quotes, and then *&* to separate the percentage and the total. (You might need to experiment with the number of spaces to ensure that the columns line up properly.) You need to calculate the second value as a negative number that's the result of multiplying the value in the Discount by the subtotal. Remember, because you're multiplying a currency value by a noncurrency value, you should use the CLng and CCur functions to round and truncate the result before you display it. So enter *Format(-CCur(CLng([Discount]*[SubTotal Cost] *100)/100),"$#,##0.00 "))*. Click OK to close the Zoom box and store the result.

Be sure that this control has the Text Align property set to Right. You can also set the Can Shrink property to Yes so that the control will "disappear" when its value is an empty string (when the Discount is 0). If you check the result in Print Preview, you should see something like Figure 17-23 when the order has a discount.

50	Laser Printer	1		$510.00	$510.00
	Printers Total:	1			$510.00

	SubTotal Cost:	$10,410.00
	Discount: 5.00%	-$520.50
	Sales Tax	$741.71
	Freight:	$37.50
	Total Due:	$10,668.71

Figure 17-23.
A Discount line is displayed in Print Preview when the customer receives a discount.

Figure 17-24 shows the result when the Discount is 0. Notice that the Discount row has disappeared and the Sales Tax and Freight values have moved up.

32	Seaweed 211MB 15	1		$471.25	$471.25
	Hard drives Total:	1			$471.25

	SubTotal Cost:	$471.25
	Sales Tax	$40.06
	Freight:	$8.29
	Total Due:	$519.60

Figure 17-24.
A Discount line is not displayed in Print Preview when the customer receives no discount.

EMBEDDING A SUBREPORT

In the Prompt Computer Solutions database, Catalog Items are set up so that you can sell an individual component (such as a video card) or whole systems. When customers purchase a packaged system, it would be nice to itemize for them all the pieces they're getting in the system. You can add that information to the Invoice–Chap 17 report by designing a subreport based on the related Item Components and Components information.

Designing the Subreport

Because you need information from more than one table, you should first design a query for the subreport. You need the Catalog Item ID and the Amount fields from the Item Components table (to determine the quantity of each component included in the system), and you need the Description field from the Components table. Because you don't need this detailed information for anything but packaged systems, you will want to include the Item Type Code field from the Catalog Items table so that you can perform a test (to determine when to shrink the subreport because an item isn't a system).

Your resulting query should look something like the one shown in Figure 17-25. Save the query and name it *Invoice Subreport Query–Chap 17* (called "Invoice Subreport Query" in the PROMPT sample database on CompuServe). Select the query in the Database window and click the New Report button on the tool bar. Click the Blank Report button in the New Report dialog box to open the Report window in Design view.

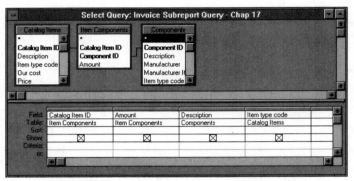

Figure 17-25.
The Invoice Subreport Query–Chap 17.

Shrink the page header and page footer sections so that they have zero height. Microsoft Access won't display report or page headers from a subreport on the main report anyway. You need only one control on the report, a text box control to display the Amount and Description fields when the value in the Item Type Code field equals 100 (the value for packaged systems). Choose the Sorting And Grouping command from the View menu. Select Description as the Field/Expression and Ascending as the Sort Order. Close the Sorting and Grouping window.

Figure 17-26 shows you the formula to enter in the Control Source property box. You want a display when the test is true, so you must define the display string in the second parameter of the IIF function. Include an empty string (" ") as the last parameter. Be sure to set the Can Shrink property to Yes for this control so that the control disappears if the Item Type Code isn't 100. Save the report and then name it *Invoice Subreport–Chap 17.* Now you're ready to embed this subreport in the main report.

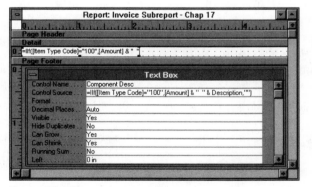

Figure 17-26.
A conditional display statement is set as the source of a subreport control.

Embedding the Subreport

Go back to the Invoice–Chap 17 report and open a small area below the Description field in the detail section. Click the Subform/Subreport tool in the toolbox, create a Subform/Subreport control in the empty space, and size it to about 0.17 inches high—high enough to display one line. See Figure 17-27.

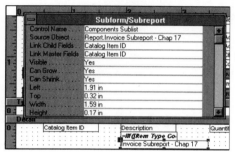

Figure 17-27.
The subreport is linked to the main report.

To insert your subreport, enter *Report.Invoice Subreport–Chap 17* in the Source Object property box of the subreport control. Because you could also include a form in the report, the *Report.* prefix tells Microsoft Access to include a report, not a form. As you did with a subform, you need to define linking fields. In this case, the Catalog Item ID field on the main report (set in the Link Master Fields property box) matches the Catalog Item ID field on the subreport (set in the Link Child Fields property box). You need to set the Can Shrink and Can Grow properties to Yes to allow the subreport to expand or shrink as necessary.

You might notice that this sample includes a text box as a "disappearing" title in a text box control above the subreport control. The title displays the word *Contains* when an item is a system. You can build the conditional display statement for this title exactly as you built one previously for the Discount control in the subreport. Figure 17-28 shows the property settings you need for this text box.

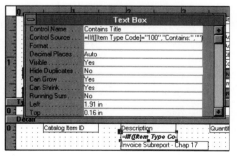

Figure 17-28.
A conditional display statement for the control that titles the subreport shown in Figure 17-26.

Viewing the Embedded Result

After you finish, the result should look similar to Figure 17-29. Notice that no sub-report shows for the individual mouse entries. The subreport and its title do appear for the 386/33 packaged system.

Category	Item No.	Description	Quantity	Unit Price	Amount
Mice, pointing devices					
	26	MBus Mouse	4	$72.50	$290.00
	25	Serial mouse	1	$15.00	$15.00
Mice, pointing devices Total:			5		$305.00
Packaged Systems					
	47	386/33 System	4	$1,599.00	$6,396.00
		Contains:			
		1 Mx 130MB 15ms			
		1 3.5" HD floppy			
		1 Ar SVGA 14" 1024x768 Monitc			
		1 Baby Tower Case			
		1 E x SVGA 1024x768 Adapter			
		1 Isset 386/33 DX			
		1 Mx 130MB 15ms			
	49	486/50 DX System	1	$3,199.00	$3,199.00
		Contains:			
		1 Isset 486/50 DX			
		1 101-keyboard			
		1 3.5" HD floppy			

Figure 17-29.
A title and a list of components are displayed in Print Preview when an invoice contains a system.

If you find that you need to make some adjustments to the subreport (or, for that matter, to any subreport or subform), you can edit it directly from the Design view of the main report or form. Be sure that the subreport isn't selected. Then double-click inside the subreport control to open it in Design view. Save and close the subreport in its Report window after you've finished. To update the subreport control to reflect these changes in the main report's Report window, select the subreport control, and then click inside it and highlight the source object name in the upper left corner of the control. Press Enter to update the subreport definition in the main report.

EMBEDDING OBJECTS

As a finishing touch, you can add an embedded picture to display the company logo. As you might suspect, you can also add a bound object frame to display pictures or graphs stored in your data. With a graph control, you can graphically represent numeric data. You embed objects in reports in the same way you embed objects in forms. For an explanation of the process, see "Working with Objects" in Chapter 14.

In the Invoice–Chap 17 example, you can remove the company title from the page header and substitute a picture logo as an unbound object frame, as shown in Figure 17-30.

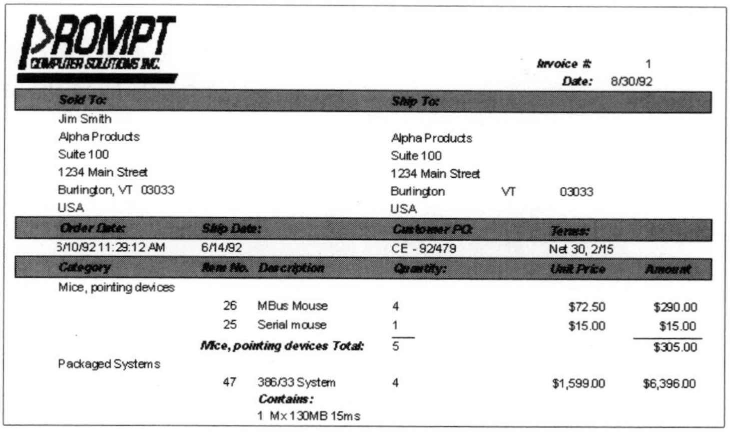

Figure 17-30.
The Invoice–Chap 17 report with an unbound picture object embedded, the Prompt Computer Solutions Inc. logo.

At this point, you should thoroughly understand the mechanics of constructing reports and working with complex formulas. The final section of this book shows you how to bring together all that you've learned to build an application.

PART VI

CREATING
AN APPLICATION

Part VI of this book teaches you the fundamentals of Microsoft Access macros and shows you how to use them to automate forms and reports and to link objects together.

Chapter 18, ``Adding Power with Macros,'' provides you with a detailed look at defining macro actions and conditional statements. After a quick tour of the macro design facility, you will learn about each of the macro actions and the events that trigger them.

The final chapter in the book, Chapter 19, ``Designing the Prompt Computer Solutions Application,'' shows you how to design reports and forms that handle specific tasks you identified when you first laid out your database design in Chapter 4. The chapter leads you through the steps required to build a portion of the Prompt Computer Solutions application.

18

Adding Power with Macros

In Microsoft Access you can define a macro to execute just about any task you would otherwise initiate with the keyboard or mouse. The unique power of macros in Access is the ability to automate responses to many types of events. The event might be a change in the data, the opening or closing of a form or report, or even a change of focus between one control and another. Within a macro, you can include multiple actions and define condition checking so that different actions are performed depending on the values in your forms or reports.

This chapter first discusses the various types of actions you can define in macros. Next you'll tour the macro design facility and learn how to build both a simple macro and a macro with multiple defined actions. You'll also learn how to manage the many macros you need for a form or report by creating a macro group. Finally you'll see how to add conditional statements to a macro to control what actions Microsoft Access performs. At the end of the chapter, you'll find summaries of the macro actions and of the events that can trigger a macro. You might find these sections useful as a quick reference when you design macros for your application.

USES OF MACROS

Microsoft Access provides various types of macro actions that you can use to automate your application.

- You can use macros to open any table, form, query, or report in any available view. You can also close opened tables, forms, and queries.

- You can use macros to open a report in Print Preview or to send a report directly to the printer.

- You can use macros to execute a select query (which opens its Datasheet view) or any action query. You can base the parameters of a query on controls in any open form.

- With macros you can base the execution of an action on any condition that tests values in your database, in an open form, or on a report. You can use macros to execute other macros or Access Basic modules. You can halt the current macro or all macros, cancel the event that triggered the macro, or quit the application.

- You can use macros to set the value of any form or report control. You can also emulate keyboard actions and supply input to system dialog boxes. With macros you can also refresh the values in any control based on a query.

- You can use macros to apply a filter to, go to any record in, or search for data in the underlying table or query of a form.

- For any form, you can use macros to define a custom menu bar that replaces the standard menus offered by Microsoft Access.

- You can use macros to execute any of the commands on any of the Microsoft Access menus.

- Using macros you can move and size, minimize, maximize, or restore any window within the Access workspace. You can change the focus to a window or any control within a window. You can select the page of a report to display in Print Preview.

- You can use macros to display informative messages and sound a computer tone to attract attention to your message. You can also disable certain warning messages when executing action queries.

- You can use macros to rename any object in your database. You can make another copy of a selected object in your database or copy an object to another Microsoft Access database. With macros you can also import, export, or attach other database tables, or import or export spreadsheet or text files.

- You can use macros to start another application, in either Microsoft Windows or MS-DOS, and exchange data with the application using Dynamic Data Exchange (DDE) or the Clipboard. You can also send keystrokes to the target application.

Consider some of the other possibilities for macros. For example, you can make it easy to move from one task to another using command buttons that open and position forms and set values. You can create very complex editing routines that validate data entered on forms, including checking data in other tables. You can even check something like the customer name entered on an order form and pop up another form so the user can enter detailed data if that customer record doesn't already exist.

THE TOOL BAR FOR THE MACRO WINDOW

Microsoft Access provides a custom tool bar for working with macros. Open the PROMPT database, click the Macro button in the Database window, and click the New button to open a new Macro window. Access opens the tool bar shown in Figure 18-1.

Figure 18-1.
The Macro window tool bar.

From left to right, the buttons on the Macro window tool bar are

 Macro Names button. Click this button to show or hide the Macro Name column in the Macro window. Within this column you can assign names to macros in a macro group.

 Conditions button. Click this button to show or hide the Condition column in the Macro window. With this column you can define conditions that must be true in order to execute the associated action.

 Run button. Click this button to run your macro. You must save the macro and give it a name before you can run it.

 Single Step button. Click this button to step through a macro one action at a time. This option is useful for debugging complex macros. Once you set this option, it remains active until you turn it off. See "Testing Your Macro" later in this chapter for details.

 Undo button. Click this button to undo the last change you made to the macro design.

Help button. Click this button to access context-sensitive Help topics.

CREATING A SIMPLE MACRO

At the end of Chapter 14, "Advanced Form Design," you learned how to create a macro that opens a form when a button is pushed on another form. This section explains the macro design facility in Microsoft Access in more detail.

Macro Window

When you opened a new Macro window to take a look at the tool bar, you saw an empty window similar to the one shown in Figure 18-2. There are two columns, Action and Comment, at the top of the window.

Notice that the area at the bottom right of the Macro window displays a short Help message. The message changes, depending on where your cursor is located in the Macro window. You can always press F1 to open a context-sensitive Help topic.

Figure 18-2.
A new Macro window.

In the Action column you can specify any one of more than 40 macro actions provided by Access. If you click anywhere in the Action column, you'll see a down arrow button. This button opens a drop-down list of the macro actions, as shown in Figure 18-3.

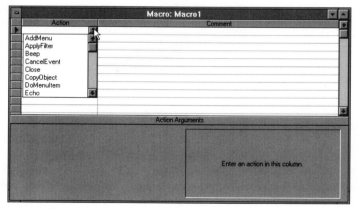

Figure 18-3.
An open drop-down list of macro actions.

To see how the Macro window works, try selecting the MsgBox action now. The MsgBox action will open a pop-up modal dialog box with a message in it. It's a great way to display a warning or an informative message or information in your database without defining a separate form.

Now assume this message will be a greeting, and type *Greeting message* in the Comment column of the Macro window. You'll find the Comment column especially useful for documenting large macros that contain many actions. In the Comment column you can enter additional comments on any blank line (any line without an action next to it).

After you select an action such as MsgBox, Access shows areas in the bottom of the Macro window in which you enter settings, called *arguments,* for the action. See Figure 18-4. As with the Table and Query windows in Design view, you can use the F6 key to move between the top and bottom portions of the Macro window.

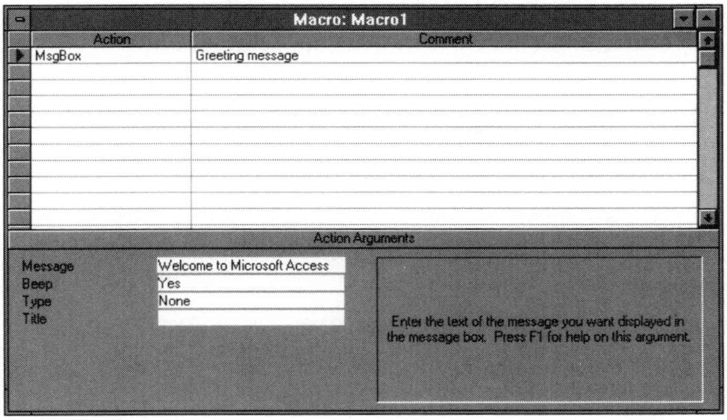

Figure 18-4.
The macro that displays a greeting message.

The setting in the Message box is the message you want Access to display in the window you're creating. The setting in the Beep box will tell Access whether to sound a beep when the message is displayed. In the Type box you can set a graphic indicator, such as a red stop sign, that will appear along with your message. In the Title box you can type the contents of your dialog box's title bar. Use the settings shown in Figure 18-4 in your macro.

Saving Your Macro

You must save any macro before you can run it. Choose the Save or Save As command from the File menu. Access opens the dialog box shown in Figure 18-5 on the next page. Enter the name *Test Greeting* and click OK to save your macro.

Figure 18-5.
The Save As dialog box for saving a macro.

Testing Your Macro

Some macros (such as the simple one you just created) can be run directly from the Database window or from the Macro window because they don't depend on controls in an open form or report. If your macro does depend on a form or report, you must link the macro to the appropriate event and run it that way. However you run your macro, Microsoft Access provides you with a good way to test it, by allowing you to single step through the macro actions.

To activate single stepping, first go to the Database window, click the Macro button, select the macro you want to test, and click the Design button. These steps will open the macro in a Macro window. You can then either click the Single Step button on the tool bar or choose the Single Step command from the Macro menu.

When you run your macro after clicking the Single Step button, Microsoft Access will open the Macro Single Step dialog box before executing each step. In the dialog box you will see the macro name, the action, and the action arguments.

Try this procedure with the Test Greeting macro you just created. Open the Macro window in Design view and click the Single Step button. Then click the Run button. The Macro Single Step dialog box opens, as shown in Figure 18-6. If you click the Step button in the dialog box, the action you can see in the dialog box will run, and you will see the modal dialog box with the message you created, as shown in Figure 18-7. Click the OK button in the message box to dismiss it. If your macro had had more than one action defined, you would return to the Macro Single Step dialog box, which would show you the next action. In this case your macro has only one action, so Access returns you to the Macro window in Design view.

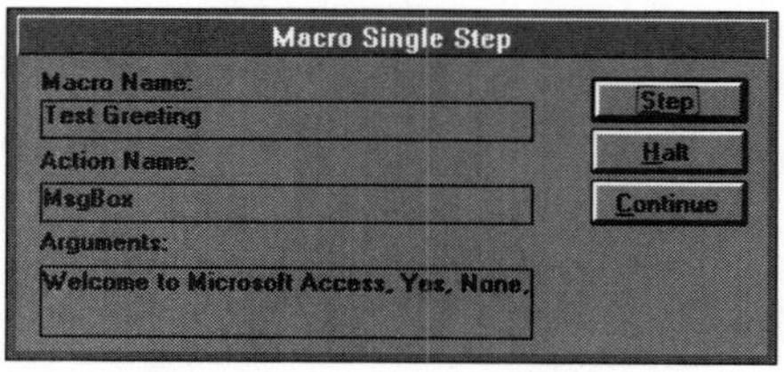

Figure 18-6.
The Macro Single Step dialog box.

Figure 18-7.
The dialog box you created with the macro in Figure 18-4.

If you encounter an error in any macro during normal execution of your application, Microsoft Access first displays a dialog box explaining the error it found. Then you'll see an Action Failed dialog box, similar to the Macro Single Step dialog box, with information about the action that caused the problem. At this point you can click only the Halt button in the Action Failed dialog box. You can then edit your macro to fix the problem. Before you read on in this chapter, you might want to return to the Macro window and click the Single Step button again so that it's no longer selected. Otherwise you will continue to single step through every macro you run in a database.

DEFINING MULTIPLE ACTIONS

In Microsoft Access you can define more than one action within a macro, and you can define the sequence in which you want the actions performed. There are several good examples in the NWIND sample database of macros containing more than one action. Open the NWIND database, click the Macro button in the Database window, and scroll down to the macro named *Sample AutoExec*. Double-click this macro with your right mouse button, or select the macro and click the Open button to open this macro in a Macro window in Design view. The macro is shown in Figure 18-8.

Figure 18-8.
The Sample AutoExec macro, which defines multiple actions in NWIND.

This macro can be used to start the Main Switchboard form in the Northwind Traders application each time you open the NWIND database. As you'll learn in the next chapter, if you create a macro and name it *AutoExec,* Access runs the macro each time you open the database in which it is stored.

In this macro you can see three actions defined. The Echo action sets Echo On to No so that you don't see any extraneous actions flashing on the screen while the macro runs. The Echo action also defines an informative message that displays on the status bar while the macro is running to tell you what's happening. The Hourglass action sets Hourglass On to Yes, so that an hourglass mouse pointer is displayed while the macro is running. The OpenForm action opens the Main Switchboard form that contains the NWIND logo and buttons to activate the various features in the application.

MACRO GROUPS

You'll find that most of the forms you design for an application require multiple macro actions—some to edit fields, some to open reports, and still others to respond to command buttons. You could design a macro for each of these actions, but you'd soon have hundreds of separate macros in your application. A simpler design is to create a macro group for each form or report. In a macro group you can define a number of macros. You give each macro in the group a name in the Macro Name column of the Macro window. When you save your Macro and give it a name, that name is the macro group name. The macro group name appears in the list of macros in the Database window.

Figure 18-9 shows the Main Switchboard form in the NWIND database. This form contains five command buttons, each of which triggers a different macro. The macros are all contained within a macro group called Main Switchboard Buttons. To look at the macro group, go to the Database window, click the Macro button, and then select Main Switchboard Buttons in the list of macros in the Database window. Click the Design button to open this macro group in a Macro window, as shown in Figure 18-10.

The Main Switchboard Buttons macro group has a Macro Name column. (If you don't see the Macro Name column, be sure the Macro Names button on the tool bar is selected.) Each of the five names in this column represents a macro within the group. The first three macros open other forms. The fourth macro moves the focus to the Database window. The last macro closes all open objects and exits Access.

If you open the Main Switchboard form in Design view and look at the properties for each of the command buttons, you'll see that the On Push property contains two names separated by a period. The name before the period is the name of the macro group. The name after the period is the name of the macro within the group.

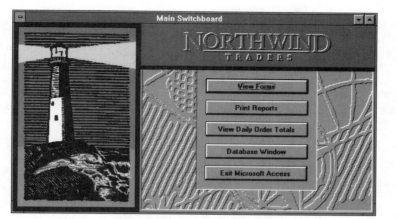

Figure 18-9.
The NWIND Main Switchboard form.

Figure 18-10.
The Main Switchboard Buttons macro group.

So, for the first command button control, the On Push property has been set to *Main Switchboard Buttons.View Forms.* When the user clicks this button, Access runs the View Forms macro in the Main Switchboard Buttons group.

CONDITIONAL EXPRESSIONS

In some macros you might want to execute some actions only under certain conditions. For example, you might want to update a record, but only if new values in the controls in a form pass validation tests. Or you might want to display or hide certain controls based on the value of other controls.

The Required Entry macro in NWIND is a good example of a macro that uses conditions to test whether an action should proceed. Select Required Entry in the NWIND macro list, and click the Design button to see the Macro window shown in Figure 18-11. If you can't see the Condition column, be sure the Conditions button on the tool bar is selected.

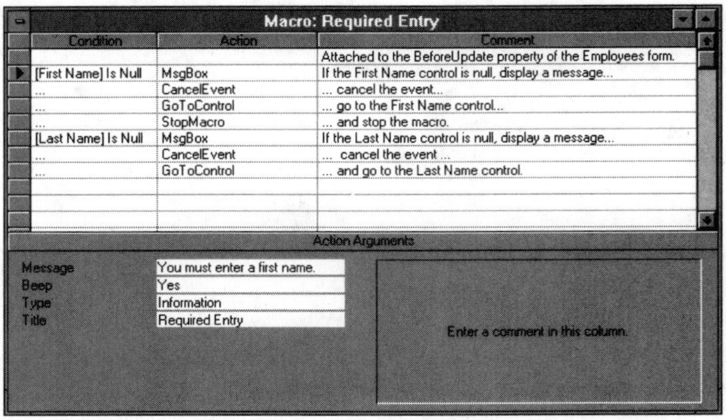

Figure 18-11.
The NWIND Required Entry macro.

This macro is triggered by the Before Update property of the Employees form. The idea is to ensure that a value exists for both the first and last name controls in the record about to be updated. The first condition checks to see whether the First Name control on the form contains a null value. Notice that the form must be open for this macro to work; the macro must be able to find the First Name control. The designer of this macro could also have used the IsNull built-in function to perform this test by typing *IsNull([First Name])* in the Condition column. If the test is true (a first name has not been entered for the record), Microsoft Access executes the action listed in the Action column of the Macro window. In this case, Access displays a message box informing you that you must enter a first name.

Notice that the three lines following the first name test each have three periods specified in the Condition column. This indicates that if the previous condition is true, you also want the actions on these lines performed. This is a handy way to group several actions that you want to run based on the results from one test. In this case, when the name is null, the CancelEvent action stops the update that triggered this macro, the GoToControl action puts the focus back on the control that has the error (to help the user fix the error), and the StopMacro action prevents Access from wasting time performing other tests. If the First Name control does contain a value, the macro performs a similar check on the Last Name control. Because the second check is the last one in the macro, you don't need another StopMacro action if the Last Name control does not contain a name.

The rest of this chapter summarizes all the actions you can include in macros and the events that trigger macros. You'll find it useful to browse through these sections on first reading to become familar with the available actions and events before going on to the final chapter in which you build a major part of the Prompt Computer Solutions application. As you build the application, you'll find these last two sections useful as a quick reference to actions and events.

SUMMARY OF MACRO ACTIONS

This section summarizes the actions available for you to use in macros. The summaries are organized in the following functional categories:

- Opening and closing tables, queries, forms, and reports
- Printing data
- Executing a query
- Testing conditions and controlling action flow
- Setting values
- Searching for data
- Building a custom menu and executing menu commands
- Controlling display and focus
- Informing the user of actions
- Renaming, copying, importing, and exporting objects
- Running another application for MS-DOS or Microsoft Windows

Opening and Closing Tables, Queries, Forms, and Reports

Close	Closes either the specified window or the active window for a table, query, form, or report.
OpenForm	Opens a form in Form, Datasheet, or Design view, or in Print Preview. You can also apply a filter or Where condition in Datasheet or Form view or in Print Preview.
OpenQuery	Opens a query in Datasheet or Design view or in Print Preview. If you specify an action query, Microsoft Access performs the updates specified by the query. See RunSQL in the section "Executing a Query" to specify parameters for a query.
OpenReport	Opens a report in Print Preview (the default), prints the report, or opens the report in Design view. For Print and Print Preview, you can also specify a filter or Where condition.
OpenTable	Opens a table in Datasheet or Design view or in Print Preview.

Printing Data

OpenForm	Can optionally open a form in Print Preview. You can specify a filter or Where condition.
OpenTable	Can optionally open a table in Print Preview.
OpenQuery	Can optionally open a query in Print Preview.
OpenReport	Prints a report or opens a report in Print Preview. You can specify a filter or Where condition.
Print	Prints the active datasheet, form, or report. You can specify a range of pages, the print quality, the number of copies, and collation. Use an Open... action first if you want to apply a filter or Where condition.

Executing a Query

OpenQuery	Runs a select query and displays the dynaset in Datasheet view or Print Preview. Executes an action query. To specify parameters for an action query, use the RunSQL action.
RunSQL	Executes the specified SQL Insert, Delete, Select...Into, or Update statement. You can refer to form controls in the statement to limit the affected records.

Testing Conditions and Controlling Action Flow

CancelEvent	Cancels the event that caused this macro to be executed. You can't use a CancelEvent action in macros that define menu commands, in the OnClose event for a report, or in macros triggered by the AfterUpdate, OnCurrent, OnEnter, or OnPush event.
DoMenuItem	Executes a command on a standard Microsoft Access menu. You can use a DoMenuItem action in a macro that defines a custom menu to make selected Access menu commands available in the custom menu.
Quit	Closes all windows and exits Microsoft Access.
RunCode	Executes an Access Basic function procedure. Other actions following this action execute after the function completes. To execute an Access Basic subprocedure, call that procedure from a function.
RunMacro	Executes another macro. Actions following this action execute after the other macro completes.
StopAllMacros	Stops all macros, including any macros that called this macro.
StopMacro	Stops the current macro.

Setting Values

Requery
Refreshes the data in a control that is bound to a query (such as a list box, combo box, subform, or a control based on a domain function such as DSum). When other actions (such as inserting or deleting a row in the underlying query) might affect the contents of a control that is bound to a query, use the Requery action to update the control values. Use Requery without an argument to refresh the data in the active object (form or datasheet).

SendKeys
Places keystrokes into the keyboard buffer. If you intend to send keystrokes to a modal form or dialog box, you must execute the SendKeys action before opening the modal form or dialog box.

SetValue
Changes the value of any control or property you can update. For example, you can use the SetValue action to calculate a new total in an unbound control or to affect the Visible property of a control (which determines whether you can see that control).

Searching for Data

ApplyFilter
Restricts the information displayed in a form or report by applying a named filter or query or SQL WHERE clause to the underlying table or query of the form.

FindNext
Finds the next record that meets the criteria previously set in the Find dialog box or by a FindRecord macro action.

FindRecord
Finds a record that meets the search criteria. You can specify in the macro action all the parameters available in the Find dialog box.

GoToRecord
Moves to a different record and makes it current in the specified table, query, or form. You can move to the first, last, next, or previous record. When you specify "next" or "previous," you can move more than one record. You can also go to a specific record number or to the new-record placeholder at the end of the set.

Building a Custom Menu and Executing Menu Commands

AddMenu
Adds a drop-down menu to a custom menu bar for a form. This is the only action allowed in a macro triggered by an OnMenu event. Each AddMenu macro action must have a name that corresponds to the menu name on the menu bar of the custom menu. The parameter to AddMenu specifies the name of another macro that contains all the named commands for the menu and the actions that correspond to those commands.

DoMenuItem
Executes a command on one of the standard Microsoft Access menus. Use this macro action within a custom menu bar to make selected Access menu commands available in the custom menu.

Controlling Display and Focus

Echo	Controls the display of intermediate actions while a macro runs.
GoToControl	Sets the focus to the specified control.
GoToPage	Moves to the specified page in a report or form.
Hourglass	Sets the mouse pointer to an hourglass icon while a macro runs.
Maximize	Maximizes the selected window.
Minimize	Minimizes the selected window.
MoveSize	Moves and sizes the selected window on the screen.
RepaintObject	Forces the repainting of the window for the specified object. Forces recalculation of any formulas in controls on that object.
Requery	Refreshes the data in a control that is bound to a query (such as a list box, combo box, subform, or a control based on a domain function such as DSum). When other actions (such as inserting or deleting a row in the underlying query) might affect the contents of a control that is bound to a query, use the Requery macro action to update the control values. Use requery without an argument to refresh the data in the active object (form or datasheet).
Restore	Restores a maximized or minimized window to its previous size.
SelectObject	Selects the window for the specified object. Restores the window if it was minimized.
SetWarnings	Causes an automatic Yes or OK response to all system warning or informational messages while a macro runs. Does not halt the display of error messages. Use this macro action with the Echo action set to Off to avoid displaying the messages.
ShowAllRecords	Removes any filters previously applied to the active form.

Informing the User of Actions

Beep	Causes a sound.
MsgBox	Displays a warning or informational message and optionally produces a sound. You must click OK to dismiss the dialog box and proceed.
SetWarnings	Causes an automatic Yes or OK response to all system warning or informational messages while a macro runs. Does not halt the display of error messages. Use this macro action with the Echo action set to Off to avoid displaying the messages.

Renaming, Copying, Importing, and Exporting Objects

CopyObject	Copies any object in the current database with a new name or with any specified name in another Microsoft Access database.
Rename	Renames the specified object in the current database.

(continued)

TransferDatabase	Exports data to or imports data from another Microsoft Access, dBASE, Paradox, FoxBase, Btrieve, or SQL database. You can also use this action to attach tables or files from other Access, dBASE, Paradox, Btrieve, or SQL databases.
TransferSpreadsheet	Exports data to or imports data from Microsoft Excel or Lotus spreadsheet files.
TransferText	Exports data to or imports data from text files.

Running Another Application for MS-DOS or Microsoft Windows

RunApp	Starts another application for MS-DOS or Microsoft Windows.

SUMMARY OF EVENTS THAT TRIGGER MACROS

Microsoft Access provides 14 events on forms and reports that can trigger macros. This section summarizes those events and organizes them in the following functional categories:

- Opening and closing forms and reports
- Changing data
- Detecting focus changes
- Printing
- Activating a custom form menu

Opening and Closing Forms and Reports

OnOpen	Runs the specified macro or user-defined function when you open a form or report but before Access displays the first record. To access a control on the form or report, the macro must specify a GoToControl action to set the focus on the control.
OnClose	Runs the specified macro or user-defined function when you close a form or report but before Access clears the screen. You can't use a CancelEvent macro action in the OnClose macro for a report. You should use caution when including a CancelEvent macro action in the OnClose for a form.

Changing Data

AfterUpdate	Runs the specified macro or user-defined function after the data in the specified form or control has been updated. You can't include a Cancel-Event macro action in a macro triggered by AfterUpdate. You can, however, use a DoMenuItem action to choose the Undo command from the Edit menu. This event applies to all forms and to combo boxes, list boxes, option groups, and text boxes, as well as to check boxes, option buttons, and toggle buttons that are not part of an option group.

(continued)

BeforeUpdate	Runs the specified macro or user-defined function before the changed data in the specified form or control has been saved to the database. You can use a CancelEvent action to stop the update and place the focus on the updated control or record. This event is most useful for performing complex validations of data on forms or in controls. This event applies to the same controls as AfterUpdate.
OnDelete	Runs the specified macro or user-defined function just before one or more rows are deleted. You can use this event to provide a customized warning message. You can also provide automatic deletion of dependent rows in another table (for example, of all the orders for the customer about to be deleted) by executing a Delete action query. Use the CancelEvent action if you need to stop the rows from being deleted.
OnInsert	Runs the specified macro or user-defined function when you type the first character in a new row. This event is useful for providing additional information to a user who is about to add records. Use the BeforeUpdate event on the form to cancel the insertion of records.

Detecting Focus Changes

OnCurrent	Runs the specified macro or user-defined function in a form when a new record receives the focus, but before Access displays that record. The macro or function specified is also triggered when you open a form. You can't use the CancelEvent action in a macro triggered by this event.
OnDblClick	Runs the specified macro or user-defined function when you double-click a bound object frame, combo box, command button, list box, option group, text box, as well as when you double-click a check box, option button, or toggle button that is not part of an option group. Access runs the macro before showing the normal result of the double-click.
OnEnter	Runs the specified macro or user-defined function when the focus moves to a bound object frame, combo box, command button, list box, option group, or text box, as well as when the focus moves to a check box, option button, or toggle button that is not part of an option group. You can't use a CancelEvent action in a macro triggered by OnEnter.
OnExit	Runs the specified macro or user-defined function when the focus moves from a bound object frame, combo box, command button, list box, option group, or text box, as well as when the focus moves from a check box, option button, or toggle button that is not part of an option group.
OnPush	Runs the specified macro or user-defined function when you choose (push) a command button. You can't use a CancelEvent action in a macro triggered by OnPush.

Printing

OnFormat   Runs the specified macro or user-defined function just before Access formats a report section to print. This event is useful for hiding or displaying controls in the report section based on data values. If Access is formatting a group header, you have access to the data in the first row of the detail section. Similarly, if Access is formatting a group footer, you have access to the data in the last row of the detail section. You can test the FormatCount property to find out if OnFormat has run a macro or function more than once for a section (due to page overflow). You can use the CancelEvent action to keep a section from appearing on the report.

OnPrint   Runs the specified macro or user-defined function just before Access prints a formatted section of a report. If you use the CancelEvent action in a macro triggered by OnPrint, Access leaves a blank space on the report where the section would have printed.

Activating a Custom Form Menu

OnMenu   Defines the macro that creates the custom menu for a form. The macro triggered by OnMenu must contain only named AddMenu actions. Each AddMenu action refers to another macro that defines the individual commands for that menu.

You should now have a basic understanding of macros and how you might use them. In the next chapter you'll see macros in action.

Designing the Prompt Computer Solutions Application

Now it's time to put all you've learned about building tables, queries, forms, and reports into action. In this chapter, you'll see how to link together some of the pieces built in previous chapters, and you'll create the four additional forms needed to complete a major portion of the Prompt Computer Solutions application.

CONNECTING TASKS TO FORMS AND REPORTS

In Chapter 4, "Designing Your Database," you saw how to lay out several key tasks for the PROMPT application, as shown in Figure 19-1 on the next page. You need to define suppliers before you can add components, and you need components in order to build items for the catalog. When you bring together customers and catalog items, you can record an order and ultimately print an invoice.

In previous chapters you created some of the objects you'll need to accomplish these tasks:

- Supplier–Chap 12

- Display/Add Components–Chap 14

- Catalog–Chap 14

- Invoice–Chap 17

In the following sections, you'll learn how to link and automate these four objects within the PROMPT database, as well as how to build, link, and automate forms that define customers, enter orders, choose an invoice to print, and select activities from a main menu. These new forms will be named

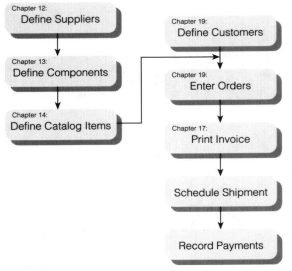

Figure 19-1.
The task flow in the PROMPT application.

- Add Customers–Chap 19

- Orders–Chap 19

- Invoice Selector–Chap 19

- Main Menu–Chap 19

In linking and automating these objects, you'll often use macros to access controls on forms and reports. To access a control, the macro must first specify whether the control is on a form or a report, then it must name the form or report, and finally it must name the control. These elements are separated by exclamation points with no spaces between them, as in the following example

```
Forms![Catalog - Chap 14]![Supplier ID]
```

This example specifies a control named Supplier ID on a form named Catalog–Chap 14.

AUTOMATING THE CATALOG FORM

At the end of Chapter 14, you learned how to build a complex catalog form with a subform and how to open another form with a command button. This is a very simple way to automate the use of forms and other objects within your database. In the sections below you'll see that Microsoft Access also allows you to automate more complex functionality. For example, you'll learn how to do the following:

- Check the values in one field against the values in another
- Enter the data from one field into another field
- Calculate new values automatically
- Cascade a deletion to delete more than one record automatically
- Open forms by double-clicking on a control
- Test whether a form is open
- Resynchronize data between two open forms

Validating Data

There's a famous old cliché in data processing: "Garbage in, garbage out." Simply stated, this means that if incorrect data is put into a process, incorrect data will result. Good database management systems such as Microsoft Access provide you with the tools to help ensure that no one enters any "garbage" in your database. Defining a simple validation rule on individual fields is easy. If you create these rules when you define your tables, Access automatically uses these rules in a form that you design when a control is bound to these fields. For example, the Description field in the Catalog Items table should never be empty. You can ensure this by typing *Is Not Null* in the Validation Rule for this field in the table. See Figure 19-2. Then open the Catalog–Chap 14 form in Design view, select the Description control, and delete it. (The change in table definition can be reflected only in a newly created control.) Create the description control again. When you look at the control's property sheet, you can see that the Is Not Null validation rule is now included in the form, as shown in Figure 19-3 on the next page.

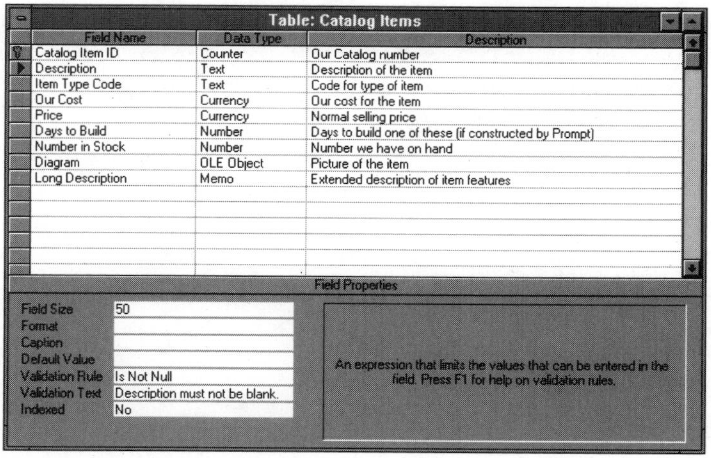

Figure 19-2.
The Catalog Items table with a validation rule on the Description field.

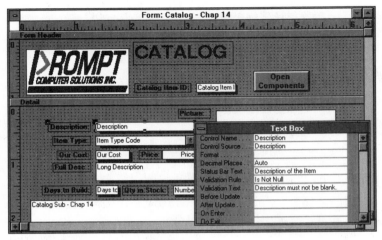

Figure 19-3.
A validation rule on the Description field is automatically copied from a table to a form.

But there are times when a simple validation rule will not suffice. You can't use a validation rule to compare the values of two fields that are in different tables. Neither can you use a validation rule to compare two fields from the same table when the values in the two fields are changed at the same time. (Microsoft Access performs any comparison against the previously saved value of the second field.)

For example, in the Catalog Items table you would expect the selling price to always be greater than or equal to what Prompt Computer Solutions pays for the sum of the components. You could include a validation rule that checks to see that the value in the Price field is always greater than or equal to the value in the Our Cost field. Assume you're starting with Our Cost set to $12 and Price set to $14. If, using the Catalog–Chap 14 form, you set Our Cost to $9 and Price to $11, the validation test would fail because the new $11 price is less than the the original cost of $12. Access checks Price against the old cost because the new cost hasn't been saved to the database yet.

To solve this problem, you need to check the value of one field against another using a macro. Figure 19-4 shows you the macro, called Check Price. It's part of what will be a macro group, here called Catalog–Chap 19. The condition for the Check Price macro is

```
[Our Cost] > [Price]
```

Add the ellipses (...) as shown in the Condition column of Figure 19-4 to apply the condition to other actions of this macro. The settings for the Check Price macro are shown in Figure 19-5.

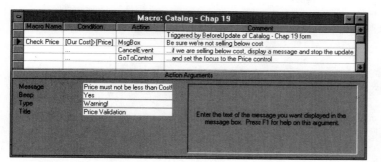

Figure 19-4.
The Check Price macro validates the Price field by comparing it to the Our Cost field.

Action	Argument Box	Setting
MsgBox	Message	Price must not be less than Cost!
	Beep	Yes
	Type	Warning!
	Title	Price Validation
CancelEvent	(none)	(none)
GoToControl	Control Name	Price

Figure 19-5.
The settings for the Check Price macro.

The macro works like this: When Our Cost is greater than Price, a dialog box issues a warning message, the CancelEvent action stops the update from proceeding, and the GoToControl action puts the focus back on the control in error. You can see that it would be easy to include several validation checks in this macro by including additional conditions.

You can trigger this macro from the Before Update property of the form that contains the control you want to check. Figure 19-6 shows the property sheet of the Catalog–Chap 14 form from which the macro called *Catalog–Chap 19.Check Price* is activated. A macro triggered by the Before Update property will run for each field in turn when you save any record that has changed.

Within the macro, you can check a new value against the current value of other fields on the form or against the old value of fields before they are changed by Access. The default is to compare a new value to the current value on the form.

Calculating Values

Macros are extremely useful for providing automatic calculations whenever certain events occur. For example, you can automatically add entries to a blank field if the field is empty when you tab into it. You can also recalculate values whenever records are added, changed, or deleted in the database.

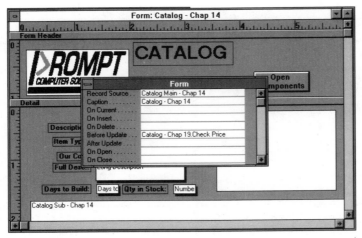

Figure 19-6.
The form's Before Update property is set to trigger the Check Price macro.

Assisting Data Entry

In the Catalog–Chap 14 form there is a Description control and a Long Description control. The entry in Long Description is usually a repeat of the entry in Description but with additional information. To make data entry easier, you can use a macro to automatically copy the entry from the Description control into the Long Description control when the Long Description control is empty. You can call this macro Long Desc and create it as part of the Catalog–Chap 19 macro group.

Figure 19-7 shows the macro. The macro condition tests to see whether the Long Description is null (has never been updated) or contains a zero-length string (might have been updated and then cleared). The full condition string is

```
IsNull([Long Description]) Or [Long Description]=""
```

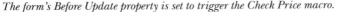

Figure 19-7.
The Long Desc macro automatically copies data from the Description control to the Long Description control.

The settings for the Long Desc macro are shown in Figure 19-8.

Action	Argument Box	Setting
SetValue	Item	Forms![Catalog - Chap 14]![Long Description]
	Expression	Forms![Catalog - Chap 14]![Description]
SendKeys	Keystrokes	{F2}
	Wait	Yes

Figure 19-8.
The settings for the Long Desc macro.

When you've finished, if either condition in the macro's Condition column is true while you're entering data in the Catalog–Chap 14 form, the SetValue macro action copies the data from the Description control to the Long Description control. (In this case you could have used only the names of the controls on the form, but it's a good practice to always fully qualify names in macro parameters with the form name and the control names unless the online Help for the macro parameter specifically states that you should not fully qualify these names.)

You can trigger this macro action either from the On Exit property of the Description control (so that data is copied when focus leaves the Description control) or from the On Enter property of the Long Description control (so that data is copied when focus enters the Long Description control). Figure 19-9 shows how to trigger the macro from the On Enter property of the Long Description control.

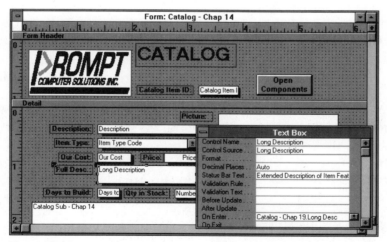

Figure 19-9.
The Long Description control's On Enter property is set to trigger the Long Desc macro.

Performing Automatic Calculations

The Catalog Sub–Chap 14 form has Our Cost and Amount fields for each component of a catalog item. There is also a Total Cost field, which multiplies Our Cost times Amount for each component and then calculates a Sum of the result, to provide a total cost of the catalog item. It would be nice if every time this total cost changed, the new cost was reflected in the Catalog–Chap 14 main form's Our Cost control. A new suggested price could also be calculated. You can perform both of these calculations by creating a macro called Set Cost and triggering it from the After Update property on the subform. See Figure 19-10.

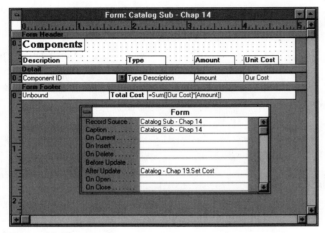

Figure 19-10.
The subform's After Update property is set to trigger the Set Cost macro.

Figure 19-11 shows the Set Cost macro that recalculates the cost in the main form, sets a new price, and saves the result. The settings are shown in Figure 19-12. The condition statement is explained below.

The first SetValue action in the Set Cost macro calls a Domain function called DSum to recalculate the total cost for all the items on the subform. You might think that you could just copy the value in the Sum Of Cost control on the subform to the main form, but this won't work. The reason you can't copy the value is that many actions in Microsoft Access happen asynchronously. The After Update event triggers the macro after any changed row is saved but before all controls on the subform might have finished recalculating. Because the Sum function takes perhaps half a second to perform, the new Sum Of Cost value isn't available when the Set Cost macro runs. So you have to do the Sum Of Cost calculation as part of the SetValue action in the macro to be sure you get the correct amount.

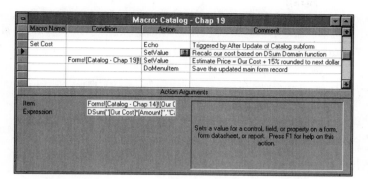

Figure 19-11.
The Set Cost macro calculates a new cost and suggested price after an item component's cost information is changed.

Action	Argument Box	Setting
Echo	Echo On	Yes
	Status Bar Text	(none)
SetValue	Item	Forms![Catalog - Chap 14]![Our Cost]
	Expression	DSum("[Our Cost]*[Amount]", "Catalog Sub - Chap 14", "[Catalog Item ID]=Forms![Catalog - Chap 14]![Catalog Item ID]")
SetValue	Item	Forms![Catalog - Chap 14]![Our Cost] Is Not Null
	Expression	Forms![Catalog - Chap 14]![Price]=CCur(CLng(Forms![Catalog - Chap 14]![Our Cost] *1.15*100)/100)
DoMenuItem	Menu Bar	Form
	Menu Name	File
	Command	Save Record
	Subcommand	(none)

Figure 19-12.
The settings for the Set Cost macro.

The second SetValue macro action adds 15 percent to the total cost to determine a suggested price. A conditional test checks to ensure that there's a value in the Our Cost control because if no components are defined, the Our Cost value will be null and the calculation will fail. The full condition statement is

```
Forms![Catalog - Chap 14]![Our Cost] Is Not Null
```

The calculation by the second SetValue macro involves a currency, so you have to convert to an integer to be sure fractional penny amounts are rounded correctly. The *[Our Cost]*1.15*100* part of the entry calculates the 15 percent margin in pennies. The CLng function converts the result to a long integer, rounding to the nearest penny. Dividing the result by 100 and converting back to a currency value (via the CCur function) yields the desired result accurate to the penny.

The DoMenuItem macro action ensures that the new subtotal value is saved to the database each time something changes on the subform.

Cascading a Delete

If you correctly defined all the relationships in the PROMPT database and turned on referential integrity, Microsoft Access makes sure you haven't entered any orders for nonexistent customers. Access also makes sure you haven't defined any components for nonexistent catalog items. Access ensures the integrity of your database, but requires that when you want to delete an obsolete Catalog Item record (the data in the Catalog–Chap 14 main form), you must first remove all the related Item Component records (the data in the Catalog–Chap 14 subform).

You can delete a Catalog item from the Catalog–Chap 14 main form by first selecting and deleting each Item Component in the subform datasheet and then selecting and deleting the Catalog Items record (using the Select Record command and the Delete command from the Edit menu). Or you can create a macro that automatically takes care of removing the related components (after first warning you) whenever you delete the Catalog Items record. Call this macro Delete Items and trigger it with the On Delete property for the Catalog–Chap 14 form, as shown in Figure 19-13.

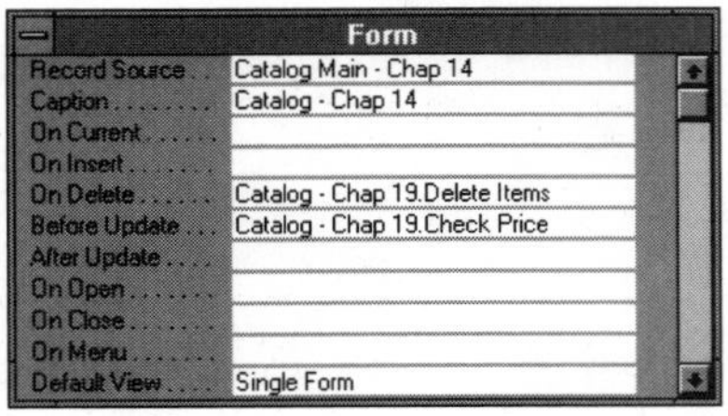

Figure 19-13.
The form's On Delete property is set to trigger the Delete Items macro.

The macro triggered by On Delete must first verify that the user intends to delete both the Catalog Items record and all the related components. If the user confirms the delete action, then the macro must run an action query that deletes all the Item Components records that match the Catalog Items record being deleted. After this action query is finished, the macro is done, and Microsoft Access can complete

410

its deletion of the Catalog Item record without violating the integrity rule. The macro is shown in Figure 19-14 and its settings are shown in Figure 19-15. The condition is explained below.

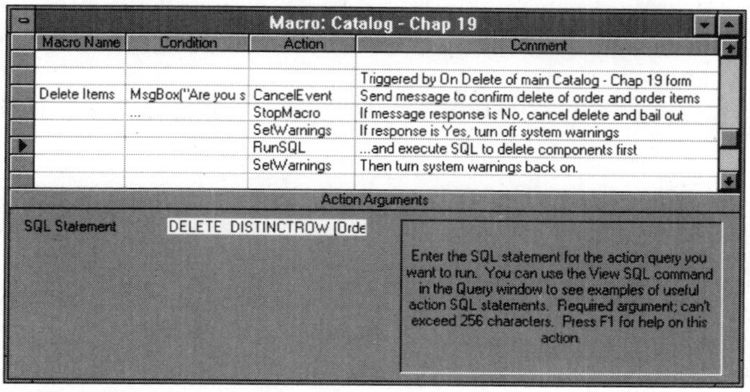

Figure 19-14.
The Delete Items macro deletes Item Component records of a Catalog Item.

Action	Argument Box	Setting
CancelEvent	(none)	(none)
StopMacro	(none)	(none)
SetWarnings	Warnings On	No
RunSQL	SQL Statement	DELETE DISTINCTROW [Item Components].[Catalog Item ID] FROM [Item Components] WHERE ((([Item Components].Catalog Item ID]=Forms![Catalog Item ID]));
SetWarnings	Warnings On	Yes

Figure 19-15.
The settings for the Delete Items macro.

Notice that the second line of the Delete Items macro uses the MsgBox function, not the MsgBox action, in the Condition column to prompt the user and return a numeric value based on the user's response. The MsgBox function has three parameters: the message to display in the dialog box, a number indicating the dialog box mode, and an optional text string to display in the title bar of the dialog box. In this case, the full condition statement is

```
MsgBox("Are you sure you want to delete
Catalog Item :Description:
and all its components?",33,"Delete Catalog Item")<>1
```

Notice that the first parameter uses the technique of embedding a control name surrounded by vertical bars to insert variable information into the message.

(You can enter this text using the Zoom edit box by placing the cursor in the Condition entry and pressing Shift-F2.) You can use the Ctrl-Enter key combination at the end of each line to create a multiple-line message. The parameter 33 is the sum of 1 (indicating a dialog box with OK and Cancel buttons) and 32 (indicating a question mark Warning icon). (See the *Microsoft Access Language Reference* for details on other mode values.) If a user clicks OK in the dialog box created by the MsgBox action, the function returns a 1. If the user doesn't click OK, the macro action on this line, a CancelEvent action, executes to stop the action that triggered this macro—the deletion of the Catalog Items record. The following line, a StopMacro action, also executes if the user doesn't click OK—to stop the deletion of the Item Component records by the macro.

If the user does click OK, the SetWarnings action disables the dialog box that Microsoft Access would normally display to inform the user that rows are about to be deleted in the Item Components table. The RunSQL action contains a delete action query to remove the matching rows from Item Components.

If you're not an SQL expert, the easiest way to create this SQL statement is to design an action query for the Item Components table to delete data. The query should use the value in the field from the Catalog–Chap 14 form to delete all records in the Item Components table that have a matching value in the Catalog Item ID field. Choose SQL from the View menu of the Query window in Design view, highlight the SQL statement created by the query, and press Ctrl-C to copy the statement to the Clipboard. Switch to the Macro window for the Catalog–Chap 19 macro, and paste the query statement into the RunSQL box. You can also save the action query you designed and run it directly from the macro with an OpenQuery action.

The final action in this macro turns SetWarnings back on. After the macro runs, Microsoft Access proceeds to delete the Catalog Items record from your form and underlying table.

Linking Forms with a Mouse Event

You learned how to open the Display/Add Components–Chap 14 form from the Catalog–Chap 14 form using a command button. Now you can link the Supplier–Chap 12 form to the Display/Add Components–Chap 14 form in a different way.

Instead of using a command button, you can open the Supplier–Chap 12 form by double-clicking in the Supplier ID field of the Display/Add Components–Chap 14 form. Figure 19-16 shows you how to set the properties for the Supplier ID control to do this. The On Dbl Click property is set to trigger a macro called New Supplier. This macro will be created in a macro group called Components–Chap 19. Notice how the control's status bar text has been changed (using the control's Status Bar Text property) to inform you that double-clicking the control will open the Supplier–Chap 12 form to add a new supplier to the list.

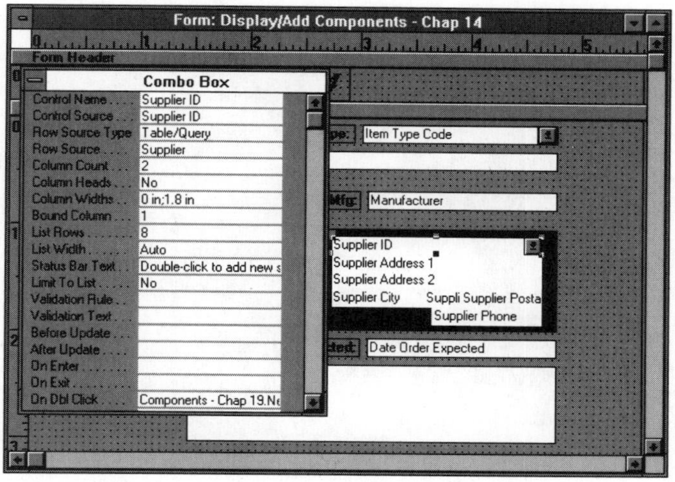

Figure 19-16.

The Supplier ID combo box's On Dbl Click property is set to trigger the New Supplier macro.

Open a new macro and save it as Components–Chap 19. The New Supplier macro is simply an OpenForm macro action to open the Supplier–Chap 12 form. You want to define a new supplier when you double-click in the Supplier ID control on the Display/Add Components–Chap 14 form, so you need to set the Data Mode box for the OpenForm action to the Add setting. See Figure 19-17. The Add setting causes the Supplier form to open ready for data entry, as shown in Figure 19-18 on the next page. You can type in your new supplier information and then close the form to save the record and return to the Display/Add Components–Chap 14 form.

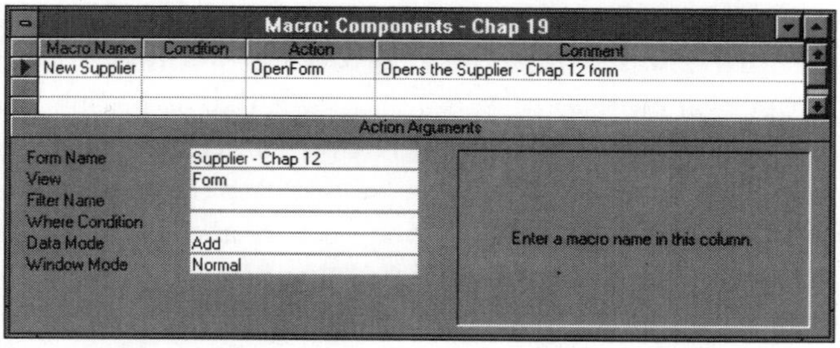

Figure 19-17.

The New Supplier macro will open the Supplier–Chap 12 form.

Testing for an Open Form and Resynchronizing Data

After you type in new supplier information and close the Supplier–Chap 12 form, it would be nice to see that new information immediately appear in your Display/Add Components–Chap 14 form. As you might imagine, you can create a macro

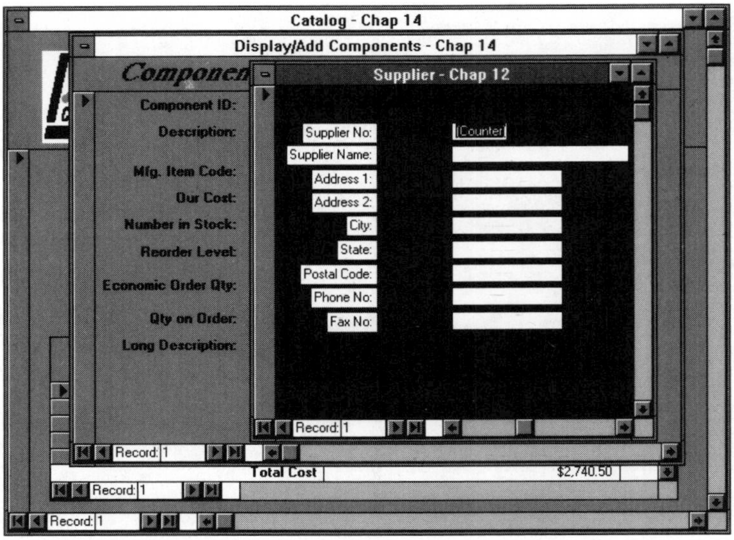

Figure 19-18.
The Supplier–Chap 12 form has been opened, ready for the addition of a new supplier.

triggered by the On Close property of the Supplier form to update the information in the Display/Add Components–Chap 14 form when Microsoft Access returns to it. However, you might want to open the Supplier–Chap 12 form by itself, so the macro needs to be able to detect whether the Display/Add Components–Chap 14 form is open. The macro will end in an error if it tries to update controls on the Display/Add Components–Chap 14 form when the form isn't open.

Testing for an Open Form—an Introduction to Modules

In this section you'll learn a little about Microsoft Access Basic modules. To be able to verify whether a form is open or not, you need a function that is not a standard function in Microsoft Access. But you can find the function you need in the NWIND module called *Introduction to Programming.* To locate it, open the NWIND database, and click the Module button in the Database window. Be sure the Introduction to Programming module is selected, and click the Design button to open the module. You'll see something similar to Figure 19-19.

In Figure 19-19 you see the declarations section of the module, in which the programmer can set global options and variables. On the tool bar, you can find a Procedure combo box. Open the list in this box and scroll until you can see a function called *IsLoaded.* Select the IsLoaded function, and the Access Basic code will appear in the Module window, as shown in Figure 19-20.

Open the Procedure combo
box to see a list of functions

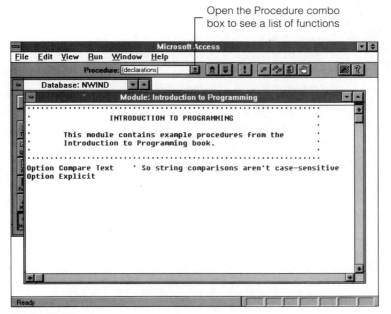

Figure 19-19.
The initial view of the Introduction to Programming module in the NWIND database.

```
Function IsLoaded (MyFormName)
' Accepts: a form name
' Purpose: determines if a form is loaded
' Returns: True if specified the form is loaded;
'          False if the specified form is not loaded.
' From: Chapter 3

Dim i
    IsLoaded = False
    For i = 0 To Forms.Count - 1
        If Forms(i).FormName = MyFormName Then
            IsLoaded = True
            Exit Function          ' Quit function once form has been found
        End If
    Next
End Function
```

Figure 19-20.
The Access Basic code for the IsLoaded function.

To copy this code to the PROMPT database, select the contents of the Module window with your mouse. Choose the Copy command from the Edit menu and close the NWIND database. Open the PROMPT database, click the Module button in the Database window, and click the New button. Choose the New Procedure command from the Edit menu. Access will open the New Procedure dialog box shown in Figure 19-21 on the next page. In the Type group box choose Function, and name your

New Procedure
Type
Sub
Function
OK
Cancel
Name:
IsLoaded

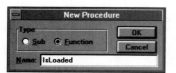

Figure 19-21.
The New Procedure dialog box.

function IsLoaded. Then choose Paste from the Edit menu to copy the code into your module. Delete the first and last lines in the Module window so that the window resembles Figure 19-20. Choose the Save command from the File menu and give your new module the name *Functions–Chap 19*. Now the custom function IsLoaded can be used anywhere in the PROMPT database in the same way you'd use any built-in function. The IsLoaded function can be used to test for open forms, as explained in the next section.

Note: *If you already have a function named IsLoaded in your database (for example, because you are working with a version of the PROMPT database that you copied from CompuServe), Microsoft Access will not let you give this new function the same name. You'll need to rename the other function or save this function with another name.*

Resynchronizing Two Forms

You can open the Supplier–Chap 12 form from the Display/Add Components–Chap 14 form. If you add a new supplier to the Supplier–Chap 12 form, you can use a macro so that the new supplier information, including Supplier ID data, appears immediately in the Display/Add Components–Chap 14 form.

Create a Supplier–Chap 19 macro group, and in the Macro window you can create the Refresh Component macro shown in Figure 19-22. The settings are shown in Figure 19-23. The conditions are explained below.

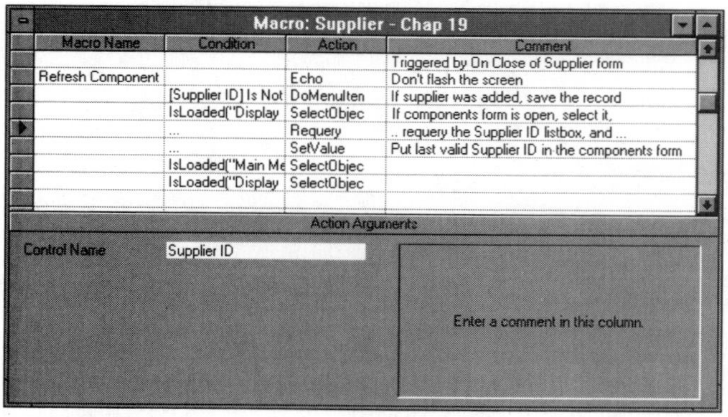
Macro: Supplier - Chap 19
Macro Name
Condition
Action
Comment
Triggered by On Close of Supplier form
Refresh Component
Echo
Don't flash the screen
[Supplier ID] Is Not
DoMenuIten
If supplier was added, save the record
IsLoaded("Display
SelectObjec
If components form is open, select it,
...
Requery
.. requery the Supplier ID listbox, and ...
...
SetValue
Put last valid Supplier ID in the components form
IsLoaded("Main Me
SelectObjec
IsLoaded("Display
SelectObjec
Action Arguments
Control Name
Supplier ID
Enter a comment in this column.

Figure 19-22.
The Refresh Component macro automatically adds new supplier information to the Display/Add Components–Chap 14 form.

Action	Argument Box	Setting
Echo	Echo On	No
	Status Bar Text	(none)
DoMenuItem	Menu Bar	Form
	Menu Name	File
	Command	Save Record
	Subcommand	(none)
SelectObject	Object Type	Form
	Object Name	Display/Add Components - Chap 14
	In Database Window	No
Requery	Control Name	Supplier ID
SetValue	Item	Forms![Display/Add Components - Chap 14]![Supplier ID]
	Expression	Forms![Supplier - Chap 12]![Supplier ID]
SelectObject	Object Type	Form
	Object Name	Main Menu - Chap 19
	In Database Window	No
SelectObject	Object Type	Form
	Object Name	Display/Add Components - Chap 14
	In Database Window	No

Figure 19-23.

The settings for the Refresh Component macro.

Because several things are happening in this macro that might be distracting, the first macro action sets Echo to No. The second line in the macro checks to see whether the current Supplier ID on the Supplier–Chap 12 form is a valid value. The condition statement is

```
[Supplier ID] Is Not Null
```

If you opened the Supplier–Chap 12 form but didn't add a new record, you don't want to copy information from an invalid Null supplier record to the Display/Add Components–Chap 19 form.

If the Supplier ID is valid, the DoMenuItem macro action chooses the Save record command from the file menu to be sure you've saved the new supplier information. The condition on the next line checks whether a valid Supplier ID was entered and whether the Display/Add Components–Chap 14 form is open. The condition looks like this:

```
IsLoaded("Display/Add Components - Chap 14") And Forms![Supplier -
    Chap 12]![Supplier ID] Is Not Null
```

If the Supplier ID is valid and the Display/Add Components–Chap 14 form is open, the macro action SelectObject will move the focus to the Display/Add

Components–Chap 14 form. Notice the ellipses in the Condition column of Figure 19-22. The ellipses mean that the condition still applies to the macro action on this line. The Requery macro action refreshes the Supplier ID control on the Display/ Add Components–Chap 14 form. Finally, the SetValue macro action copies the Supplier ID from the Supplier–Chap 12 form to the Display/Add Components– Chap 14 form.

The next line in the macro action will check to see whether the Main Menu– Chap 19 form is open. At the end of this chapter, you'll see how to design the Main Menu–Chap 19 form that you can use to select all the options in this part of the Prompt Computer Solutions application. When the Display/Add Components– Chap 14 form is not open, you'll want Access to return to the Main Menu–Chap 19 form when the Supplier–Chap 12 form is closed. (Be sure to set the On Close property of the Supplier–Chap 12 form to Supplier–Chap 19.Refresh Components.) The condition statement for this first macro action is

```
IsLoaded(Main Menu - Chap 19)
```

The last macro action will move the focus to the Display/Add Components– Chap 14 form if it is open. Its condition statement is

```
IsLoaded(Display/Add Components - Chap 14)
```

CREATING THE ADD CUSTOMERS FORM

In this section, you'll build a form to add and display customer information, one of four additional forms you need in order to complete the PROMPT application. The easiest way to create the Add Customers–Chap 19 form is to go to the Database window in PROMPT and select the Customer table. Then click the New Form button on the tool bar. When the New Form dialog box opens, click the FormWizards button. Use the single-column FormWizard.

Add the fields shown in Figure 19-24, choose the Standard look for your form, and name your form *Add Customers–Chap 19*. When the FormWizard has finished, move some of the fields on the form to create a second column and size the controls so that they display all of the information. Add an unbound object frame control to display the PROMPT logo. Your result should look something like Figure 19-25.

You'll notice that at the bottom of the Add Customers–Chap 19 form in Figure 19-25 there's a combo box with the company name. The combo box wasn't created by the FormWizard, of course, but you can create it yourself now. This unbound control is tied to a macro to help you pick the record you want to see. The underlying query for this control is called *Company List–Chap 19*; the query contains company names in ascending alphabetic sequence. Start by creating the query, as shown in Figure 19-26 on page 420.

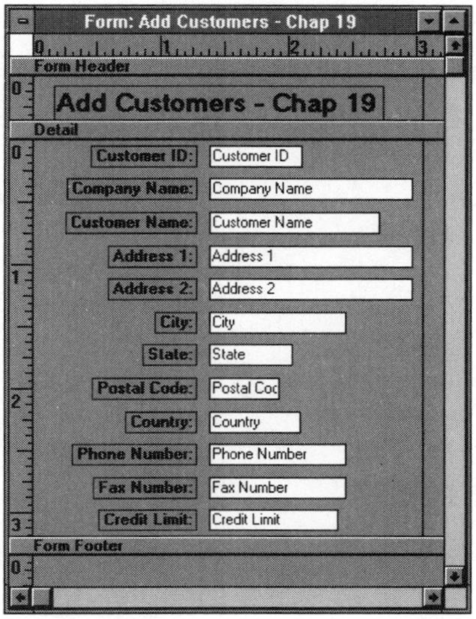

Figure 19-24.
The fields on the single-column Add Customers form.

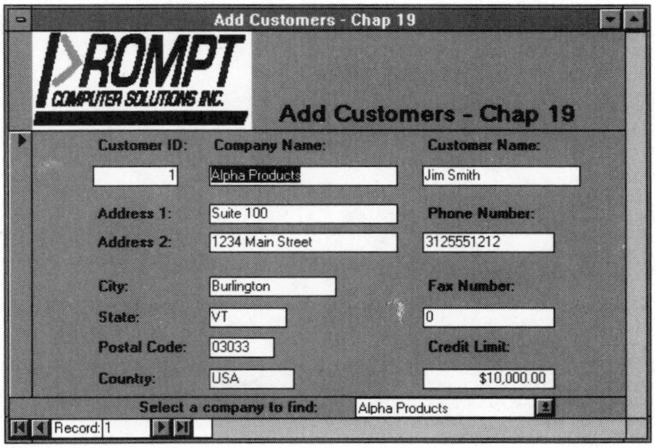

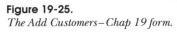

Figure 19-25.
The Add Customers–Chap 19 form.

After you've created the query, open the Add Customers–Chap 19 form in Design view and add the unbound combo box control. Open the property sheet for the control, set the Control Name property to Company Pick List, and set the Row Source property to the Company List–Chap 19 query. The property sheet is shown in Figure 19-27 on the next page. Set the After Update property so that it triggers a macro called Find Company from a macro group called Customers–Chap 19. You'll create this macro below.

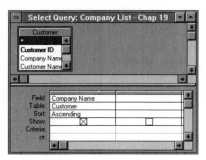

Figure 19-26.
The Company List query.

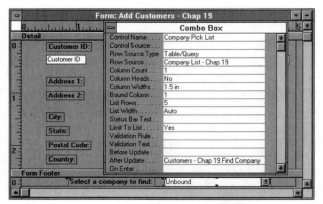

Figure 19-27.
The property sheet for the Company Pick List combo box.

To create the Find Company macro, first open a new Macro window and save it as *Customers–Chap 19.* Enter the macro as shown in Figure 19-28. The macro's settings are shown in Figure 19-29.

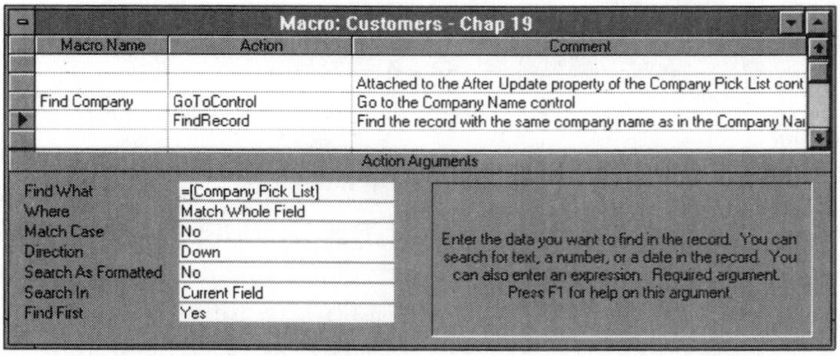

Figure 19-28.
The Find Company macro searches for the record that matches the selection in the Company Pick List combo box.

In the Find Company macro, the GoToControl action moves the focus to the Company Name control on the form. The FindRecord action then goes to the record whose company name matches the name that has been selected in the Company Pick List combo box.

Action	Argument Box	Setting
GoToControl	Control Name	Company Name
FindRecord	Find What	=[Company Pick List]
	Where	Match Whole Field
	Match Case	No
	Direction	Down
	Search As Formatted	No
	Search In	Current Field
	Find First	Yes

Figure 19-29.
The settings for the Find Company macro.

BUILDING THE ORDERS FORM

If you've followed along in the book to this point, you should feel comfortable with the techniques for building a complex form and subform based on queries that combine information from multiple tables. You built such a form to maintain catalog entries in Part IV of this book, and you learned how to use macros to automate that form earlier in this chapter. You'll want a similarly complex form and set of macros to enter orders for Prompt Computer Solutions. This section shows you the major features of the Orders–Chap 19 form in the PROMPT database and shows you a couple of new techniques you can use to automate forms.

In the PROMPT database there are an Orders table containing summary information about each order (with entries such as shipping address and discount) and an Order Items table that contains an entry for each catalog item included in the order. Each order can have multiple items, so it makes sense, in designing an Orders form, to create a main form to hold the order summary information with an embedded subform for the order details.

The Orders table contains the Customer ID as a foreign key to link back to the customer information. Therefore, you can verify information from the Customer table at the same time you create or review orders if you include the Customer table along with the Orders table in the query you'll use for the Orders main form. The query should look something like Figures 19-30 and 19-31. A bit later in this chapter, in the section called "Orders Form Properties," you'll set a property on the Orders form to allow you to update the address information for the customer even though the Customer table is on the "one" side of the relationship between customers and orders.

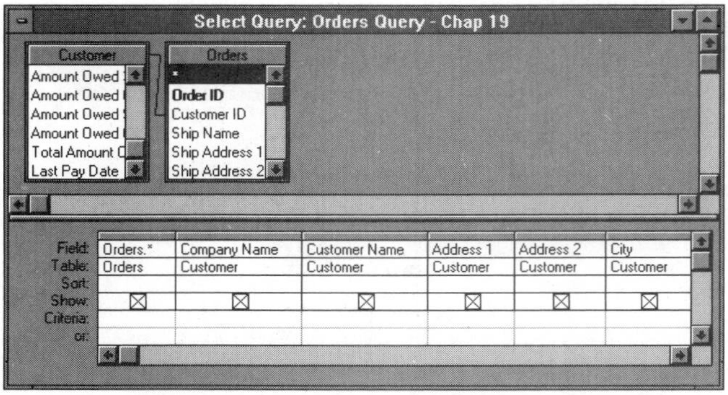

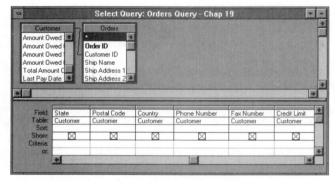

Figure 19-30.
Some of the fields in the QBE grid of the Orders Query–Chap 19 query.

Figure 19-31.
The rest of the fields in the QBE grid of the Orders Query.

Using the Order Items Query that underlies the subform in the main Orders form, you'll be updating information in the Order Items table in the subform. This table contains the Order ID (linked via properties in the subform control to Order ID in the Orders table), Catalog Item ID, Quantity, and Quoted Price fields that you'll want to update in the subform. Catalog Item ID isn't very informative by itself, so it's a good idea to include the Catalog Items table so that you can show the item's Description field easily. Also, from the Catalog Items table, you'll need the Our Cost and Price fields to help the user decide on the actual price to charge the customer in this order, and you'll need the Number in Stock field to show whether this item can be shipped to the customer right away. If you include the Types table, your Orders subform can show other items of the same type as the item that the customer wants to order. The resulting query should look something like Figure 19-32.

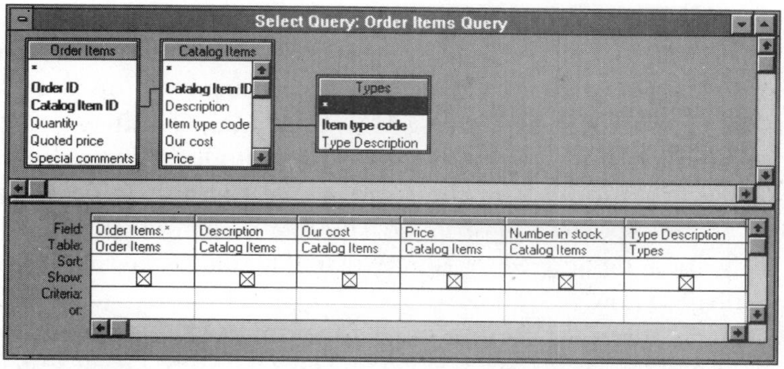

Figure 19-32.
The Order Items Query on which the Order Details Subform is based.

After you've created the Orders Query and the Order Items Query, you're ready to start building the main part of the Orders form. You can call the main form *Orders–Chap 19*, and you can call the subform *Order Details Sub–Chap 19*. Figure 19-33 shows you the completed form and subform. On the main form in the form header, include controls for Order ID, Customer PO, and Order Date from the Orders table (by way of the Orders Query). Set the Link Child Fields and Link Master Fields properties of the subform to Order ID. Later in this chapter, in the section called "Triggering an Invoice," you'll see how to create a macro to print the related invoice using the command button you can see in this sample.

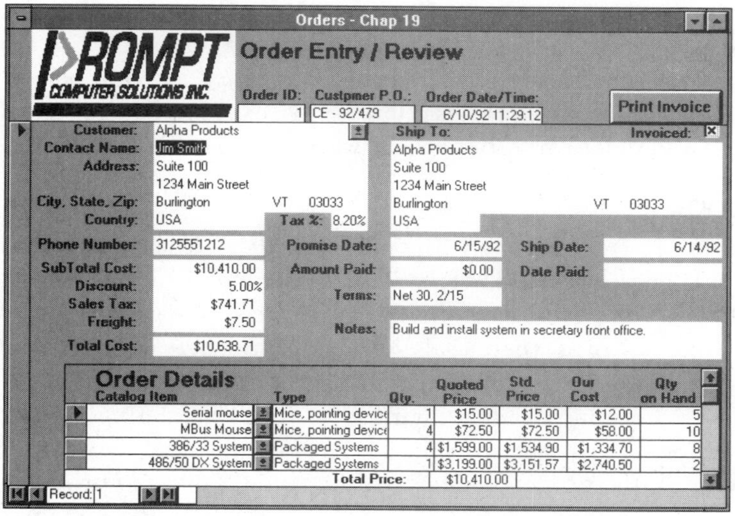

Figure 19-33.
The Orders–Chap19 form in Form view.

On the main form, in the detail section, there is a combo box bound to the Customer ID field of the *Orders* table to show the related customer name from the *Customer* table. See the section below called "Picking a Customer on the Orders Form" for details. The Contact Name, Address, City, State, Zip, Country, and Phone Number fields all come from the Customer table in the underlying query. Something that's not obvious from looking at the form is that there's a hidden control bound to Company Name next to the Ship To label. You include this control to make it easy to copy in a default Ship Name using a macro, as explained in "Automating Data Entry" below.

The detail section of the main form also uses four macros to calculate values: Update Cost, Set Tax, Calc Tax, and Calc Total. The Update Cost macro recalculates the subtotal on the main form when there's a change on the subform. The Set Tax macro sets the sales tax percentages for different states, and the Calc Tax macro calculates the tax amount. The Calc Total macro calculates the value for the Total Cost field (an unbound text box) each time the form displays a new record. The macro is triggered from the On Current property for the main form. See the section "Calculating Values" for an explanation of these four macros.

The subform is automated in several ways. The design for the Order Details Sub–Chap 19 is similar to the Catalog Sub–Chap 14 form you built previously. You need a combo box to display Catalog Item descriptions, designed so that you can also update the Catalog Item ID field in the Order Items table. The Type Description comes from the Type table in the query, and you should set this control's Enabled property to No and its Locked property to Yes so that no one will be able to change data in this field. Also, a macro in the subform sets the initial Quoted Price value to the catalog price, as explained in the "Automating Data Entry" section below.

Finally, the "Cascading a Delete" section below explains the Delete Items macro that enables you to delete an order record with all its associated order items.

Orders Form Properties

There are several interesting property settings on the Orders–Chap 19 form that are worth examining. See Figure 19-34. There's a macro attached to the On Current property that recalculates the total cost whenever you view a new order record. As with the Catalog–Chap 19 form, there's also a macro attached to the On Delete property that automatically removes all matching Order Items rows if you decide to delete an order. (These two macros are explained in the "Calculating Values" and "Cascading a Delete" sections, respectively.)

You'll also notice on the property sheet that the Allow Updating property is set to Any Tables. Normally, because the Customer table is related one-to-many to the Orders table, you wouldn't be able to update any information in the Customer table through the query used in this form. Updating the "one" side of a query is usually

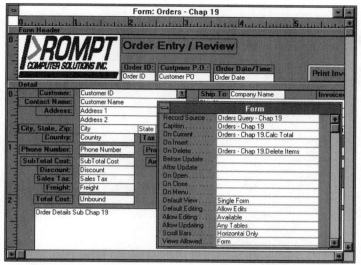

Figure 19-34.
The property sheet for the Orders–Chap 19 form.

a bad idea because it could potentially affect many more records than the one you change. In this case, however, you'll probably always want to reflect the latest customer address information for *all* orders for this customer, so allowing the query to update information in the Customer table is acceptable. Also, you've carefully restricted the fields you will allow to be updated in the Customer table via the Orders–Chap 19 form, so you won't be harming the integrity of your data. By setting the Allow Updating property to Any Tables you can update the Customer table data using Orders table fields.

Picking a Customer on the Orders Form

You created a combo box in the Components–Chap 13 form that was used for picking a Supplier ID. The Customer ID combo box on the Orders form works in much the same way. You can use the Customer table as the setting for the Row Source property of this control because the first column in the Customer table contains the Customer ID for the bound value of this control and the second column contains the Company Name that provides meaningful data from which to pick the Customer ID. See Figure 19-35. Notice that the Column Count property is set to 2, pointing to the two columns Customer ID and Company Name. The Column Width settings are 0 inches and 2 inches. The 0 setting determines that the first column, Customer ID, is not displayed. You can see the property settings for the combo box in Figure 19-35. Since the Customer ID (to which the control is bound) is a number, you also need to set the alignment left to display the characters in the Company Name field properly aligned.

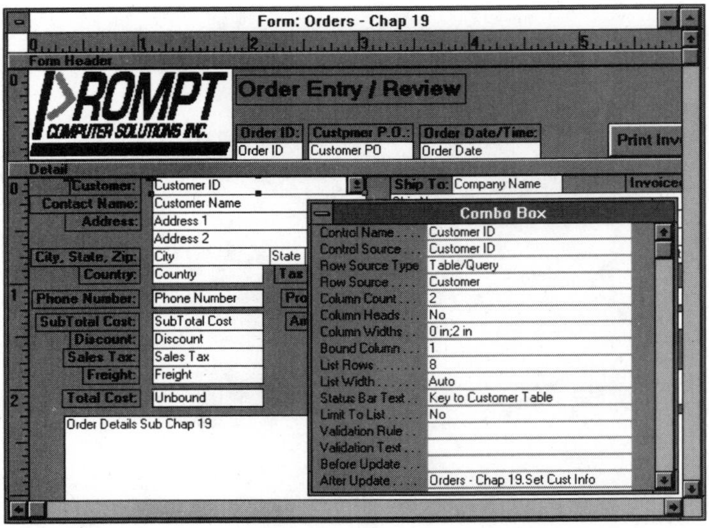

Figure 19-35.
The property sheet for the Customer ID combo box.

As mentioned earlier, the Allow Updating property for this form is set to Any Tables, enabling you to update the customer name and address information on the Orders–Chap 19 form. However, when you choose Any Tables, Microsoft Access will not automatically fill in the contact name and address information when you choose a new Customer ID via the Customer ID combo box. You'll need a macro attached to the control's After Update property to do the job for you. You'll see later that you also need an actual control bound to Company Name in order to fill in supplier information automatically. If you look closely at Figure 19-35, you can see a control for this next to the Ship To label. Because the Customer ID combo box normally displays this information, this control has its Visible property set to No so that you don't display the information twice.

Figure 19-36 shows the macro that updates customer name, address, and phone information in the Orders–Chap 19 form. This macro is called *Set Cust Info*, and it has been created within a macro group called *Orders–Chap 19*. To pull individual field values from a table or query in your database, you can use a handy built-in function of Microsoft Access called *DLookUp*. The parameters you supply to this function are the name of the column, the name of the table or query, and a condition statement to get the record you want. In this example, you can get each of the several fields in the Customer table by including a condition to match that field with the Customer ID that's just been selected on the form. For example, to update Customer Name you would use a SetValue macro action with the Item box set to this:

```
Forms![Orders - Chap 19]![Customer Name]
```

```
Orders - Chap 19.Set Tax
```

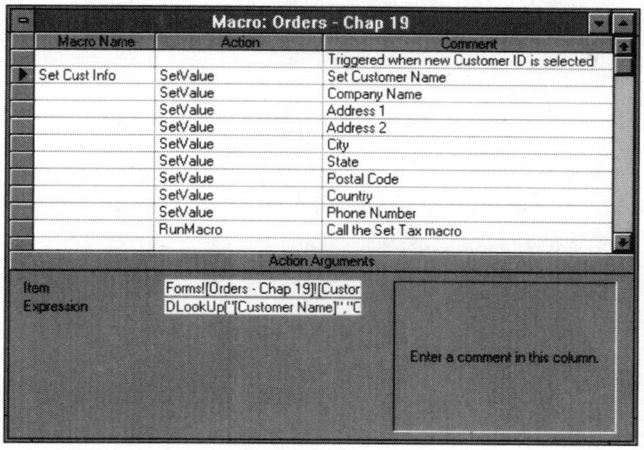

Figure 19-36.
The Set Cust Info macro updates fields of customer information in the Orders–Chap 19 form.

You would then set the Expression box to this:

```
DLookUp("[Customer Name]","Customer","[Customer ID]=Forms![Orders-
   Chap 19]![Customer ID]")
```

You need one SetValue action for each field you want to fill in from the Customer table, using the appropriate field name. The RunMacro action (at the end of this macro) runs the Set Tax macro that calculates the state sales tax percentage. You'll look at the Set Tax macro later in this chapter. The RunMacro macro action has the following setting in the Macro Name box:

Automating Data Entry

There are a couple of opportunities on the Orders–Chap 19 form to help make entering data simpler. The first opportunity occurs in the main form. When you tab to the Ship Name control, it would be nice if that information were filled in automatically from the customer data (when you haven't already typed in a new value). You can make this happen by setting the On Enter property of the Ship Name control so that it triggers the macro shown in Figure 19-37.

In this macro, the condition checks to see if the Ship Name control is empty or contains a null value. The condition statement looks like this:

```
IsEmpty([Ship Name]) Or IsNull([Ship Name]) Or [Ship Name]=""
```

Notice the ellipses in the Condition column; the condition statement applies for each SetValue macro action. If the Ship Name control does meet these conditions, the SetValue macro actions will copy the appropriate customer name and

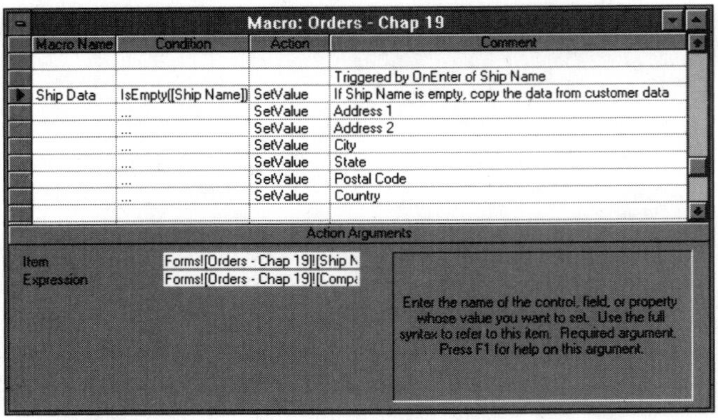

Figure 19-37.
The Ship Data macro sets empty "ship to" fields to the customer name and address information.

address fields to the shipping information fields in the Orders table record. It's easy then to either tab to other fields if you're shipping to the main address for the customer, or correct the address if you're not. To define each SetValue macro action in this Ship Data macro, you can follow the example below for the Ship Name control. The Item box setting for the Ship Name control is like this:

```
Forms![Orders - Chap 19]![Ship Name]
```

The Expression box setting for the Ship Name control is like this:

```
Forms![Orders - Chap 19]![Company Name]
```

The second opportunity to make it easier to enter data is on the subform. Each time you pick a different catalog item on the subform, it would be handy if the initial Quoted Price value were set to the normal price you charge for the item as reflected in the catalog. You could then adjust the price on the form if necessary to get the sale. Attach a macro to the After Update property of the Catalog Item ID control in the subform and use a SetValue macro action to set the Quoted Price value equal to Price.

Calculating Values

There are several calculations occurring in the Orders–Chap 19 form and subform. First, any time you add, change, or delete an order item, the cost needs to be recalculated and copied to the SubTotal Cost field in the Orders table record. In addition, the sales tax based on any new subtotal must be calculated and a new grand total displayed.

To further complicate matters, any time a customer's State is changed, there might be a new sales tax percentage which affects the sales tax stored in the Orders table record as well as the grand total displayed on the form.

To deal with these calculations, you need four macros:

- An Update Cost macro that calculates a new subtotal any time you make a change in the subform

- A Set Tax macro that determines the new sales tax rate whenever you change the customer's State field

- A Calc Tax macro that calculates the sales tax whenever the subtotal, the discount, or the sales tax rate changes

- A Calc Total macro that calculates the grand total owed each time the subtotal, sales tax, discount, or freight rate changes

You can see the macros you need for these four calculations in Figures 19-38 and 19-40.

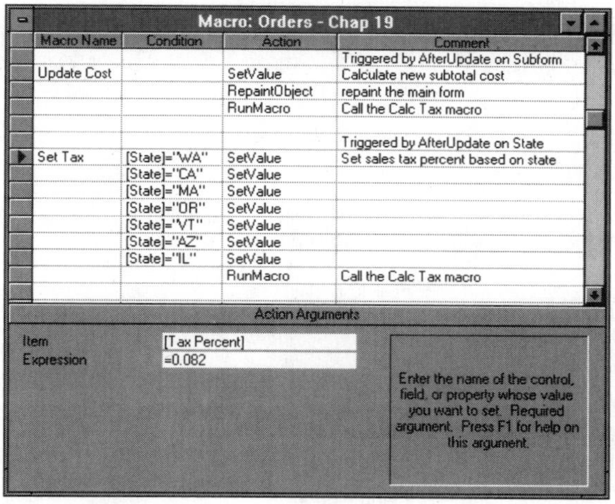

Figure 19-38.
The Update Cost and Set Tax macros are used to calculate values on the Orders–Chap 19 form.

The first macro, called Update Cost, is triggered whenever any record changes on the subform. The After Update property on the Orders Details Sub–Chap 19 form is set to Update Cost. This macro uses the DSum function to calculate the sum of the Quantity times Quoted Price values for all items in the order; it then places the result in the SubTotal Cost control on the main form. Because any change to the subtotal affects sales tax and the grand total, this macro calls the macro that calculates sales tax. The settings for the Update Cost macro are shown in Figure 19-39.

The second macro, Set Tax, is triggered whenever the value for the customer's State field changes. The sample shown in Figure 19-38 handles only seven states with simple condition checks. You could also construct a sales tax table based on State and use a DLookUp function to set the new sales tax rate. The RunMacro action is set to call the Orders–Chap 19.Calc Tax macro.

Action	Argument Box	Setting
SetValue	Item	Forms![Orders - Chap 19]![Subtotal Cost]
	Expression	DSum("[Quantity]*[Quoted Price]", "Order Items-Chap 19","[Order ID]= Forms![Orders-Chap 19]![Order ID]")
RepaintObject	Object Type Object Name	Orders - Chap 19
RunMacro	Macro Name Repeat Count Repeat Expression	Orders - Chap 19 (none) (none)

Figure 19-39.
The settings for the Update Cost macro.

The third macro, Calc Tax, shown in Figure 19-40, calculates a new sales tax amount whenever the value changes in the SubTotal Cost, the Sales Tax Percent, or the Discount control. This macro is executed from the Update Cost and Set Tax macros. The After Update property on the Discount control also executes this macro.

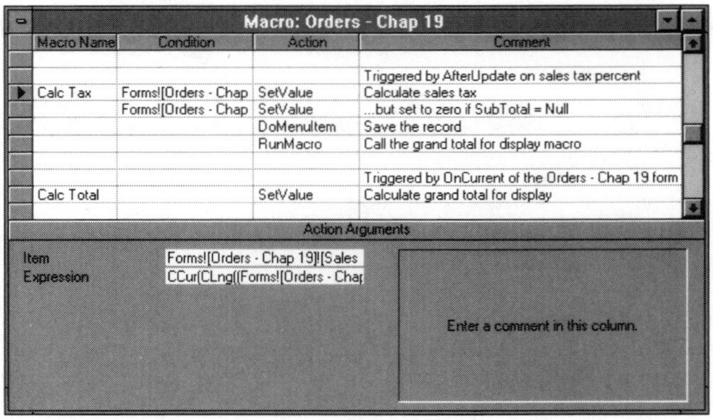

Figure 19-40.
The Calc Tax and Calc Total macros are used to calculate values on the Orders–Chap 19 form.

There are two condition statements in the Calc Tax macro. The first is

```
Forms![Orders - Chap 19]![SubTotal Cost] Is Not Null
```

This first condition statement checks whether the SubTotal Cost value is not null, in which case it initiates the first SetValue action, the calculation of the sales tax. The second condition is

```
Forms![Orders - Chap 19]![SubTotal Cost] Is Null
```

430

This second condition statement checks whether the SubTotal Cost value is null, in which case it initiates the SetValue action that sets the tax to zero. The settings for the Calc Tax macro are shown in Figure 19-41.

Action	Argument Box	Setting
SetValue	Item Expression	Forms![Orders - Chap 19]![Sales Tax] CCur(CLng((Forms![Orders-Chap 19]![SubTotal Cost]*(1-Forms![Orders- Chap 19]![Discount]))*Forms![Orders- Chap 19]![Tax Percent]*100)/100)
SetValue	Item Expression	Forms![Orders-Chap 19]![Sales Tax] 0
DoMenuItem	Menu Bar Menu Name Command Subcommand	Form File Save Record (none)
RunMacro	Macro Name Repeat Count Repeat Expression	Orders - Chap 19.Calc Total (none) (none)

Figure 19-41.
The settings for the Calc Tax macro.

NOTE: *Because the first SetValue action calculates sales tax based on a percentage of a currency amount, you need to use the CLng and CCur functions to ensure that there aren't any penny-rounding errors. See the setting for the Expression box of the first SetValue action in Figure 19-41.*

The fourth and final calculation macro, Calc Total, creates the grand total you see on the form. This grand total value isn't stored in any table. The macro runs whenever the subtotal changes, the sales tax rate changes, or you update either the Discount or Freight control. Calc Total also executes each time you move to a new order record (triggered by the On Current property for the form). The settings for the Calc Total macro are shown in Figure 19-42.

Action	Argument Box	Setting
SetValue	Item Expression	Forms![Orders-Chap 19]![SubTotal Cost] CCur(CLng((Forms![Orders-Chap 19]![SubTotal Cost]*(1-Forms![Orders-Chap 19]![Discount])) *100)/100)+Forms![Orders-Chap 19]![Sales Tax]+Forms![Orders-Chap 19]![Freight]

Figure 19-42.
The settings for the Calc Total macro.

Cascading a Delete

Referential integrity protects the relationship between Orders and Order Items data in the Orders–Chap 19 form. That is, an Order Item record cannot exist without being connected to an Order record. So if you want to delete an order, you must either delete all the Order Items first or create a macro to do it for you automatically.

The macro you need to do this job must be attached to the On Delete property of the Orders–Chap 19 form. The macro used for cascading a delete is shown in Figure 19-43. In this case, the Condition setting for the CancelEvent action should look like this:

```
MsgBox("Are you sure you want to delete
Order Number ;[Order ID];
for ;[Company Name];?",33,"Delete Order")<>1
```

Notice the ellipses in the Condition column, in the line beneath the condition statement. The settings for the Delete Items macro are shown in Figure 19-44.

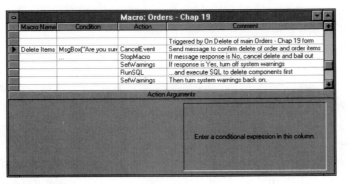

Figure 19-43.
The Delete Items macro.

Action	Argument Box	Setting
CancelEvent	(none)	
StopMacro	(none)	
SetWarnings	Warnings On	No
RunSQL	SQL Statement	DELETE DISTINCTROW [Order Items].[Order ID] FROM [Order Items] WHERE ((([Order Items].[Order ID]=Forms![Orders-Chap 19]![Order ID]));
SetWarnings	Warnings On	Yes

Figure 19-44.
The settings for the Delete Items macro.

Triggering an Invoice

What if you're ready to ship an order and you need to print an invoice? In Chapter 17, "Advanced Report Design," you learned how to create the Invoice–Chap 17 report. You can add a command button on the Orders–Chap 19 form to format and print an invoice for the current order.

In the Orders table, a Yes/No field called Invoiced indicates whether you've previously printed the invoice for an order. You shouldn't need to print an invoice more than once. You should set the Enabled property of this field to No and the Locked property to Yes so that you can't set the field from the form. You'll set this field from a macro instead. Notice the Print Invoice button on the Orders form in Figure 19-33. The On Push property for this button is set to trigger the Print Invoice macro. The macro is shown in Figure 19-45.

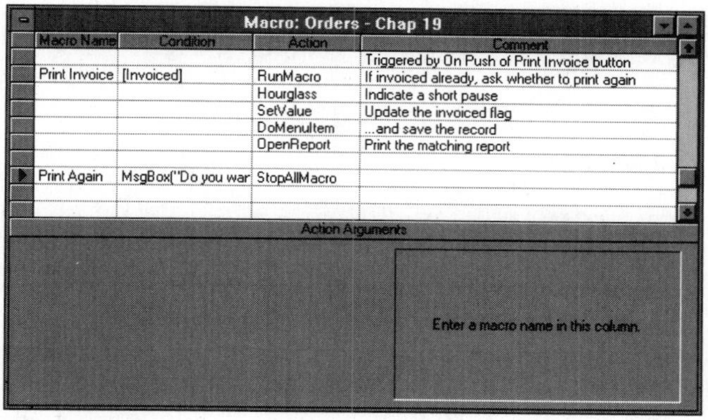

Figure 19-45.
The Print Invoice and Print Again macros are used to print the invoice for an order.

The first line in this macro tests to see whether the Invoiced field has previously been set to Yes. You can see the macro's condition statement in Figure 19-45. The settings for the Print Invoice macro are shown in Figure 19-46.

When an order hasn't had its invoice printed previously, or if you choose the Yes button in the dialog box opened by the MsgBox function, the Print Invoice macro changes the mouse pointer to an hourglass shape (because formatting a report takes a few seconds). The macro then sets the Invoiced field in the record to Yes, saves the record, and prints the report. The Where condition for the OpenReport macro action restricts the report to the Order ID value that matches the order currently displayed on the form. In this example, the macro opens the report in Print Preview, but you could use a DoMenuItem action with a Print command to send the report directly to the printer.

If Invoiced is set, the RunMacro action executes another macro, the Print Again macro, that is also shown in Figure 19-45. This macro uses the MsgBox

Action	Argument Box	Setting
RunMacro	Macro Name	Orders - Chap 19.Print Again
	Repeat Count	(none)
	Repeat Expression	(none)
Hourglass	Hourglass On	Yes
SetValue	Item	Forms![Orders - Chap 19]![Invoiced]
	Expression	Yes
DoMenuItem	Menu Bar	Form
	Menu Name	File
	Command	Save Record
	Subcommand	(none)
OpenReport	Report Name	Invoice–Chap 19
	View	Print Preview
	Filter Name	(none)
	Where Condition	[Order ID]=Forms![Orders - Chap 19]![Order ID]

Figure 19-46.

The settings for the Print Invoice macro.

function in the Condition field to determine whether you want to print this invoice again. The MsgBox function looks like this:

```
MsgBox("Do you want to print the invoice
for Order Number :[Order ID]: again?",292,"Re-Print Invoice")=7
```

In this case, the second parameter value of 292 is the sum of option value 4 to display Yes and No buttons, option value 32 to display the Warning icon (a question mark), and option value 256 to make the second button (No) the default. If you choose the No button, the MsgBox function returns a 7, which would normally cause the action in the Print Again macro to run. You need to use the StopAllMacros action in this case to stop not only the Print Again macro but also the Print Invoice macro that called Print Again.

SETTING UP A PRINT INVOICE MENU

You might find it convenient to print a group of invoices at a time. The Invoice Selector–Chap 19 form is shown in Design view in Figure 19-47. Using the option buttons on the form, you can print all uninvoiced orders or you can print a group of orders you select. When you choose the Print Selected Orders option, a subform appears. The subform is shown in Design view in Figure 19-48.

The subform is a continuous form that displays the Order ID, Company Name, and Invoiced fields, using a query called Orders List that sorts the information in ascending order by Company Name and Order ID. Set the Default Editing property of the subform to Read Only so that you can view and select rows but can't change the data. You could have used a combo box or a list box that displays just Company Name to select an order to print, but since a company might have several outstanding orders, this form shows both Company Name and Order ID fields along with the Invoiced control. You could also add a filter to this subform to show orders for only the current month.

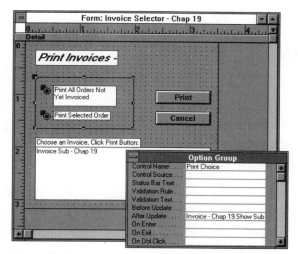

Figure 19-47.
The Invoice Selector–Chap 19 form in Design view.

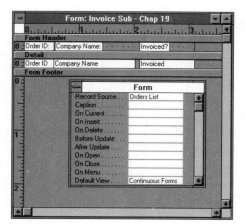

Figure 19-48.
The Invoice Sub–Chap 19 form.

Three macros are needed in order to automate the Invoice Selector–Chap 19 form. These macros are Show Sub, Print It, and Cancel, and they are defined within the Invoice–Chap 19 macro group, as shown in Figure 19-49. Notice that in the Condition column of this macro group there are references to two conditions: *[Print Choice]=1* and *[Print Choice]=2*. These conditions refer to the choices in the option group of the form, in which the Print All Orders Not Yet Invoiced option is print choice 1 and the Print Selected Order option is print choice 2. Ellipses are used three times in the Condition column, when a previous condition applies to the next macro in the Action column.

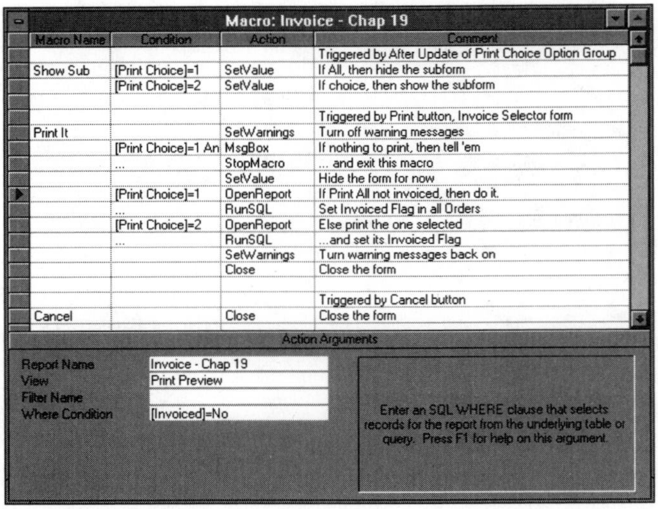

Figure 19-49.
The Show Sub, Print It, and Cancel macros are used on the Invoice Selector–Chap 19 form.

The Show Sub macro runs each time you choose a new option in the form's option group. If you select the Print All Orders Not Yet Invoiced option (print choice 1), the macro hides the subform by setting its Visible property to No. If you select the Print Selected Order option (print choice 2), the macro sets the subform's Visible property to Yes. The settings for the Show Sub macro are shown in Figure 19-50.

The Print It macro runs when you click the Print command button on the form. The macro first checks to see whether the Print All Orders Not Yet Invoiced option (print choice 1) has been selected and whether there are any orders that haven't been invoiced. The full condition statement for this MsgBox action is this:

```
[Print Choice]=1 And DCount("[Order ID]","Orders","[Invoiced]=No")=0
```

The DCount function returns a count of the number of records in the Orders table that have the Invoiced field set to No. If all records in the Orders table have

Action	Argument Box	Setting
SetValue	Item	Forms![Invoice Selector - Chap 19]![Invoice Sub - Chap 19].Visible
	Expression	No
SetValue	Item	Forms![Invoice Selector - Chap 19]![Invoice Sub - Chap 19].Visible
	Expression	Yes

Figure 19-50.
The settings for the Show Sub macro.

their Invoiced field set to Yes, there will be no invoices to print, and a dialog box will notify the user. If some records have not been invoiced (and so meet the Where condition of Invoiced=No), the macro prints those invoices and uses an SQL update statement to change the Invoiced field of those records to Yes.

When you have selected the Print Selected Order option (print choice 2) and clicked the Print command button, the Print It macro will print the records that match the Order ID you selected on the Invoice Sub–Chap 19 subform. Again, an SQL update statement changes the Invoiced field to Yes for those records. See the settings for the Print It macro in Figure 19-51.

The final macro in the Invoice–Chap 19 group is the Cancel macro, and it is triggered by the Cancel button on the form.

DEFINING THE MAIN MENU

The last form that you need to build in order to link your application together is called the Main Menu. This is a simple form with a logo, a title, and six command buttons. The command buttons open the forms you've defined in the application. You can see the form in Design view in Figure 19-52.

One new feature worth mentioning here is the use of the special ampersand character (&) in the setting for each control's Caption property, to define an access key for the control. In the Caption property for the Customers command button, for example, the character precedes the letter *C*. The letter *C* becomes the access key, which means that you can "push" the Customers button by pressing Alt-C as well as by using the more traditional methods of clicking with your mouse or tabbing to the control and pressing the spacebar or the Enter key. You must be careful, however, not to choose a duplicate access key letter. Note that the access key for the Catalog command button in this example is *G*, to avoid conflict with the C access key for the Customers command button.

Action	Argument Box	Setting
SetWarnings	Warnings On	No
MsgBox	Message	An Invoice has been printed for all orders.
	Beep	No
	Type	Information
	Title	All Orders Have Been Invoiced
StopMacro	(none)	
SetValue	Item	Forms![Invoice Selector - Chap 19].Visible
	Expression	No
OpenReport	Report Name	Invoice - Chap 17
	View	Print Preview
	Filter Name	(none)
	Where Condition	[Invoiced]=No
RunSQL	SQL Statement	UPDATE DISTINCTROW Orders
		SET Orders.Invoiced = Yes
		WHERE Invoiced = No;
OpenReport	Report Name	Invoice - Chap 17
	View	Print
	Filter Name	(none)
	Where Condition	[Order ID]= Forms![Invoice Selector - Chap 19]!
		[Invoice Sub - Chap 19].Form![Order ID]
RunSQL	SQL Statement	UPDATE DISTINCTROW Orders
		SET Orders.Invoiced = Yes
		WHERE ((Orders.[Order ID]=Forms![Invoice
		Selector - Chap 19]![Invoice Sub - Chap
		19].Form![Order ID]));
SetWarnings	Warnings On	Yes
Close	Object Type	Form
	Object Name	Invoice Selector - Chap 19

Figure 19-51.
The settings for the Print It macro.

You can use an access key to make it simpler to select any control that has a label caption. For command buttons, the caption is part of the control itself. For most other controls, you can find the caption in the attached label. For example, you could define access keys to select option or toggle buttons in an option group.

Create a macro group called *Main Menu–Chap 19*, and create a macro for each command button (Customers, Orders, and so on). Then give each macro a single OpenForm macro action. Follow the example shown in Figure 19-53. In Figure 19-52 you'll see that the On Push property for the Customers command button has been set to trigger the Customers macro you just defined.

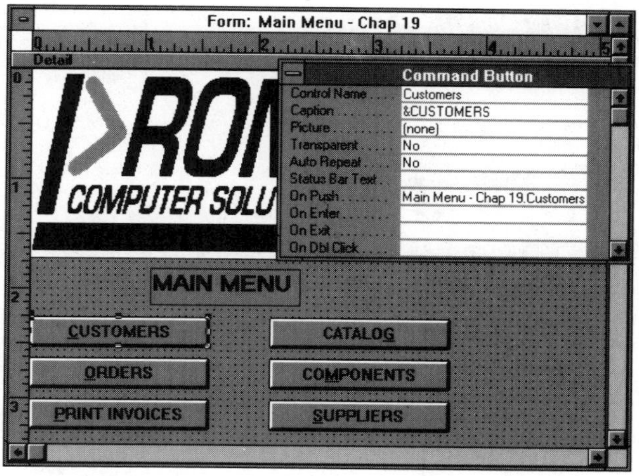

Figure 19-52.
The Main Menu – Chap 19 form in Design view, showing the property sheet of a command button.

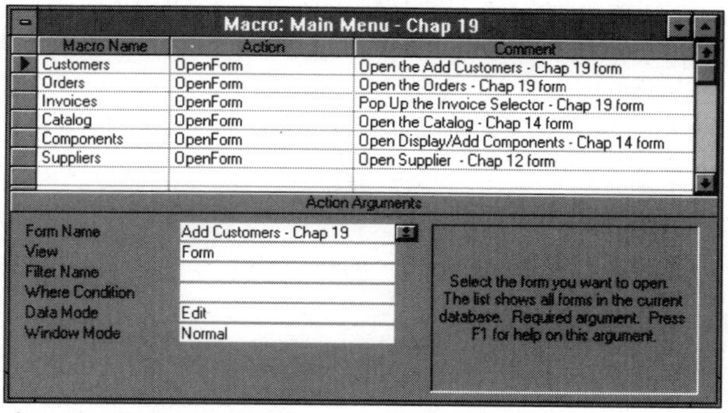

Figure 19-53.
The macros that open forms from the command buttons on the Main Menu – Chap 19 form.

USING AUTOEXEC TO START YOUR APPLICATION

At this point you have all the pieces you need to fully implement the first six tasks of the PROMPT database, as diagrammed in Figure 19-1 at the beginning of this chapter. But there's an additional Microsoft Access feature you might want to employ. You can create a macro called Autoexec in your database, and Access will automatically run Autoexec when the database is opened. An Autoexec macro for PROMPT, such as the one shown in Figure 19-54, can be used to automatically open the Main Menu form.

In Figure 19-54, you can see that there are six macro actions in the sample PROMPT Autoexec macro. The Echo action disables the display of intermediate steps.

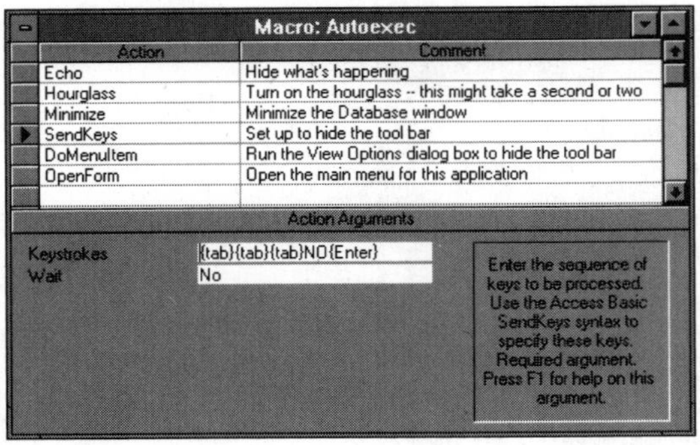

Figure 19-54.
An Autoexec macro for PROMPT that will automatically open the Main Menu form.

When you use the Hourglass action to change the mouse pointer to an hourglass, you give the database user a visual cue that the actions that follow might take a few seconds. The Minimize action minimizes the Database window to an icon.

Because the user of the application has no need for any of the tool bars, you can hide them using the Autoexec macro. The SendKeys macro action tabs down to the Show Tool Bar option, types *NO* as a setting for the option, and presses the Enter key to remove the tool bar. The DoMenuItem action opens the View Options dialog box. Because this dialog box is modal, you need to "prime" the key buffer with the keystrokes you want executed in the dialog box before you open it. The last macro action, Open Form, opens the PROMPT Main Menu–Chap 19 form.

Figure 19-55 shows the settings for the six macro actions described above.

Action	Argument Box	Setting
Echo	Echo On	No
	Status Bar Text	(none)
Hourglass	Hourglass On	Yes
Minimize	(none)	
SendKeys	Keystrokes	{tab}{tab}{tab}NO{Enter}
	Wait	No
DoMenuItem	Menu Bar	Database
	Menu Name	View
	Command	Options
	Subcommand	(none)

Figure 19-55. *(continued)*
The settings for the Autoexec macro.

Figure 19-55. *continued*

Action	Argument Box	Setting
OpenForm	Form Name	Main Menu - Chap 19
	View	Form
	Filter Name	(none)
	Where Condition	(none)
	Data Mode	Edit
	Window Mode	Normal

NOTE: *If you need to open a database without running its Autoexec macro, choose the Open command from the file menu, click on the name of the database in the Open Database dialog box, and then press Shift+Enter.*

I hope you're as impressed as I am by the power and simplicity of Microsoft Access as an application development tool. As you have seen in this book, you can quickly build fairly complex applications for the Windows operating system without having to learn the sophisticated Access Basic programming language. You can use the relational database in Access to store and manage your data locally or on a network, or you can "access" information in other popular database formats or in any server-hosted or mainframe-hosted database that supports the emerging Open Database Connectivity (ODBC) standard. Whether you use Microsoft Access to build your own personal applications or to create applications for others to use, I'm confident you'll find it one of the most powerful and easy-to-use products you've ever experienced.

PART VII

APPENDIXES

This part provides you with additional information to help you work with Microsoft Access and the exercises in this book.

Appendix A shows you the minimum machine and operating software configuration required to run Microsoft Access successfully. Included are tips on installing Access and setting up ODBC drivers.

Appendix B contains the complete table definitions and the sample data for the Prompt Computer Solutions application. You can also find suggested table designs for four other applications.

Appendix C describes how to install and use the Database Analyzer utility included with Microsoft Access. The Database Analyzer is essential for managing complex database and application development projects.

A
Installing
Microsoft Access

To install Microsoft Access for a single user, you need the following personal computer configuration:

- A Microsoft Windows-compatible computer with

  - An 80386 or higher microprocessor (80386SX-20 recommended as a minimum)

  - At least 4 MB of RAM

  - A hard-disk drive with at least 11 MB of free space

  - A high-density floppy-disk drive (1.44 MB 3.5 inch or 1.2 MB 5.25 inch)

  - A mouse or other pointing device

  - A VGA or higher display

- MS-DOS version 3.1 or later (version 5.0 or later recommended)

- Microsoft Windows version 3.0 or later (version 3.1 or later recommended)

To run Microsoft Access as a server on a network, you need the following:

- Network software supporting named pipes such as Microsoft LAN Manager, Novell NetWare, or Banyan VINES

- A Microsoft Windows-compatible computer with at least 11 MB of free disk space for the Microsoft Access software plus additional space for user databases

- User workstations configured as specified above for a single user

Before you run the Microsoft Access Setup program, be sure that no other applications are running on your computer, and then start the Windows operating system. If you are installing Access from floppy disks, place the first installation disk in your high-density floppy-disk drive, and choose the Run command from the File menu in Program Manager. Type *a:\setup* in the command line text box (where *a:* is the drive letter for your high-density floppy-disk drive) and press Enter. To install from a network drive, use File Manager to find the directory where your system manager has copied the Microsoft Access setup files. Run SETUP.EXE in that directory. If you are installing Access from a Master License Pack, include a /L switch in the command line when you run Setup, as in *a:setup /L*. If you are installing from a network, (without a Master License Pack), include a /N switch in the command line when you run setup, as in *a:setup /N*.

The Microsoft Access Setup program asks for your name and your company name, and then lets you choose the directory in which you want the Access files installed. Setup then asks if you want a Complete, Custom, or Express setup. A Complete setup installs all the Access options. A Custom setup lets you pick which Access options you'd like installed, including program files, Help files, Cue Cards, database drivers, Microsoft Graph, and the NWIND sample database. An Express setup installs only the Access program files. A Complete setup requires 11 MB of hard-disk drive space; an Express installation requires 5 MB of hard-disk space. If you've installed network software on your computer, Setup gives you an opportunity to join existing workgroups.

INSTALLING ODBC SUPPORT

If you want to use Microsoft Access to connect to SQL databases that support the Open Database Connectivity (ODBC) standard, you must install the ODBC driver for that database and the Microsoft ODBC administrator. Microsoft provides the ODBC driver for Microsoft SQL Server with Access. You can find this driver and an ODBC installation program on the last installation disk or in the ODBC subdirectory on your network setup drive. To install the Microsoft SQL Server driver, run the separate ODBC Setup program from the ODBC floppy disk or subdirectory on your network setup drive.

After you complete ODBC Setup, you'll find a program group in File Manager called Microsoft ODBC. This program group contains the Microsoft ODBC Administrator icon. Double-click this icon to install or modify your ODBC Setup. You'll see the Microsoft ODBC administrator dialog box, as shown in Figure A-1.

To add new data sources, you must first define a logical name for each available ODBC server type. Select an available ODBC driver in the bottom of the window, and then click the Add New Name button to see the dialog box shown in Figure A-2. Enter a unique alias name for each server that you want to access through this ODBC driver. Click the Add button to add each name to the list. Click Cancel to return to the first dialog box.

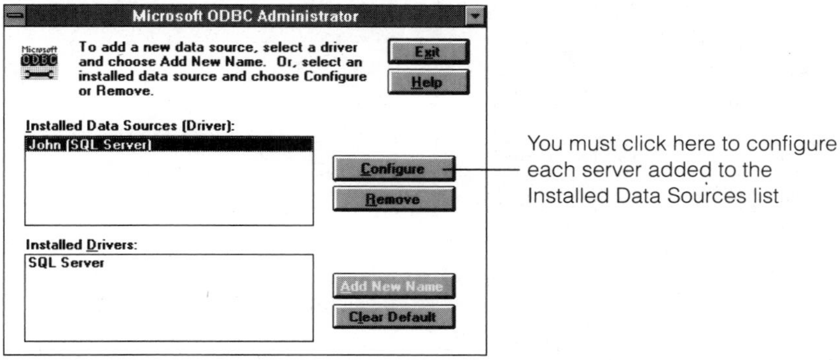

Figure A-1.
The Microsoft ODBC Administrator dialog box.

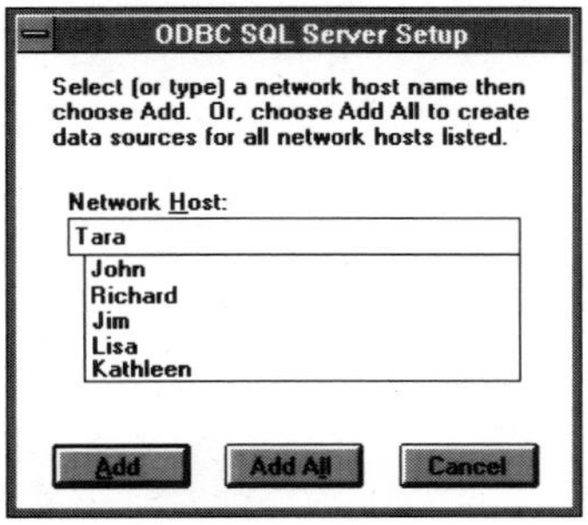

Figure A-2.
The ODBC Administrator dialog box that defines a network host.

After you have defined an alias name for each network server that you want to access, you'll see the names listed in the top window of the dialog box shown in Figure A-1. Select each one in turn and click the Configure button to define the specific network address and driver library for each alias name. See Figure A-3 on the next page.

Within Microsoft Access, you'll use the data source name to attach to each SQL ODBC server. See Chapter 10, "Importing, Attaching, and Exporting," for details.

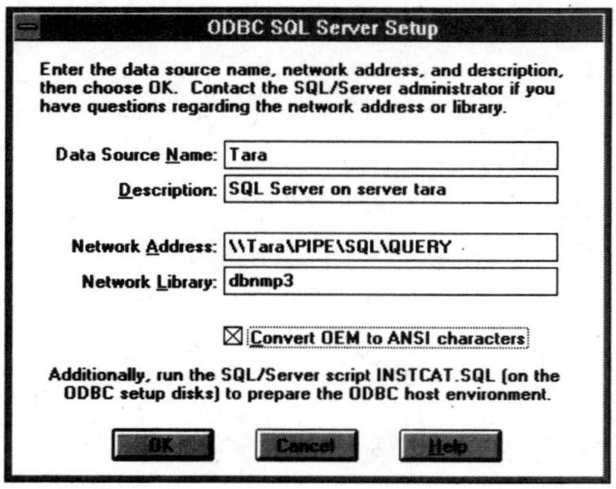

Figure A-3.
The ODBC Administrator dialog box that configures a network address.

Sample Database Schemas

This appendix contains two categories of information. First, it contains the table designs and data for the PROMPT database (a database for a company named Prompt Computer Solutions, Inc.). These are the tables you'll use to develop a full database application in the course of this book. The whole database, with its tables, is also available on CompuServe, as described below. I recommend you obtain PROMPT from CompuServe.

The second category of information in this appendix is a series of four database schemas. These schemas contain the table designs that you can use as the foundation for the following types of databases:

- Music collection or music store database

- Cooking or restaurant database

- Bookstore database

- Human resources database

PROMPT COMPUTER SOLUTIONS DATABASE

This section contains the table designs and data for the PROMPT database. The PROMPT database is used in the examples throughout Running Microsoft Access. Before building these tables, you should be familiar with Chapter 5 ("Building Your Database in Microsoft Access") and Chapter 6 ("Modifying Your Database Design") of this book. Companies, names, and data used in the PROMPT database are fictitious.

You don't have to build these tables yourself; the complete database, including the tables, queries, forms, reports, and macros, can be found in the Microsoft Access forum on CompuServe. To access this forum, type *Go Microsoft* at any ! prompt. For an introductory CompuServe membership kit specifically for users of Microsoft software, call (800) 848-8199 and ask for operator 230. As you'll see in the pages that follow, it's a big job to create the PROMPT tables. I recommend you get the database from CompuServe.

Figure B-1 depicts the PROMPT database schema. It shows a Microsoft Access query that contains field lists for the nine PROMPT tables. The names of the tables are shown in the title bars of the boxes. The relationships between the tables are shown below.

First Table	Relationship	Second Table
Customers	One-to-Many	Orders
Orders	One-to-Many	Order Items
Catalog Items	One-to-Many	Order Items
Catalog Items	One-to-Many	Item Components
Components	One-to-Many	Item Components
Suppliers	One-to-Many	Item Components
Types	One-to-Many	Catalog Items
Types	One-to-Many	Components
Catalog Items	One-to-Many	Monthly Sales

Each table's fields are listed below the title bar. Some lists of fields are too long to be shown in their entirety. Notice that there are lines connecting the field lists. These lines show the relationships between the tables.

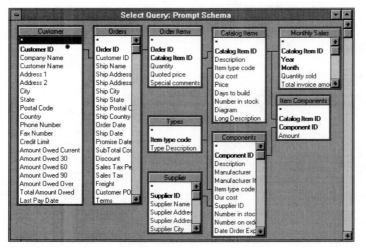

Figure B-1.
The Prompt Computer Solutions database schema.

There are 18 sets of information in this section on the PROMPT database, two for each table. The first set of information about each table is the table definition (e.g., "Components Table: Definition"). The next set of information is the table data (e.g., "Catalog Items Table: Data"). The instructions below are not detailed, but they summarize the procedures that are explained fully in the text of the book. Here's what you do:

1. Create a new database in Microsoft Access.

2. Open a new Table window in Design view for each table below.

3. Create each table definition (for example, for the Components table) using the information below on table design (for example, Components Table: Definition).

4. Switch to the Datasheet view of your table, and enter the appropriate data in the fields (for example, Components Table: Data).

Because the tables you're creating are based on an actual existing database, there are some things you should understand about the data in this appendix:

- The numbers in some columns (for example, Component ID) are of the Counter data type. These numbers are generated automatically by Microsoft Access. All you have to do as you're entering data is to tab through the field that has the Counter data type, and then input your data in the other fields in the record. When you move to another record, a number will be generated automatically.

- Some tables show gaps in the sequence of records. You will have to create and delete some dummy records so that the correct number appears in the field that has the Counter data type. This is easy. Type inside a field other than the field that has the Counter data type, and then press the down arrow key. A dummy record has been created with the next number in the Counter sequence.

- In the Customer table you will enter some data and be referred to a section in Chapter 9 called, "Inserting Data From Another Table." Chapter 9 explains how to append a large amount of data from the NWIND database that comes with Microsoft Access.

- Some fields are defined but do not always contain data. In the data below, empty (null) values are indicated by ellipses (...).

- If you define relationships between tables and activate referential integrity, be sure you enter all data in "parent" tables before adding data to "child" tables. For example, define all customers in the Customers table before attempting to insert data in the Orders table.

CATALOG ITEMS TABLE: DEFINITION

Field Name	Description	Type	Length	Primary Key
Catalog Item ID	Our Catalog number	Counter	4	√
Description	Description of the item	Text	50	
Item type code	Code for type of item	Text	3	
Our cost	Our cost for the item	Currency	8	
Price	Normal selling price	Currency	8	
Days to build	Days to build one of these (if constructed by Prompt)	Integer	2	
Number in stock	Number we have on hand	Long Integer	4	
Diagram*	Picture of the item	OLE Object	0	
Long Description	Extended description of item features	Memo	0	

*In the complete PROMPT database on CompuServe this field in the Customer table is linked to a graphic object that was created in the Paintbrush application in Microsoft Windows.

CATALOG ITEMS TABLE: DATA

Catalog Item ID*

1
    Description: Ex SVGA 1024×768 Adapter   *Price:* 114.00
    Item type code: 008   *Days to build:* 0
    Our cost: 98.70   *Number in stock:* 5
    Long Description: Excellent Top VGA - SVGA 1024×768 1MB memory

2
    Description: Gn VGA 800×600   *Price:* 204.00
    Item type code: 008   *Days to build:* 0
    Our cost: 177.00   *Number in stock:* 5
    Long Description: Genie VGA 512K 800×600 Interlaced & Non-interlaced

3
    Description: Gn VGA 1024×768   *Price:* 338.00
    Item type code: 008   *Days to build:* 0
    Our cost: 294.00   *Number in stock:* 5
    Long Description: Genie SVGA 1024×768 1MB memory Interlaced & non-interlaced

4
    Description: VGA Wonder XL   *Price:* 243.00
    Item type code: 008   *Days to build:* 0
    Our cost: 211.00   *Number in stock:* 3
    Long Description: VGA Wonder XL 1MB memory Interlaced & non-interlaced

*The numbers in the Catalog Item ID column are automatically generated by Microsoft Access because the Catalog Item ID field is defined with the Counter data type. As you're entering data in Datasheet view, tab through the Catalog Item ID field; the Catalog Item ID numbers will automatically appear.

CATALOG ITEMS TABLE: DATA *(continued)*

Catalog Item ID

---

5   *Description:* VRAM II 512   *Price:* 273.00
     Item type code: 008   *Days to build:* ...
     Our cost: 237.00   *Number in stock:* 5
     Long Description: Vira SVGA VRAM II 512KB memory Interlaced & Non-interlaced

---

6   *Description:* VRAM II 1M   *Price:* 353.00
     Item type code: 008   *Days to build:* 0
     Our cost: 307.00   *Number in stock:* 8
     Long Description: Vira SVGA VRAM II 1MB memory Interlaced & non-interlaced

---

7   *Description:* Ar SVGA 14" 1024×768 Monitor   *Price:* 286.35
     Item type code: 002   *Days to build:* 0
     Our cost: 249.00   *Number in stock:* 10
     Long Description: Arrowhead SVGA 14" monitor 1024×768 Interlaced and non-interlaced

---

8   *Description:* S 14" 1024×768 .28mm   *Price:* 423.75
     Item type code: 002   *Days to build:* 0
     Our cost: 339.00   *Number in stock:* 5
     Long Description: Superscreen 1304 14" 1024×768 .28 mm Interlaced & non-interlaced

---

9   *Description:* S 17" shielded   *Price:* 1175.00
     Item type code: 002   *Days to build:* 0
     Our cost: 940.00   *Number in stock:* 2
     Long Description: Superscreen 1304S 17" Level II shielding

---

10   *Description:* Sk 14" 1024×768   *Price:* 608.75
     Item type code: 002   *Days to build:* 0
     Our cost: 487.00   *Number in stock:* 2
     Long Description: Skandis 14" 1024×768 .25mm Interlaced & non-interlaced

---

11   *Description:* NC MultiSync 3-D 16"   *Price:* 411.25
     Item type code: 002   *Days to build:* 0
     Our cost: 329.00   *Number in stock:* 2
     Long Description: New Computer MultiSync 3-D 16" 1024×768 Interlaced

---

12   *Description:* NC MultiSync 3FGX 15"   *Price:* 430.00
     Item type code: 002   *Days to build:* 0
     Our cost: 344.00   *Number in stock:* 2
     Long Description: New Computer MultiSync 3FGX 15" .28mm

(continued)

CATALOG ITEMS TABLE: DATA *(continued)*

Catalog Item ID

13	*Description:* NC MultiSync 4FG	*Price:* 680.00
	Item type code: 002	*Days to build:* 0
	Our cost: 544.00	*Number in stock:* 1
	Long Description: New Computer MultiSync 4FG 15" .28mm 70Hz	

14	*Description:* Sg monochrome	*Price:* 345.00
	Item type code: 002	*Days to build:* 0
	Our cost: 276.00	*Number in stock:* 0
	Long Description: Sugar Portrait Monochrome Adapter included	

15	*Description:* Z 2400 & ProComm	*Price:* 90.00
	Item type code: 016	*Days to build:* 0
	Our cost: 78.00	*Number in stock:* 5
	Long Description: Zorro 2400 half-card modem & Comm software	

16	*Description:* Z 9600 modem	*Price:* 485.00
	Item type code: 016	*Days to build:* 0
	Our cost: 419.00	*Number in stock:* 2
	Long Description: Zorro 9600 V.32 V.42bis	

17	*Description:* P P 9600 modem	*Price:* 475.00
	Item type code: 016	*Days to build:* 0
	Our cost: 411.00	*Number in stock:* 2
	Long Description: PP Tech 9600 baud V.32 V.42bis	

18	*Description:* Z 9600/2400 fax	*Price:* 178.00
	Item type code: 016	*Days to build:* 0
	Our cost: 155.00	*Number in stock:* 4
	Long Description: Zorro send/receive fax, 9600 fax; 2400 data modem, Includes Windows fax software	

22*	*Description:* 3.5" HD floppy	*Price:* 96.25
	Item type code: 005	*Days to build:* 0
	Our cost: 77.00	*Number in stock:* 20
	Long Description: Terry 1.44MB 3.5" HD floppy	

23	*Description:* 5.25" HD Floppy	*Price:* 96.25
	Item type code: 005	*Days to build:* 0
	Our cost: 77.00	*Number in stock:* 20
	Long Description: Terry 5.25" High density floppy drive	

*The Catalog Item ID field is missing three numbers in the sequence (19-21). You'll have to create and delete three dummy fields to obtain the correct Catalog Item ID value of 22.

CATALOG ITEMS TABLE: DATA *(continued)*

Catalog Item ID

---

24   *Description:* Tape backup drive   *Price:* 83.00
         Item type code: 015   *Days to build:* 0
         Our cost: 72.00   *Number in stock:* 5
         Long Description: Mountain 40/120MB tape backup

---

25   *Description:* Serial mouse   *Price:* 15.00
         Item type code: 010   *Days to build:* 0
         Our cost: 12.00   *Number in stock:* 5
         Long Description: MSFT-compatible serial mouse

---

26   *Description:* MBus Mouse   *Price:* 72.50
         Item type code: 010   *Days to build:* 0
         Our cost: 58.00   *Number in stock:* 10
         Long Description: Microsoft Bus Mouse

---

27   *Description:* L Serial mouse w. Windows   *Price:* 106.25
         Item type code: 010   *Days to build:* 0
         Our cost: 85.00   *Number in stock:* 10
         Long Description: Lovell Serial mouse w. Windows 3.0

29*   *Description:* Maximum Drive 130MB 15ms   *Price:* 285.00
         Item type code: 006   *Days to build:* 0
         Our cost: 228.00   *Number in stock:* 10
         Long Description: Maximum Drive 130MB IDE 15ms

---

30   *Description:* Seaweed 130MB 16ms   *Price:* 283.75
         Item type code: 006   *Days to build:* 0
         Our cost: 227.00   *Number in stock:* 20
         Long Description: Seaweed 130MB 16ms

---

31   *Description:* Constant 174MB 18ms IDE   *Price:* 391.25
         Item type code: 006   *Days to build:* 0
         Our cost: 313.00   *Number in stock:* 20
         Long Description: Constant 174MB 18ms IDE

---

32   *Description:* Seaweed 211MB 15ms IDE   *Price:* 471.25
         Item type code: 006   *Days to build:* 0
         Our cost: 377.00   *Number in stock:* 5
         Long Description: Seaweed 211MB 15ms IDE

(continued)

*The Catalog Item ID field is missing one number in the sequence (28). You'll have to create and delete one dummy field to obtain the correct Catalog Item ID value of 29.

CATALOG ITEMS TABLE: DATA *(continued)*

Catalog Item ID

33		
Description: Constant 212MB 16ms IDE 64K cache	*Price:* 566.25	
Item type code: 006	*Days to build:* 0	
Our cost: 453.00	*Number in stock:* 5	
Long Description: Constant 212MB 16ms IDE 64K cache		

34		
Description: Constant 510MB 12ms IDE	*Price:* 1228.75	
Item type code: 006	*Days to build:* 0	
Our cost: 983.00	*Number in stock:* 5	
Long Description: Constant 510MB 12ms IDE		

35		
Description: Ultra 8MB cache controller	*Price:* 425.00	
Item type code: 013	*Days to build:* 0	
Our cost: 370.00	*Number in stock:* 2	
Long Description: Ultra 8MB cache controller		

42*		
Description: 101-keyboard	*Price:* 96.25	
Item type code: 003	*Days to build:* 0	
Our cost: 77.00	*Number in stock:* 20	
Long Description: 101-keyboard - Northwind		

43		
Description: MultiMedia Kit	*Price:* 775.00	
Item type code: 011	*Days to build:* ...	
Our cost: 654.00	*Number in stock:* 2	
Long Description: MultiMedia Kit: CD-ROM Sound board driver software		

44		
Description: 386/25 SVGA System	*Price:* 1438.00	
Item type code: 100	*Days to build:* 2	
Our cost: 1250.70	*Number in stock:* 1	
Long Description: 386/25 System		

46**		
Description: 386/40 System	*Price:* 1645.00	
Item type code: 100	*Days to build:* 2	
Our cost: 1430.70	*Number in stock:* 5	
Long Description: 386/40 System		

47		
Description: 386/33 System	*Price:* 1534.90	
Item type code: 100	*Days to build:* 2	
Our cost: 1334.70	*Number in stock:* 8	
Long Description: 386/33 System		

*The Catalog Item ID field is missing six numbers in the sequence (36-41). You'll have to create and delete six dummy fields to obtain the correct Catalog Item ID value of 42.

**The Catalog Item ID field is missing one number in the sequence (45). You'll have to create and delete a dummy field to obtain the correct Catalog Item ID value of 46.

CATALOG ITEMS TABLE: DATA *(continued)*

Catalog Item ID

48
Description: 486/33 System	*Price:* 1958.56
Item type code: 100	*Days to build:* 3
Our cost: 1703.10	*Number in stock:* 5
Long Description: 486/33 System	

49
Description: 486/50 DX System	*Price:* 3151.57
Item type code: 100	*Days to build:* 3
Our cost: 2740.50	*Number in stock:* 2
Long Description: 486/50 DX System	

50
Description: Laser Printer	*Price:* 549.00
Item type code: 009	*Days to build:* 0
Our cost: 477.00	*Number in stock:* 3
Long Description: Laser Printer	

51
Description: 1 MB 70ns RAM	*Price:* 50.00
Item type code: 007	*Days to build:* 0
Our cost: 38.70	*Number in stock:* 0
Long Description: 1 MB 70ns RAM	

COMPONENTS TABLE: DEFINITION

Field Name	Description	Type	Length	Primary Key
Component ID	Unique component ID	Counter	4	√
Description	Description of the item	Text	50	
Manufacturer	Item manufacturer	Text	50	
Manufacturer Item Code	Manufacturer's catalog code	Text	20	
Item type code	Code for type of item	Text	3	
Our cost	Our cost for the item	Currency	8	
Supplier ID	Regular supplier of this component	Long Integer	4	
Number in stock	Number we have on hand	Long Integer	4	
Number on order	Number we have on order	Long Integer	4	
Date Order Expected	When next order will arrive	Date/Time	8	
Reorder level	Reorder when stock drops below this value	Long Integer	4	
Economic Order Qty	Best amount to order at one time	Long Integer	4	
Long Description	Extended description of item features	Memo	0	

COMPONENTS TABLE: DATA

Component ID*

1

Description:	Ex SVGA 1024×768 Adapter	*Number in stock:*	1000
Manufacturer:	Excellent	*Number on order:*	0
Manufacturer Item Code:	XP693M	*Date Order Expected:*	7/15/92 0:00:00
Item type code:	008	*Reorder level:*	2
Our cost:	98.70	*Economic Order Qty:*	5
Supplier ID:	5		

Long Description: Excellent Top VGA - SVGA 1024×768 1MB memory Interlaced and non-interlaced Up to 256 colors One year manufacturer warranty.

2

Description:	Gn VGA 800×600	*Number in stock:*	5
Manufacturer:	Genie	*Number on order:*	0
Manufacturer Item Code:	GP512VG	*Date Order Expected:*	…
Item type code:	008	*Reorder level:*	2
Our cost:	177.00	*Economic Order Qty:*	5
Supplier ID:	1		

Long Description: Genie VGA 512K 800×600 Interlaced & Non-interlaced

3

Description:	Gn VGA 1024×768	*Number in stock:*	5
Manufacturer:	Genie	*Number on order:*	0
Manufacturer Item Code:	GP1024VG	*Date Order Expected:*	…
Item type code:	008	*Reorder level:*	2
Our cost:	294.00	*Economic Order Qty:*	5
Supplier ID:	1		

Long Description: Genie SVGA 1024×768 1MB memory Interlaced & non-interlaced

4

Description:	VGA Wonder XL	*Number in stock:*	3
Manufacturer:	Wonder	*Number on order:*	0
Manufacturer Item Code:	WVG001	*Date Order Expected:*	…
Item type code:	008	*Reorder level:*	1
Our cost:	211.00	*Economic Order Qty:*	3
Supplier ID:	2		

Long Description: VGA Wonder XL, 1MB memory Interlaced & non-interlaced

5

Description:	VRAM II 512	*Number in stock:*	5
Manufacturer:	Vira Display	*Number on order:*	0
Manufacturer Item Code:	VR0512-II	*Date Order Expected:*	…
Item type code:	008	*Reorder level:*	1
Our cost:	237.00	*Economic Order Qty:*	3
Supplier ID:	3		

Long Description: Vira SVGA VRAM II 512KB memory Interlaced & Non-interlaced

*The numbers in the Component ID column are automatically generated by Microsoft Access because the Component ID field is defined with the Counter data type. As you're entering data in Datasheet view, tab through the Component Item ID field; the Component ID numbers will automatically appear.

COMPONENTS TABLE: DATA *(continued)*

Component ID

6		
Description:	VRAM II 1M	*Number in stock:* 8
Manufacturer:	Vira Display	*Number on order:* 0
Manufacturer Item Code:	VR1024-II	*Date Order Expected:* ...
Item type code:	008	*Reorder level:* 2
Our cost:	307.00	*Economic Order Qty:* 4
Supplier ID:	3	
Long Description:	Vira SVGA VRAM II 1MB memory Interlaced & non-interlaced	

7		
Description:	Ar SVGA 14" 1024×768 Monitor	*Number in stock:* 10
Manufacturer:	Arrowhead	*Number on order:* 0
Manufacturer Item Code:	AR-14	*Date Order Expected:* ...
Item type code:	002	*Reorder level:* 3
Our cost:	249.00	*Economic Order Qty:* 5
Supplier ID:	4	
Long Description:	Arrowhead SVGA 14" monitor 1024×768 Interlaced and non-interlaced	

8		
Description:	S 14" 1024×768 .28mm	*Number in stock:* 5
Manufacturer:	Superscreen	*Number on order:* 0
Manufacturer Item Code:	S-1304	*Date Order Expected:* ...
Item type code:	002	*Reorder level:* 2
Our cost:	339.00	*Economic Order Qty:* 5
Supplier ID:	2	
Long Description:	Superscreen 1304 14" 1024×768 .28 mm, Interlaced & non-interlaced	

9		
Description:	S 17" shielded	*Number in stock:* 2
Manufacturer:	Superscreen	*Number on order:* 0
Manufacturer Item Code:	S1304S	*Date Order Expected:* ...
Item type code:	002	*Reorder level:* 1
Our cost:	940.00	*Economic Order Qty:* 1
Supplier ID:	2	
Long Description:	Superscreen 1304S 17" Level II shielding	

10		
Description:	Sk 14" 1024×768	*Number in stock:* 2
Manufacturer:	Skandis	*Number on order:* 0
Manufacturer Item Code:	CM1450	*Date Order Expected:* ...
Item type code:	002	*Reorder level:* 1
Our cost:	487.00	*Economic Order Qty:* 1
Supplier ID:	1	
Long Description:	Skandis 14" 1024×768 .25mm Interlaced & non-interlaced	

(continued)

COMPONENTS TABLE: DATA *(continued)*

Component ID

11		
Description:	NC MultiSync 3-D 16"	*Number in stock:* 2
Manufacturer:	New Computer	*Number on order:* 0
Manufacturer Item Code:	MS 3-D	*Date Order Expected:* ...
Item type code:	002	*Reorder level:* 1
Our cost:	329.00	*Economic Order Qty:* 1
Supplier ID:	3	
Long Description:	New Computer MultiSync 3-D 16" 1024×768 Interlaced	

12		
Description:	NC MultiSync 3FGX 15"	*Number in stock:* 2
Manufacturer:	New Computer	*Number on order:* 0
Manufacturer Item Code:	3FGX	*Date Order Expected:* ...
Item type code:	002	*Reorder level:* 1
Our cost:	344.00	*Economic Order Qty:* 1
Supplier ID:	3	
Long Description:	New Computer MultiSync 3FGX 15" .28mm	

13		
Description:	NC MultiSync 4FG	*Number in stock:* 1
Manufacturer:	New Computer	*Number on order:* 0
Manufacturer Item Code:	4FG	*Date Order Expected:* ...
Item type code:	002	*Reorder level:* 0
Our cost:	544.00	*Economic Order Qty:* 1
Supplier ID:	3	
Long Description:	New Computer MultiSync 4FG 15" .28mm 70Hz	

14		
Description:	Sg monochrome	*Number in stock:* 0
Manufacturer:	Sugar	*Number on order:* 0
Manufacturer Item Code:	SM-PT	*Date Order Expected:* ...
Item type code:	002	*Reorder level:* 0
Our cost:	276.00	*Economic Order Qty:* 1
Supplier ID:	4	
Long Description:	Sugar Portrait Monochrome Adapter included	

15		
Description:	Z 2400 & Comm	*Number in stock:* 5
Manufacturer:	Zorro	*Number on order:* 0
Manufacturer Item Code:	ZR2400	*Date Order Expected:* ...
Item type code:	016	*Reorder level:* 2
Our cost:	78.00	*Economic Order Qty:* 5
Supplier ID:	2	
Long Description:	Zorro 2400 half-card modem & Comm software	

COMPONENTS TABLE: DATA *(continued)*

Component ID

16		
Description: Z 9600 modem	*Number in stock:* 2	
Manufacturer: Zorro	*Number on order:* 0	
Manufacturer Item Code: ZR9600	*Date Order Expected:* ...	
Item type code: 016	*Reorder level:* 1	
Our cost: 419.00	*Economic Order Qty:* 1	
Supplier ID: 2		
Long Description: Zorro 9600 V.32, V.42bis		

17		
Description: P P 9600	*Number in stock:* 2	
Manufacturer: P P Technologies	*Number on order:* 0	
Manufacturer Item Code: PP9600A	*Date Order Expected:* ...	
Item type code: 016	*Reorder level:* 1	
Our cost: 411.00	*Economic Order Qty:* 1	
Supplier ID: 1		
Long Description: PP Tech 9600 baud V.32, V.42bis		

18		
Description: Z 9600/2400 fax	*Number in stock:* 4	
Manufacturer: Zorro	*Number on order:* 0	
Manufacturer Item Code: ZR9600F	*Date Order Expected:* ...	
Item type code: 016	*Reorder level:* 2	
Our cost: 155.00	*Economic Order Qty:* 1	
Supplier ID: 2		
Long Description: Zorro send/receive fax 9600 fax; 2400 data modem Includes Windows fax software		

19		
Description: 1 MB Ram	*Number in stock:* 20	
Manufacturer: Memory Tech	*Number on order:* 0	
Manufacturer Item Code: MB1024	*Date Order Expected:* ...	
Item type code: 007	*Reorder level:* 5	
Our cost: 38.70	*Economic Order Qty:* 10	
Supplier ID: 1		
Long Description: 1 MB 70ns RAM simm		

20		
Description: Baby Tower Case	*Number in stock:* 10	
Manufacturer: Unknown	*Number on order:* 0	
Manufacturer Item Code: Baby-1	*Date Order Expected:* ...	
Item type code: 001	*Reorder level:* 3	
Our cost: 119.00	*Economic Order Qty:* 5	
Supplier ID: 4		
Long Description: Baby Tower case w. 200w power supply		

(continued)

COMPONENTS TABLE: DATA *(continued)*

Component ID

21			
Description: Full Tower Case		*Number in stock:* 10	
Manufacturer: Unknown		*Number on order:* 0	
Manufacturer Item Code: FTCASE		*Date Order Expected:* ...	
Item type code: 001		*Reorder level:* 2	
Our cost: 177.00		*Economic Order Qty:* 3	
Supplier ID: 4			
Long Description: Full Tower w. 230 watt supply			

22			
Description: 3.5" HD floppy		*Number in stock:* 20	
Manufacturer: Terry		*Number on order:* 0	
Manufacturer Item Code: TE 3.5HD		*Date Order Expected:* ...	
Item type code: 005		*Reorder level:* 10	
Our cost: 77.00		*Economic Order Qty:* 10	
Supplier ID: 3			
Long Description: Terry 1.44MB 3.5" HD floppy			

23			
Description: 5.25" HD Floppy		*Number in stock:* 20	
Manufacturer: Terry		*Number on order:* 0	
Manufacturer Item Code: TE 5.25HD		*Date Order Expected:* ...	
Item type code: 005		*Reorder level:* 10	
Our cost: 77.00		*Economic Order Qty:* 10	
Supplier ID: 3			
Long Description: Terry 5.25" High density floppy drive			

24			
Description: Tape backup drive		*Number in stock:* 5	
Manufacturer: Mountain		*Number on order:* 0	
Manufacturer Item Code: MT-TAPE		*Date Order Expected:* ...	
Item type code: 015		*Reorder level:* 2	
Our cost: 72.00		*Economic Order Qty:* 5	
Supplier ID: 3			
Long Description: Mountain 40/120MB tape backup			

25			
Description: Serial mouse		*Number in stock:* 5	
Manufacturer: Mouse House		*Number on order:* 0	
Manufacturer Item Code: FBN-mouse		*Date Order Expected:* ...	
Item type code: 010		*Reorder level:* 2	
Our cost: 12.00		*Economic Order Qty:* 2	
Supplier ID: 1			
Long Description: MSFT-compatible serial mouse			

COMPONENTS TABLE: DATA *(continued)*

Component ID

---

26   *Description:* Microsoft Bus Mouse

Description:	Microsoft Bus Mouse
Manufacturer:	Microsoft
Manufacturer Item Code:	MS-Mouse-Bus
Item type code:	010
Our cost:	58.00
Supplier ID:	1
Long Description:	Microsoft Bus Mouse

Number in stock:	10
Number on order:	0
Date Order Expected:	...
Reorder level:	5
Economic Order Qty:	5

27

Description:	L Serial mouse w. Windows
Manufacturer:	Lovell
Manufacturer Item Code:	L-Mouse
Item type code:	010
Our cost:	85.00
Supplier ID:	1
Long Description:	Lovell Serial mouse w. Windows 3.0

Number in stock:	10
Number on order:	0
Date Order Expected:	...
Reorder level:	2
Economic Order Qty:	5

28

Description:	Desktop case
Manufacturer:	Unknown
Manufacturer Item Code:	Case-Desk
Item type code:	001
Our cost:	137.00
Supplier ID:	4
Long Description:	Desktop case w. 220w power supply

Number in stock:	5
Number on order:	0
Date Order Expected:	...
Reorder level:	2
Economic Order Qty:	5

29

Description:	Mx 130MB 15ms
Manufacturer:	Maximum Drive
Manufacturer Item Code:	MX-130
System type code:	006
Our cost:	228.00
Supplier ID:	2
Long Description:	Maximum Drive 130MB IDE 15ms

Number in stock:	10
Number on order:	0
Date Order Expected:	...
Reorder level:	4
Economic Order Qty:	5

30

Description:	Sg 130MB 16ms
Manufacturer:	Seaweed Technologies
Manufacturer Item Code:	SG-130
Item type code:	006
Our cost:	227.00
Supplier ID:	2
Long Description:	Seaweed 130MB 16ms

Number in stock:	20
Number on order:	0
Date Order Expected:	...
Reorder level:	5
Economic Order Qty:	10

(continued)

COMPONENTS TABLE: DATA *(continued)*

Component ID

31		
Description: Cn 174MB 18ms IDE	*Number in stock:* 20	
Manufacturer: Constant	*Number on order:* 0	
Manufacturer Item Code: CR-174	*Date Order Expected:* ...	
Item type code: 006	*Reorder level:* 5	
Our cost: 313.00	*Economic Order Qty:* 10	
Supplier ID: 2		
Long Description: Constant 174MB 18ms IDE		

32		
Description: Seaweed 211MB 15ms IDE	*Number in stock:* 5	
Manufacturer: Seaweed	*Number on order:* 0	
Manufacturer Item Code: SG-211	*Date Order Expected:* ...	
Item type code: 006	*Reorder level:* 2	
Our cost: 377.00	*Economic Order Qty:* 5	
Supplier ID: 2		
Long Description: Seaweed 211MB 15ms IDE		

33		
Description: Constant 212MB 16ms IDE 64K cache	*Number in stock:* 5	
Manufacturer: Constant	*Number on order:* 0	
Manufacturer Item Code: CR-212/64	*Date Order Expected:* ...	
Item type code: 006	*Reorder level:* 2	
Our cost: 453.00	*Economic Order Qty:* 2	
Supplier ID: 2		
Long Description: Constant 212MB 16ms IDE 64K cache		

34		
Description: Constant 510MB 12ms IDE	*Number in stock:* 5	
Manufacturer: Constant	*Number on order:* 0	
Manufacturer Item Code: CR-510	*Date Order Expected:* ...	
Item type code: 006	*Reorder level:* 1	
Our cost: 983.00	*Economic Order Qty:* 1	
Supplier ID: 2		
Long Description: Constant 510MB 12ms IDE		

35		
Description: Ultra 8MB cache controller	*Number in stock:* 2	
Manufacturer: Ultra	*Number on order:* 0	
Manufacturer Item Code: US-8	*Date Order Expected:* ...	
Item type code: 013	*Reorder level:* 1	
Our cost: 370.00	*Economic Order Qty:* 1	
Supplier ID: 2		
Long Description: UltraStore 8MB cache controller		

COMPONENTS TABLE: DATA *(continued)*

Component ID

36
Description:	AMM 386/25 SX	*Number in stock:*	10
Manufacturer:	AMM	*Number on order:*	0
Manufacturer Item Code:	AM-386/25	*Date Order Expected:*	...
Item type code:	004	*Reorder level:*	2
Our cost:	354.00	*Economic Order Qty:*	2
Supplier ID:	1		
Long Description:	AMM 386/25 SX 2MB Ram		

37
Description:	Issat 386/25 DX	*Number in stock:*	5
Manufacturer:	Issat	*Number on order:*	0
Manufacturer Item Code:	IN-386/25	*Date Order Expected:*	...
Item type code:	004	*Reorder level:*	2
Our cost:	402.00	*Economic Order Qty:*	2
Supplier ID:	1		
Long Description:	Issat 386/25 DX 2 MB ram		

38
Description:	Issat 386/33 DX	*Number in stock:*	5
Manufacturer:	Issat	*Number on order:*	0
Manufacturer Item Code:	IN-386/33	*Date Order Expected:*	...
Item type code:	004	*Reorder level:*	2
Our cost:	486.00	*Economic Order Qty:*	2
Supplier ID:	1		
Long Description:	Issat 386/33 DX 2MB ram, 64K cache		

39
Description:	AMM 386/40 DX	*Number in stock:*	5
Manufacturer:	AMM	*Number on order:*	0
Manufacturer Item Code:	AM-386/40	*Date Order Expected:*	...
Item type code:	004	*Reorder level:*	2
Our cost:	582.00	*Economic Order Qty:*	2
Supplier ID:	1		
Long Description:	AMM 386/40 DX 2MB Ram, 64K cache		

40
Description:	Issat 486/33 DX	*Number in stock:*	3
Manufacturer:	Issat	*Number on order:*	0
Manufacturer Item Code:	IN-486/33	*Date Order Expected:*	...
Item type code:	004	*Reorder level:*	1
Our cost:	777.00	*Economic Order Qty:*	3
Supplier ID:	1		
Long Description:	Issat 486/33 DX 4MB ram, 256K cache		

(continued)

COMPONENTS TABLE: DATA *(continued)*

Component ID

41	*Description:* Issat 486/50 DX	*Number in stock:* 2
	Manufacturer: Issat	*Number on order:* 0
	Manufacturer Item Code: IN-486/50	*Date Order Expected:* ...
	Item type code: 004	*Reorder level:* 1
	Our cost: 982.00	*Economic Order Qty:* 1
	Supplier ID: 1	
	Long Description: Issat 486/50 DX 4MB ram, 256K cache	

42	*Description:* 101-keyboard	*Number in stock:* 20
	Manufacturer: Northwind	*Number on order:* 0
	Manufacturer Item Code: KEY101	*Date Order Expected:* ...
	Item type code: 003	*Reorder level:* 5
	Our cost: 77.00	*Economic Order Qty:* 10
	Supplier ID: 4	
	Long Description: 101-keyboard - Northwind	

43	*Description:* MultiMedia Kit	*Number in stock:* 2
	Manufacturer: Media Unlimited	*Number on order:* 0
	Manufacturer Item Code: MPC - 001	*Date Order Expected:* ...
	Item type code: 011	*Reorder level:* 1
	Our cost: 654.00	*Economic Order Qty:* 1
	Supplier ID: 2	
	Long Description: MultiMedia Kit: CD-ROM, sound board, driver software	

45*	*Description:* Laser Printer	*Number in stock:* 1
	Manufacturer: Laseronics	*Number on order:* 0
	Manufacturer Item Code: LP-101	*Date Order Expected:* ...
	Item type code: 009	*Reorder level:* 0
	Our cost: 477.00	*Economic Order Qty:* 1
	Supplier ID: 2	
	Long Description: Laser Printer, 6 ppm	

46	*Description:* Word Processing	*Number in stock:* 3
	Manufacturer: Software Unlimited	*Number on order:* 0
	Manufacturer Item Code: WP-101	*Date Order Expected:* ...
	Item type code: 012	*Reorder level:* 2
	Our cost: 129.00	*Economic Order Qty:* 2
	Supplier ID: 2	
	Long Description: ...	

---

*The Component ID field is missing one number in the sequence (44). You'll have to create and delete a dummy field to obtain the correct Component ID value of 45.

CUSTOMER TABLE: DEFINITION

Field Name	Description	Type	Length	Primary Key
Customer ID	Customer Identifier	Counter	4	√
Company Name	Customer Company Name	Text	30	
Customer Name	Name of Company Contact	Text	25	
Address 1	Street Address Line 1	Text	30	
Address 2	Street Address Line 2	Text	30	
City	City	Text	20	
State	State or Province	Text	12	
Postal Code	Zip or Postal Zone Code	Text	10	
Country	Country Name	Text	6	
Phone Number	Phone Number	Text	20	
Fax Number	Fax machine phone number	Text	20	
Credit Limit	Maximum credit allowed	Currency	8	
Amount Owed Current	Total amount currently owed	Currency	8	
Amount Owed 30	Amount owed 30-59 days	Currency	8	
Amount Owed 60	Amount owed 60-89 days	Currency	8	
Amount Owed 90	Amount owed 90-119 days	Currency	8	
Amount Owed Over	Amount owed 120 days	Currency	8	
Total Amount Owed	Total amount owed	Currency	8	
Last Pay Date	Date of last payment	Date/Time	8	

CUSTOMER TABLE: DATA

Customer ID*

1			
	Company Name: Alpha Products		*Fax Number:* 0
	Customer Name: Jim Smith		*Credit Limit:* 10000.00
	Address 1: Suite 100		*Amount Owed Current:* 1197.00
	Address 2: 1234 Main Street		*Amount Owed 30:* 370.00
	City: Burlington		*Amount Owed 60:* 263.00
	State: VT		*Amount Owed 90:* 584.00
	Postal Code: 03033		*Amount Owed Over:* 33.00
	Country: USA		*Total Amount Owed:* 2447.00
	Phone Number: 3125551212		*Last Pay Date:* ...

(continued)

*The numbers in the Customer ID column are automatically generated by Microsoft Access because the Customer ID field is defined with the Counter data type. As you're entering data in Datasheet view, tab through the Customer ID field; the Customer ID numbers will automatically appear.

CUSTOMER TABLE: DATA *(continued)*

Customer ID

2		
Company Name:	Beta Consulting	*Fax Number:* 0
Customer Name:	George Roberts	*Credit Limit:* 15000.00
Address 1:	...	*Amount Owed Current:* 1462.00
Address 2:	7891 44th Avenue	*Amount Owed 30:* 765.00
City:	Redmond	*Amount Owed 60:* 46.00
State:	WA	*Amount Owed 90:* 87.00
Postal Code:	98052	*Amount Owed Over:* 67.00
Country:	USA	*Total Amount Owed:* 2427.00
Phone Number:	2066781234	*Last Pay Date:* ...

3		
Company Name:	Condor Leasing	*Fax Number:* 0
Customer Name:	Marjorie Lovell	*Credit Limit:* 13000.00
Address 1:	44th floor	*Amount Owed Current:* 270.00
Address 2:	901 E. Maple	*Amount Owed 30:* 513.00
City:	Chicago	*Amount Owed 60:* 589.00
State:	Il	*Amount Owed 90:* 210.00
Postal Code:	60606	*Amount Owed Over:* 275.00
Country:	USA	*Total Amount Owed:* 1857.00
Phone Number:	3126665544	*Last Pay Date:* ...

95*		
Company Name:	Thompson's Bookstop	*Fax Number:* ...
Customer Name:	Mike Thompson	*Credit Limit:* 18000.00
Address 1:	...	*Amount Owed Current:* 1078.00
Address 2:	7895 Hollow Road	*Amount Owed 30:* 846.00
City:	New Bedford	*Amount Owed 60:* 498.00
State:	MA	*Amount Owed 90:* 128.00
Postal Code:	02013	*Amount Owed Over:* 69.00
Country:	USA	*Total Amount Owed:* 2619.00
Phone Number:	...	*Last Pay Date:* ...

*The Customer ID field is missing 91 numbers in the sequence (4-94). You *don't* have to create and delete 91 dummy fields. To complete the Customer table you need to append 91 customer records from the NWIND dtabase that comes with Microsoft Access. The query you use to append the entries from NWIND is described in Chapter 9 in a section called "Inserting Data From Another Table." After you append the missing records, you can enter record number 95 for Thompson's Books.

ITEM COMPONENTS TABLE: DEFINITION

Field Name	Description	Type	Length	Primary Key
Catalog Item ID	Our Catalog number	Long Integer	4	√
Component ID	Unique component ID	Long Integer	4	√
Amount	Amount of this component in the item	Integer	2	

ITEM COMPONENTS TABLE: DATA

Catalog Item ID	Component ID	Amount
1	1	1
2	2	1
3	3	1
4	4	1
5	5	1
6	6	1
7	7	1
8	8	1
9	9	1
10	10	1
11	11	1
12	12	1
13	13	1
14	14	1
15	15	1
16	16	1
17	17	1
18	18	1
22	22	1
23	23	1
24	24	1
25	25	1
26	26	1
27	27	1
29	29	1
30	30	1

(continued)

ITEM COMPONENTS TABLE: DATA *(continued)*		
Catalog Item ID	*Component ID*	*Amount*
31	31	1
32	32	1
33	33	1
34	34	1
35	35	1
42	42	1
43	43	1
44	1	1
44	7	1
44	20	1
44	22	1
44	29	1
44	37	1
44	42	1
46	1	1
46	7	1
46	20	1
46	22	1
46	29	1
46	39	1
46	42	1
47	1	1
47	7	1
47	20	1
47	22	1
47	29	1
47	38	1
47	42	1
48	1	1
48	7	1
48	19	2
48	20	1
48	22	1
48	29	1

ITEM COMPONENTS TABLE: DATA *(continued)*

Catalog Item ID	Component ID	Amount
48	40	1
48	42	1
49	1	1
49	7	1
49	19	4
49	20	1
49	22	1
49	34	1
49	41	1
49	42	1
50	45	1
51	19	1

MONTHLY SALES TABLE: DEFINITION

Field Name	Description	Type	Length	Primary Key
Catalog Item ID	Our Catalog number	Long Integer	4	✓
Year	Year of Sale	Integer	2	✓
Month	Month of Sale	Integer	2	✓
Quantity sold	Total sold in this month	Long Integer	4	
Total invoice amount	Total invoiced for this item	Currency	8	
Total cost	Total cost for this item	Currency	8	

MONTHLY SALES TABLE: DATA

Catalog Item ID	Year	Month	Quantity sold	Total invoice amount	Total cost
1	1991	12	4	542.85	394.80
1	1992	1	5	616.8750	493.50
1	1992	2	8	987.00	789.60
1	1992	3	4	493.50	394.80
1	1992	4	3	370.13	296.10
1	1992	5	6	740.25	592.20

(continued)

MONTHLY SALES TABLE: DATA *(continued)*

Catalog Item ID	Year	Month	Quantity sold	Total invoice amount	Total cost
1	1992	6	3	370.13	296.10
1	1992	7	8	987.00	789.60
1	1992	8	9	1110.37	888.30
1	1992	9	4	493.50	394.80
1	1992	10	7	863.63	690.90
1	1992	11	5	616.87	493.50
1	1992	12	10	1233.75	987.00
2	1992	1	2	442.50	354.00
2	1992	2	4	885.00	708.00
2	1992	3	7	1548.75	1239.00
2	1992	4	1	221.25	177.00
2	1992	5	3	663.75	531.00
2	1992	7	3	663.75	531.00
2	1992	8	2	442.50	354.00
2	1992	9	5	1106.25	885.00
2	1992	10	4	885.00	708.00
2	1992	11	3	663.75	531.00
2	1992	12	5	1106.25	885.00
2	1992	6	4	885.00	708.00
3	1992	1	1	367.50	294.00
3	1992	2	2	735.00	588.00
3	1992	3	6	2205.00	1764.00
3	1992	4	2	735.00	588.00
3	1992	5	4	1470.00	1176.00
3	1992	6	3	1102.50	882.00
3	1992	7	2	735.00	588.00
3	1992	8	7	2572.50	2058.00
3	1992	9	4	1470.00	1176.00
3	1992	10	4	1470.00	1176.00
3	1992	11	7	2572.50	2058.00
3	1992	12	4	1470.00	1176.00
6	1992	1	3	1151.25	921.00
6	1992	2	5	1918.75	1535.00

MONTHLY SALES TABLE: DATA *(continued)*

Catalog Item ID	Year	Month	Quantity sold	Total invoice amount	Total cost
6	1992	3	2	767.50	614.00
6	1992	5	1	383.75	307.00
6	1992	6	8	3070.00	2456.00
6	1992	7	4	1535.00	1228.00
6	1992	8	3	1151.25	921.00
6	1992	9	6	2302.50	1842.00
6	1992	10	2	767.50	614.00
6	1992	11	9	3453.75	2763.00
6	1992	12	11	4221.25	3377.00
7	1992	1	30	9337.50	7470.00
7	1992	2	25	7781.25	6225.00
7	1992	3	36	11205.00	8964.00
7	1992	4	22	6847.50	5478.00
7	1992	5	29	9026.25	7221.00
7	1992	6	1	311.25	249.00
7	1992	7	4	1245.00	996.00
7	1992	8	8	2490.00	1992.00
7	1992	9	9	2801.25	2241.00
7	1992	10	4	1245.00	996.00
7	1992	11	8	2490.00	1992.00
7	1992	12	4	1245.00	996.00
10	1991	12	7	4261.25	3409.00
11	1992	1	11	4523.75	3619.00
11	1992	2	14	5757.50	4606.00
11	1992	3	9	3701.25	2961.00
11	1992	4	17	6991.25	5593.00
11	1992	5	13	5346.25	4277.00
15	1992	1	22	2145.00	1716.00
15	1992	2	35	3412.50	2730.00
15	1992	3	25	2437.50	1950.00
15	1992	4	38	3705.00	2964.00
15	1992	5	44	4290.00	3432.00

(continued)

MONTHLY SALES TABLE: DATA *(continued)*

Catalog Item ID	Year	Month	Quantity sold	Total invoice amount	Total cost
16	1992	6	1	500.00	419.00
17	1991	12	5	2568.75	2055.00
22	1991	12	18	1732.50	1386.00
22	1992	1	34	3272.50	2618.00
22	1992	2	28	2695.00	2156.00
22	1992	3	44	4235.00	3388.00
22	1992	4	37	3561.25	2849.00
22	1992	5	26	2502.50	2002.00
22	1992	6	2	192.50	154.00
22	1992	7	12	1155.00	924.00
22	1992	8	16	1540.00	1232.00
22	1992	9	14	1347.50	1078.00
22	1992	10	21	2021.25	1617.00
22	1992	11	18	1732.50	1386.00
22	1992	12	27	2598.75	2079.00
24	1992	1	5	450.00	360.00
24	1992	3	7	630.00	504.00
25	1991	12	12	180.00	144.00
26	1992	1	34	2465.00	1972.00
26	1992	2	45	3262.50	2610.00
26	1992	3	27	1957.50	1566.00
26	1992	4	38	2755.00	2204.00
26	1992	5	41	2972.50	2378.00
26	1992	6	4	292.50	232.00
26	1992	7	23	1667.50	1334.00
26	1992	8	32	2320.00	1856.00
26	1992	9	29	2102.50	1682.00
26	1992	10	31	2247.50	1798.00
26	1992	11	28	2030.00	1624.00
26	1992	12	25	1812.50	1450.00
29	1991	12	22	6270.00	5016.00
29	1992	1	22	6270.00	5016.00
29	1992	2	12	3420.00	2736.00

MONTHLY SALES TABLE: DATA *(continued)*

Catalog Item ID	Year	Month	Quantity sold	Total invoice amount	Total cost
29	1992	3	15	4275.00	3420.00
29	1992	4	19	5415.00	4332.00
29	1992	5	12	3420.00	2736.00
29	1992	6	12	3420.00	2736.00
29	1992	7	3	855.00	684.00
29	1992	8	6	1710.00	1368.00
29	1992	9	7	1995.00	1596.00
29	1992	10	5	1425.00	1140.00
29	1992	11	4	1140.00	912.00
29	1992	12	9	2565.00	2052.00
31	1992	1	3	1173.75	939.00
31	1992	2	2	782.50	626.00
31	1992	3	5	1956.25	1565.00
31	1992	4	3	1173.75	939.00
31	1992	5	8	3130.00	2504.00
31	1992	6	1	391.25	313.00
31	1992	7	11	4303.75	3443.00
31	1992	8	9	3521.25	2817.00
31	1992	9	10	3912.50	3130.00
31	1992	10	8	3130.00	2504.00
31	1992	11	11	4303.75	3443.00
31	1992	12	9	3521.25	2817.00
32	1992	1	15	7068.75	5655.00
32	1992	2	9	4241.25	3393.00
32	1992	3	11	5183.75	4147.00
32	1992	4	7	3298.75	2639.00
32	1992	5	9	4241.25	3393.00
32	1992	6	1	471.25	377.00
32	1992	7	3	1413.75	1131.00
32	1992	8	2	942.50	754.00
32	1992	9	1	471.25	377.00
32	1992	10	3	1413.75	1131.00
32	1992	11	4	1885.00	1508.00

(continued)

MONTHLY SALES TABLE: DATA *(continued)*

Catalog Item ID	Year	Month	Quantity sold	Total invoice amount	Total cost
32	1992	12	2	942.50	754.00
35	1992	1	34	15725.00	12580.00
35	1992	2	22	10175.00	8140.00
35	1992	3	28	12950.00	10360.00
35	1992	4	39	18037.50	14430.00
35	1992	5	24	11100.00	8880.00
35	1992	6	13	6012.50	4810.00
35	1992	7	10	4625.00	3700.00
35	1992	8	15	6937.50	5550.00
35	1992	9	12	5550.00	4440.00
35	1992	10	18	8325.00	6660.00
35	1992	11	16	7400.00	5920.00
35	1992	12	21	9712.50	7770.00
42	1992	1	43	4138.75	3311.00
42	1992	2	39	3753.75	3003.00
42	1992	3	31	2983.75	2387.00
42	1992	4	27	2598.75	2079.00
42	1992	5	55	5293.75	4235.00
42	1992	6	1	96.25	77.00
42	1992	7	22	2117.50	1694.00
42	1992	8	27	2598.75	2079.00
42	1992	9	19	1828.75	1463.00
42	1992	10	23	2213.75	1771.00
42	1992	11	34	3272.50	2618.00
42	1992	12	22	2117.50	1694.00
43	1992	2	3	2452.50	1962.00
43	1992	4	2	1635.00	1308.00
43	1992	6	3	2452.50	1962.00
44	1991	12	9	12591.00	11256.30
44	1992	1	5	22750.00	16785.00
44	1992	2	8	36400.00	26856.00
44	1992	3	9	40950.00	30213.00
44	1992	4	7	31850.00	23499.00

MONTHLY SALES TABLE: DATA *(continued)*

Catalog Item ID	Year	Month	Quantity sold	Total invoice amount	Total cost
44	1992	5	12	54600.00	40284.00
44	1992	6	5	16448.00	6253.50
44	1992	7	3	4197.00	3752.10
46	1992	6	1	1599.00	1430.70
47	1992	6	1	1599.00	1334.70
48	1991	12	11	23639.00	18734.10
48	1992	6	1	2149.00	1703.10
49	1992	6	3	7197.00	7989.30
50	1992	6	3	1530.00	1431.00
51	1992	6	4	200.00	154.80

ORDER ITEMS TABLE: DEFINITION

Field Name	Description	Type	Length	Primary Key
Order ID	Unique Order identifier	Long Integer	4	✓
Catalog Item ID	Our Catalog number	Long Integer	4	✓
Quantity	Amount ordered	Integer	2	
Quoted price	Price quoted for this order	Currency	8	
Special comments	Any special terms quoted to customer	Memo	0	

ORDER ITEMS TABLE: DATA

Order ID	Catalog Item ID	Quantity	Quoted price	Special comments
1	25	1	15.00	...
1	26	4	72.00	...
1	47	4	1599.00	...
1	49	1	3199.00	...
1	50	1	510.00	...
2	43	1	817.00	...
2	44	2	1399.00	...
3	1	1	123.38	...

(continued)

Order ID	Catalog Item ID	Quantity	Quoted price	Special comments
3	7	1	311.00	…
4	44	1	1369.00	…
5	46	1	1599.00	…
6	27	1	106.00	…
6	43	1	817.00	…
6	48	1	2149.00	…
7	32	1	471.00	…
8	26	1	72.00	…
8	43	1	817.00	…
8	44	1	1399.00	…
9	26	1	72.00	…
9	49	1	2899.00	…
9	50	1	510.00	…
10	26	1	72.00	…
10	47	1	1599.00	…
10	51	2	50.00	…
11	49	2	2399.00	…
11	50	1	510.00	…
12	44	1	1399.00	…
12	50	1	510.00	…
12	51	2	50.00	…
13	43	1	817.00	…
13	49	2	3199.00	…
13	50	1	510.00	…
15	48	2	1959.00	…
15	26	2	70.00	…

ORDER ITEMS TABLE: DATA *(continued)*

ORDERS TABLE: DEFINITION

Field Name	Description	Type	Length	Primary Key
Order ID	Unique Order identifier	Counter	4	√
Customer ID	Key to Customer Table	Long Integer	4	
Ship Name	Name of person or company to receive the shipment.	Text	40	
Ship Address 1	Street address only—no post-office box allowed.	Text	30	
Ship Address 2	Street address only—no post-office box allowed.	Text	30	
Ship City	Shipping city	Text	20	
Ship State	Shipping State or province.	Text	12	
Ship Postal Code	Shipping Zip or Postal Code	Text	10	
Ship Country	Shipping Country	Text	15	
Order Date	Date order was placed	Date/Time	8	
Ship Date	Date order was shipped/installed	Date/Time	8	
Promise Date	Date order was promised to be ready	Date/Time	8	
SubTotal Cost	Cost of items in the order	Currency	8	
Discount	Discount % on this order	Double	8	
Sales Tax Percent	Tax percent for this order	Double	8	
Sales Tax	Total sales tax for this order	Currency	8	
Freight	Shipping charge for this order	Currency	8	
Customer PO	Customer Puchase Order Number	Text	15	
Terms	Payment terms	Text	20	
Invoiced	Flag to indicate if order has been invoiced	Yes/No	1	
Amount Paid	Amount paid to date	Currency	8	
Date Paid	Date of last payment	Date/Time	8	
Notes	Special notes about this order	Memo	0	

ORDERS TABLE: DATA

Order ID	Customer ID				
1	1	*Ship Name:* Alpha Products	*SubTotal Cost:* 10410.00		
		Ship Address 1: Suite 100	*Discount:* 0.05		
		Ship Address 2: 1234 Main Street	*Sales Tax Percent:* 0.075		
		Ship City: Burlington	*Sales Tax:* 741.71		
		Ship State: VT	*Freight:* 7.50		
		Ship Postal Code: 03033	*Customer PO:* CE - 92/479		
		Ship Country: USA	*Terms:* Net 30, 2/15		
		Order Date: 6/10/92 11:29:12	*Invoiced:* 1		
		Ship Date: 6/14/92 0:00:00	*Amount Paid:* 0		
		Promise Date: 6/15/92 0:00:00	*Date Paid:* ...		
		Notes: Build and install system in secretary front office			
2	2	*Ship Name:* Beta Consulting	*SubTotal Cost:* 3615.50		
		Ship Address 1: ...	*Discount:* 0		
		Ship Address 2: 7891 44th Avenue	*Sales Tax Percent:* 0.082		
		Ship City: Redmond	*Sales Tax:* 296.47		
		Ship State: WA	*Freight:* 0		
		Ship Postal Code: 98052	*Customer PO:* ...		
		Ship Country: USA	*Terms:* ...		
		Order Date: 6/10/92 12:22:57	*Invoiced:* 0		
		Ship Date: ...	*Amount Paid:* 0		
		Promise Date: 6/10/92 0:00:00	*Date Paid:* ...		
		Notes: ...			
3	29	*Ship Name:* Frugal Feast Comestibles	*SubTotal Cost:* 434.63		
		Ship Address 1: Evans Plaza	*Discount:* 0		
		Ship Address 2: 531 - 2nd Ave.	*Sales Tax Percent:* 0		
		Ship City: Eugene	*Sales Tax:* 0		
		Ship State: OR	*Freight:* 0		
		Ship Postal Code: 97403	*Customer PO:* ...		
		Ship Country: USA	*Terms:* ...		
		Order Date: 6/10/92 12:31:33	*Invoiced:* 0		
		Ship Date: ...	*Amount Paid:* 0		
		Promise Date: 6/10/92 0:00:00	*Date Paid:* ...		
		Notes: ...			

ORDERS TABLE: DATA *(continued)*

Order ID	Customer ID				
4	46	*Ship Name:* Lazy K Kountry Store		*SubTotal Cost:* 1399.00	
		Ship Address 1: ...		*Discount:* 0	
		Ship Address 2: 12 Orchestra Terrace		*Sales Tax Percent:* 0.082	
		Ship City: Walla Walla		*Sales Tax:* 114.72	
		Ship State: WA		*Freight:* 0	
		Ship Postal Code: 99362		*Customer PO:* ...	
		Ship Country: USA		*Terms:* ...	
		Order Date: 6/10/92 12:32:45		*Invoiced:* 0	
		Ship Date: ...		*Amount Paid:* 0	
		Promise Date: 6/10/92 0:00:00		*Date Paid:* ...	
		Notes: ...			
5	57	*Ship Name:* Oceanview Quickshop		*SubTotal Cost:* 1599.00	
		Ship Address 1: Franklin Mall		*Discount:* 0	
		Ship Address 2: 231 N. Ukiah Rd		*Sales Tax Percent:* 0	
		Ship City: Aloha		*Sales Tax:* 0	
		Ship State: OR		*Freight:* 0	
		Ship Postal Code: 97006		*Customer PO:* ...	
		Ship Country: USA		*Terms:* ...	
		Order Date: 6/10/92 12:02:43		*Invoiced:* 0	
		Ship Date: ...		*Amount Paid:* 0	
		Promise Date: 6/10/92 0:00:00		*Date Paid:* ...	
		Notes: ...			
6	61	*Ship Name:* Pedro's Bodega		*SubTotal Cost:* 3072.50	
		Ship Address 1: ...		*Discount:* 0	
		Ship Address 2: 7 Nachoes Way		*Sales Tax Percent:* 0.073	
		Ship City: Phoenix		*Sales Tax:* 224.31	
		Ship State: AZ		*Freight:* 0	
		Ship Postal Code: 85021		*Customer PO:* ...	
		Ship Country: USA		*Terms:* ...	
		Order Date: 6/10/92 12:04:28		*Invoiced:* 0	
		Ship Date: ...		*Amount Paid:* 0	
		Promise Date: 6/10/92 0:00:00		*Date Paid:* ...	
		Notes: ...			

(continued)

ORDERS TABLE: DATA *(continued)*

Order ID	Customer ID				
7	44	*Ship Name:*	La Tienda Granda	*SubTotal Cost:*	471.25
		Ship Address 1:	...	*Discount:*	0
		Ship Address 2:	12345 - 6th St.	*Sales Tax Percent:*	0.085
		Ship City:	Los Angeles	*Sales Tax:*	40.0563
		Ship State:	CA	*Freight:*	8.29
		Ship Postal Code:	91406	*Customer PO:*	...
		Ship Country:	USA	*Terms:*	...
		Order Date:	6/10/92 12:07:31	*Invoiced:*	0
		Ship Date:	...	*Amount Paid:*	0
		Promise Date:	6/10/92 0:00:00	*Date Paid:*	...
		Notes:	...		
8	25	*Ship Name:*	Fitzgerald's Deli and Video	*SubTotal Cost:*	2289.0000
		Ship Address 1:	Eastgate Center	*Discount:*	0
		Ship Address 2:	14 E. Eastway	*Sales Tax Percent:*	0.082
		Ship City:	Bellevue	*Sales Tax:*	187.67
		Ship State:	WA	*Freight:*	0
		Ship Postal Code:	98006	*Customer PO:*	...
		Ship Country:	USA	*Terms:*	...
		Order Date:	6/10/92 12:08:45	*Invoiced:*	0
		Ship Date:	...	*Amount Paid:*	0
		Promise Date:	6/10/92 0:00:00	*Date Paid:*	...
		Notes:	...		
9	3	*Ship Name:*	Condor Leasing	*SubTotal Cost:*	2981.50
		Ship Address 1:	44th floor	*Discount:*	0
		Ship Address 2:	901 E. Maple	*Sales Tax Percent:*	0.074
		Ship City:	Chicago	*Sales Tax:*	220.63
		Ship State:	Il	*Freight:*	2981.50
		Ship Postal Code:	60606	*Customer PO:*	...
		Ship Country:	USA	*Terms:*	...
		Order Date:	6/10/92 12:13:04	*Invoiced:*	0
		Ship Date:	...	*Amount Paid:*	0
		Promise Date:	6/10/92 0:00:00	*Date Paid:*	...
		Notes:	...		

ORDERS TABLE: DATA *(continued)*

Order ID	Customer ID				
10	95	*Ship Name:* Thompson's Bookstop		*SubTotal Cost:* 1771.50	
		Ship Address 1: ...		*Discount:* 0	
		Ship Address 2: 7895 Hollow Road		*Sales Tax Percent:* 0.086	
		Ship City: New Bedford		*Sales Tax:* 152.35	
		Ship State: MA		*Freight:* 0	
		Ship Postal Code: 02011		*Customer PO:* ...	
		Ship Country: USA		*Terms:* ...	
		Order Date: 6/10/92 12:14:34		*Invoiced:* 0	
		Ship Date: ...		*Amount Paid:* 0	
		Promise Date: 6/10/92 0:00:00		*Date Paid:* ...	
		Notes: ...			
11	3	*Ship Name:* Condor Leasing		*SubTotal Cost:* 6308.00	
		Ship Address 1: 44th floor		*Discount:* 0	
		Ship Address 2: 901 E. Maple		*Sales Tax Percent:* 0.074	
		Ship City: Chicago		*Sales Tax:* 466.79	
		Ship State: Il		*Freight:* 0	
		Ship Postal Code: 60606		*Customer PO:* ...	
		Ship Country: USA		*Terms:* ...	
		Order Date: 6/10/92 12:28:27		*Invoiced:* 0	
		Ship Date: ...		*Amount Paid:* 0	
		Promise Date: 6/10/92 0:00:00		*Date Paid:* ...	
		Notes: ...			
12	57	*Ship Name:* Oceanview Quickshop		*SubTotal Cost:* 2009.00	
		Ship Address 1: Franklin Mall		*Discount:* 0	
		Ship Address 2: 231 N. Ukiah Rd		*Sales Tax Percent:* 0	
		Ship City: Aloha		*Sales Tax:* 0	
		Ship State: OR		*Freight:* 0	
		Ship Postal Code: 97006		*Customer PO:* ...	
		Ship Country: USA		*Terms:* ...	
		Order Date: 6/12/92 12:47:34		*Invoiced:* 0	
		Ship Date: ...		*Amount Paid:* 0	
		Promise Date: 6/12/92 0:00:00		*Date Paid:* ...	
		Notes: ...			

(continued)

ORDERS TABLE: DATA *(continued)*

Order ID	Customer ID				
13	95	*Ship Name:*	Thompson's Bookstop	*SubTotal Cost:*	7725.50
		Ship Address 1:	...	*Discount:*	0.02
		Ship Address 2:	7895 Hollow Road	*Sales Tax Percent:*	0.086
		Ship City:	New Bedford	*Sales Tax:*	740.00
		Ship State:	MA	*Freight:*	0
		Ship Postal Code:	02011	*Customer PO:*	...
		Ship Country:	USA	*Terms:*	...
		Order Date:	7/13/92 12:08:47	*Invoiced:*	0
		Ship Date:	7/14/92 0:00:00	*Amount Paid:*	0
		Promise Date:	7/15/92 0:00:00	*Date Paid:*	...
		Notes:	...		
15*	2	*Ship Name:*	Beta Consulting	*SubTotal Cost:*	4058.00
		Ship Address 1:	...	*Discount:*	0.05
		Ship Address 2:	7891 44th Avenue	*Sales Tax Percent:*	0.082
		Ship City:	Redmond	*Sales Tax:*	316.12
		Ship State:	WA	*Freight:*	0
		Ship Postal Code:	98052	*Customer PO:*	...
		Ship Country:	USA	*Terms:*	Net 30, 2/15
		Order Date:	7/31/92 12:25:40	*Invoiced:*	0
		Ship Date:	...	*Amount Paid:*	0
		Promise Date:	7/31/92 0:00:00	*Date Paid:*	...
		Notes:	...		

*The Order ID field is missing one number in the sequence (14). You'll have to create and delete a dummy field to obtain the correct Order ID value of 15.

SUPPLIER TABLE: DEFINITION

Field Name	Description	Type	Length	Primary Key
Supplier ID	Unique Supplier ID	Counter	4	√
Supplier Name	Supplier's Name	Text	50	
Supplier Address 1	Supplier address line 1	Text	50	
Supplier Address 2	Supplier address line 2	Text	50	
Supplier City	Supplier city name	Text	50	
Supplier State	Supplier state code	Text	2	
Supplier Postal	Supplier postal or zip code	Text	10	
Supplier Phone	Supplier phone number	Text	20	
Supplier Fax	Supplier fax number	Text	20	

(continued)

SUPPLIER TABLE: DEFINITION *(continued)*

Field Name	*Description*	*Type*	*Length*	*Primary Key*
Owed to supplier	Amount currently owed to this supplier	Currency	8	
Date payment due	Date of next payment	Date/Time	8	
Payment amount	Amount of next payment	Currency	8	

SUPPLIER TABLE: DATA

Supplier ID

1
Supplier Name: AAA Computer Supply	*Supplier Phone:* 2065591212
Supplier Address 1: Cedar Industrial Park	*Supplier Fax:* 2065591234
Supplier Address 2: 12345 NE 87th	*Owed to Supplier:* ...
Supplier City: Redmond	*Date payment due:* ...
Supplier State: WA	*Payment amount:* ...
Supplier Postal: 98052	

2
Supplier Name: Best Computer Wholesale	*Supplier Phone:* 2139991200
Supplier Address 1: Suite 900	*Supplier Fax:* 2139991201
Supplier Address 2: 9000 Sepulveda	*Owed to Supplier:* ...
Supplier City: Los Angeles	*Date payment due:* ...
Supplier State: CA	*Payment amount:* ...
Supplier Postal: 97000	

3
Supplier Name: Computer Wholesale, Inc.	*Supplier Phone:* 4088881233
Supplier Address 1: Noble Industrial Park	*Supplier Fax:* 4088881234
Supplier Address 2: 3999 Central Expressway	*Owed to Supplier:* ...
Supplier City: Santa Clara	*Date payment due:* ...
Supplier State: CA	*Payment amount:* ...
Supplier Postal: 95050	

4
Supplier Name: Lovell Electronics Supply	*Supplier Phone:* 7137775454
Supplier Address 1: 15th Floor, Johnson Tower	*Supplier Fax:* 7137775455
Supplier Address 2: 1900 Bayou Parkway	*Owed to Supplier:* ...
Supplier City: Houston	*Date payment due:* ...
Supplier State: TX	*Payment amount:* ...
Supplier Postal: 74062	

5
Supplier Name: New Age Computing	*Supplier Phone:* 5097671234
Supplier Address 1: Suite 359	*Supplier Fax:* 5097671299
Supplier Address 2: 755 NE 132nd	*Owed to Supplier:* ...
Supplier City: Walla Walla	*Date payment due:* ...
Supplier State: WA	*Payment amount:* ...
Supplier Postal: 98345	

TYPES TABLE: DEFINITION

Field Name	Description	Type	Length	Primary Key
Item type code	Item type code	Text	3	✓
Type Description	Description for this class of items	Text	100	

TYPES TABLE: DATA

Item type code	Type Description	Item type code	Type Description
001	Cases, Power Supplies	010	Mice, pointing devices
002	Monitors	011	Multimedia
003	Keyboards	012	Software
004	Mother boards	013	Controllers
005	Floppies	014	Cables
006	Hard drives	015	Tape drives
007	RAM	016	Modems
008	Video boards	100	Packaged Systems
009	Printers		

MUSIC COLLECTION OR MUSIC STORE DATABASE

Here's a Music database for keeping track of all your favorite recordings. It could also serve as the basis for an inventory database for a music store. The relationships between tables are shown in Figure B-2.

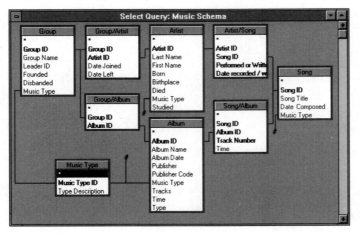

Figure B-2.
The Music database schema.

ALBUM TABLE DEFINITION

Field Name	Description	Type	Length	Primary Key
Album ID	Unique ID for this album	Counter	4	✓
Album Name	Name of this album	Text	50	
Album Date	Date this album was published	Date/Time	8	
Publisher	Name of album publisher	Text	50	
Publisher Code	Publisher's item number	Text	20	
Music Type	Main type of music on album	Long Integer	4	
Tracks	Number of tracks on album	Integer	2	
Time	Total running time in minutes	Double	8	
Type	Media type: C = CD, T = Tape, V = Vinyl disk	Text	1	

ARTIST TABLE DEFINITION

Field Name	Description	Type	Length	Primary Key
Artist ID	Unique ID for artist	Counter	4	✓
Last Name	Artist's last name	Text	25	
First Name	Artist's title, first name, etc.	Text	25	
Born	Artist's birth date	Date/Time	8	
Birthplace	Place artist was born	Text	50	
Died	Date artist died	Date/Time	8	
Music Type	Main type of music for this artist	Long Integer	4	
Studied	Place where artist studied music	Text	50	

ARTIST/SONG TABLE DEFINITION

Field Name	Description	Type	Length	Primary Key
Artist ID	Unique artist ID	Long Integer	4	✓
Song ID	Unique song ID	Long Integer	4	✓
Performed or Written	P = Artist performed this song; W = Artist wrote this song	Text	1	✓
Date recorded/ Written	Date artist recorded or wrote this song	Date/Time	8	✓

GROUP TABLE DEFINITION

Field Name	Description	Type	Length	Primary Key
Group ID	Unique identifier for the group	Counter	4	√
Group Name	Name of the group or orchestra	Text	50	
Leader ID	ID of the lead artist (or conductor)	Long Integer	4	
Founded	Date the group was founded	Date/Time	8	
Disbanded	Date the group disbanded (or changed leader)	Date/Time	8	
Music Type	Main type of music produced by the group	Long Integer	4	

GROUP/ALBUM TABLE DEFINITION

Field Name	Description	Type	Length	Primary Key
Group ID	Unique ID of the group	Long Integer	4	√
Album ID	Unique ID of the album	Long Integer	4	√

GROUP/ARTIST TABLE DEFINITION

Field Name	Description	Type	Length	Primary Key
Group ID	ID of the group	Long Integer	4	√
Artist ID	ID of the artist	Long Integer	4	√
Date Joined	Date the artist joined the group	Date/Time	8	
Date Left	Date the artist left the group	Date/Time	8	

MUSIC TYPE TABLE DEFINITION

Field Name	Description	Type	Length	Primary Key
Music Type ID	Unique ID for music type	Counter	4	√
Type Description	Description of music type	Text	30	

SONG TABLE DEFINITION				
Field Name	*Description*	*Type*	*Length*	*Primary Key*
Song ID	Unique identifier for song	Counter	4	✓
Song Title	Name of the song	Text	50	
Date Composed	Date this song was written	Date/Time	8	
Music Type	Type of music for this song	Long Integer	4	

SONG/ALBUM TABLE DEFINITION				
Field Name	*Description*	*Type*	*Length*	*Primary Key*
Song ID	ID of the song	Long Integer	4	✓
Album ID	ID of the album	Long Integer	4	✓
Track Number	Track number on the album that contains this song	Long Integer	4	✓
Time	Length of this song on this album in minutes	Double	8	

COOKING OR RESTAURANT DATABASE

You can use this database to keep a record of your favorite recipes—or to run a restaurant. The relationships between the tables are shown in Figure B-3.

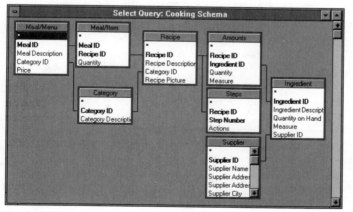

Figure B-3.
The Cooking or Restaurant database schema.

AMOUNTS TABLE DEFINITION

Field Name	Description	Type	Length	Primary Key
Recipe ID	Recipe that this amount applies to	Long Integer	4	✓
Ingredient ID	Ingredient identifier	Long Integer	4	✓
Quantity	Amount of ingredient required for this recipe	Double	8	
Measure	Measurement type (tbs., tsp., lb., etc.)	Text	10	

CATEGORY TABLE DEFINITION

Field Name	Description	Type	Length	Primary Key
Category ID	Unique ID for this category	Counter	4	✓
Category Description	Description: Breakfast, Brunch, Lunch, Dinner; Meat, Poultry, Seafood, Salad, Appetizer, etc.	Text	50	

INGREDIENT TABLE DEFINITION

Field Name	Description	Type	Length	Primary Key
Ingredient ID	Unique ingredient ID	Counter	4	✓
Ingredient Description	Description of this ingredient	Text	50	
Quantity on Hand	Amount we have in stock	Double	8	
Measure	Normal measure (tbs., tsp., lb., cup, etc.)	Text	10	
Supplier ID	ID of the usual supplier of this ingredient	Long Integer	4	

MEAL/MENU TABLE DEFINITION

Field Name	Description	Type	Length	Primary Key
Meal ID	Unique ID for this meal	Counter	4	✓
Meal Description	Full description of this meal	Memo	0	
Category ID	Category for this meal	Long Integer	4	
Price	Price of meal if a restaurant	Currency	8	

MEAL/ITEM TABLE DEFINITION

Field Name	Description	Type	Length	Primary Key
Meal ID	Link to Meal/Menu table	Long Integer	4	✓
Recipe ID	Link to Recipe table	Long Integer	4	✓
Quantity	Quantity of this item in this meal	Integer	2	

RECIPE TABLE DEFINITION

Field Name	Description	Type	Length	Primary Key
Recipe ID	Unique ID for this recipe	Counter	4	✓
Recipe Description	Description of this recipe	Text	255	
Category ID	Category for this recipe	Long Integer	4	
Recipe Picture	Picture of prepared dish	OLE Object	0	

STEPS TABLE DEFINITION

Field Name	Description	Type	Length	Primary Key
Recipe ID	Recipe that uses this step	Long Integer	4	✓
Step Number	Step number in this recipe	Long Integer	4	✓
Actions	Description of what to do	Memo	0	

SUPPLIER TABLE DEFINITION

Field Name	Description	Type	Length	Primary Key
Supplier ID	Unique Supplier ID	Counter	4	✓
Supplier name	Supplier's name	Text	50	
Supplier Address 1	Supplier address line 1	Text	50	
Supplier Address 2	Supplier address line 2	Text	50	
Supplier City	Supplier city name	Text	50	
Supplier State	Supplier state code	Text	2	
Supplier Postal	Supplier zip or postal code	Text	10	
Supplier Phone	Supplier phone number	Text	11	
Supplier Fax	Supplier fax number	Text	11	
Owed to Supplier	Amount currently owed to this supplier	Currency	8	
Date Payment Due	Date of next payment	Date/Time	8	
Payment Amount	Amount of next payment	Currency	8	

BOOKSTORE DATABASE

Use this database as the basis for a bookstore application, or use it to save information about each book in your personal library. The relationships between the tables are shown in Figure B-4.

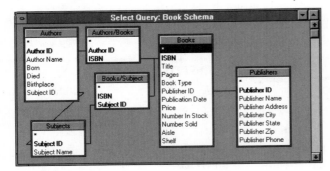

Figure B-4.
The Bookstore database schema.

AUTHORS TABLE DEFINITION

Field Name	Description	Type	Length	Primary Key
Author ID	Unique ID for this author	Long Integer	4	√
Author Name	Name of the author	Text	50	
Born	Date author was born	Date/Time	8	
Died	Date author died	Date/Time	8	
Birthplace	Author place of birth	Text	100	
Subject ID	Author's main subject specialty	Long Integer	4	

AUTHORS/BOOKS TABLE DEFINITION

Field Name	Description	Type	Length	Primary Key
Author ID	Link to Authors table	Long Integer	4	√
ISBN	Link to Books table	Long Integer	4	√

BOOKS TABLE DEFINITION

Field Name	Description	Type	Length	Primary Key
ISBN	Unique book identifier	Long Integer	4	√
Title	Title of the book	Text	110	

(continued)

BOOKS TABLE DEFINITION *(continued)*

Field Name	Description	Type	Length	Primary Key
Pages	Number of pages	Long Integer	4	
Book Type	P=Paperback; H=Hardback; T=Trade paperback	Text	1	
Publisher ID	ID of the publisher	Long Integer	4	
Publication Date	Date of first publication	Date/Time	8	
Price	Cover price	Currency	8	
Number In Stock	Number in inventory	Long Integer	4	
Number Sold	Number sold to date	Long Integer	4	
Aisle	Aisle ID in the bookstore	Text	5	
Shelf	Shelf number	Integer	2	

BOOKS/SUBJECT TABLE DEFINITION

Field Name	Description	Type	Length	Primary Key
ISBN	Link to Books table	Long Integer	4	✓
Subject ID	Link to Subjects table	Long Integer	4	✓

PUBLISHERS TABLE DEFINITION

Field Name	Description	Type	Length	Primary Key
Publisher ID	ID for this publisher	Counter	4	✓
Publisher Name	Name of the publisher	Text	50	
Publisher Address	Street address	Text	50	
Publisher City	City name	Text	30	
Publisher State	State abbreviation	Text	2	
Publisher Zip	Zip or postal code	Text	12	
Publisher Phone	Phone number	Text	12	

SUBJECTS TABLE DEFINITION

Field Name	Description	Type	Length	Primary Key
Subject ID	Unique Subject ID	Counter	4	✓
Subject Name	Description of the subject area	Text	120	

HUMAN RESOURCES DATABASE

This database provides the skeleton for a human-resources application. The relationships between the tables are shown in Figure B-5.

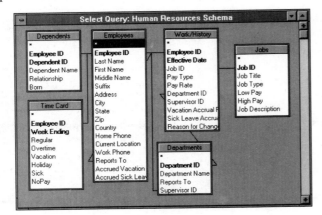

Figure B-5.
The Human Resources database schema.

DEPARTMENTS TABLE DEFINITION

Field Name	Description	Type	Length	Primary Key
Department ID	Unique department number	Counter	4	✓
Department Name	Name of this department	Text	50	
Reports To	Self-link	Long Integer	4	
Supervisor ID	Pointer to Employees table	Long Integer	4	

DEPENDENTS TABLE DEFINITION

Field Name	Description	Type	Length	Primary Key
Employee ID	Link to Employees table	Long Integer	4	✓
Dependent ID	Unique dependent number	Double	8	✓
Dependent Name	Name of the dependent	Text	50	
Relationship	Relationship of dependent	Text	50	
Born	Birth date of dependent	Date/Time	8	

EMPLOYEES TABLE DEFINITION

Field Name	Description	Type	Length	Primary Key
Employee ID	Unique ID for employee	Counter	4	✓
Last Name	Employee last name	Text	25	
First Name	Employee first name	Text	25	
Middle Name	Employee middle name	Text	25	
Suffix	Jr., Sr., III, Ph.D., etc.	Text	10	
Address	Street address	Text	40	
City	City name	Text	30	
State	State abbr.	Text	2	
Zip	Zip or postal code	Text	11	
Country	Country	Text	25	
Home Phone	Home phone number	Text	12	
Current Location	Current location ID	Text	30	
Work Phone	Work phone number	Text	12	
Reports To	Self-referencing key	Long Integer	4	
Accrued Vacation	Number of hours of vacation available	Double	8	
Accrued Sick Leave	Number of hours of sick leave available	Double	8	

JOBS TABLE DEFINITION

Field Name	Description	Type	Length	Primary Key
Job ID	Unique Job ID	Counter	4	✓
Job Title	Title for this job	Text	50	
Job Type	E = Exempt, N = Nonexempt	Text	50	
Low Pay	Bottom of normal pay range	Currency	8	
High Pay	Top of normal pay range	Currency	8	
Job Description	Full description of this job	Memo	0	

TIME CARD TABLE DEFINITION

Field Name	Description	Type	Length	Primary Key
Employee ID	Link to Employees table	Long Integer	4	✓
Week Ending	Week ending date	Date/Time	8	✓
Regular	Regular hours	Double	8	
Overtime	Overtime hours	Double	8	
Vacation	Vacation hours	Double	8	
Holiday	Holiday hours	Double	8	
Sick	Sick leave hours	Double	8	
No Pay	Time off without pay	Double	8	

WORK/HISTORY TABLE DEFINITION

Field Name	Description	Type	Length	Primary Key
Employee ID	Link to Employees table	Long Integer	4	✓
Effective Date	Date position effective	Date/Time	8	✓
Job ID	Link to Jobs table (0 = termination record)	Long Integer	4	
Pay Type	H=Hourly; S=Salaried; T=Temp hourly	Text	1	
Pay Rate	H, T = Hourly pay; S = Monthly pay	Currency	8	
Department ID	ID of department where working	Long Integer	4	
Supervisor ID	Link to Employees table	Long Integer	4	
Vacation Accrual Rate	Hours per pay period	Double	8	
Sick Leave Accrual Rate	Hours per pay period	Double	8	
Reason for Change	New Hire, Raise, Promotion, Transfer, etc.	Text	25	

C

The Database
Analyzer

One of the toughest tasks in building and modifying an application is tracking the potential impact of a change to all your tables, queries, forms, reports, macros, and modules. Fortunately, one of the Microsoft Product Support specialists created a library of utilities called the Database Analyzer to help you with this task.

After you install Microsoft Access, you'll find a file called ANALYZER.MDA in your Access subdirectory. This file contains the utilities that help you to analyze your database. The Microsoft Access online Help describes one method of activating the Database Analyzer; here's an even easier method. You must make a couple of small changes to your MSACCESS.INI file to activate the Database Analyzer.

Before you start Access, you need to locate the file called MSACCESS.INI in your Windows subdirectory. Open that file with a text editor such as Notepad and search for the Libraries section. (It starts with a line that reads [Libraries].) You should find one line in this section that reads *wizard.mda=ro*. (This line loads the Form-Wizards and ReportWizards.) Add one line below this line to activate the Database Analyzer. Assuming that your Access files are located in a directory named ACCESS on your C drive, your Libraries entry should look like this:

```
[Libraries]
C:\ACCESS\wizard.mda=ro
C:\ACCESS\analyzer.mda=rw
```

Next scroll down to the end of the initialization file and add a blank line and the following two lines:

```
[Menu Add-Ins]
&Database Analyzer==StartAnalyzer()
```

Note that you can give this menu action any name you like. Include an ampersand (&) before the character that you want to act as the keyboard shortcut. Be sure not to use "C," "S," "U," or "A" as the keyboard shortcut action letter (because the

Help menu already contains commands that use these characters as keyboard shortcuts). Save MSACCESS.INI and start Microsoft Access. Next open the Help menu, and you'll see a new entry for the Database Analyzer, as shown in Figure C-1.

Figure C-1.
The Database Analyzer entry appears when you add it to the Help menu.

Open the database you want to analyze, and then choose Database Analyzer from the Help menu. If you create a macro to run the Database Analyzer, select that macro in the database window and click the Run button. The Database Analyzer opens a selection dialog box, as shown in Figure C-2.

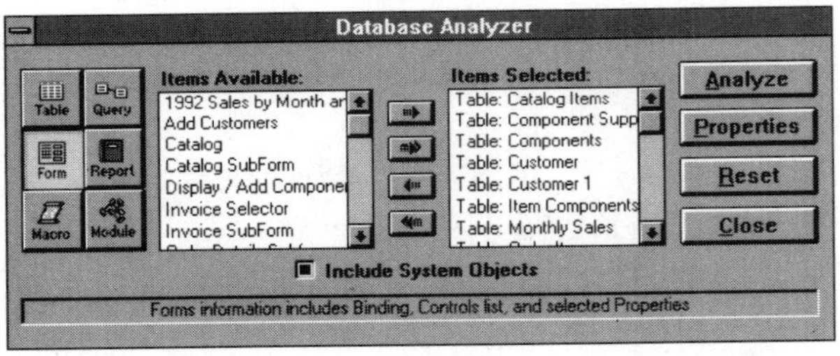

Figure C-2.
The Database Analyzer selection dialog box.

In this dialog box you can click the buttons at the far left to choose the type of object you would like analyzed. The Database Analyzer dialog box displays the available items in the current database in the Items Available list box. Use the double right arrow button to move all objects from the Items Available list box to the Items Selected list box. Or select an individual object and click the single right arrow button to move the object to the Items Selected list box. You can also select objects in the Items Selected list box and click the left arrow button to move the objects back to the Items Available list box.

For forms and reports, you can select additional properties that you would like analyzed. When you have clicked either the Form button or the Report button, you can click the Properties button to open the Properties dialog box, which is shown in Figure C-3 for Form. You can modify the list of selected properties by selecting property names in either list box and clicking the appropriate arrow button to add or remove properties. Click the Close button when your list is complete.

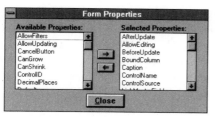

Figure C-3.
The Form Properties dialog box allows you to modify the list of selected properties.

When you have selected all the objects and the properties you want analyzed, click the Analyze button in the Database Analyzer dialog box. The Database Analyzer opens the dialog box shown in Figure C-4 so that you can specify where you want the output analysis tables saved. The analysis tables can be saved in any available Microsoft Access database.

Figure C-4.
The Database Analyzer Output Database dialog box allows you to specify where you want to save the output analysis tables.

Depending on the object types and properties you choose, the Database Analyzer can create up to 10 output tables. You can create queries and forms that use the data in these tables and produce custom reports about the structure of your database. The 10 tables are as follows:

@FormControls	One record for each control on the forms you requested to be analyzed. The Database Analyzer creates one field for each property you selected.
@FormProperties	One record for each form you requested to be analyzed. The fields in the table contain the property settings for the form.
@MacroDetails	One record for each line that contains a non-blank Action in the macros you requested to be analyzed. Fields show you the Label, Condition expression, Action, and all parameters.
@ModuleProcedures	One record for each procedure name within each module you requested to be analyzed. Fields show you the procedure name and its parameters.

(continued)

@ModuleVariables	One record for each declared variable in each procedure within each module you requested to be analzyed, showing you the declared type of the variable.
@QueryDetails	One record for each output field in each query you requested to be analyzed, showing you the source table, the data type, and the field length.
@QuerySQL	One record for each query you requested to be analyzed, with the full SQL statement for that query.
@ReportControls	One record for each control on the reports you requested to be analyzed. The Database Analyzer creates one field for each property you selected.
@ReportProperties	One record for each report you requested to be analyzed. The fields in the table contain the property settings for the report.
@TableDetails	One record for each field in each table you requested to be analyzed. The fields include the field name, field type, field length, and index information.

Index

Special Characters

John L. Viescas

John L. Viescas, a specialist in systems analysis and relational database management systems, is a consultant for Tandem Computers, Incorporated. He has more than 24 years of industry experience, including information security management and database software product development. He regularly lectures on relational database issues for Tandem customers, third-party vendors, industry consultants, and various information processing user groups. Viescas graduated *cum laude* from the University of Texas at Dallas with a degree in business finance. He resides in Redmond, Washington, with his wife.

The manuscript for this book was prepared and submitted to Microsoft Press in electronic form. Text files were processed and formatted using Microsoft Word.

Principal editorial compositor: Barb Runyan
Principal proofreader/copy editor: Kathleen Atkins
Principal typographer: Lisa Iversen
Interior text designer: Kim Eggleston
Principal illustrator: Lisa Sandburg
Cover designer: Rebecca Geisler-Johnson
Cover color separator: Color Service, Inc.

Text composition by Microsoft Press in New Baskerville with display type in Avant Garde Demi, using the Magna composition system and the Linotronic 300 laser imagesetter.

Printed on recycled paper stock.

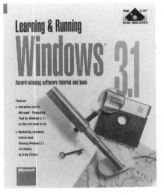
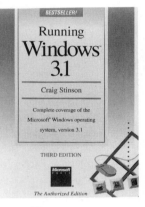

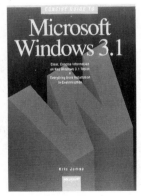